DATE DUE

DEMCO 38-296

TROUBLED TIGER

TROUBLED TIGER

TIGER

Businessmen,

Bureaucrats,

and Generals

in South Korea

Revised Edition

MARK L. CLIFFORD

An East Gate Book

M.E. Sharpe

Armonk, New York

London, England

An East Gate Book

Library of Congress Cataloging-in-Publication Data

Clifford, Mark L., 1957–
Troubled tiger: businessmen, bureaucrats, and generals in South Korea
by Mark L. Clifford.—Rev. ed.
p. cm.
"An East gate book."
Includes bibliographical references and index.
ISBN 0-7656-0140-0 (cloth : alk. paper). ISBN 0-7656-0141-9 (paperback)
1. Korea (South)—Economic policy. 2. Korea (South)—Economic
conditions—1948–1960. 3. Korea (South)—Economic conditions—1960– .
4. Korea (South)—Politics and government—1948—1960.
5. Korea (South)—Politics and government—1960– I. Title.
HC467.C6486 1997
338.95195—dc21 97-35048
CIP

Printed in the United States of America

The paper used in this publication meets the minimum requirements of
American National Standard for Information Sciences—
Permanence of Paper for Printed Library Materials,
ANSI Z 39.48-1984.

BM (c) 10 9 8 7 6 5 4 3 2 1
BM (p) 10 9 8 7 6 5 4 3 2 1

For Melissa, Anya, and Ted

Contents

Acknowledgments

Somewhere beyond the video clips of rock-slinging demonstrators and the idealized photographs of what once was the land of Morning Calm is a country filled with some of the world's most extraordinary people, one whose demonic energy alternately chills and seduces those who know it.

This book is an attempt to sketch a more nuanced picture of one of the world's most extraordinary economies than that which appears in either popular or academic accounts. It does not pretend to put forward any theory about development, although I am particularly interested in the relation between Korea's authoritarian politics and social structure and the country's rapid economic growth. I am also interested in the tensions between and among business, government and the military and how the balance of power has shifted over time.

I must thank my erstwhile co-author Tony Michell for starting out with me on what has been a much more ambitious project than either of us imagined or intended. Tony helped plot the general structure of the book and contributed research for an initial draft before other commitments forced him to bow out.

Jim West read this book in several subsequent drafts; his intellectual rigor, encyclopedic knowledge of modern Korea, and natural skepticism made for a reader of the sort that all authors long for. I would also like to thank Professor Song Sang Hyun for an incisive reading and numerous factual corrections as well as sharing his perceptive analysis of Korea with me since I met him in 1987. Other readers who struggled through all or part of the manuscript, and whose insights I have benefited from, include Ron Rodgers, Miguel Gonzalez, John Bernson and Chung Hoon Mok. Special thanks for everything, including a sharp copy editor's eye, to my mother, Marty Carlock.

I was fortunate enough to be in Korea during what was, even by Korean standards, an unusually tumultuous period and to be there with an extraordinary group of foreign correspondents. I must particularly thank those people with whom I worked—my colleagues at the *Far Eastern Economic Review* in Seoul, John McBeth and, later, Shim Jae Hoon, as well as the bureau's assistant, Lee Kyung Ja. Jae's willingness to share much of what he has seen in more than three decades of reporting in Korea made this a richer book.

I am grateful to the many hundreds of Koreans and foreigners who helped me understand one of the world's most enigmatic and fascinating countries, especially those who sat for extended interviews while I poked and prodded into the dark corners of the past. I am grateful to Ed Baker, Steve Brull, John Bennett, Bob Carter, Cho Sung Il, John Gittlesohn, Kim Ki Hwan, Kim Mahn Je, Kim Suk Won, Lee Hahn Been, Lee Sang Hi, Lee Soon Ja, Carol Mann, Holly Ornstein, Alan Plumb, Nam Duck Woo, Park Tae Joon, Park You Kwang, David Satterwhite, and Yoo Chang Soon as well as many others who asked not to be named but whose contributions proved every bit as valuable.

But my biggest debt is to my son, Ted, my daughter, Anya, and my wife, Melissa, who is, along with so much more, an acute observer of Korea and an incisive editor.

Hong Kong
May 1997

* * *

I have used the Korean convention of referring to the family name first followed by the two given names spelled as separate words. This decision leads to at least one anomaly alert readers may notice: My interviews and descriptions refer to Kim Ki Hwan; citations to Dr. Kim's published work follow his preferred spelling, Kim Kihwan. Sakong Il is another anomaly: His family name (Sakong) is made up of two characters; his given name consists of one.

CHINA

RUSSIA

North Korea

Taedong
River

Sea of Japan

Pyongyang

D M Z

Kangnung

Seoul
Inchon

South Korea

Yellow Sea

Taejon •

Pohang •
Taegu •
Ulsan •
Masan
• Pusan

• Kwangju
Mokpo

Korea Strait

0 ——— 100
km

Cheju Island

JAPAN

TROUBLED
TIGER

1

Uneasy Alliances

Enrich the Nation and Strengthen the Army.
—Park Chung Hee[1]

Wearing a suitably conservative dark suit, seventy-seven-year-old Chung Ju Yung sat quietly in the courtroom, looking as if he were just another business-man caught up in the usual sorts of commercial disputes that perpetually filter through the court.

In reality, Chung's trial was one of the more remarkable events in Korea in the past thirty years. The founder and the chairman of the Hyundai group, one of the world's biggest corporations, sat in a Seoul courtroom in late 1993 because he had dared to challenge the established order in Korea, one that held that government mandarins should rule the affairs of business and workers. Chung Ju Yung was a businessman but he was also a revolutionary, for this former peasant wanted nothing more than to pull down the old order, to change the twisted Confucian rules of Korea, Inc., which decreed that business exists to serve the government. The judge's sentence reflected the gravity of the threat: three years in prison.[2]

It might seem strange in a country that to all outward appearances is a show-place of capitalist development that a businessman like Chung Ju Yung could spark this sort of political retribution, one clearly designed to force his company back into line. But Chung's humiliation is telling. Although Korea, Inc. is cele-brated as a successful example of a business-government partnership, the reality is that of a chronically strained alliance. Government officials have always be-lieved that they should enjoy the upper hand and that business exists at the sufferance of—and often to do the bidding of—government. And relations between government and business, always uneasy, have deteriorated sharply as the country has become wealthier and more politically tolerant. At the same time, the rate of economic growth has been slowing thanks to higher costs and increased international competition.

Periodic political convulsions have left the underlying structure of control largely untouched. Although the inauguration of Kim Young Sam, a former dissident, as South Korea's president in February 1993 was a watershed in democratic development, it also marked the start of a sweeping purge that saw hundreds of officials, including some of the most powerful in the country, driven from power. While many of them no doubt deserved their punishment, there were also personal attacks that carried the unmistakable signs of a very traditional Korean manner of settling scores—and not only in the case of Chung Ju Yung.

Park Tae Joon, the founder and long-time chairman of Pohang Iron and Steel (Posco), another icon of Korea's economic success, was driven from the country and had his house seized by the government. Although the ostensible charge was tax evasion, Park's real crime was his temerity in challenging Kim Young Sam for the presidency and the continued control that the former Posco head exercised over the ruling party's secret fund-raising apparatus. Then there was the respected president of the central Bank of Korea, Cho Soon, a long-time fixture in the nation's economic policy-making circles. He was banished unceremoniously from power in the hiatus between Kim's election and his inauguration, in large part because he had refused to punish the Hyundai group for Chung's activities and because he wanted to pursue an independent interest rate policy. And the president of the country's most prestigious think tank, the government-funded Korea Development Institute, Song Hee Yhon, found himself looking for work after he criticized Kim's economic stimulus program.

Although business is powerful, and getting more so, it is still the government that dominates the landscape in the Korean economy. In Korea almost everything that is not explicitly permitted can at any moment be forbidden. This sounds like a joke from the old Communist world, but in the case of Korea it is a reality, often enshrined in law. People protest against the government, but they also expect the government to take care of them, with the modern state expected to look after its subjects in much the same way that a paternalistic monarch would.

Although the enforced discipline of Korea, Inc. is fraying, most of the country's leaders have, at best, a lukewarm commitment to a new way of doing business. The old order is shriveling, but the new one has yet to be born. It is both Korea's greatest strength and its greatest weakness that it has chosen to follow a coarser version of the Japanese model, one that has led to a good deal of international success but that is now increasingly a victim of its self-imposed rigidity. Land policy, the tax system, the dominance of a single political party and the structure of Korean firms all have echoes of Japan. But rather than taking

Japan's difficulties as a warning, Koreans are determined to press ahead on the same path. Even Kim Young Sam, a former dissident and South Korea's first civilian president in more than three decades, has been unable to make the sorts of sweeping reforms necessary to prevent Korea from running into an economic dead-end. Korea does not face an immediate crisis threatening its prosperity. But the old model, which worked so well for three decades, isn't right anymore. Its three decades of nearly 9 percent compound annual growth are past, a victim of what Koreans themselves ruefully term their "high-cost, low-efficiency" economy. Given the looming crisis in North Korea, which will mean additional burdens on the South, it's short-sighted to imagine that Seoul can continue business as usual.

South Korea's dilemma is simple: If it continues to follow the bureaucratic, government-dominated approach of the past thirty-plus years, it risks becoming a second, but lesser, Japan, inheriting many of the inefficiencies that make much of everyday life in Japan so dismal, before it has developed the manufacturing prowess and huge capital surpluses that have made Japan a world economic power. Korean companies, their size notwithstanding, will be pushed to the sidelines of the international economy as its politicians and bureaucrats squabble over the spoils of a corrupt economic and political system.

Yet if the country tries to make the leap to a more flexible, entrepreneurial economy, it will be taking an unprecedented risk. It will be a painful reckoning, one that will require opening the domestic economy to increased international competition and almost certainly leading to the dissolution of some of Korea's largest business groups.

Because government and business are so intertwined, dramatic reform is unlikely absent the threat of a crisis. Korea's officials will find it hard to relax their obsessive and highly personalized control of the economy and its companies are likely to continue celebrating size over efficiency and profitability. Simply put, it will be difficult for this tiger to change its stripes.

To describe Korea as a paternalistic, authoritarian society does not, of course, explain Korea's enviable record of economic growth. Fear alone does not produce prosperity, as the successors to Stalin and Mao learned to their regret.

Korea succeeded in large part because the government got the fundamentals right. High levels of literacy, high savings and investment levels, an inflation rate that stayed within bounds and an outward orientation to the economy helped provide an essential foundation. A population control program that bordered on the coercive helped push birth rates down rapidly and minimized the impact of a post–Korean War baby boom on schools and, later, the labor market.

There is a great deal of debate about how much of Korea's success reflects getting the basics right and how much stems from tinkering at the edges, from nonmarket forces. This book does not directly address that debate. Rather it looks at the relationship between authoritarian politics and rapid economic growth, particularly at the often ignored or misunderstood tensions between government and business, and within the government itself, and the prospects for this system to continue contributing to high economic growth.

For it is what Korea did differently, how it took basic tools like universal literacy and high investment rates and used them to construct a modern economic power, that makes the country both seductive and chilling to anyone trying to figure out the puzzle of East Asia's extraordinary economic growth. Starting at the top, its authoritarian political leaders have promoted and presided over a cult of outward-looking economic growth that has animated the country. Korea's strategy included huge rewards—in the form of money, power, and prestige—for businesses that could carry out government policies, and the country has been able to marry the power of top-down, centralized planning with the need for flexibility and competition that characterize capitalist economies. It has done this through a strong state, which has used its control of the financial system in a credit-starved economy both to dominate the private sector and to channel the tremendous energy and ambitions of Koreans anxious to rebuild their country after war and partition.

This statist approach was successful in stimulating economic growth only because it went hand in hand with fierce competition at the individual enterprise level and a consistent export policy. Exports have been vital to Korea's economic success, because they both earned foreign currency and forced companies to achieve international levels of quality and competitiveness. The government ensured that those companies that did not make it in foreign markets were turned over to other owners or did not survive.

Company owners were alternately bullied and cajoled into going along with government strategies for growth. Although sound economic policies underlay most of these strategies, this was in no sense an impersonal, market-oriented process, for money and power are woven together differently in Korea than they are in the West. In Korea, business exists at the pleasure of the government and, when called upon, is expected to put national development ahead of private greed. Government officials extract corporate donations for their projects, whether in the form of cash or employees, and nudge companies into one business or discourage them from another.

Thanks to government favors and a policy of building up capital-intensive industry, the Korean economy is dominated by fewer than a dozen big business groups, with the four largest alone accounting for 22 percent of the market value of the Korea Stock Exchange.[3] These firms, the *chaebol*, are the heart of Korea, Inc., the multibillion-dollar companies that make everything from automobiles to underwear. The biggest groups, Samsung and Hyundai, each have group combined sales of more than $80 billion a year, making them among the largest conglomerates in the world. These companies and their smaller peers grew up under the protective umbrella of former presidents Park Chung Hee and Chun Doo Hwan, neither of whom had any hesitation about showing business who was boss. Two of Park's first acts were to jail many of the country's leading businessmen and to nationalize banks. When Chun came to power he forced a highly political restructuring of the chaebol, shuffling businesses as if they were playing cards.

The government lent the chaebol money at cheap rates, jailed and blacklisted workers who tried to organize unions, allowed the companies to earn oligopolistic profits in the domestic market and helped them beg, buy, and steal needed technology from abroad. In return, the government demanded that business put most of its energies into manufacturing, rather than simple zero-sum activities such as real estate speculation, and persuaded businessmen to keep their drinking and carousing discreet enough to convince ordinary Koreans that everybody was sacrificing together. Political repression and a tightly controlled economic world kept this system intact and allowed the president to dominate businessmen, bureaucrats, and workers.

In Korea, as in Japan, corporate profits have been guzzled by a cash-hungry political system. For the better part of forty years, government has used money extorted from businesses—both foreign and Korean—to lubricate the economy and fund lavish election campaigns. Businessmen rose on the strength of not only their skill but their political connections. They were political entrepreneurs. Companies that did not play along were not always punished, but they could not expect favors, such as access to bank loans, or emergency help. Those that did were usually rewarded, provided—and this was critical—that they remained competitive in export markets.

Corruption, coercion, and favoritism are the dark side of Korea, Inc., the militarized economy that has shot from poverty to prosperity in a single generation. Unlike Japan, the rise of Korea is a story not of consensus or harmony, but of bitter battles in the boardrooms and on the shop floors, in the heavily fortified presidential palace and the grimly utilitarian ministry offices, of Korea. It is a story of struggle among the generals, businessmen, bureaucrats, technocrats, and, now, the workers who have shaped the economy.[4] Until the internal struggle comes to an end, Korea's international competitiveness is likely to suffer. But the divisions run so deep, and the tug of the old ways is so strong, that even a reform-oriented president is unlikely to make the necessary changes without a crisis.

Too Hard a State

Korea was vaulted into the modern world following the chaos of the peninsula's division and a bitter fratricidal war. The Korean War destroyed the old social and political order and paved the way for the forced-march growth that followed. Now, having achieved a reasonable level of prosperity, Korea's former flexibility seems to be hardening into a rigidity that undercuts its ambitions to become a major player in the international political and economic arena.

Strength in times of adversity and weakness in times of peace characterize Korea's twisting road of development. As a result, its leaders have helped ensure that Korea is in a state of permanent crisis, one with few parallels outside Communist or fascist countries. It is among the most authoritarian and interventionist state among the high-powered East Asian countries that have led the economic growth tables for the past three decades.[5]

Since Park Chung Hee took power in 1961 the energies of the country have been directed toward economic growth with a remarkable intensity. It is easy to see why South Korea has been, and continues to be, obsessed with economic growth. The country is, as Koreans themselves like to put it, "a shrimp among whales," hemmed in by powerful neighbors—its former colonial ruler, Japan, its former tributary master, China, and Russia. On its northern border, just a little more than 30 miles from Seoul (less than three minutes flying time), is North Korea, one of the world's most unpredictable and isolated countries. South Korea survived the North's 1950 invasion only because of United Nations (mostly U.S.) soldiers and generous amounts of international aid. Even today, 37,000 U.S. troops are still in South Korea, and the border separating it from North Korea remains one of the tensest in the world.

Since the late 1980s there have been moves toward liberalization in government, in business, and especially in politics, but Korea is still a country of tremendous conformity and astounding narrowness. For example, while even prissy Singapore let superstar Michael Jackson perform in late 1993 as part of his world tour, Korea, alone in Asia, refused to let the singer stage a show.

Korea remains a country of elite control, one in which the state oversees everything from wedding ceremonies to corporate investment. The courts have limited independence and rule of law still counts for little: Tax audits often are used to mete out politically motivated punishment to individuals who step out of line.

The bolder press and the more open political structure that have been evident since the late 1980s are significant, but they do not herald democracy as it is known in the West. There are almost 500,000 local government officials—more than one for every hundred people in the country—and through them the hand of the state reaches down into every household in monthly neighborhood propaganda meetings. Social campaigns sing the virtues of thrift and hard work. Government buildings are plastered with huge signs urging Koreans to strive for vague goals like "new order, new life."

Typical is a campaign launched at the end of 1991 urging citizens to work more (an extra thirty minutes a day), save more (another 10 percent of income), export more, produce more, and live a more frugal life. The so-called Five Mores campaign was launched by all major business organizations with the backing of the government. "Unless we rearm ourselves with a hard-working spirit, the country, far from joining advanced countries, will fall back to the less-developed nations group," warned Minister of Trade and Industry Lee Bong Suh at a rally to kick off the campaign. The signs extolling these propaganda campaigns are better-painted and replaced more often than in China or the old Soviet bloc, but the message is the same—a Stakhanovite campaign to raise production and investment.

Despite the slogans calling for sacrifice, Seoul probably has more chauffeured cars than any other city in the world. Every senior executive must have his own driver. Government ministries and large companies have private elevators, operated by attractive young women, reserved for executives, ministers, and other VIPs. At the same time, other elevators in the same buildings are taken out of service or stop only on alternate floors in line with ineffectual government energy-saving campaigns.

In 1960, South Korea had a per capita gross national product of $80 a year, a figure putting it on roughly the same level as Ghana and Sudan and a bit behind India. In Seoul, people were sleeping and even starving in the streets. Koreans were still numbed by the Korean War, which had killed some three million of their countrymen—nearly one out of every ten people—and sealed the division between North and South for decades. Private cars were a novelty and electricity and running water still luxuries of the well-to-do. Asia's up-and-comers included Burma and the Philippines. South Korea seemed destined to remain a perennial mendicant.[6]

Since then, South Korea has been near the top of the world's growth charts, with thirty years of growth averaging almost 9 percent a year, doubling, doubling, doubling, again and again in a fantastic exponential explosion of economic growth. Except in neighboring Taiwan, this sustained boom has no parallel in history—not in the United States or Europe during their high-growth stages, not even in postwar Japan.[7]

Korea's growth was more like a nuclear explosion than the usual dull, plodding course of barely perceptible economic progress. Boys who grew up working in rice paddies found themselves building oil tankers and designing semiconductor chips. And not just a few of them: A whole nation of people who were born in a backward, isolated agricultural country that had been smothered by colonialism and torn by war were catapulted into the global market.

In 1996, South Korea was the world's eleventh-largest economy.[8] For a mid-sized country, it is unusually obsessed with big, capital-hungry industries. Korea is the second-largest shipbuilder, trailing only Japan, and Hyundai Heavy Industries' Ulsan shipyard is the world's single largest. Korea is the fourth-largest electronics maker (behind only the United States, Japan, and Germany); Samsung Electronics in 1992 passed its Japanese competitors to become the world's largest manufacturer of DRAMs, the workhorse semiconductor memory chips that power personal computers and a host of other devices. It is the world's sixth-largest steelmaker: State-owned Posco is the second largest steel company in the world—and one of the most efficient.

South Korea is only about the size of Indiana. Yet until high costs drove its labor-intensive industries offshore, it for a time had the world's biggest single textile facility, the biggest tire factory, and the biggest shoe factory. Its Big Three car companies make it the world's seventh-largest automaker, ahead of Britain, and its auto companies plan to keep up a ferocious expansion program during the

1990s by investing more than $10 billion in new facilities at a time when most of their global competitors are cutting back.

South Korea's population alone is one-quarter larger than the other three of Asia's celebrated four tigers (Hong Kong, Singapore, and Taiwan), which have been the major economic success stories of the last thirty years. Its strength in heavy industry is also greater than its three rivals put together. This size made it big enough to develop a broad range of industries, but not so big as to be seduced for more than a few years by the sorts of import-substitution strategies that hurt bigger countries like Indonesia, India, and Brazil. A relatively small size also made political and economic control far easier than in large countries.

Order and Opportunity

In politics and in business, South Korea is a country not of laws but of a few very powerful men, not of political parties but of strong personalities. There is pressure for order and conformity, pressure that begins in the family and is buttressed by a rigid educational system and, at times, naked force. Koreans, like Japanese, say of their society that "the nail that sticks out gets hammered down." Koreans swing the hammer harder and more often than just about any other people in the world.

The glue for this system comes in the form of a rigid hierarchy, a residue of Confucianism that has been concentrated and magnified by the military-style discipline enforced on the country since 1961. Even with the election of Kim Young Sam, the military bias in Korean culture remains.

There are the obvious signs of this militaristic tint, like the riot police, and the less obvious ones, like workers literally running to work. Every day except Sunday, morning strollers in downtown Seoul will see secretaries and managers alike jostling passers-by as they sprint through the streets so they can cram onto an overloaded elevator in order to be at their desks by the start of the workday. What matters is that they are at work on time, for soon the more senior executives may head out for a spell in the sauna and the more junior men a prolonged trip to the lavatory, both reflections of the frequent Korean tendency to put form ahead of substance.

Powerful personal relations, revolving around the extended family and elite schools but extending deep into the workplace, are the cornerstone of this culture of authoritarianism. Personal loyalty, to both superiors and subordinates, typically outweighs loyalty to the organization and is far more pronounced than in Japan. Every aspect of Korean society is rigidly organized according to title, which often reflects seniority. Behavior toward seniors is extremely deferential, and requires special forms of speech, while that toward juniors can often be rough and crude. Even among twins, the younger one typically defers to the older one and uses an honorific form of speech.

To be in a group is to have a sense of place. The lapel pins worn by Korean men and the uniforms worn by women office workers are less a sign of militaristic conformity than a desire to show that they belong. Someone who is alone in Korea—such as a solitary hiker—is quizzed by puzzled Koreans who imagine that to be alone is to be lonely.

Those who are outside an organization and who want something from inside have to push through a dense bamboo forest of relations. A Korean who wants information from a company or the government will have a much more difficult time getting it than a Westerner would. Typically, a Korean man will try to figure out whom he knows in an organization (or whom he knows who knows someone) rather than make a direct approach. This reliance on personal connections means that even within organizations information is not shared freely—another competitive disadvantage in an information-intensive age.

Although foreigners are the most obvious outsiders, most Koreans, in fact, are also excluded from the elite group of mandarins and bureaucrats, businessmen and generals, who have controlled the country for the past three decades. The fact that blue-collar workers can almost never jump the social chasm to become managers reinforces this sense of otherness and alienation. Although hierarchical systems are generally accepted—even by radical unionists and opposition politicians—many Koreans think that they personally deserve to be closer to the pinnacle of power.

In general, this structure is quite similar to that in Japan, although Koreans are much franker and do not have the same degree of outward politeness. Koreans are more emotional, more openly distrustful, and more willing to act on that distrust. The unwillingness to accept a subordinate position in Korea is quite different from the case in Japan. Koreans often display an indifferent—even hostile—attitude toward service, which is also quite different from the Japanese attention to customers.

Fortunately, there is a ladder of upward mobility—education. The reverence for education—and the equation of education with the ability to pass standardized tests—is a holdover from Confucianism. Literacy is nearly universal, and the average skill level in Korea is higher than in many Western countries—sometimes strikingly so. In mathematics tests administered by the Educational Testing Service to thirteen-year-old students from a variety of countries, including the United States, Korean students ranked first in each of the five categories of problems. The gap between the Koreans and the others was higher for more complex problems.[9] Economic growth has provided tremendous opportunities and an educational system that is largely merit-oriented has ensured that the best and the brightest have had a better chance of rising in the last forty-five years than at any other time in Korea's history. It is this odd combination of authoritarianism and merit, flawed though it is, that has helped power Korea, Inc. into the ranks of the world's major economies.

A Culture of Rage

There is a popular saying: "When cousin gets a house, I get a stomach ache." It hints at the radical egalitarianism that makes South Korea's affluence so politically troubling. Social tensions were muted when the country was poor and everyone suffered more or less together. But with riches has come resentment at the widening gap between rich and poor.

Asia's growth economies are, by and large, relatively tame places politically. That is not the case in Korea, where bitterness and anger are close to the surface of everyday life, often bursting out in spasms of shouting or in the head-shaving, hostage-taking, and humiliations that are part of the country's union movement.

Roh Tae Woo, the president from 1988 to 1993 and the self-admitted recipient of $650 million in under-the-table payments, is serving a 17-year jail sentence on charges related to corruption and his part in a successful military coup. Roh's predecessor, Chun Doo Hwan, was hounded into two years of exile at a remote Buddhist monastery after leaving office. He is serving a life sentence for mutiny, treason and corruption charges growing out of his successful grab for power in late 1979 and early 1980. Park Chung Hee, who preceded Chun, was murdered by the head of the Korean Central Intelligence Agency, a man whom he had known for more than thirty years and counted as one of his closest associates. His predecessor, Yun Po Sun, who had headed a weak civilian government in 1960–61, was relatively lucky: Although he was pushed to the political sidelines, he escaped jail.

Syngman Rhee, the founder of the Republic of Korea, was driven from office and sought refuge in Hawaii, where he died. Cho Bong Am, mastermind of the agrarian land reform that saved Korea from Communist revolution on the eve of the Korean War, was, ironically, executed as a purported Communist for daring to challenge Syngman Rhee in the 1955 presidential election.

Korea has endured a brutal century. The trunk of the peninsula was sliced in half, creating two Koreas and splitting several million families. The Republic of Korea (South Korea) is a young country, founded only in 1948, and for decades it was an extremely poor one. It is in many senses one of the most unified nations in the world—probably only the Japanese are comparably homogeneous in terms of racial origins and national identity—and it uses this nationalistic sentiment to fuel economic growth. Yet when not facing an external threat, South Koreans are splintered by regional tensions, class divisions, and a brutal mistrust between rulers and ruled.

Government and business by no means have a monopoly on coercion. Students at the Hankuk University of Foreign Studies, one of the country's most prestigious universities, pelted the prime minister—a former professor—with eggs and dumped flour on him when he visited their campus in June 1991. Unionists frequently held managers hostage during bargaining sessions in the late 1980s. Their targets ranged from Hyundai's Chung Ju Yung to expatriates at Citibank and Barclays Bank.

This rage is not limited to campuses or companies. A track coach who said he treated a young track star "like my own daughter" ruptured her eardrum in a beating said by athletic officials to be typical of the treatment that many athletes receive from their coaches.[10] In another incident, some 300 employees of a food company invaded the hospital at the nation's most prestigious university, Seoul National, and staged an overnight sit-in. They were angry because a doctor at the hospital had published an article criticizing one of their company's products, a cod-liver preparation. At another hospital, relatives of a boy killed in an auto accident tried to attack a surgeon they said was incompetent with broken beer bottles and other weapons. While the doctor and hospital staff huddled in the intensive care section for protection, the relatives and friends of the dead boy staged a sit-in demanding that the doctor be turned over to them. In another incident, a group of disabled Koreans rolled their wheelchairs into the middle of a busy street and set a fire to dramatize their unhappiness with remarks made by the head of their (state-sponsored, of course) organization.

Even religion is not immune to this sort of blind anger, a recognition that raw power is what counts in this fast-moving society. The country's largest Buddhist sect, which is centered at Chogye temple in Seoul, has been torn apart by fighting between two well-armed groups of monks—often using chains and shovels in their brawls—who have battled for control of the temple for a decade.

This culture of rage is part of the harvest that the South Korean miracle has produced. The old village bonds have been broken by the tumult of the city, but there is no legitimate way of resolving the conflicts—which, in any event, Koreans believe are not supposed to occur among a homogeneous group of people with a unique 5,000-year history. But conflicts do occur. Americans are fond of decrying their country's excess of lawyers, but South Korea dramatically shows the dangers of trying to move toward democracy when both law and legitimacy are in short supply.

This ill-concealed anger sets Korea apart from its wealthier neighbor to the east, Japan. There is often a tendency to lump the two countries together, and for a time in the late 1980s it was popular to imagine that Korea was the "next Japan." Korea is in fact closer to the Japanese model than any other country in the world. Korea patterned its economy on the Japanese one, with a large role for government and an emphasis on large business groups and a strong manufacturing sector. In both Korea and Japan the line dividing the state from the private sector is blurred. But "Korea, Inc." is perhaps more apt than "Japan, Inc." In Korea, unlike Japan, the government has controlled and dominated business for the past thirty years.

A more important difference is that Japan has managed to build, or enforce, a social consensus that has so far eluded Korea. For example, in spite of a ritual spring wage offensive, Japanese unions have been extremely cooperative in working with employers to raise productivity and improve quality. Japan's rapid adjustment to the 1985–87 yen shock, when the yen appreciated nearly 50 percent against the dollar, is one example of how Japan works. Koreans, at least since 1987, have often been too busy fighting one another to get down to the hard work of improving productivity and quality.

Perhaps nowhere is the difference more pronounced than in the perception of business. Despite the key role business has played in growth, Koreans have a view of big business that is closer to the way Americans looked at the robber barons of a century ago than to the benign view that postwar Japanese have taken toward big business. That all the largest companies in Korea have prospered because of government help, in the form of preferential credit and lax regulatory and tax treatment, fuels the anger and ambivalence. But, despite this antipathy, a job with one of the big business groups is the dream of virtually every top graduate.

Corrupted Confucianism

Korea's success is often laid at the feet of Confucius, but Korea's is a twisted, perverted form of Confucianism. Confucius believed in the idea that power and authority should cascade down a natural hierarchy, from fathers to sons, from husbands to wives, from elder to younger. But with authority came responsibility: Confucius would never have condoned the abuse of subordinates, the systematic stifling of workers, the sacrifice of dignity in the name of development, or the chronic wife-beating for which Koreans are notorious.

Confucianism is often cited as a reason for the lack of concern for human rights and individual welfare, which is seen in everything from torture cases to Korea's horrible record on worker health and safety. It is a misguided analysis, for Confucianism is extremely concerned with individual welfare. Moreover, William Shaw, the editor of an insightful work on law and human rights in Korea, points out that the fashionable use of Confucianism to explain the lack of concern with human rights is logically inconsistent, for rapid industrial growth, huge industrial corporations, government by military elites, urbanization, and long executive working hours are certainly not Confucian concepts.[11]

Confucianism in Korea has been transformed almost beyond recognition in the past hundred years. Japanese colonialism in the first half of the century, the division of the country in 1945, and a horrible civil war in the early 1950s destroyed many of the traditional buffers against absolute power that existed in traditional Korean society. The violent century helped raise the military from a position of inferiority to one of supremacy.

It is tempting to think of Korea as a country that glorifies military culture. In fact, the military was traditionally looked down upon as a second-class calling, far below that of a scholar or government bureaucrat. It was only during the Japanese period that the military became a route of upward mobility and acquired some prestige as a profession. The power and image of the army was enhanced further after the Korean War and the establishment of the Korean Military Academy. Park Chung Hee's seizure of power then put the military in a pivotal position and yet more ambitious young men flocked to the army.

The three former generals who ruled the country from 1961 until 1993—Park, Chun Doo Hwan, and Roh Tae Woo—used this distorted legacy to build a powerful economic system, yet they never enjoyed full legitimacy, the "mandate of heaven" that a wise and just Confucian ruler needs. President Kim Young Sam began his tenure with overwhelming public support but he has been unable to push through needed structural reforms and his popularity has withered in the face of repeated scandals. The stereotypical Asian ideals of consensus and harmony do exist in Korea, especially among classmates and in some working situations, but much of what passes for consensus in Korea is actually coercion. There is little room in most factories and offices for these classical Confucian ideals, except as decorative calligraphy on the wall. Hyundai chairman Chung Ju Yung hurling an ashtray at a senior executive or slapping him in the face is every bit as typical of the Korean business milieu as this idealized notion of harmony.

It is better to think of Korea as a system of military authoritarianism laid on top of a rigid hierarchical society, one that draws in many senses on this older Confucian legacy. While this hierarchy stifled economic growth for hundreds of years, in the past three decades it has been reoriented and channeled toward economic growth. This economic juggernaut has destroyed traditional Korean society.

Thanks partly to Confucianism, there is a deep ambivalence toward business, which in the Korean mind is grubby in a way that scholarship or government service is not. When Roh Tae Woo made a state visit to Mexico in 1991, Mexican President Carlos Salinas de Gortari wanted to invite Roh and the business leaders who had accompanied him on the state visit to breakfast. Word came back from the Korean side that it would be unseemly for Roh to be at a gathering set up for "merchants," even though one of the main purposes of the trip had been to spur economic exchanges between the two countries. So Roh sat in his hotel suite for two hours rather than be involved in such worldly affairs.[12]

Something is askew. The president of a country with one of the world's highest growth rates does not want to have a dialogue with business. His administration and that of his successor pursue criminal charges against one of the country's most successful entrepreneurs on what are at heart political grounds. Workers who have enjoyed one of the most rapid rises in real wages in history are in ferment. And a government that has presided over rapid growth now pursues policies that seem designed to thwart further economic expansion. This is Korea, Inc., the bitter fruit of a painful past.

Notes

1. This was a popular slogan of the Park Chung Hee years. Quoted in Lee-Jay Cho and Yoon Hyung Kim (eds.), *Economic Development in the Republic of Korea*, p. 163.
2. The jail sentence was suspended on account of Chung's age.
3. *Korea Economic Weekly*, October 25, 1993, quoting the Securities Supervisory Board. Data as of September 15, 1993. The top 30 groups accounted for 44 percent of the market capitalization. Sales data is imprecise because Korean groups typically combine sales for group companies, rather than consolidating them to eliminate double-counting. For Hyundai and Samsung, the difference was between being $30 billion groups and being $50 billion ones in 1992.
4. Technocrats are government officials who hold graduate degrees, usually Ph.D.s,

earned abroad. Many of them work in research institutes affiliated with the government; some are employed as working-level officials in the bureaucracy, but they often do not go through the normal testing procedure to enter the civil service. At their best, they are more concerned with long-term policies than short-term political fixes. At their worst, they are theoretical and abstruse and their policies bear little relation to the world.

Technocrats have been very important in South Korea's economy because of the country's reverence for scholarship. South Korea has an extraordinary number of Ph.D.s, especially in economics. South Korea has more than twice as many United States-trained Ph.D. economists as Japan, although its population is only one-third as large. From 1970 through 1990, 801 Koreans and 305 Japanese economists published their doctoral disser- tations in the United States. The trend accelerated in the mid-1980s: 425 Koreans pub- lished their dissertations from 1986 to 1990 compared with 87 Japanese. (This information comes from Alice H. Amsden, in "The Specter of Anglo-Saxonization Is Haunting South Korea," in *Korea's Political Economy: An Institutional Perspective*, ed. Lee-Jay Cho and Yoon Hyung Kim, p. 92.) It is often said that Koreans have more Ph.D.s in economics per capita than any other country in the world. This may or may not be apocryphal.

5. For comparative data and analysis see two World Bank studies: *East Asia and the Pacific Regional Development Review: Sustaining Rapid Development* and *The East Asian Miracle: Economic Growth and Public Policy.*

6. The World Bank's Economic Report in November 1957 singled out the Philippines and Burma as the two most promising economic upstarts of the region.

> By comparison with most underdeveloped countries, the basic economic position of the Philippines is favorable. It has a generous endowment of arable land, forest resources, minerals and normal potential. Through a comparatively high level of expenditure on education, transport, communications and industrial plant over the past 50 years, the Philippines has achieved a position in the Far East second only to Japan, both in respect to its level of literacy and to per capita production capacity. . . . The prospects of the Philippine economy for sustained long-term growth are good.

In 1958 the Bank's report lauded Burma: "In her first 10 years of independence, Burma has made remarkable economic progress. . . . Burma's long-run potential compares favorably with those of other countries in Asia."

When South Korea's first development plan was introduced in 1961, the World Bank commented pessimistically: "There can be no doubt that this development program by far exceeds the potential of the Korean economy. . . . It is inconceivable that exports will rise as much as projected."

Cited in World Bank, *East Asia and the Pacific Regional Development Review*, p. 11.

7. The World Bank calculates that gross domestic product (GDP) in Korea grew an average of 9.9 percent from 1965 to 1980 and 9.7 percent from 1980 to 1990. The manufacturing sector grew even more rapidly—18.7 percent per year in 1965–80 and 12.7 percent in 1980–90.

The only countries that came close to that rate were Singapore, which grew at an average annual rate of 10 percent in 1965–80 but slowed to a 6.4 percent clip in the following decade, and China, which grew at a 9.5 percent rate in 1980–90, following 6.8 percent growth in the preceding 15 years. Hong Kong's figures were 8.6 percent and 7.1 percent, respectively. (The World Bank does not include figures for Taiwan because of political sensitivities.)

By comparison, Japan grew 6.4 percent in 1965–80 and 4.1 percent in 1980– 90. The United States grew 2.7 percent in the earlier period and 3.4 percent in the 1980s. World Bank, *East Asia and the Pacific Regional Development Review.*

It took South Korea only 11 years (from 1966) to double its real income per person; it took Japan 34 years (1885–1919). The United States took 47 years (1839–86) and Britain took 58 years (1780–1838). *Economist*, October 16, 1993, citing Angus Maddison, *Dynamic Forces in Capitalist Development: A Long-Run View*. Britain's economic growth averaged 1.2 percent a year between 1830 and 1910; Taiwan and Korea each averaged about 9 percent a year from 1962 to 1992. Both countries have showed lower growth rates since then.

8. World Bank, "East Asia & Pacific Region Country Briefing Note." Washington, D.C., 1993, p. 1.

9. World Bank, *The East Asian Miracle,* pp. 70–71. See also pp. 43–46 for a comparative discussion of education in Korea and East Asia.

10. Lim Choon Ae, a gold medal winner in the 1986 Asian Games, said after the incident: "I blame myself for not having done my best to improve my record. . . . This accident will only contribute to a better chemistry between us." An official of the Korean Amateur Sport Association said that the incident was "unfortunate" but that there was no reason for punitive action against the coach. "It is an open secret that coaches slap and whip their athletes on the buttocks during training." *Korea Herald*, June 4, 1987.

11. William Shaw (ed.), *Human Rights in Korea*, p. 2.

12. This information was provided to the author by a high-level official involved in the visit.

2

Bone Ranks, Buddhas,
and Slaves

Ours has been a history of stagnation, idleness, complacency, accommodation and feudalism . . . an annal of foreign oppressions,
conquests and misery.

—Park Chung Hee[1]

Koreans are fond of saying that they are a people with a unique 5,000-year
history. There is a sliver of truth in this sweeping claim to a special identity. But
it conceals almost as much as it reveals.

The simple fact of Korea's existence as a nation, even a divided one, is
extraordinary. Jutting south from China toward Japan like an extended finger,
or, as one Japanese put it, "a dagger pointed at the heart of Japan," the peninsula has long been considered a strategic prize by its powerful neighbors. Han
and Tang Chinese, Mongolian, Manchu, and Japanese invaders have fought in
and over Korea for more than two thousand years. Mongolian occupation in the
thirteenth century, two brutal Japanese invasions in the 1590s, and Manchu
incursions in the 1620s and 1630s hammered home to Koreans their vulnerability. Korea's ability to survive as a nation, albeit a divided one, would not have
been possible without a ferocious national pride.[2]

Understanding this past helps make sense out of what otherwise seems inex-
plicably bizarre behavior in contemporary Korea. It is a past of conquest, factionalism, and rigid social divisions in a country that was—except for
invaders—almost completely isolated from the non-Chinese world. For most of
its history Korea was a tributary state of China, with active relations to the court

18

of the Chinese emperor. But except for some contact with Japan, Koreans had no trade or political relations with any other country. Foreigners who happened to land on Korea's shores were usually killed, so it was no exaggeration when colonial adventurers dubbed it the Hermit Kingdom.

A brief tour through Korean history provides important clues for understanding contemporary Korean politics and economics. For more than a thousand years, a succession of centralized, authoritarian governments spawned a winner-take-all style of political rule that left little room for dissent. Although Confucianism allowed for remonstrances by dissident elites, the very idea of a loyal opposition is anathema to the Korean ideal of statecraft, and rivals have often been ruthlessly eliminated. However, a strong state again and again carried the germ of its own destruction, as inflexible rulers and bureaucrats were unable to reform or to share power even with other members of the elite.

A bloody history of invasions and factionalism has instilled a deep fear of disorder and disintegration among many Koreans and, even today, Koreans often fear that pluralism will lead to chaos. Koreans are taught to prize stability in order to guard against the country's powerful neighbors that could threaten the nation's very survival. Yet destabilizing factions dominate the political terrain precisely because power is so centralized.

Like most small nations, Korea has had a strong love-hate relationship with the large country that borders it. Chinese influence has been strong throughout Korean history, and it has often dominated Korean politics and culture. Koreans have looked up to the Chinese as a superior culture, but they often had reason to fear Chinese power. The Han Chinese invaded the peninsula in 109 B.C. and established fortified towns that gave them loose control over the northern part of the peninsula. At the time of the Chinese incursion, rice cultivation already had been under way for nearly a thousand years, and the first period of organized political life was evident. In a foretaste of what was to come, the ruling elite lived in walled towns apart from the rest of the population.

Chinese rule was not harsh, although the Chinese did use native laborers for cutting timber and mining iron ore. Leaders of states in the southern part of the peninsula paid formal subservience to the Chinese, who were regarded as a more advanced culture, but the tributary system was seldom antagonistic. This concept of subservience to a great power *(sadejuui)* still has a powerful impact on contemporary politics, given the interests of four great powers (the United States, Japan, China, and Russia) in the Korean peninsula. For reasons of survival, leaders have relied on powerful foreign patrons, even though this often has undercut their domestic legitimacy.

Birth of a Nation

During the period of the Chinese commanderies, four rival kingdoms were formed on the peninsula. They forged alliances with and against each other as they struggled for dominance. Eventually, the Shilla kingdom (57 B.C.–A.D. 935), located in the southwest, triumphed over its rivals. Unification came in 618, but only with the help of the Tang Chinese who helped Shilla subdue its rivals. The Tang then tried to dominate Shilla, which successfully resisted incorporation into the Chinese empire. Shilla was nonetheless forced to become a tributary state, paying formal homage to Chinese dominance.

The unification of Korea under Shilla was a pivotal moment in Korean history, for if the peninsula had fallen under Chinese domination, Korea as we know it probably would not exist. Chinese history is littered with the conquest and subjugation of proud, independent cultures, such as those of Mongolia and Tibet. If the Shilla had been less determined, Korea could easily have become an outlying area assimilated into the greater Chinese empire, especially given the powerful attraction of Sinic culture for the Koreans.

The Shilla dynasty pioneered an authoritarian, centralized elite state in Korea. Shilla's hierarchical society was built around a bloodline system known as a "bone rank." Important military positions or ministries could be held only by the so-called true bone ranks, who were related to the royal family. Even within the bone ranks there were important barriers to advancement, with the highest positions generally reserved for those most closely related to the ruler. Grades, which descended through a series of six "head ranks" held by commoners, placed a rigid straitjacket over every aspect of life.

Birth determined not only a man's station in life, but what kind of house he could live in, what color clothes he wore, what sort of horse and carriage he had (if indeed he was one of the privileged few who were allowed to own a horse), and even what eating utensils he could use. A state civil service examination, patterned on the Chinese model, introduced in 788, was limited to nobles (until 1894) and failed to open up this insular monarchy. Ambitious aristocrats and commoners alike grew increasingly frustrated.

Shilla was a wealthy culture. The official history of China's Tang dynasty said of the Shilla capital of Kyongju: "Emoluments flow unceasingly into the houses of the highest officials, who possess as many as 3,000 slaves, with corresponding numbers of weapons, cattle, horses and pigs."[3] With a population of perhaps one million at its peak, Kyongju was one of the great cities of Asia. The city's surviving art treasures, notably the stunning stone Buddha in the Sokkuram grotto, testify to a sophisticated artistic sensibility.

Shilla's rulers faced chronic political instability, the result of an overly centralized monarchy that was unable to share power even among the rest of the country's elite. Between 750 and 890, twenty revolts or palace coups took place. "It comes as no surprise that of the last twenty monarchs of Shilla, only nine died apparently natural deaths, the remainder dying violently or under suspicious circumstances," writes William Henthorn in his history of Korea.

> It seems doubtful that the rulers of any other nation have been subjected to the vicissitudes which have befallen the kings and princes of the various states of

Korea. They have been murdered by all imaginable means, including the sword, poison and drowning. They have been dethroned, kept captive, sent into exile, and upon occasion munificently been permitted to take their own lives.[4]

One king, Kungye, was driven from power by his own generals and then killed by his subjects as he tried to flee. It all sounds distressingly familiar to anyone familiar with more modern Korean history.

Koryo

Shilla's factionalism ensured its eventual collapse. The Koryo dynasty (918–1392) that succeeded Shilla was more fluid, and there was more upward mobility for talented aristocrats and even the occasional commoner. The Censorate acted as a check on royal power. Koryo was an age of great landed estates and a refined culture that combined Buddhism and Confucianism. Buddhist monasteries were exempt from taxes and from the *corvée* (forced labor for the state), and they amassed power and wealth. Some monasteries were so large that they formed private armies made up of monk-soldiers. Private estates also flourished, with local gentry growing wealthy thanks to the 50 percent share they took of the crop.

The Koryo dynasty faced a series of invasions by the Mongols in the mid-thirteenth century. It eventually had to cede dominance to the Mongols (who proclaimed the Yuan dynasty in China in 1271), but formal political control still remained with Koryo.

> A succession of Koryo kings was required to take princesses of the Yuan imperial house as primary consorts, while sons born to these queens normally would succeed to the Koryo throne. Koryo thus became a 'son-in-law' nation to Yuan and the Koryo king was no longer the independent ruler of his kingdom. . . . Moreover, Yuan's economic levies on Koryo sorely afflicted a nation laid bare by prolonged warfare. Yuan demanded Koryo gold, silver, cloth, grain, ginseng and falcons, and at times even young women and eunuchs.[5]

Artistically, Koryo was highly developed. A renowned Koryo legacy is the entire thirteenth-century Buddhist canon, known as the *tripitaka*, which was carved onto more than 80,000 wooden blocks in the vain hope of warding off another Mongol invasion. Beautiful celadon pottery was one of Koryo's greatest achievements, but fine bronze pieces and sophisticated stone carvings were also a feature of the period. Buddhist art was highly developed; the capital of Kaesong boasted more than seventy temples.

Chosun

Koryo disintegrated in the late fourteenth century, and General Yi Song Gye seized power in 1392. He founded the Chosun dynasty, which lasted more than five hundred years, until the Japanese seized Korea in 1910. Land reform was at the top of Yi's list of changes. He purged the Buddhist legacy of the Koryo period and established a Confucian order that became even more ritualistic than the Chinese example it was modeled on. The system was characterized by a rigid hierarchy, where bloodline, age, and rank strictly determined power and influence. Although in China the rigid civil service exams were nominally open to all men, in Korea even the ability to take the exam was limited to a relatively small elite.[6]

The Chosun dynasty tried to control its subjects through a primitive national identity system. Beginning in 1413, virtually every Korean had to wear name tags, which were permanent, graded badges with an identification number and personal information. The highest officials wore ivory tags. Outcasts and slaves wore large square wooden ones. Commoners' badges had information on their name, birthplace, and birth date; those of slaves and outcasts also had information on the complexion and height of the bearer. These breastplate passports formalized the class structure of the Chosun dynasty. They were also used to control movement and gather tax and census information.

Korea's rulers prized control, order, and stability above all else. A direct line of sight ran from the king's throne room out the royal palace, through the great Kwanghwamun (Kwanghwa Gate, which still stands in downtown Seoul) and down a royal boulevard that was flanked by government ministries. It was a physical line, but it was foremost a line of power symbolizing the ruler's authority throughout the land. Although the checks on the monarch's authority often limited his power, this symbol was an appropriate metaphor for the structure of Korean authority. After the Japanese colonized Korea in 1910, they built a huge capitol building between the palace and the gate to block this reminder of Korean royal dominion. It still stands, although President Kim Young Sam announced shortly after his inauguration in February 1993 that this graphic reminder of Japanese domination would be razed.

The monarch controlled the appointments that led to prestige and wealth; he could coerce obedience through the use of secret censors and show trials. Yet there was a shifting, uneasy balance of power between the monarch and the aristocracy. The Confucian literati were able to exercise a good deal of control over the royal monarch. In Confucian thought these scholars were the purveyors of ultimate wisdom, and the best of them tried to hold the Yi dynasty kings and queens to higher moral and ethical standards. Others sought factional advantage.[7] A monarch who acted unjustly ran the risk of remonstrance by scholars and the loss of the mandate of heaven, the legitimacy needed to rule. This is the origin of student demonstrations, the first of which occurred more than three hundred years ago.

In reality, the king's power was quite circumscribed by the bureaucracy. "Implementing a decision was a lengthy procedure which involved numerous offices, and every petty detail, including the style of the missive and procedural correctness, was deliberated, criticized, and wrangled over to the extent that the process resembles legislation by negotiation," notes William Henthorn.[8]

Factionalism played a prominent role from the beginning of the Chosun dynasty. When it came time for Yi Song Gye to pick a successor, his two sons from his second wife were presented as candidates. Angered, two of Yi's sons from his first wife killed their half-brothers. The following year, in 1399, their father abdicated the throne. These two brothers quarreled between themselves and four months later yet another brother assumed the throne; one of the killers was exiled and another deposed.[9]

Bloody factional strife among officials reached absurd proportions as different groups fought for coveted government appointments. Factions were based on familial loyalty and were economically supported by vast agricultural estates. Lee Ki Baik, in his highly regarded history of Korea, gives a flavor of the intractable feuding that plagued the Yi dynasty.

> The descendants of those identified with a particular faction inherited their factional affiliation generation after generation, and their clansmen joined in factional politics with them. . . . Even if a faction was ousted from power for a time, from the stronghold of their lands in the countryside the descendants of the victims would await the time when they might again rise to office in the capital and vindictively exonerate their ancestors.[10]

Park Chung Hee was more scathing in his criticism and ridicule of factionalism.

> Factional fights in our case are almost without precedent in world history, so infantile and puerile. . . . For example, a petty difference which originated between Sim Ui Gyom and Kim Hyo Won later gave birth to the Easterner and Westerner factions which ramified into Southerners and Northerners. Still later this division split again into Big North and Little North; Big North in to Flesh North, Muddy North and Little North into Clear Little North and Muddy Little North. The Southerners split into Clear South and Muddy South; the Westerners into Clear West, Muddy West and Young South, Old South. Junior and Senior factions arose, with the former again bifurcating into Pyok and Si factions.[11]

Revenge was severe. Ancestors' graves were dug up and desecrated, a terrible fate in an ancestor-dominated society, while the living were typically exiled or executed. The brutality of executions was limited only by the imagination of the executioners.

A struggle for the throne in the mid-fifteenth century, which came close to tearing apart the dynasty, saw the sons and grandsons of the losing faction killed by the victorious clique. Between 1498 and 1545 four violent purges of literati occurred. The first purge was capped when the body of Kim Chong Jik, who had died six years earlier, was exhumed and his skeleton was chopped to bits as posthumous punishment for some imagined crime.

There were a few incandescent moments in the history of the Yi dynasty. The early fifteenth century rule of King Sejong witnessed a period of rapid technological and cultural development. An innovative indigenous phonic alphabet was invented, replacing Chinese ideograms. Widely used today, it smoothed the way for universal literacy. Astronomy, meteorology, and cartography flourished during this period. Cast metal movable type had been developed in Korea as early as the thirteenth century—predating Gutenberg; these printing techniques were improved during Sejong's rule.

Sejong, unfortunately, proved little more than a brilliant exception to what became an increasingly moribund and splintered dynasty. A period of peace between 1630 and 1876 did not spur economic progress in Korea, in contrast to the development occurring during this period in Tokugawa Japan. The population grew, thanks to important agricultural advances, but the result was only a precarious balance in times of good harvests and starvation when the crops failed. During this time Korea probably had the highest ratio of population to arable land in Asia.

Like China, Korea became mired in a developmental bog because of its rigid social structure and a bias against innovation. Agricultural surpluses were skimmed off by non-productive officials, scholars, and nobles, most of whom were exempt from paying taxes. Some, in fact, were tax collectors who built huge fortunes by keeping some of the funds they collected on behalf of the state.

Increasing numbers of applicants passed the state civil service exams. But there were too few government posts for them, so most became little more than parasites in a society that revered the Confucian ideal of scholarship and looked down on any form of physical work. Pak Chi Won (1737–1805) described this sense of class privilege in his *Tale of a Yangban*.

> Even though a scholar *[yangban]* be poor and rusticate in the country, he is still a law unto himself; a man who can demand his neighbor's cow so that his fields be plowed first, and who may require the people of the district to weed his fields. Should someone slight the yangban, the wretch will be seized and lye will be poured down his nose, and he will be tied down by his topknot and his beard will be torn out hair by hair, and no one will attend his grievances.[12]

While these putative scholars enjoyed numerous privileges, peasants' lives were rigorously controlled. To take only one example of how minutely privileges were maintained, a peasant was allowed to ride a horse on only two occasions— his marriage and his funeral. Given the country's poverty, however, most peasants would probably be lucky ever even to see a horse. Below the free peasants were large numbers of slaves: Slavery was not abolished until 1894.

The Chosun dynasty faced periodic threats from the bottom. When the Korean court fled Seoul during the Japanese invasion in 1592, royalty and retainers were stoned by the people of Kaesong, the old Koryo capital where they sought refuge. The slaves who stayed behind in Seoul burned official records and government buildings. Today, numerous historical plaques in Seoul record this destruction, simply noting that it was caused during the Japanese invasion and implying that the carnage was all caused by the invaders. To state otherwise would undercut the myth of Korean unity.

The enduring combination of factionalism, a brittle class structure and economic torpor produced an unsustainable situation by the early 1800s. After particularly severe subsistence crises around 1810–1812, coupled with prolonged peasant rebellions, the population seems to have shrunk about 20 percent. By the middle of the century Korea was clearly very backward by the standards of not only Europe and America, but also many non-European countries. Korea's isolation was enforced by a rigid royal ban on all trade or contact with outsiders except emissaries to or from the Chinese emperor. Foreigners who landed in Korea, whether by design or chance, were killed or jailed. The first Americans to sail to Korea were killed in 1866, when a crowd burned their ship on the Taedong River near Pyongyang. It was not an auspicious start for what has sometimes been a troubled relationship.

As the imperial powers nibbled away at Korea's isolation, a furious and typically fractious debate about modernization began. Most of the country's Confucian bureaucrats rejected commercial development and no business class developed. Officials resisted the introduction of money, severely limiting economic growth. Until the 1890s, the only common currency was a cumbersome single-denomination copper coin. Rice prices were strictly controlled, inhibiting the growth of a merchant class. Peddling, which started during the nineteenth century as handicraft production increased, was the only remotely modern economic activity. It is typical of the Chosun dynasty that officials used the peddlers as spies.

A group of prominent reformers, known as the Progressives, tried to push through radical changes. Like their counterparts in China and Japan, the Progressives thought it was possible to use Western technology to spur economic development without sacrificing traditional culture altogether. The Progressives wanted to abolish class distinctions, reform the political process (Japan's Meiji Restoration was their model), and end Chinese interference in Korean affairs. However, the failed Kapshin coup in 1884 (which the Japanese military stationed in Seoul had promised to support but did not) destroyed the Progressives' hopes and strengthened Chinese influence over Korea.

Some limited progress in modernizing the economy was nonetheless made in the late 1800s. By the turn of the century, Korea had limited electric power, a handful of mining operations, a rudimentary tram system in Seoul, and new crops and handicraft industries. But Korea's internal economic and political weaknesses left the country with little room for maneuver. Modern economic development simply began too late to prevent the country from being seized as a colonial trophy.

Japanese Colonization

Korea was victimized by China's weakness at the end of the nineteenth century. Because the Chosun dynasty was a Chinese tributary state, Chinese troops three centuries earlier had helped repel the Japanese invasions of the 1590s. In 1894 the Korean monarch called on China again, this time to put down the Tonghak rebellion, a peasant uprising that swept through much of the country and could have brought down the king. The Japanese used this as a pretext to return their troops to Korea, for the first time since the failed Kapshin coup, and to redouble their attempts to win control of the strategic peninsula. As China tottered, the Koreans finally went it alone and in October 1897, on the site of what is now the Chosun Hotel in downtown Seoul, a Korean king finally dared to pray directly to the heavens and thus elevate himself to the same status as the Chinese emperor. But by then it was too late for even divine intervention. Korea was caught up in the whirlwind of colonialism and war.

As China stood on the brink itself, it could no longer keep Korea within its sphere of influence and the country was prey for whoever was strongest. The Russo-Japanese War, in which the Japanese vanquished the Russian navy in 1905, established Japan as the dominant power on the peninsula. Theodore Roosevelt, in a secret 1905 agreement, traded Japanese hegemony in Korea for Tokyo's acquiescence in U.S. control of the Philippines. Some Koreans still regard the Taft-Katsura agreement, as it is known, as a betrayal of the country by the United States, which they complain has consistently put U.S. security interests ahead of the national aspirations of Koreans.

When Japan formally annexed Korea as a colony in 1910, the attitude of the great powers was best summed up by the German consul in Seoul who is supposed to have said: "It is a shame no doubt, but no one I think will send a gunboat." Western treaty ports were closed, a tobacco monopoly imposed, and foreign mining companies were put under pressure to sell to the Japanese. About all that was left of Western influence was a rudimentary educational system run by Christian missionaries, many of whom actively worked for Korean independence.

The Japanese ran their new colony with the ruthlessness of a young colonial power determined to outdo its European teachers, trying to forcibly pull Korea into the orbit of the modern world. It was a brutal period, but one that arguably— and most Koreans *would* argue with this interpretation—had the virtue of laying the foundation for subsequent economic development. Landholdings were expropriated by the Japanese and worked by tenant sharecroppers. Railways and ports were built, so that Korea's rice farmers could feed Japanese industrial workers. The Japanese also made substantial investments in other infrastructure projects, such as roads and power supply systems, and began rapid industrial development during the 1930s.

More than simple physical development was at work, for thousands of Koreans were involved in managing and supporting these new enterprises. The civil service was modernized. Koreans were taught the basics of business, such as bookkeeping, in retail, financial, and industrial companies. The first Korean business groups were formed. Korean officers attended Japanese military academies, where they learned modern fighting strategy and imbibed the anti-capitalist, fascist ideology that dominated Japanese military thinking during the 1930s and early 1940s. Some of these Korean soldiers also went to the Japanese puppet state of Manchukuo (Manchuria) and witnessed the massive economic plans made and carried out under the authority of the Japanese military government. One of these officers was future president Park Chung Hee, who saw in Manchukuo the role that a military government could play in development.

Many of the elite of Korea assimilated to colonial rule, and the relationship between the well-to-do of Korea and the Japanese was relatively cordial. For most Koreans, however, the costs of Japanese colonization were heavy. After a brief but impressive boom during World War I, when Korea produced a wide range of manufactured exports for China, the rural economy of Korea was ruthlessly exploited as Japanese and Korean landlords attempted to extort the maximum agricultural output for export to Japan. The rice consumption of Koreans fell progressively. In good years the peasants ate imported millet from Manchukuo, and in bad years they starved. Industrial development had little effect on the majority of Koreans and millions migrated—or were forcibly relocated—to Japan and Manchukuo.

Chun Doo Hwan's family was one of thousands that moved to Manchukuo to take advantage of the economic opportunities opened by the Japanese conquest of the northeastern corner of China. A flattering biography of Chun, who became president in 1980, tells the story of how the family was forced to flee after his father—a local official—tried to kill a Japanese official and of the desperate life that the family and many other Koreans lived in Manchuria.

> Poverty was the order of the day for most Korean migrants in Manchuria, but they managed to survive. Worse than poverty were the lawless bandits. The local police and even military authorities could not do much to prevent the bandits from raiding the Manchurian towns and villages. Every time the villagers heard the frightening gallop of the bandits' horses they immediately ran from their houses and hid in the reed fields surrounding the villages.

As the villagers were hiding from one of these raids, younger brother Chun Ki Hwan began to cry. " 'Quiet him,' said one of the neighbors in a low but desperate voice. 'Strangle him or we'll all be killed by the bandits!' said another, who was holding a silk band in his hand. He was just about to lay the band on the baby's neck when the baby stopped crying miraculously."[13] After this brush with her baby's death, Chun's mother was said to have insisted that the family move back to Korea.

Korea's fierce sense of national identity had been forged by centuries of battling foreign invaders. So it was little surprise that the Japanese colonial period, too, was punctuated by periodic political resistance. A peaceful independence rally on March 1, 1919, was a watershed in the opposition to Japanese rule. More than 7,000 Koreans were killed in a savage crackdown that followed the independence protests.

Colonial rule became harsher during the fascist period of the 1930s, culminating in policies forcing Koreans to adopt Japanese names and allowing only Japanese to be spoken. During the late 1930s and early 1940s hundreds of thousands of Koreans were drafted into the Japanese military, and between 100,000 and 200,000 women were pressed into service as prostitutes, known euphemistically as "comfort women," for Japanese soldiers at the front.[14] Men were forced to take on dangerous work as miners or prison guards. Tens of thousands of Koreans died during the war, including, ironically, several thousand who were killed when the United States dropped its atomic bomb on Hiroshima.

Liberation and Division

World War II, or what the Koreans call the Pacific War, brought new stresses to Korea, including extreme shortages of clothing and food and increasing inflation. However, the country was not bombed by the Allies (except by the Russians on the northern frontier) and, while badly run down, was intact after the war. Koreans were every bit as happy as Americans when the Japanese surrendered in August 1945, and numerous factions jostled for influence in a country they expected would soon be independent. Unfortunately, international politics intervened yet again to dash their hopes of freedom.

At the Cairo conference of Allied leaders in December 1943 it had been proposed that Korea become independent immediately after the war. However, British authorities, concerned about the precedent that Korea might set for their colonies, opposed immediate independence for Korea. As a result, the Allies decided that Korea would become independent "in due course," and Korea was occupied after the Japanese defeat by the Russians in the north and the United States in the south. The victors were supposed to establish a trusteeship as a prelude to independence. Instead, the cold war rivalry between the United States and the Soviet Union, coupled with the splintering of domestic political groups, conspired to divide the country for the first time since the seventh century.

Seoul was at the center of a country in a race against time that it was doomed to lose. The capital, remembers former diplomat Gregory Henderson, was a city that combined intimacy and excitement. When a car went down the street, "you leaned out of a third story and said, 'Oh, there goes Mr. Lee. He's going to visit Governor Koo.' You knew everyone who owned a car in Seoul in 1948 and you usually knew where he was going."[15]

Tragically, dreams of liberation gave way to the brutality of division. Superpower rivalries magnified local ones and the country was caught in the whirlwind of change. The U.S. military authorities had no time for a fledgling coalition of nationalists and leftists and instead supported conservative politicians, many of them wealthy landowners. In the north, Soviet troops helped former guerrilla leader Kim Il Sung consolidate his power.

U.S. military authorities turned to Korean military and police officials, who had earlier collaborated with the Japanese, in an attempt to impose rule on the country. Leftists encouraged strikes and even armed uprisings by urban workers and farmers; between 1945 and 1948 the south drew closer to civil war. Peasants wanted to topple an oppressive agricultural system that forced them to turn over 50 percent or more of their crops to landowners. Dedicated leftists merged with nationalists in the south, riding a wave of revulsion on the part of urban workers and farmers against an elite tainted by its association with the Japanese.

Even before the Korean War, prospects for the Korean economy were bleak. In February 1948, American general Charles Helmick (who had served as deputy military governor with the occupation forces) predicted: "Korea can never attain a high standard of living. There are virtually no Koreans with the technical training and experience required to take advantage of Korea's resources and effect an improvement over its rice-economy status." Helmick also predicted that after the U.S. forces withdrew, as they did the following year, South Korea would become nothing but a "bull cart" economy and that nine million nonfood producers would face starvation.[16]

The view that the Koreans would never amount to much was widely shared. Two years later, Alec Adams, the British chargé d'affaires in Korea, described Koreans as "sorry, contemptible and dishonest." Adams also called Koreans "the thievingest people, and the greatest 'gimme' exponents of all time. Folk who live here mostly entertain the lowest opinion of Korean intelligence, mores, ability and industry. It is hard to believe, I gather, that they will ever be able successfully to govern themselves."[17]

A combination of ignorance and willful misunderstanding caused the United States to badly mismanage its military occupation of Korea. The United States reflexively sided with the well-dressed, English-speaking conservative landowners and, on many occasions in the early days of U.S. occupation, U.S. military authorities proved more comfortable with the former Japanese rulers than with aspiring Korean leaders.

Relations between north and south quickly deteriorated, thanks to local rivalries and superpower tensions. Both South (Republic of Korea) and North (Democratic People's Republic of Korea) declared their independence in 1948. Soviet troops left Korea in late 1948. The United States, which had no clear strategic policy in Korea, pulled its last forces out in mid-1949.

The North invaded the South on June 25, 1950. The attack came against a background of hostility on both sides, with Syngman Rhee in the months before the invasion threatening to march north, but it was Kim Il Sung who struck first, backed by China and the Soviet Union. It was a brutal conflict, one that killed some 3 million people. The end result was a tense stand-off almost exactly where the fighting began.

After the 1953 armistice, South Korea struggled to rebuild, but Syngman Rhee proved unequal to the task. The conservative patriot turned increasingly dictatorial and corrupt. Anyone with government connections could easily exploit them for profit during the 1950s. Graft was pervasive, perhaps equal to about $140 million, a significant sum given the tiny size of the economy. It was a time, remembers one Korean, "when we all stole from one another." But some stole more than others.

In the 1952 "Tungsten Dollar" incident, $3 million in foreign exchange earned from tungsten exports was given to favored firms for imports of grain and fertilizer. Huge profits were earned, some of which were recycled in the form of campaign contributions to Syngman Rhee's Liberal Party. A similar incident occurred just before the 1956 election, when the Commercial Bank of Korea made large loans to twelve industries. The money was then surreptitiously donated to the ruling party.[18]

In another example of corrupt government-business ties, an entrepreneur with good government connections was able to buy a textile mill left abandoned by the Japanese for a fraction of its value, financing most of the purchase through low-interest loans. Using almost none of his own capital, a shrewd, talented, and well-connected businessman could parlay his contacts with politicians into a business empire.

Although some people did well, most people counted themselves lucky just to scrape by. Kim Woo Choong, who later went on to found the huge Daewoo group, had lost his father in 1950, when North Korean soldiers took him away from the family dinner table in Seoul. Kim's family fled to Taegu, where Kim Woo Choong eked out a subsistence living by peddling newspapers. It was a time, he remembers, when "people were so destitute that it was easier to die than to live. We were constantly hungry."[19]

South Korea was short of everything. The U.S. military brought in ships equipped with large generators to provide electricity for the U.S. forces. The country's only auto producer built cars using cast-off U.S. military jeeps. The bodies were made of metal drums, also U.S. throwaways, which were beaten flat. The economy and the country, too, had been flattened. Unfortunately, Syngman Rhee proved unable to put the country convincingly on the road to recovery and reconstruction.

"Syngman Rhee was a patriot and in some sense a revolutionary but not in any sense an administrator," says one of Rhee's former cabinet ministers, who held an economic portfolio. "Rhee was born in the nineteenth century. He hadn't seen modern Korea. He spent most of his time in the U.S. in exile. He thought that if he [simply] appealed to the people's sense of patriotism they would follow him."[20] That worked for a time, but Rhee became increasingly isolated. Following a rigged presidential election in 1960 and the murder of a student activist by the government, large demonstrations by students and intellectuals forced Rhee to step down on April 19, 1960.

The Second Republic, which succeeded him, was marked by indecision and uncertainty, and the country continued to drift along through 1960 and into the spring of 1961. Park Kwon Sang, a leading South Korean journalist who was harassed, exiled, and arrested by the Park and Chun governments, is no friend of the military. But he remembers how dispirited the country was at the end of the 1950s and in the chaotic year after the overthrow of the Rhee regime.

> On the eve of the coup it was almost total chaos, economically, politically, socially. North Korea was far ahead of us. They had ten years of tough mobilized action. They worked hard and there were visible results.
>
> The North Korean military, too, was stronger than ours. They felt they were victorious, that they had fought not only South Korea but also the U.S. and had not been defeated.
>
> In South Korea, from the president down to the street beggar there was a mendicant mentality. The general attitude was "we need more aid, we need more American help." Half of our government budget relied on government aid.[21]

Thus was the stage set for the May 1961 military coup and 18 years of rule by Park Chung Hee.

Notes

1. Park Chung Hee, *The Country, The Revolution and I*, p. 166.
2. Korean sources sometimes use a much higher figure. Donald Stone Macdonald's history, *The Koreans*, cites a Korean figure of 900 invasions (p. 2). This is a good indication of the vulnerability Koreans feel, but it is misleading, elevating as it does border clashes and incursions into invasions.
3. Quoted in Carter J. Eckert et al., *Korea Old and New: A History*, p. 49.
4. Quoted in William E. Henthorn, *A History of Korea*, pp. 79, 83. Henthorn does, of course, indulge in some hyperbole, for the Byzantines and the Venetians could easily match the Koreans in their treatment of kings and princes.
5. Eckert, *Korea Old and New*, pp. 96, 97.
6. See James B. Palais, *Politics and Policy in Traditional Korea*, p. 7, for a discussion of this point. Palais's seminal book spurred intense debate among scholars of Korea about centralization, factionalism, the role of the elite, the power of the monarchy, and related issues.
7. This discussion of monarchy and literati draws on Palais's analysis in *Politics and Policy in Traditional Korea*, especially pp. 9–16.
8. Henthorn, *A History of Korea*, p. 159.
9. Ibid., p. 137; Macdonald, *The Koreans*, p. 32.
10. Lee Ki Baik, *A New History of Korea*, p. 209.
11. Park, *The Country, The Revolution and I*, p. 167.
12. Quoted in Frederica M. Bunge, *South Korea, A Country Study*, p. 69.
13. Cheon Kum Sung, *Chun Doo Hwan, Man of Destiny*, pp. 16–17.
14. Most of the women were too humiliated to talk about their experiences, and it was

almost half a century after the war before details began emerging about the systematic use of forced prostitution by the Japanese military. Kim Hak Sun was one of the first women *teishintai* to ever testify publicly. Born in Manchukuo in 1924, she was sold by her step-father to the Japanese military when she was 17. She and three other Koreans worked as forced laborers during the day and were forced to sleep with 5 or 6 soldiers during the night. "We Korean girls lived like animals. We felt like a public lavatory and nothing more than tools for Japanese soldiers' catharsis," she told Korean reporters in 1991. She eventually escaped and moved first to Shanghai and later to Seoul, where she worked as a house maid and menial laborer. *Korea Herald*, August 16, 1991.

Later, in December 1991, when documents surfaced proving Japanese government complicity, the issue became a major point of contention between the two governments. One of the few extended treatments of this subject is George Hicks' *The Comfort Women*.

15. Gregory Henderson, "Korea 1950," in James Cotton and Ian Neary (eds.), *The Korean War in History*, p. 175.

16. U.S. State Department, *Foreign Relations of the United States*, 1948, VI, p. 1092. I am grateful to Professor Lee Chong-Sik for this citation.

17. These are from two letters, dated December and October 1950, respectively, quoted in Ra Jong-yil, "Political Settlement in Korea: British Views and Policies, Autumn 1950," in Cotton and Neary, *The Korean War in History*, p. 54.

18. Alice Amsden, *Asia's New Giant*, p. 39; Leroy P. Jones and Sakong Il, *Government, Business and Entrepreneurship in Economic Development: The Korean Case*, pp. 272–73.

19. Kim Woo Choong, *Every Street Is Paved with Gold*, p. 158.

20. Author interview, November 1991.

21. Author interview, November 1991.

3

Economic Warrior

The people of Asia today fear starvation and poverty more than the oppressive duties thrust upon them by totalitarianism.[1]
—Park Chung Hee

Park Chung Hee's slight, slender build may have simply reflected his family's poverty and the reality that the last child had less to eat in a family where there was not much to begin with. Or perhaps it was a legacy of his mother's legendary attempt to induce an abortion by drinking raw soybean paste and willow bark soup when she was pregnant with her seventh child. In any event, from the time he was a young schoolboy Park's ferocious physical and intellectual intensity compensated for his physique. "He was half the size of his opponent, but he made up for it by bellowing all the time he was going for the other man," a military academy classmate remembers of watching Park in fencing matches. Much the same might be said of South Korea's improbable emergence as an economic wunderkind during Park's tenure, making up for its small size and natural weaknesses with a convincing mixture of courage and bluster.

If there is one day that marks the beginning of the history of modern Korea, it is May 16, 1961. At five o'clock on that late spring morning, an intense forty-three-year-old general who had flirted with communism in his younger days seized power. Park Chung Hee took over Korea promising to do away with the "evil legacies" of Korean history, end corruption, rebuild national pride, and spur economic development. During his eighteen years of rule Park converted most of these hazy revolutionary slogans into reality with remarkable thoroughness—with the striking exception of his pledge to end corruption. From the May 16 coup until his assassination in 1979, Park Chung Hee was the nation's school-master and its chief economist.

Park was a nation-builder with few peers in the modern world. None of the better-known national architects of the twentieth century—Ataturk, Nasser, or Lenin—have built a more durable and prosperous country than Park. Like any assembler of state power, the young president had no qualms about crushing people in the process of realizing his goals. Park was obsessed with economic growth and, in turn, he used economic development and the threat from North Korea to legitimize his often harsh rule. Workers were sacrificed on the altar of industrialization, as Korea racked up one of the world's highest rates of indus-trial accidents and deaths. Dissidents were jailed, tortured, and occasionally even executed for their attempts to assert human rights. Even the businessmen, gener-als, and politicians who prospered under Park's long shadow were not always safe from retribution, for he sometimes turned on his closest allies, purging them and destroying their careers.

Teacher, Soldier, Patriot, Collaborator

Park Chung Hee was born into a poor family in a farming village in southeastern Korea, not far from Taegu. He grew up walking to school in straw shoes over a mountain path. But even in the poverty and the plainness of village life, the family felt the powerful cross-currents buffeting the country. His father had been caught up in the Tonghak rebellion, the late nineteenth century uprising of tens of thousands of discontented farmers that nearly toppled the Korean monarchy.

Some accounts say that Park's father was one of the rebels and was sentenced to death before being granted clemency. Others say that he helped put down the rebels and was rewarded with a government post as a county magistrate, which he later resigned. In any event, by the time Park was born in 1917, the family was so poor that "his birth gave the family no cause for congratulation." [2]

Park was smart, and he won one of 90 places (competing with about 1,900 applicants) to the Taegu Normal School, the equivalent of an American high school and one of only three such schools in Japanese-occupied Korea. Friendly biographers have tried to paint him as a Korean nationalist who was opposed to Japanese rule, but in fact Park's youth and early adulthood is one of extraordi-nary success, which was gained by cooperating with the Japanese.

A sympathetic foreign biographer of Park, Michael Keon, writes:

> By the time he had come to middle school, he was well aware from his father of how the Japanese had suppressed the Tonghak uprising and brought his father to near-execution. There are those who can remember from among the little group of Koreans in the Taegu dormitory how at night the talk would be of Korean history and wrongs suffered and freedoms lost, and how Park persis-tently took part in this talk. [3]

In 1937, at the age of nineteen, Park graduated from this school and went to teach in the nearby village of Mungyong. Teaching is a revered profession in Korea because of the country's obsession with education, and had Park risen no further he still would have been the most successful member of his family. A Korean nationalist might have been happy to bide his time in the mountains, withdrawing from the affairs of the world until liberation from the Japanese was achieved. But instead the ambitious young Park Chung Hee joined the Japanese military.

At the age of twenty-three, Park won admission to the Japanese Manchukuo Academy for military training in the Manchurian capital of Changchun, and in the spring of 1940 he took the long train ride from Taegu to begin his studies at the academy. At the end of the two-year program he graduated at the top of his class, an accomplishment that was rewarded by the puppet emperor of Manchukuo, Pu Yi, who presented the young cadet with a gold wristwatch. Next, Park became part of an even more elite group of Koreans who were sent to Tokyo for two years of training at the Tokyo Military Academy. He first saw battle only in 1944 and spent the waning months of World War II in skirmishes with Chinese Communist guerrillas.

The Japanese army during this period had a strong anticapitalist streak running through its ranks, one that mixed Marxist-Leninist ideas about state control with rightist military ones. In 1934 the Army Ministry had called for increased state control of the economy and decried "classes that live by unearned profit." In Manchuria, the military's ideas were put to the test; Manchukuo became a training ground for the Japanese state's involvement in postwar economic development.[4]

The Manchuria of the 1930s was a new frontier for the Japanese and Koreans who moved there, and it was to have a huge impact on Park and on the subsequent course of Korean development. Grand plans to build dams, factories, and power stations were drawn up and, with varying degrees of success, implemented by the Japanese military and the business groups that were allied with it, such as the South Manchurian Railway Company.[5] Park's exposure to state-dominated economic development, especially of heavy industry, later had a profound impact on Korea.

Park was caught up in the chaos and political confusion that followed the liberation. Park's older brother was killed as he took part in a leftist uprising in Taegu in 1946. During this period, the history of the family is extremely murky, as is the development of Park Chung Hee's political beliefs. He was, however, an intense and well-trained young soldier in a pressure-cooker of political conflict. In one of the most serious infiltrations of the Korean military during the 1945–50 interwar years, a group of army officers that included Park formed a Communist cell. Park was a cell leader, not simply a member, and in 1948 he took part in an aborted military mutiny known as the Yosu Rebellion. He was sentenced to death, but won a reprieve after helping investigators.[6]

Park Chung Hee served for the South in the Korean War, when a questionable past was less important than the ability to lead troops. However, when he took power thirteen years later, his background was questionable enough that Kennedy adminis-tration officials initially worried that a Communist takeover had occurred in South Korea.[7] Park, as it turned out, was not a Communist, although statements like "Economics precedes politics or culture," sometimes made him sound like one.[8]

By the time the Korean War ended, Park Chung Hee was a brigadier general. After the war he spent a year training with the U.S. Army at Fort Sill, Oklahoma, and came home as commander of artillery in the Korean Army and commandant of its artillery school.

In January 1960 Park took over the Logistics Base Command in Pusan and tried to cleanse it of the systematic corruption that was typical of the Korean military at that time. A description of him by a local Pusan businessman, who was involved in supplying the army, reveals much about the kind of figure Park cut.

> Vaguely frightening, that's the best way I can describe General Park's arrival on the Pusan scene. Though plenty of people claimed to know all sorts of things about him, I doubt many of us had heard anything at all about him until he appeared.
>
> It was those dark glasses of his that first got me. I had gone to the base on business and Park was pointed out to me, standing outside some office. Just standing there. In fatigues. A stocky figure of a fellow. And doing nothing. Or seeming to do nothing. Just staring.
>
> [I later met Park on] a minor matter that I was afraid might be a bigger one in the making. . . . Park actually spent very little time questioning me; just two or three questions, key ones all right, and he was through with me. He was neither pleasant nor unpleasant. That is what I think I meant by vaguely frightening.
>
> Afterwards, I realized that there had been no threat, not even a reprimand, nothing. But I figured the writing was on the wall. I fixed things up right away, and certainly in the remaining time Park was in the Pusan job everything went perfectly well for me.
>
> Only it was all somehow unsatisfactory. If Park had cursed me out as a crook, or talked about saving the country from economic ruin, or shown some feeling of some kind, I would have felt better. But that time I best remember, and the two or three other times I ran into him to talk to, he just looked at you—or rather you *presumed* he was looking at you—through those great black glasses of his.[9]

This description is characteristic of the righteous, wise man who periodically overturns Korean society, a man who usually is portrayed as aloof, enigmatic, and a man of few words. Invariably, no one knows anything for certain about him, although many claim to.

Sweeping Out Parasites and Profiteers

After Syngman Rhee's ouster in April 1960, the country drifted for a chaotic and indecisive thirteen months. Then Park made his move. Along with Colonel Kim

Jong Pil (Park's nephew) and a group of about a dozen other officers, Park seized control of the capital. The civil government was forced to step down and the top ranks of the military were purged. No one knew what to make of Park behind his dark glasses. The local press corps dubbed him "Parkov" because of his menacing manner and, apparently, a suspicion that he might be pro-Soviet.[10]

Park's extraordinary logistical and organizational ability was evident during the coup, his ability to see things, as one senior officer later said, "all connected-up."

> The extent to which General Park had his own arrangements, of which we were an important part, but only a part, did not become clear to us until well after the revolution started off. . . . Pusan is our second biggest city. Well, when we moved to secure it, we found that it had already been secured by Colonel Kim Hyun Ok, who was not one of us at all. And Kim had secured Pusan for General Park, on General Park's direct order. And that's how it went. Bit by bit, it came out that the President had his operations plans, contingency plans, arrangement with troop commanders, air force operations officers, communications personnel, that we had either not known about or had not seen as all connected-up.[11]

Because of their training in the fascist-corporate state of the wartime Japanese empire, the military men of Park's generation had a clearer idea of how a state could organize capitalism than did either their seniors or their juniors. Park and other Koreans of his age, the "Japanese generation" that had matured in the 1930s and early 1940s, returned to Korea with a pragmatic philosophy dedicated to getting things done. As a group they had scant regard for the intricacies of etiquette, which all too often limited action in Korea. They also placed much less importance on the family and more importance on the organization—both the nation and the corporation. In this sense they were much less typically Korean than the generations that preceded and followed them. It is hard to overemphasize their importance in Korean development.

After the coup Park quickly formed a Supreme Council for National Reconstruction. This ruling council, made up of thirty-two military officers, suspended the constitution and did away with the legislature. Politicians, businessmen, and "profiteers" were jailed, and many were stripped of their wealth. The military forced a group of speculators who had grown wealthy during the Syngman Rhee years to parade through the Kwanghwamun intersection in central Seoul wearing signs with slogans such as, "I am a parasite." Freedom, complained Park, had been abused, with people mistaking it for "freedom to engage in smuggling, freedom to accept bribes and freedom to amass illegal fortunes."[12]

Two dozen of the nation's leading businessmen were arrested almost immediately by the military government. Samsung founder Lee Byung Chull, the country's richest businessman, remained in Japan until he could negotiate a truce with the new government. "Lee Byung Chull was out of the country when the coup broke out," says Yoo Chang Soon, who was in the research department of the Bank of Korea at the time and later became deputy prime minister for economic affairs. "He was called back to Korea, and when he landed at Kimpo some [military] people met him and escorted him to a place where Park Chung Hee waited for him and asked him to cooperate [in economic development]. Lee Byung Chull was saved. Park Chung Hee knew he was the leader."[13]

This incident showed Park's pragmatism at work, for he forced Lee and the rest of the business community to work with him. On June 14, the military passed a law designed to punish anyone who had illicitly grown rich in the previous eight years. It was, fittingly enough for a military nationalist like Park Chung Hee, more a license to prosecute anyone with money than a finely crafted piece of legislation. The law promised punishment for anyone who had, beyond a certain minimum threshold, earned profits through using government property; obtained government loans or foreign exchange licenses; made more than token political donations; earned profits for public works projects; evaded taxes, or illegally sent money abroad.[14] Five days later, on June 19, Lee Byung Chull "voluntarily" offered to donate his entire fortune to the government; within the next week eight other prominent businessmen followed suit.

On the Sunday after the coup, paratroopers shepherded 167 "hoodlums" through the street. In the sort of public abasement that is so popular in Korea, the purported criminals were forced to wear large name tags and signs with slogans such as, "We will quit being hooligans and will become workers for the revolution." In the first six days after the coup, 4,212 "hoodlums" were arrested, according to police figures.

The new regime initiated a social morality campaign. On May 21 police rounded up forty-seven dancers and charged them with dancing in an unlicensed dance hall "in broad daylight." The new national police director, brigadier general Cho Hung Man, said that one of his top priorities would be to eliminate foreign cigarettes, which he said cost the country 8 billion hwan annually. Authorities also warned that smugglers could be subject to capital punishment. Police in late May proudly announced that 9,822 packs of foreign cigarettes had been confiscated. Coffee and other "luxurious goods" were banned from the country, and smugglers were threatened with the death penalty.[15]

Park quickly conducted an extensive purge after he seized power. Purges are a common feature of the Korean political landscape, just as they are in China, and they are typical of new leadership. However, the upheaval that followed the May 1961 coup was exceptionally large. Two thousand military officers were dismissed, and hundreds of civilians were banned from political activities. Fifteen political parties and 238 social organizations were dissolved.[16] Under the headline "MILITARY COURTS BUSY IN CLEAN-UP DRIVE" the *Korea Times* noted that judicial authorities were busily sending "hooligans, reporters, thieves and other suspected criminals" to prison.

The unluckiest victims were put to death. At the end of 1961 the military government executed Choi In Kyu, who had served as Syngman Rhee's last home minister; a motion picture producer-*cum*-political hoodlum; a newspaper publisher; and a leftist leader.

The U.S. government looked askance at these young generals. The Kennedy administration briefly withheld support for the new leaders and the *New York Times*, in one of its less prescient editorials, urged that Korea's new leaders "look to the example of General Ne Win, commander of military forces in Burma," who the paper said had quickly restored political power to civilians after a military coup.[17]

Only Japan offered any guide for what Park should do to promote economic development after finishing his purges. Syngman Rhee had presided over a corrupt dictatorial government while Prime Minister Chang Myon's administration had been a weak democratic one. Neither accomplished much in the way of development and both were dependent on U.S. assistance.

Park's response was characteristically pragmatic. Having threatened the rich with jail, fines, and loss of their property, he then offered to cut a deal. Ten businessmen were summoned by Park. He offered to exempt most of those under investigation from criminal prosecution and allowed them to keep most of their assets. The young military leaders fined the businessmen, but, significantly, told businessmen that they could pay off the assessments by establishing new companies and donating the shares to the government.

The *Korea Annual*, a semi-official publication, gave this account of how the wealthy were treated. "The Military Government carried out criminal punishment, through the revolutionary trial, of those involved in illegal amassment of wealth so as to meet and alleviate the people's [indignation] against such hated millionaires and former high-ranking government officials and generals." This is the sort of rhetoric expected from a budding Communist state, not a country that would be heralded as a triumph of capitalist growth, but it is a revealing illustration of the mistrust—even hatred—that many Koreans had for businessmen.

The *Annual* went on to describe how the assets seized from the wealthy would be put at the service of economic growth, as directed by the government. "The confiscation [of illegally amassed wealth] shall be materialized through forced reinvestment in the specific plant projects that the 5-year Economic Development Plan envisaged. Thus, a number of plant projects including a cement plant, an oil refinery, an iron works, a fertilizer plant, etc. were designated as the target projects for the confiscatory investment."

In the end, most of the factories were not built, no shares were turned over to the government, and businessmen settled their obligations by paying only about $16 million in fines. Nonetheless, it was a classic example of Confucian coercion. But it is almost certain that this sort of bullying would have failed to produce economic growth in most other countries.[18]

Park's action set the pattern for a close, if stormy, marriage between business and government. He was determined to discourage wasteful economic activities by forcing businessmen to invest in the productive economy of the country, especially by building factories. His revolutionary fervor led to intermittent crackdowns on real estate speculation, corruption and black marketeering throughout his two decades in power.

Development by Decree

Economic growth, Park knew, would legitimize his rule by raising living standards. Development would also allow Korea to wean itself from its humiliating dependence on U.S. aid. But his experience in Manchukuo had taught Park that governments needed business to produce wealth. For their part, businessmen needed Park to provide the money and stability necessary for development. The fate of the state and of business were joined, and neither would survive without the other. But it was a marriage of convenience, not of love, and it was one in which the state dominated.

After agreeing to cooperate in national economic development, business leaders formed the Federation of Korean Industries (FKI) in August 1961. "This organization was founded by those business people whom Park had labeled as 'illicit profiteers,' " says Yoo Chang Soon, who became chairman of the FKI in 1989. Similar to the Japanese *keidanren*, the FKI was the main institutional transmission belt for corporate-government communication. Although the president was willing to listen to businessmen's advice, such as Lee Byung Chull's suggestion to promote exports, no one questioned Park's ultimate authority. Park in the 1960s was good at listening to suggestions, but orders ran in only one direction, from Park's presidential Blue House to the bureaucracy and business.

This top-down approach was very different from that used in Japan, where government-business relations were based more on consensus. In Japan, both business and the bureaucracy had built up independent power bases during a century of development; they were forced to work cooperatively. In Japan the large business groups typically included a bank. These banks, which collected low-cost deposits from individual savers, funneled money to other companies in the group, who used it for capital investment. This control of low-cost funding sources was key to the success of Japanese business groups.

The situation in Korea was altogether different, thanks to Park's decision to confiscate large shareholdings in banks. The five major Seoul-based banks, including one owned by Samsung's Lee Byung Chull, were nationalized within a year of Park's taking power. That gave the government almost total control over the financial system and, through it, over industrial development. Control of credit remains the government's most powerful economic tool even today.

A year after the military coup, the Bank of Korea was put under the control of the Ministry of Finance, which further increased the centralized power Park enjoyed over economic development. Financial authorities adopted a grading system to ensure that money was channeled to productive investment. If an industrialist applied for a bank loan to expand his plant and it was in a priority industry, such as producing textiles for the export market, he would almost automatically get the money. If the business was in a low-priority category, such as noodle production for domestic consumption, a bank loan was virtually impossible to obtain, no matter how good the business prospects were. The noodle manufacturer would have to rely on retained earnings or private sources of loans, such as the informal, or curb, market, which were significantly more expensive. The textile exporter not only received cheap loans but also enjoyed access to óther special funds that made expansion even easier. Moreover, he could usually count on preferential treatment from local officials if he needed to bend rules.

Park justified his control in the name of economic development, contrasting his plans for development with the poverty and chaos of the 1960–61 experiment with democracy. In forcing the business community to assist his nation-building enterprise, Park showed that he had learned an important lesson from his experience in Manchukuo: The state alone could not simply will economic development into occurring. The Japanese Army in Manchukuo had started with an anticapitalist, anti–big business philosophy, but had found that developing a country required both capital and professional management.

This is where Park and his counterparts in Japan and Taiwan, no matter how harsh their political regimes, diverged from Communist states: they recognized the importance of nurturing business. They were always suspicious of business and they always tried to control it for their own purposes, but they also knew that government could never substitute for profit-seeking businessmen.

Park managed that delicate balancing act with consummate skill. On one side he controlled business through loans, periodic tax investigations and anticorruption campaigns. But he also presided over the explosive growth of the chaebol, which were both fiercely competitive private companies—in the export sector—and privileged recipients of domestic oligopolies and monopolies.

Park incorporated the private sector into the state; it became impossible to tell where one ended and the other began. This was the essence of Korea, Inc. It allowed the state to manage the big picture, and business and workers to labor in the trenches. It also gave foreign bankers the confidence to lend tens of billions of dollars with relatively little risk of default.

That Park was able to pull off this highwire act so successfully is testimony to his logistical and political skills. But it also shows his pragmatic nationalism. Park was willing to test the patience of the United States Agency for International Development (AID) advisers who were helping to bankroll the country. He was also willing to break with the rules of traditional Korea. He set up a centralized, militarized state that was far more powerful than any that had preceded it. He grafted the powerful growth-oriented bureaucratic structure of the Japanese colonial era onto the Korean political structure. He did this by drawing on what he knew best of Japan; the militarized, top-down approach that he had seen in Manchukuo during the war.

Jung-en Woo, a scholar who has written on the relationship between the state and finance in South Korea, had this to say about the men who engineered the coup:

> These were men of peasant origin and harbored, like ultranationalist Japanese officers in the 1930s, a peasants' suspicion of the wealthy. When they thought of capitalism, they thought of a conspiracy of the rich; when they entertained the notion of economic development, they thought of a rich nation and a strong army, and wartime Japan came to their minds; and when they awakened to the need for domestic resource mobilization, they badgered the rich and forced citizens, through campaigns and edicts, to salt away chunks of their salaries.[19]

The military revolutionaries had plenty of hazy slogans, but they quickly found out that trying to run Korea would require far more than rhetoric. Park liked bold actions and occasionally tried shock therapy for the economy. On June 9, 1962, barely a year after he seized power, he attempted a snap currency exchange in an effort to tease money out of the underground economy.

All currency had to be surrendered by the following business day, with one new won issued for 10 old hwan, and all bank accounts were frozen. This basically shut the economy down. The idea was to pull money out of hoarding—and to ensure that political opponents did not have access to funding—but it was a disaster of the sort usually promulgated by anticapitalist revolutionaries. The main impact was to confirm businesses' suspicion of the new administration.

It was a measure, says economist and former Prime Minister Nam Duck Woo, that

> came from a basic lack of economic knowledge. People [around Park] thought Korea needed investment resources but [imagined] those resources were in the hand of pirates, people who were trying to hold the money instead of using it. He thought the money was under the mattress or under the roof. That was nonsense. People had been suffering from chronic inflation so money value was deteriorating every day. People had their money in the bank. I told him it was an illusion that you can find money.[20]

Park and the people around him "were a little confused at the beginning," says Nam, a technocrat who became a leading economic minister in the 1970s. "He was guided by several different thoughts. They were influenced by some academics who had a socialist approach." This was partly academic jealousy, for Nam was at Sogang University's economics department at the time. The Sogang professors thought that Seoul National University's economics department was a hothouse of economic radicalism.

The *Korea Annual* criticized the currency change as an example of Korean Central Intelligence Agengy (KCIA) politics, attacking Kim Jong Pil for his role in this secretive, half-baked attempt at reform. It was, as Jung-en Woo points out, an amateur attempt to mimic a similar measure in postwar Germany. The difference is that the currency reform in Germany was accompanied by sweeping economic liberalization of the sort that South Korea never had.

South Korea was desperately poor when Park took over. Song In Sang, a minister of reconstruction in the late 1950s, counted it as a major victory that by the end of the Rhee years most people were hungry only in the "barley hill" (late spring, before the barley crop came in) rather than all year round. By virtually any economic measure, Korea ranked near the bottom of the list. For example, per capita electricity consumption was only about 2 percent that of the United States.

Shortly after he took power, Park complained that South Korea, a country of 24 million people, produced less electricity than Ford Motor Company did in Detroit. "How can we even dream of independence? How dare we cry out for the industrialization of Korea?"[21] Park exhorted Koreans to "exhaust every ounce of our strength to develop electricity. Without electricity there can be no production. Without production we cannot hope for the growth of the national economy."

The North was far stronger than the South in many economic areas and remained so until the early 1970s.[22] The per capita GNP in the South was less than $100 a year, among the poorest in the world. Even this figure masks the true level of poverty, because Korea's harsh climate required more resources for heating and housing than was the case in countries like India or the Philippines, which had similar per capita incomes.

Seoul, which had been captured twice by the Communists during the war, had almost no basic infrastructure. Even in the capital, electricity was a luxury and telephones were limited to the elite. In 1960, the entire country had only 627 public telephones. Peter Bartholomew, an American who went to Korea with the Peace Corps in 1967, remembers that in the late 1960s some people used to put electricity meters outside their houses, although they had no electrical connections, simply as a sign of affluence.[23]

When Park seized power in 1961, South Korea was an overwhelmingly rural country. Nearly three out of every five Koreans lived on a farm, most simply eking out a subsistence living. The sweeping land reform of the 1950s had displaced the old landowning class, so that industrialization could not be funded with surpluses from agriculture, as it was in many other countries. It was largely to solve this problem of rural poverty that Park decided to jump-start the development process by concentrating on industrialization. "The strategy of our economic plan was to develop key industries and infrastructure industries," remembers Park Tae Joon, who was a young colonel in 1961 and later went on to found Pohang Iron and Steel (Posco). In 1961, however, industrialization was only a dream, one made more poignant by the primitive conditions in the countryside.[24]

Notes

1. Park Chung Hee, *Our Nation's Path*, p. 204.
2. Kim Chong Shin, *Seven Years with Korea's Park Chung-hee*, p. 214.
3. Michael Keon, *Korean Phoenix*, p. 43. Much of this section is drawn from Keon's account. Other sources include Gregory Henderson, *Korea, The Politics of the Vortex*, p. 108, and Kim Chong Shin, *Seven Years with Korea's Park Chung-hee*.
4. Chalmers Johnson, *MITI and the Japanese Miracle*, pp. 124–25.

5. Ibid., p. 130.

6. Paik Sun Yup, *From Pusan to Panmunjom*. Brassey's, a Division of Maxwell Macmillan, Washington, D.C.: 1992 (my source is pp. 813, 829–32 in manuscript of the English translation provided to me by translator Bruce Grant. This section was deleted from the published book. The original is *Kun Gwa Na* [Army and I]. Seoul: Daehan Textbook, 1989). Paik says Park Chung Hee was the only one sentenced to death who was spared. Like so much of the history of this period, however, Paik's account cannot be regarded as authoritative.

7. Jon Halliday and Bruce Cumings, *Korea: The Unknown War*, p. 41. The Kennedy administration was angry enough at Park's snuffing of Korea's embryonic democracy that it withheld $25 million in aid for a time. This is cited in Jung-en Woo, *Race to the Swift*, p. 106. Park had notoriously bad relations with U.S. diplomats in Seoul immediately after he took power.

8. Park Chung Hee, *The Country, the Revolution and I*, p. 26.

9. Quoted in Keon, *Korean Phoenix*, pp. 49–50.

10. Kim Chong Shin, *Seven Years With Korea's Park Chung-hee*, pp. 125–27, describes the use of the "Parkov" nickname and its prohibition by the military.

11. Keon, *Korean Phoenix*, p. 64.

12. Park Chung Hee, *Our Nation's Path*, p. 174.

13. Author interview, November 1990.

14. Leroy P. Jones and Sakong Il, *Government, Business and Entrepreneurship in Economic Development: The Korean Case*, pp. 280–82.

15. *Korea Times*, May 27, 1961, on cigarettes; the other material comes primarily from contemporary newspaper accounts.

16. Henderson, *Korea, The Politics of the Vortex*, p. 357 on military officers; Donald Stone Macdonald, *The Koreans*, p. 54, on politicians; *Far Eastern Economic Review*, September 7, 1961, on political parties and social organizations.

17. Cited in *Korea Times*, May 24, 1961.

18. Quotations are from *Korea Annual*, 1964 (the first edition of the annual); the data on fines paid is from Jones and Sakong, *Government, Business and Entrepreneurship in Economic Development*, pp. 69–70, 272.

19. Woo, *Race to the Swift*, p. 81.

20. Author interview, December 1991.

21. Park, *The Country, the Revolution and I*, p. 43.

22. Nicholas Eberstadt, one of the few scholars who has made a comparative study of both economies, made this point in a personal communication, October 1991. Song Byung-nak, *The Rise of the Korean Economy*, p. 206, quotes a Swedish source as saying that in 1960 the North led the South in 17 areas of the economy, "including the production of electricity, cement, coal, fertilizer and tractors."

23. The figure on public telephones is from Park, *The Country, the Revolution and I*, p. 87. The anecdote about electricity meters came in a personal communication from Peter Bartholomew, October 1989.

24. A good discussion of the problems South Korea faced in agriculture in the 1960s and 1970s is found in Edward S. Mason et al., *The Economic and Social Modernization of the Republic of Korea*, pp. 209–43. South Korea faced particular problems in agriculture because it had one of the lowest ratios of arable land per person in the world, far lower than that of even India or China.

4

To Build a Nation

In human life, economics precedes politics or culture.
—Park Chung Hee[1]

The young military revolutionaries were determined to make their impoverished country prosperous and autonomous. It was an improbable goal for a country still suffering from the brutal civil war that had sealed the peninsula's division a decade earlier. South Korea was an international mendicant, with half its government budget and most of its investment financed from abroad, mostly in the form of U.S. aid.

Economic growth since the end of the Korean War had been sluggish and, following cuts in U.S. assistance at the end of the 1950s, threatened to disappear altogether by the time Park staged his coup. "I felt, honestly speaking, as if I had been given a pilfered household or a bankrupt firm to manage," Park later wrote. "Around me I could find little hope. The outlook was bleak."[2]

Looking back on this period thirty years later, Park Tae Joon, one of Park Chung Hee's juniors who took part in the coup, underscored the army's concern with Korea's economic misery.

> The Korean people suffered from hunger. In the spring just before the barley harvest people had to eat pine bark. Korea was entirely dependent on U.S. assistance but that assistance was not enough. We didn't have any capital facilities or natural resources. . . . At that time the whole country was completely ruined and destroyed. We didn't know when the North Koreans would attack us again. The civilian government was totally relying on U.S. assistance. They were not interested at all in developing the country's economy.[3]

Worse yet, Korea did not have much in the way of a glorious past to back up Park Chung Hee's hopes of standing tall. The sclerotic Chosun dynasty had been a tributary state of the Chinese and, ever since Korea had been pried open by imperial powers, its weakness had been displayed to the world. During the twentieth century the Japanese had brutally colonized the country, and liberation in 1945 had proved to be a cruel hoax.

Park Chung Hee was scathing in his critique of Korean history. "When did our ancestors, even once, dominate the territories of others, seek foreign civilization in order to reform our national society, demonstrate our power of unity to the outside world and act with independence in the face of others? Always, it has been we who have been mauled by the big Powers, assimilated by foreign cultures, impeded by primitive forms of industry, indulged in fratricidal squabbles. Ours has been a history of stagnation, idleness, complacency, accommodation and feudalism."[4]

Yet, against the odds, South Korea has managed to carve out a fair amount of prosperity and independence by pursuing a high-growth economic strategy. Park took accepted economic theory, mixed in what he had seen of the wartime Japanese economic model, and topped this concoction off with his fervent nationalistic exhortations. This recipe would not work in many countries, but it did in Korea, thanks to a willingness to accept and obey legitimate—and sometimes even illegitimate—authority.

The secrets of the economic system Park put in place are deceptively simple: brutally long work hours, high rates of savings and investment, and a hierarchical, authoritarian system that rewarded those who succeeded and punished those who did not cooperate. Park was able to squelch most dissent, and he was smart enough to add the discipline of the international export market to make sure that companies were competitive. Moreover, for all his talk about independence, he was pragmatic enough to see that industrial expansion needed to be financed by foreign bankers and that foreign companies were the best source of competitive technology.

Perhaps his greatest achievement was the intangible one of convincing Koreans that economic growth was both important and possible, and that this was a historic goal worth suffering for. "Unless we can establish an 'economy first' consciousness, our dream of building a strong national state will end in a dream and nothing more," Park warned Koreans. "I want to emphasize, and re-emphasize, that the key factor of the May 16 Military Revolution was to effect an industrial revolution in Korea."[5]

Some of his speeches and writings have an almost hysterical quality to them, as if he wanted the lower classes to rise against the rich. Here is a quintessential passage from *The Country, the Revolution and I*:

> To the sound of churning machines, sweat!
> You, a young girl sitting in the second class compartment, your white hands holding a book of French poetry. Your white hands I abhor.

We must work.

One cannot survive with clean hands.

Clean hands have been responsible for our present misery. One cannot hate a clean pair of hands, but have you seen the hands of the privileged class which comprises but one percent of our population? Smooth hands are our enemy.

Let us fire our bullets of hatred against such politicians; let us never give them a chance to rule over us.[6]

In fact, many of the colonels who made the coup went into politics, and Park failed in his goal of fundamentally changing the character of Korean politics. Although the new generation may have been less corrupt than its predecessor during the 1950s, it was nonetheless corrupt by almost any other standard.

Bureaucrats, Technocrats, and Generals

Park was every bit as strong on bureaucratic organization as he was on rhetoric. He skillfully used what he had learned in the military, especially the Japanese wartime military, to build the foundations of Korea's powerful state apparatus. Under Park, the state controlled virtually all economic activities in South Korea. The government approved all bank loans, granted licenses for virtually all businesses, and controlled many prices. In this, the Korean economy copied much of the Japanese model, but with a heavier emphasis on political and military influence in the running of the economy.

Some Koreans said that Park was more comfortable speaking Japanese than Korean. Certainly Park did not share Syngman Rhee's loathing for the Japanese, and one of his top priorities was to normalize diplomatic relations with Japan, which had been cut in 1945. In Japan, Park had a familiar model for Korea to follow. It was the Japan of the 1930s and 1940s that Park was familiar with, however, and this militarized model left a stain on the path of Korean development that remains even today.

Park's vision, his willingness to see in Japan what Korea could one day become, was probably one of his best and most surprising qualities. No one, however, should have been surprised at Park's organizational talents, for his entire career had equipped him to build and run an organization like Korea, Inc. His training as a Japanese cadet and his experience in managing logistics in Pusan gave him the confidence and organizational abilities to manage a small, primitive economy like Korea's. His experience in Manchukuo allowed him to see how the state could direct economic growth, and how government needed the cooperation of private businesses to be successful.

The Park government quickly acted to shape the government and the economy along Japanese lines. In June 1961, only a month after the military coup, the Economic Planning Council, later to become the Economic Planning Board (EPB), was established. The EPB was to become the brains of the new economy, and it allowed Park control of a sort that had not been possible before. It centralized economic information, taking over planning powers from the former Ministry of Reconstruction, responsibility for the budget from the Ministry of Finance, and statistical collection from the Ministry of Home Affairs. Information is power, and nowhere more so than in hierarchical societies such as Korea where information is not shared freely.

Even the prime minister's office of planning and coordination had to report to the EPB, as did assistant ministers in charge of policy implementation at other ministries. Later the EPB took over responsibility for price policy, fair trade administration, and reviews of projects. The EPB also sent mid-level officials to other bureaus, establishing a powerful network of personal connections that gave the ministry a window into most nooks and crannies of the country's economic bureaucracy. (This did not extend to the military and security area, however. A powerful planning official, Kim Jae Ik, complained to a U.S. diplomat as late as the mid-1970s that the EPB had no idea what the military was doing with its money.[7])

The planning procedure became increasingly elaborate during the 1960s and early 1970s. Based on the five-year plan, the government issued an annual economic management plan each year. The EPB circulated the draft of this plan to ministries, which then based their policies on these projections.

Economic policy was coordinated through this extensive administrative function. But simply setting up a planning bureaucracy in itself may do little for economic growth, as many countries with elaborate planning procedures have found. One reason that Korea was different was Park's personal involvement. He chaired monthly export meetings, monthly economic reviews, and quarterly science and technology promotion meetings. Koreans are often willing to slack off, to do just enough to get by and keep up appearances. But when the boss calls, especially one as demanding as Park Chung Hee, business and the bureaucracy have little choice but to respond. Park's fondness for asking blunt and detailed questions kept even the most senior officials alert and well-prepared. In a typical example, Park once embarrassed the minister of home affairs during a live televised press conference by asking him what the planned rural family income was in Kyongsang Province. It did not take too many incidents like that one for officials to improve their preparations dramatically in order to be ready for even the most arcane inquiry.[8]

Park also had a regular system of visiting ministries. His background as a military supply officer served him well in Korea's simple economy, for Park could easily become familiar with details and suggest ways for bottlenecks to be eased. Joel Bernstein, an American adviser during the 1960s, remembers that Park surprised bureaucrats with how much he knew about what they were doing, "so his presence was felt not only in terms of general policy but very specific directional push. He probably never left one of these ministries without leaving some new instruction with them, which would generally be in the nature of doubling their goals for the next year."[9]

With the government now dedicated to industrialization, the power of the Ministry of Commerce and Industry (the MCI, later known as the Ministry of Trade and Industry, or MTI) was greatly strengthened. The nationalization of the banks and the centralization of the financial system also made the Ministry of Finance (MoF) extremely powerful. If the Economic Planning Board was the brains of economic policy, the MCI and the MoF were its hands. It was MCI and MoF officials who had day-to-day contact with businessmen who wanted approval for projects.

These men were part of a small elite. Almost all had attended Seoul National University, which had originally been set up by the Japanese. They had passed rigorous entrance examinations and, as in Japan, while many students did not study particularly hard at university, they formed lifelong contacts. Classmates usually meet formally at least once a year for the rest of their lives. Smaller, informal groups meet more frequently. An attorney in Seoul who graduated from SNU's law college describes the university's importance:

> SNU is a school where you have a certificate of being in an elite group just by graduating. Most of the time the motive [for going to SNU] was to become a government official. Traditionally, the only position that the Korean elite could enjoy was government officials. Engineers went to work at the Ministry of Commerce and Industry or the Construction Ministry. Law students became judges or prosecutors. It was a way of social mobility [in a country where] status is so important. Do the teachers teach well? No. Does the school have enough facilities to experiment? No. But you are given some privilege and responsibility to behave.[10]

Two other universities, Yonsei and Korea, supplemented SNU's role in providing the country's technocratic, bureaucratic, and business cadre. This sense of attending the right school is so extreme that during the 1987 election a senior ruling party official asserted that his party was more suited to running the country because party members had gone to better schools.

Guided Capitalism

The men who framed policy in Korea in 1961 after Park took power made no secret of their belief that the country was not ready for a free market system. The first five-year economic development plan, which was written during the summer of 1961 and released later that year, betrayed this socialist-militarist approach to the economy:

> Throughout the plan period, the economic system will be a form of "guided capitalism," in which the principle of free enterprise and respect for the freedom and initiative of free enterprise will be observed, but in which the government will either directly participate in or indirectly render guidance to the basic industries and other important fields.

Government officials quickly said that the cabinet would be directly involved in investment decisions and, in fact, it was not until 1982 that the government gave banks the legal freedom to make their own loan decisions.[11]

Even now, that freedom remains highly circumscribed. An early draft of the plan had "socialist overtones and near xenophobic nationalistic characteristics," says scholar David Satterwhite. Satterwhite believes that the "command economy" aspects of the plan were toned down and exports emphasized partly as a way of appeasing the United States. "The official reaction from Washington would likely have been rapid and intense rejection, with serious policy implications for U.S. recognition and eventual support of the junta, given grave suspicions entertained by the United States that the coupmakers were 'closet socialists' intent on communizing the Republic."[12]

Yoo Chang Soon, who had been involved with a development plan drafted in the late 1950s at the Ministry of Reconstruction (the forerunner of the Economic Planning Board), which formed the starting point for Park's five-year plan, described the thinking behind this pivotal document.

> Broadly, there were two schools of thought. One side wanted balanced growth. ... The other favored unbalanced growth, with more emphasis on industrialization and lighter emphasis on agriculture. Park Chung Hee chose the [path of] unbalanced growth for industrialization. That's what Japan did in the Meiji era. They built a factory with the national budget and expected the benefits would come later. That was exactly the model we took.[13]

The first five-year plan was thrown together rather hastily, in spite of the groundwork that had been done by the Economic Development Council at the Ministry of Reconstruction. On July 22, 1961, less than ten weeks after the coup, the Supreme Council for National Reconstruction (SCNR) announced the establishment of the Economic Planning Board and unveiled the five-year economic growth plan.

Satterwhite believes that the quick adoption of a plan reflected the desire of the military to project an image of action as well as its ability to draw on the planning work that had already taken place under the Syngman Rhee and Chang Myon administrations. "In order to accomplish this in a politically acceptable manner the upper stratum of planners was lopped off and their assistants were fully consulted and brought into the SCNR's economic discussion."[14]

The plan was a product of wishful thinking as much as careful planning, and it was derided by many domestic critics as being overly optimistic. However, actual economic performance far outpaced the plan, with annual GNP growth from 1962 through 1966 averaging 8.3 percent, compared with a planned 7.1 percent. After it became apparent that the plan would exceed its goals, it was criticized because it worsened inflation, destroyed small and medium industries, increased rural poverty, magnified income disparities, and increased unemployment.[15]

The government's desire to ensure that this was not a short-lived economic boom forced it to listen to the handful of foreign-educated economists and their allies in the U.S. AID complex, which stood literally next door to the economic ministries in an identical building. (The two buildings, eight-story, green concrete monstrosities built by the United States, still stand on Sejong-no as a monument to the U.S. aid effort.) As a result, broad reforms were put through in 1964 and 1965, eliminating some of the grosser imbalances in the Korean economy. American advisers wanted market-oriented interest rates, better tax collection, more balanced budgets, and realistic growth targets. As a result, the won was devalued, exchange rates simplified, interest rates raised, and import tariffs cut.

David Cole and Princeton Lyman, two scholars who worked as part of the U.S. economic assistance team in Korea during the 1960s and later wrote an authoritative account of the era, described the Military Government (1961–63) as "revolutionary in tone and strongly nationalistic," but observed that "it was also pragmatic and managerial, rather than ideological in its emphasis."[16]

Cole and Lyman noted that although Park's Military Government had more younger, better-trained administrators than previous ones, it quickly became clear that the problems of national development were too complicated for revolutionary exhortation alone. By the time that civilian government was inaugurated at the end of 1963, "it had become clear that many of the Military Government reforms had gone awry and that the tasks of national development were more complex than early prognostication had indicated."[17] The Military Government was plagued with familiar problems, such as inflation, rural poverty, and scandals involving Park confidant Kim Jong Pil, who had started the KCIA as part of an effort to build a one-party state. Kim tried to raise money that would be used to control politics, allegedly through stock market manipulation and abuse of his privileged access to foreign exchange.

The leaders of the 1961 coup saw economics as a sector that with bold, sweeping measures could be straightened out in a short period of time. But their practical program was rather vague and, although the military was managerially much more adept than the previous rulers, it had little economic knowledge. "As a result, despite the importance at first laid upon economic problems by the Military Government, the overall economic decline that had begun in 1958, on the whole continued through 1962, aggravated by both political instability and some of the economic measures taken by the new leaders," note Cole and Lyman.[18]

A man who held a senior position at the Blue House during most of the 1970s and early 1980s says that it is too easy to romanticize Park's decisiveness with the benefit of thirty years' hindsight.

> People nostalgically say he was a man of strength, that he was decisive. I remind them of the early period in Park's presidency, in 1961, 1962, 1963. That period is marked by continuing reversal of decisions by President Park himself. For example, in the morning he would tell the press he was not a

candidate [in the 1963 presidential election], in the afternoon he was and the next morning he was not.[19]

But, increasingly, with the return to a civilian government in 1963, economics became the government's measure of its success. In 1964 and 1965 opposition to normalization of relations with Japan came close to toppling the government. Having survived that political crisis, and apparently convinced that he needed to gain legitimacy some other way, Park turned to economic growth. Cole and Lyman write that:

> [I]nstead of being a piece of a larger nationalistic program of somewhat vague dimensions, as had been the case with the military government, concrete economic performance became the touchstone of political performance and economic progress.
>
> The movement under the Park administration toward a political strategy emphasizing economic performance, that is, one in which internal political strategy and foreign policy would be shaped and redefined almost entirely around the economic emphasis of the administration, was thus not entirely natural or altogether inevitable.[20]

The second five-year plan was even more successful than the first. Annual GNP growth was expected to average 7 percent, but actual output on average grew a stunning 11.4 percent. These numbers were far beyond expectations, not only for Korea but for any country. Economist Tony Michell underscores how unexpected this growth was: "I know of a number of consultants who wrote reports in the 1960s based on estimated growth of 8–10 percent [a year] who were shot down with bureaucratic red pencils stating, 'Countries do not grow this fast!' "[21] In Korea, these economic plans—and their successful fulfillment—demonstrated the government's commitment to growth, and they were key to helping overcome the pessimism and economic lethargy that had plagued the country for hundreds of years.

Park's drive to convince Koreans that they could stand tall was paying off more quickly than he could have hoped. Planners drawing up the third economic plan, which ran from 1972 to 1976, boasted that "the successful completion of the first two plans has instilled new hope in the minds of the people whose attitude has been plagued by negativism and pessimism. . . . It has given them the courage to say, 'We, too, can be rich and strong.' "[22]

Although economic planning was supported by U.S. advisers, Park had, of course, earlier been exposed to state planning in Manchukuo and in wartime Japan. The idea for the five-year Manchurian development plan came, ironically enough, from the Soviet Union and focused on development of industrial and natural resources. The plan drew on the pseudo-Leninist ideas of Takahashi Kamekichi (1891–1977). Takahashi was a self-educated Marxist who based his analysis of Japan and Northeast Asia on books such as Lenin's *Imperialism, the Highest Form of Capitalism* and Bukharin's *Economics of the Transition Period*.

Takahashi believed that Japanese capitalist development had been stymied by the crises of the 1920s and that the deadlock needed to be broken by deliberate state policies. The government would help capitalism to develop and, according to Leninist theories, eventually decline.[23] Odd as Takahashi's ideas now seem, he was simply the most prominent of a group of Japanese thinkers in the 1920s and 1930s who blended Marxist analysis of the world economy with the thesis that state and big business must work together. These ideas were put to the test in Manchukuo, and Takahashi himself was invited as a consultant to the Japanese colonial administrations in both Manchukuo and Taiwan.

Like the Japanese, Park was captivated by big, capital-intensive projects that would allow the country to become economically more self-sufficient and also give Koreans a new self-confidence. In early 1962, just as the new five-year plan began, he declared that Ulsan, on the southeastern coast, would become a special industrial zone. "As the Aswan Dam stands for Nasser's revolution, so must the Ulsan Industrial Complex and the first Five-Year Plan for Economic Development stand for our May Revolution," Park proclaimed.[24] This became the site for South Korea's first petrochemical complex and later the place where Hyundai built its huge shipyard and auto factory.

Later, realizing that the country needed to be linked by road, Park decided to build the Seoul-Pusan highway. The World Bank and other international agencies told him that the road made no economic sense. Park responded by saying that "expressways would be a better investment of our limited funds than railroads and harbors for solving our transportation bottleneck." This was Park the logistics man speaking. But the highway also tugged at the emotions of Park the nation-builder. The successful construction of the highway, wrote Park, "gave the Korean people a new confidence that they can do whatever they want to do."[25]

A former engineer who worked on the highway said of Park's involvement:

> Mr. Park is not an easy man at the best of times, and he certainly was far from that during our project. But, after a while, I found myself thinking of him, of all things, as a sort of conductor of an orchestra—with his helicopter as his baton. Up and down he would go, this time with a team of geologists to figure out what was wrong with some mountainside that had crumbled on our tunnel-makers, the next time with a couple of United Nations hydrologists to figure out how our surveyors had got some water-table wrong. If he didn't know the answer on Tuesday, Mr. Park was back with it on Thursday or Saturday.[26]

When the Seoul-Pusan highway was officially dedicated on July 7, 1970, Park asked the nation, "How much energy do our people have? How much technology do we have? We will test our nation's potential by this expressway."

To anyone who has lived in Korea, these stories sound eerily like Kim Il Sung's exhortations and famous "on-the-spot guidance" that North Koreans claim to be so proud of. The difference is that this approach worked in South Korea—at least for a while.

Building the Export Machine

The success that Korea, Taiwan, Singapore, and Hong Kong have had in promoting economic growth has generated a conviction that export-led development is the best route for countries that want to get on a high-growth track. In Korea's case, however, the decision to adopt an export-oriented strategy came about almost by accident.

The experts who wrote the first five-year plan had a long draft document on the economy that the previous administration had been working on for more than three years. One section examined how exports could be expanded. The members of the revolutionary council initially deleted this section, for they saw little hope for growth.

Not only was there little initial concern with exports, but virtually no thought given to manufactured exports. "More than 80 percent of our exports are composed of agricultural, forestry and fishery products and raw ores," wrote Lee Hwal, president of the Korea Traders Association in early 1962. "This commodity structure [will] undergo no changes during the five-year program period."[27]

Seoul was effectively cut off from the rest of the world. No passenger ships made scheduled calls to Korea, and the total capacity for arriving and departing passengers was a mere 674 a week, not including U.S. military troops. Land routes were cut: South Korea occupied the southern tip of a peninsula, blocked by North Korea. The specter of Communist China hovered to the north and west. To the east was Japan, former colonizer and still a country with which Korea had no diplomatic relations.

Beginning in the 1950s, the Korean government had developed a series of measures and institutions to assist in the development of exports, generally with little success. After the first five-year plan was under way, however, the shortage of foreign exchange focused the government's attention on exports. Samsung founder Lee Byung Chull reputedly was influential in pushing for government support of exports.[28] Because Park Chung Hee bitterly opposed indefinite reliance on U.S. aid, which he understandably believed gave the United States too large a say in the running of the country, increasing export earnings looked attractive as a way of guaranteeing Korea's independence. As foreign exchange holdings dwindled to less than $100 million in the early 1960s and forced the postponement of some investment projects, increasing exports took on a new urgency.

Yet with the value of imports seven times that of exports, the chances of even a balanced trade account, much less a surplus, looked very slim indeed. This gloomy prospect was confirmed by the problems of the cotton industry, which was one of the economy's few modern sectors. Experience in the first two years of Park's administration seemed to show conclusively that merely devaluing the won did not stimulate exports. Devaluation also had serious inflationary effects. Import costs for raw materials rose as a result of the devaluation, but there was no support for would-be exporters. Few Koreans had ever been abroad, and fewer still had any knowledge of foreign markets.[29]

Nonetheless, Park quickly turned back to the measures that had been developed during the 1950s to spur exports. From 1962 to 1965 export promotion schemes were expanded and regularized. Preferential loans, favorable tax and tariff measures, and other supports were all used to encourage exporters. Exports became the measure of economic performance, as David Cole and Princeton Lyman noted.

> South Korea's export performance, long dormant, was a symbol of its capacity or lack of capacity for economic independence. Along with its international character, it was also one set of statistics that could not be readily faked. It thus became not only a measure of growth but a means of overcoming doubt and cynicism. The administration did not hesitate to make exporting into a national campaign, almost a patriotic duty. Export producers were given priority in investment decisions, credit allocations, and other benefits. Each province set its own export target. And each year the administration's year-end targets became an object of watchful waiting and, when made, the subject of widespread public discussion.[30]

Park ruled the country from behind the walls of the Blue House, named for its royal blue-tiled roof, which was located behind Kyongbok Palace in downtown Seoul. The presidential mansion is at the foot of the spectacular range of low mountains, which lies on the northern edge of Seoul and provides the natural fortifications that made the site so attractive as a capital to General Yi Song Gye when he founded the city at the end of the fourteenth century.

During Park's rule, all the major government ministries still lined the huge boulevard that began in front of Kwanghwamun, and Park could summon almost any official in a matter of minutes. There was a strong element of coercion in the export drive. Those companies that were not interested in the export market found government officials discriminating against them. Yonhap Steel, for example, was one of Korea's largest steel companies in the mid-1960s. The company was competitive only in the protected local market, however, because it did not have an integrated steel-making facility. Exporting, its owner knew, would be suicidal. "Yonhap refused to join with other companies to cooperate in the export drive because it was losing money on exports," company founder Kwon Chul Hyun said later. "That displeased President Park, who almost destroyed the company."

Kwon ran into serious legal trouble in the late 1970s. His teenage daughter suffered a brain tumor and, seeking better medical care than he could find in Korea, he took her to Sloan-Kettering Memorial Hospital in New York. Her total medical expenses were $120,000, but strict currency controls made it impossible for Kwon legally to transfer that much money abroad. So he turned to Seoul's thriving black market to change money for the medical expenses. As a result, the KCIA accused him of capital flight and arrested him.

"I believe the real reason the government arrested me on [allegations of] capital flight was because of my refusal to cooperate with the government export promotion program," Kwon said. Business executives protested the charges, which were later dropped, and the Supreme Court eventually found him not guilty of lesser tax fraud violations. Nevertheless, government pressure forced Kwon to sell his share of the steel company to the Kukje group at only 10 percent of its value.[31]

Although few businessmen suffered as much as Kwon, his reluctance to join the export drive was shared by many other companies. Alice Amsden, a scholar who has studied the development of Korea's business groups, cites data showing that in the mid-1970s half the companies polled thought that export targeting had negative effects for them. Problems included unprofitable export sales, diversion of production from the domestic to overseas markets and price cutting. But what companies lost on export sales they usually made up in profits in the protected domestic market. This strategy of forcing domestic consumers to subsidize exports was Korea, Inc.'s way of allowing Korean firms to amass the profits necessary for continued expansion. It reflects Korea's decision to organize an economy to benefit national development. That policy favored companies, not consumers.[32]

The early success of exports caught Park's attention, and in typical fashion he instituted a monthly export promotion meeting for businessmen, academics, journalists, and responsible government officials. These meetings, which symbolized the president's commitment to exports, were held in the conference room in the economic ministries' building just outside Kwanghwamun in central Seoul. The export promotion meetings, and the smaller luncheons that Park also hosted, could quickly open the door for needed loans or provide ministers with authority to issue commands "on the president's orders."

Nothing accelerated action more than a president willing to make immediate decisions at these regular meetings. If anything, Park's intervention was sometimes excessive. Every performance glitch seemed to Park to call for instant action. This trigger-happy response led the bureaucracy to be cautious about what it reported to its hyperactive boss, and persuaded many bureaucrats to hesitate before calling the president's attention to problems that might work themselves out without his involvement.

Beginning in the mid-1960s, the nation annually celebrated Export Day on November 30, marking the day in 1964 when annual exports reached $100 million for the first time. (Annual exports now are more than *eight hundred* times as large.) Park celebrated Export Day by awarding "export towers" of gold, silver, and bronze to businesses that had turned in the best performances. These ceremonies were a celebration of Korea, Inc., linking president, bureaucracy, and business in a patriotic celebration of national economic development.

Export Day photo opportunities also allowed businessmen to portray themselves as national capitalists, working for the good of the country rather than for selfish reasons. But the unceasing attention given to exports also convinced most

Koreans that overseas sales are a talisman of success, and that the country will suffer dismal economic performance if sizable export growth is not achieved. Coupled with the chronic hectoring to save more and buy less, this export-oriented policy made Korea a country that was hostile to imports and cruel to consumers.

The president's exhortations to export were backed with the lure of easy credit. Korean companies, like those in most developing countries, were—and still are—chronically short of working capital. Companies that received an overseas order backed by a letter of credit could automatically borrow against it at a domestic bank. This guaranteed approval was critical, since such loans were for many companies the only certain source of cash—and one that did not require bribes, kickbacks, or personal connections with a bank executive. The system was extremely effective in spurring exports, but it also turned out to be a major contributor to inflation in the 1970s.

Other export promotion measures during the Park era included customs duty rebates on imported items used for export products, tax relief, and import licenses conditional on export performance. The government also set up a series of associations to coordinate exports. The most important of these was the Korea Traders Association, a quasi-government agency that coordinated export activities of business in conjunction with the government. Like many other associations, it claimed to be private, but it was in reality a government-controlled organization.

The association's government counterpart was the state-owned Korea Trade Promotion Association (Kotra), which acted as an extension of the Ministry of Commerce and Industry. This association had the extraordinary power to tax all imports at a rate of 0.55 percent of their value. The revenues were supposedly used to develop international relations, especially in the trade field, although they could also be a handy source of political funds. Kotra agents scoured the world from Nairobi to New York looking for possible export markets, helping inexperienced Korean salesmen learn how to do business in each country, showing Korean companies how to prepare samples, package goods, and steer products through customs. By the 1980s this heroic phase was over, but Kotra was key to overcoming the obstacles Korean exporters, especially small ones, faced in the 1960s and 1970s.

South Korea also exported people, using the money they earned abroad to service a chronic external deficit. In December 1963, manpower exports began with the shipment of 132 miners to West Germany. In 1965, Park approved the decision to send Korean troops to Vietnam. Just as the Korean War had spurred the Japanese economy at a crucial moment in postwar development, so the Vietnam War boosted the Korean economy.

Vietnam became South Korea's first overseas profit center. In 1966 revenues from the war made up 40 percent of South Korea's foreign exchange earnings. Hyundai and Hanjin were the two chaebol that benefited most directly from the war. Hyundai won sizable construction contracts, giving the firm its first substantial overseas experience. Hanjin expanded its transport business, first assuming responsibility for operating the port of Qui Nhon and later, in 1969, taking over the feeble state-owned Korea Air Lines (KAL) from the government.[33]

Unlike Japan, which was prevented by its postwar constitution from sending troops to fight in Korea, Seoul sent soldiers to Vietnam, among them future presidents Chun Doo Hwan and Roh Tae Woo. Sending fighting forces to Vietnam provoked mixed feelings, for although Koreans felt proud that they could give as well as take in the international arena, many intellectuals were unhappy that Koreans were being sent to kill other Asians. In terms of relations with Washington, however, the dispatch of troops was a coup, winning Park a great deal of goodwill from the embattled Lyndon Johnson.

The export success Korea enjoyed in the early 1960s gratified Park, but he did not want to be known as the leader of a nation that flourished by exporting wigs, plywood, cotton fabrics, and knitwear. To Park and those around him, economic development was synonymous with heavy industries like steel and machinery. "Steel is national power," the president was fond of saying. But the problem was that these industries require frustratingly large amounts of capital investment and high degrees of technical skill, both of which were in short supply.

Wigs or Steel: The Fight for Korea, Inc.

Park Chung Hee had set his heart on building two major industrial complexes, a refinery at the Ulsan special industrial zone and an iron and steel works in another east coast fishing village about an hour's drive to the north, in Pohang. Such large-scale investment looked like a poor bet: It took much more investment and had far less prospect of earning or saving foreign exchange than did light industries. Cheap clothes might not be glamorous, but they earned hard currency more reliably than did heavy industries.

The first five-year plan, which ran from 1962 to 1966, had been a rushed affair. Surprisingly, most targets were not only met but exceeded. By the end of 1964, it was clear that Korea could achieve at least short bursts of growth, but officials were uncertain about how to sustain anything more than these expansionary boomlets. The driving, military style of Park Chung Hee's generation needed to be supplemented by more sophisticated planning. In 1965 a remarkable team of younger Koreans that was to form the nucleus of the technocracy teamed up with a group of foreign development economists to work on the second five-year plan, which ran from 1967 to 1971.

Planning began in earnest in 1965 and was taken extremely seriously, with generous support provided by the U.S. AID and the World Bank. The bureaucracy wanted to set very high targets and, encouraged by the president, to move into machine tools and heavy industry. The foreign advisers and the budding Korean technocrats soon developed serious disagreements with the main power centers of the Korean government.

The technocrats and the international economic advisers thought the heavy industry strategy was foolish. They worried about the post–Korean War baby boom generation, which would be hitting the employment market in large numbers between 1975 and 1985. Unless the economy expanded rapidly enough to provide about 500,000 new jobs every year, unemployment would increase to dangerous levels. The technocrats believed that the country was in a race against this demographic time bomb, which could be defused only by quickly developing the labor-intensive light manufacturing sector.

Light industries like textiles and wigs provided plenty of jobs and thus seemed eminently more sensible to the technocratic planners than the grand notions of building up heavy industry. In this debate, the technocrats were helped in their battle against the president by the deputy prime minister and head of the Economic Planning Board, Chang Ki Yong. "Chang Ki Yong was the liaison between us and Park Chung Hee," says Kim Mahn Je, who headed the Korea Development Institute in the 1970s and later became deputy prime minister for economic planning. Kim claims that through the 1960s Park "despised" American-trained economists.

In order to have a better chance of winning Park's approval, Chang would often lead Park to believe that the ideas he proposed were his own, when in fact they came from the World Bank, the Sogang University technocrats, or U.S. AID officials. "Chang Ki Yong had to work with the U.S. government," says Kim. "Otherwise there would be no aid."[34]

Chang was the first civilian to serve as the top economic policymaker under Park. He was also, as a businessman and newspaper publisher, a defender of the rights of private enterprise and a believer in market forces. He outflanked the bureaucracy in other ministries and supported those who wanted labor-intensive industries to come before heavy industries. In the financial sector, Chang pushed through important reforms, most notably one in 1965 that coaxed funds out of the underground economy and into banks by substantially increasing interest rates on savings deposits.

In his way, Chang was as action-oriented as Park. Once, frustrated over the refusal of the Ministry of Agriculture to liberalize imports of certain products, Chang broke all rules of bureaucratic etiquette by first calling a press conference inside the ministry to announce liberalization and only then bursting in on the minister to tell him what he had done. Another time he stunned a group of housewife and consumer representatives by urging that the market for consumer appliances be liberalized to allow imports. "It was a shock to the ladies," remembers Park You Kwang, who at that time was a young official at the EPB. "The primary work they were doing was to love and to cherish Korean goods and keep foreign ones out."

As long as Chang was deputy prime minister, Park Chung Hee's dreams of heavy industrial might were kept within the bounds of reality. Chang persuaded Park to go slowly on the plan to build up heavy industries. The president agreed that most of the country's resources would go into light industry, such as textiles and consumer electronics, for the first three years of the second plan. Heavy industries, including iron and steel, machinery, oil refineries, and chemical plants, would be developed only at the end of the second five-year plan.

By the end of the 1960s the Korean economy had come a long way, far enough for visitors from abroad to be impressed with the changes. Journalist Derek Davies visited the first Korea Trade Fair in 1968. Although the outspoken Welshman found the stifling formality of Korean officials and the heavy military presence in the economy distasteful, he was impressed by the range of goods Korean companies were making even at that time.

Davies noted that, unlike Hong Kong, Korea "is turning out a large proportion of the parts of its cars, tractors and lorries, is manufacturing marine diesels and the impressive Daedong power tillers, [as well as] Korean-made fertilizers, pharmaceuticals, pesticides, textile machinery and synthetic textiles."[35]

However, even as late as 1970, plywood was the second-largest export, trailing textiles. Wigs were third. Korea had a long way to go to fulfill its ambitions. A U.S. official, who was to become intensively involved with Korea over the next quarter-century, remembers the first time that he visited Korea, in September 1968. "I had lived in Japan for nine years and I had seen a lot of Korea through Japanese eyes. I was really struck by the place. At that time high-tech was hot water faucets and hot water boilers. The hills were still sere and brown. Reforestation was just beginning. [But] the vitality of the place and the ferociousness of the people were very striking to me."

The tension between the technocrats, who wanted an outward-looking economy, and the more inward-looking bureaucrats supported by President Park became increasingly intense during this period. Although rarely articulated, the tension between the two camps has been at the heart of economic policy-making for nearly three decades. The technocrats, many of them with doctorates from American universities, have usually favored textbook approaches, designed to capitalize on Korea's supposed comparative advantages. When labor was cheap, as it was in the 1960s, they wanted to stay in labor-intensive industries. They thought it was impossible for Korea to somehow violate economic rules by, for example, building a steel industry. Later they opposed autos and semiconductors.

Park, although he understood economics well enough, refused to be constrained by accepted wisdom. He was a nation-builder, not a textbook economist. Because he could draw on the frustrated Korean nationalism both in the bureaucracy and among Koreans generally, a nationalism that favored autarkic development, he ensured that his grand vision had a chance of success.

It is worth emphasizing that most countries pursuing this strategy of a big push in heavy industrial development failed. Only the powerful authoritarianism of the South Korean system allowed the ideas of the man at the top to be translated into action. The technocrats provided necessary ballast.

One of the most prominent technocrats of the 1960s and 1970s, Nam Duck

Woo, said that the job of the technocrats was to try to translate Park's dreams into reality without violating all the rules of neoclassical economics.

> He had a really strong desire to free the country from this poverty. The whole motivation [for his economic development program] stemmed from that. He was very pragmatic. He was not an economist, but he listened to the economists' view. He had a good sense of judgment. He didn't talk very much but he carefully listened.
>
> He used foreign-trained technocrats for the purposes of economic administration. The role of the technocrat was to accommodate his intentions, or his plans, in such a way that the side effects may be minimized. We [often] knew that his request was too much but somehow we tried to accommodate his wishes in an economic way.[36]

Financial Repression and Political Control

Park Chung Hee's understanding of finance was primitive when he took power. He had a deep distrust of financiers and suspected them of being involved in illicit activities.[37]

Park quickly, and shrewdly, seized control of the financial system. This control extended down to the operating level: From the early 1960s until the 1990s the government approved the appointment of top bank management and vetted the annual budget.

The funds that business needed to expand were available only through the state-owned banks, and for the next twenty years the government approved every significant loan that was made. The idea of credit analysis as it is known in the West was unheard of in Korea. Companies borrowed on the strength of personal relationships. The government guaranteed the banks that they would be taken care of if a borrower went bankrupt. Favored borrowers knew that they could get the credit they needed, often by running long-term overdrafts (known as "over-borrowing") at the banks. It was in the financial sector that private and public interests merged almost completely.[38]

Park Young Chul, an economist who later served as Chun Doo Hwan's senior secretary for economic affairs, underscores this lack of normal credit standards in the Korean financial system. "Economic efficiency has seldom been the major criterion in the allocation of credit. Instead, government credit allocation policy was dictated by, and carried out to accommodate, the development strategies and investment policies set forth in the four successive five-year development plans."[39]

These government guarantees extended to foreign borrowing as well. Companies could negotiate agreements with foreign banks and, after approval, they would be guaranteed by the Korean government. This cozy financial system was the heart of Korea, Inc. State and private interests needed one another, but it was the state that held far greater power. A senior lawyer in Seoul, a graduate of

Seoul National University and a former judge, expresses a common view of how this control of the financial system worked.

> What does a growth economy mean? It means you need money. In a fast-growing economy, no matter how indebted you are, in ten years it's nothing. Those who had access to money could succeed. Like King Midas, everything you touch turns to gold, if you have money. Who controls the banks? The government. Did it choose correctly? In general, yes, but looking at the details there were many mistakes.[40]

Later experiments worked better than the 1962 currency reform. In 1965, under the influence of U.S. advisers, Deputy Prime Minister Chang Ki Yong adopted a successful interest rate reform. Interest rates were doubled on savings accounts, to as much as 30 percent for one-year deposits. Bank loan rates were raised, but only to a maximum of 26 percent. Banks, in other words, lost substantial amounts of money on every loan they made.

The Bank of Korea made up the negative interest rate spread to banks through other concessions. The measure is generally claimed as a huge success, although other factors (such as greater foreign borrowing) no doubt contributed to rapid, noninflationary expansion. Deposits grew an average of 72.5 percent a year from 1966 through 1969. Economic growth expanded an average of 12 percent a year during the same time, and inflation was a low 3.5 percent compared with 17.5 percent a year for the previous five years. This was, as one academic dubbed it, "financial reform without tears."[41]

In fact, South Korea's financial system was more like a corner store run out of a cigar box than the sort of system one would expect from a country with the pretense to modernity that Park Chung Hee had. There was a variety of banks, including a clutch of specialized banks left over from the Japanese era, but all these institutions simply did the government's bidding. In the late 1960s, yet more specialized banks were set up, including the Korea Exchange Bank (to borrow money abroad), the Korea Housing Bank (for housing), and Korea Long Term Credit Bank (to provide long-term loans to favored industries.) At the same time, ten local banks were established, one for each province.

Not surprisingly, given the flood of money into banks and a government decision to ease limits on borrowing abroad, businesses piled on loans. Debt as a percentage of equity rose from 56 percent in 1965 to 113 percent in 1968. In other words, for every $1 in capital a company carried $1.13 in debt.

There is nothing inherently evil about a high debt:equity ratio, and it can be a good thing for a rapidly growing company. One benefit is that it allows owners to retain ownership of more shares. But highly leveraged companies are badly hurt when the economy turns down, because so much of their cash flow must be devoted to interest repayments. Just this happened in the early 1970s.

Making Business Serve the State

One of the key ingredients of the restructuring Park forced on the country in the early 1960s was to force all businesses, from chemical producers to truck companies, to join associations. The associations were then assigned to appropriate ministries, which then had an easy way to regulate business activities. Very small companies could conceal from the government and the association what they were doing, and very big companies could browbeat the associations, but for the most part this structure gave the government extremely effective control over the economy.

These organizations, which are a key part of the Korean (and to some extent Japanese) economy, have no modern counterparts in the United States, where industry associations are set up to promote the interests of their members. In Korea they functioned primarily as a way for government to control business. They also made it easy for businesses to form cartels and other arrangements to guard against "excessive competition"—in other words, market forces.

The list of these associations is almost endless. Automakers and architects have their associations, as do canned goods exporters and cadastral surveyors. Maritime pilots and marine products exporters, dairy farmers, and deep-sea fishers each have an association reporting to the appropriate ministry. Orders, informal regulations, and guidelines can be passed quickly from the ministry to companies. The labyrinth of associations means that government officials in effect have subordinate bureaucracies made up of association staff paid for by member companies.

After Park took power, some of these associations, particularly those connected with the construction and transportation ministries, were staffed with a heavy component of retired military officers. In some cases these jobs were sinecures intended to defuse any opposition to the new military rulers, but others drew on the military's expertise in logistical planning. The Korea Highway Corporation and the Korea Cement Industry Association became strongholds of military influence.

This system of associations was modeled on the Japanese wartime industrial structure. However, the power of the EPB was much greater than that of the Japanese Economic Planning Agency (EPA), reflecting the centralization of Korean political power and the direct involvement of the president in economic development. Conversely, the Ministry of Commerce in Korea had much less power than did the Ministry of Trade and Industry (MITI) in Japan.

The politicization of business was the biggest difference between Korea and Japan. Although the EPB was more powerful than its Japanese counterpart, it was the Blue House that held ultimate authority. In Japan, politicians had little to do with business, other than collecting campaign contributions from them. In Korea, Blue House staffers personally oversaw most loans to companies and were intimately involved in micromanaging the economy. So powerful is this tendency that even as late as 1991 a group of hustlers was arrested for impersonating Blue House officials and promising to arrange foreign loans in exchange for political funding, another in a long line of scandals involving impersonators of Blue House staff.[42]

The ultimate expression of guided capitalism and government control was the power to grant business licenses. Whereas in Western economies most activities are legal unless expressly prohibited, the Korean bureaucracy sometimes views all activities as illegal unless they are explicitly licensed. Even today, this difference is at the root of many mistakes made by foreign businessmen in Korea.

The combination of military organization and top-down state control of the economy were obvious from the early months of the Park administration, but so too was the technical competence of the new military rulers. When Park and his associates took power, the military with its logistical experience was the most modern part of South Korean society. In the absence of a developed business class, the military alone had the managerial skills to oversee the economy. "It was the biggest education institution I can imagine," the chairman of the Kumho group, Park Seong Yawng, later said. "People shed their old Korean clothes for uniforms. They learned how to lead an organized life, learned about technology."[43] It was, in fact, a military man who was to create one of the most successful South Korean corporations ever, a giant state-owned steel company named Posco.

Notes

1. Park Chung Hee, *The Country, the Revolution and I*, p. 26.
2. Park Chung Hee, *To Build a Nation*, p. 105.
3. Author interview, October 1991.
4. Park Chung Hee, *The Country, the Revolution and I*, p. 166.
5. Ibid., pp. 172–73.
6. Ibid., pp. 178–79. Punctuation and paragraph indentation follow the English translation.
7. I am grateful to John Bennett for this anecdote.
8. This incident is cited in Kim Seok Ki, "Business Concentration and Government Policy: A Study of the Phenomenon of Business Groups in Korea, 1945–1985," p. 105.
9. U.S. Congress, House, *Hearings before the Subcommittee on International Organization of the Committee on International Relations*, part 6, hearings July 19 and August 2, 1978, p. 74.
10. Author interview, October 1991.
11. *Far Eastern Economic Review*, September 7, 1961, p. 449.
12. Personal communication from David Satterwhite, February 1992. This information is drawn from his Ph.D. dissertation, "The Politics of Economic Development: Coup, State, and the Republic of Korea's First Five-Year Economic Development Plan (1962–66)."
13. Author interview, November 1990. Separately, in an interview with Kim Seok Ki, Yoo Chang Soon said that the bureaucracy presented Park with two different plans, one centered on manufacturing and the other on agriculture. Park's only concern was "How fast can we grow?" Kim Seok Ki, *Business Concentration and Government Policy: A Study of the Phenomenon of Business Groups in Korea, 1945–1985*, p. 104.

14. Personal communication from David Satterwhite, February 1992.

15. David C. Cole and Princeton N. Lyman, *Korean Development, The Interplay of Politics and Economics*, p. 82. The critique comes from a professor who is said to be representative of the domestic critics of the plan.

16. Ibid., p. 37.

17. Ibid., p. 43.

18. Ibid., p. 85.

19. Author interview, January 1991.

20. Cole and Lyman, *Korean Development, The Interplay of Politics and Economics*, p. 80 and pp. 85–86.

21. Personal communication from Tony Michell, April 1990.

22. Quoted in Leroy P. Jones and Sakong Il, *Government, Business and Entrepreneurship in Economic Development: The Korean Case*, p. 51.

23. Germaine A. Hoston, *Marxism and the Crisis of Development in Prewar Japan*, pp.76–94.

24. Park Chung Hee, *The Country, the Revolution and I*, p. 177.

25. Park Chung Hee, *To Build a Nation*, p. 121.

26. Michael Keon, *Korean Phoenix*, p. 79.

27. *Korean Affairs* (April–May 1962), p. 14.

28. Kim Mahn Je, in a November 1990 interview with the author, credited Lee Byung Chull with the emphasis on exports.

29. Alice H. Amsden, *Asia's Next Giant*, pp. 64–72, has a good section on the development of export policy, concentrating on the textile industry. She shows that devaluation alone did not help, for devaluation raised the cost of imported inputs. Interestingly, labor costs in Korea and Japan were about the same in the textile industry at this point.

30. Cole and Lyman, *Korean Development*, p. 90.

31. Kwon's account comes primarily from a press luncheon at the Seoul Foreign Correspondents' Club in May 1989. Kwon's problems may also have stemmed from the continuing struggles between a faction loyal to Kim Jong Pil and one allied with KCIA head Lee Hu Rak—with Yonhap punished because of Kwon's loyalties to the Lee Hu Rak faction.

32. Amsden, *Asia's Next Giant*, p. 69.

33. Carter J. Eckert et al., *Korea Old and New, A History*, pp. 398–99.

34. Kim Mahn Je author interview, November 1990, for this and the following section.

Kim Mahn Je, in a separate November 1990 author interview, said of Park's attitude toward the United States, "He was always very suspicious of the U.S. government." Park's speeches are full of references to the need to break free of dependence on foreign powers, that is, the United States.

It worked both ways, for the United States had initially been very unhappy with Park's coup. Lee Hahn Been remembers being in Washington at the time of the May 1961 coup and of the Kennedy administration's concern at the military takeover. The U.S. embassy in Seoul greeted the coup with little enthusiasm and initially refused to issue visas for senior Korean officials to go to Washington to justify the coup.

Yet the United States footed much of the bill for Korea. South Korea received $12.6 billion in economic and military assistance between 1946 and 1976, with international financial institutions providing an additional $1.9 billion and Japan approximately $1 billion. The per capita assistance figure of $600 for the three decades was the highest in the world, after Israel and South Vietnam, for a major country. Edward S. Mason et al., *The Economic and Social Modernization of the Republic of Korea*, pp. 165 and 182.

35. *Far Eastern Economic Review*, January 9, 1969.

36. Author interview, December 1991.

37. This section is drawn from Lee-Jay Cho and Kim Yoon Hyung (eds.), *Korea's Political Economy: An Institutional Perspective*; Mason et al., *The Economic and Social Modernization of the Republic of Korea*; and Woo Jung-en, *Race to the Swift*.

38. Cho and Kim, *Korea's Political Economy*, has a useful discussion of this practice, especially on how the reliance on overborrowing facilitated political control of nominally private firms. It also notes that both the budgets and top management of banks were vetted—or chosen—by the Ministry of Finance, although there was no law to this effect. The study also has a good discussion of the interest rate reform of 1965 and the debate over its role in stimulating economic growth.

39. Lee-Jay Cho and Kim Yoon Hyung (eds.), *Economic Development in the Republic of Korea*, pp. 56–57.

40. Author interview, October 1991.

41. Cho and Kim, *Korea's Political Economy*.

42. *Korea Herald* and *Korea Times*, October 3, 1991. The impersonators promised to arrange 4 trillion won in loans—more than $5 billion.

43. Author interview, March 1991.

5

The High Priest of Steel

Steel is national power.
— Park Chung Hee[1]

Even after he became president, Park Chung Hee often still sounded as if he were the commander of the Pusan military logistics center. The young leader talked with evangelical fervor about increasing electricity production, developing tungsten mines, and building cement and fertilizer plants. His speeches and writings are full of exhortations to increase production.

The force of Park's personality, coupled with a hard-working bureaucracy and billions of dollars in U.S. assistance, saw much of what Park envisioned for the first five-year plan completed on schedule. Cement and fertilizer plants, sugar refineries and flour mills, electrical stations and coal and tungsten mines were the building blocks that Park put in place during these early years. Because the economy was so primitive and its problems were so obvious, a military logistics man with a flair for leadership was perhaps the best sort of economist Korea could have had.

Park did not succeed in everything, of course. Steel was an area of conspicuous failure during the first five-year plan. For Park, steel was a sign of national power, useful for building weapons and tangible proof that Korea could master a technologically complex, capital-intensive process. As a result, the construction of an integrated steelworks took on a mystical, religious significance for Korea.

The mother church of this new religion was to be in Pohang, a fishing town built on a sandy beach in the southeastern part of the country about 250 miles from Seoul. The chief priest of the cult of steel was to be another military man named Park.

Park Tae Joon, a young colonel eleven years younger than the president, had also taken part in the May 16 coup that brought Park Chung Hee to power in 1961. His star rose with the coup leader's; he quickly became chief secretary to Park, and in August 1961, Park Tae Joon was promoted to the rank of brigadier general. The next month he was appointed as a member of the finance and economy committee of the Supreme Council for National Reconstruction, the military's ruling council. In 1964 Park, who by that time had been promoted to a two-star general, was dispatched to run the Korea Tungsten Corporation. Park Tae Joon turned around the scandal-ridden company, and in 1967 the president gave him the seemingly impossible task of financing and building a steel industry, a job that he accomplished with stunning success.

Most of the men who led the May 16 Revolution have long since faded into history. Some ran afoul of Park and were purged by the late president or by his successor, Chun Doo Hwan. Park Tae Joon not only survived the tumult of Korean economics and politics for three decades, but he rode the crest of the wave for an unusually long time by the brutal standards of South Korea.

Although he was one of Park Chung Hee's confidants, Park Tae Joon escaped the purge that occurred when Chun Doo Hwan seized power. Park Tae Joon's daughter married Chun's son, yet Park escaped the turmoil that followed Chun's regime and emerged more powerful than ever in the administration of Roh Tae Woo. It was only when political ambition lured him in 1992 to make an unsuccessful bid to succeed Roh as president that Park was destroyed.

But until 1992, Park Tae Joon was chairman of the Pohang Iron and Steel Company, one of the world's largest and most efficient steelmakers. At the same time he was a powerful politician, a member of the National Assembly and, from 1990 until 1992, the co-chairman of the ruling Democratic Liberal Party. General, engineer, businessman, and politician, a confidant of Park Chung Hee, Chun Doo Hwan, and Roh Tae Woo, Park Tae Joon was one of the most remarkable members of the generation that built the Korean economy.

Park Tae Joon was born in North Kyongsang Province, the eldest of six children, in 1928. Like Park Chung Hee, Park Tae Joon came from a poor, landless family and rose through the Japanese educational system on the strength of his intellect.[2]

"I personally had a very difficult childhood and adolescence. As a child, my family owned a very small amount of both dry fields and paddy land, but we lost it to the Japanese and so were very poor. Thus, when I look back at my childhood, I remember our very poor country house, the tiny kitchen, the torn paper windows, the roof that was falling in here and there, [and] the filthy outhouse."[3] Although he was younger than Park Chung Hee, Park Tae Joon was still a member of the Japanese generation. His family moved to Japan, where his father worked as an engineer.

To hear Park recount it, the family was quite poor even though his father held a professional job. "When I was studying in Japan as a youth, I was so poor I could not afford to change my underwear very often," he later told Posco managers in a lecture emphasizing the importance of high standards for quality. "It is kind of embarrassing, but there were times when I did not change my underwear for a month or more."[4]

After graduation from a Japanese high school he studied mechanical engineering at Waseda, one of Japan's most prestigious universities. World War II ended just months before Park's scheduled graduation. As U.S. bombers pounded Tokyo, "I spent my days running back and forth from the air raid shelter because of the continual bombings, and I was only able to study when I used a flashlight to read inside the shelter."[5]

"At the end of the war I was overcome with emotion as I saw some Korean students give vent to their pent-up anger by attacking returning Japanese soldiers who had been disarmed by the victorious forces. Even though I felt similar impulses, I believed that I must return to my homeland and contribute something to the development of our newly liberated nation, and so I overcame my rage."[6] In another account he described returning home "after several crises with the threats, temptations and violence of left-wing students."[7] Like Park Chung Hee, Park Tae Joon was intensely ambivalent toward Japan and the Japanese. However much he resented the Japanese colonization of Korea—and if, indeed, as he claimed, his family lost its small landholding to the Japanese, this resentment must have burned deeply—he was also inspired by the power and wealth of this country, which in some ways was so similar to Korea. Japan, like Korea, had been pried open by the West in the late nineteenth century. Through selective technological and managerial borrowing from abroad, a strong Japanese state was able to cajole business into cooperating in the cause of national economic development. This was the model that Park Chung Hee and Park Tae Joon were to follow.

After returning, Park Tae Joon joined the military and attended the Korea Military Academy, graduating after an accelerated three-month course in 1948. Although this was a period of U.S. military rule in the South, the military academy was still run along Japanese lines. When the Korean War broke out, Park had a chance to put his training to use. He fought with distinction during the Korean War, winning three medals.

Although Park Tae Joon took part in the May 16 coup, he was not a core member of the coup leadership. However, four days after the uprising, the young colonel was appointed as Park's chief secretary. Park Tae Joon then ran the Korea Tungsten Company from 1964 until 1967, when President Park asked him to take over a moribund plan to build a steel mill.

Park Chung Hee had included plans for an integrated steel mill in the first five-year plan. The Economic Planning Board had formed an agreement with an international consortium of European and U.S. companies, which would provide technical assistance and the necessary capital equipment to construct an integrated iron and steelworks. But the World Bank and the U.S. Export-Import

(Exim) Bank refused to finance the project. Almost no one took Korea's dreams of becoming a steelmaker seriously.

Park Chung Hee, frustrated at the lack of progress, took away responsibility for the imaginary steel industry from the Economic Planning Board and in November 1967 named Park Tae Joon head of the steel-making effort. "The strategy of our [first] economic plan was to develop key industries and infrastructure industries," remembered Park Tae Joon in an interview thirty years after the 1961 coup and eighteen years after he and President Park fired up the blast furnace. "The steel industry was included in the first five-year economic plan along with other key industries, such as cement and fertilizer, which were necessary to develop our country." There was, he added, a military as well as an economic reason for building a steel mill. After the Korean War armistice was signed in 1953, "the North increased its military power and forces. We had to increase our own military power. We could not rely on the United States 100 percent. Steel was necessary to produce weapons."

Note Park Tae Joon's contention that even in the early 1960s there was a fear that the United States could not be fully trusted and that South Korea had to become more self-reliant. This theme was an important part of President Park's thinking, one that became more important in the 1970s as the United States pulled ground forces out of South Korea and later ceded Vietnam to the communist North. But from the earliest days of power, South Korea's new military leaders wanted to become more self-reliant. Their distrust of the United States was stoked by Washington's cool initial reaction to the coup. Park Tae Joon:

> During the first five-year economic development plan President Park formed a team [to study our entrance into the steel industry]. Although at that time we didn't have any good industries there were some people who had experiences in industries [from the Japanese colonial period].
> Park Chung Hee instructed the team to develop a steel industry. The result was that in the [course of carrying out the] first five-year development plan, all other key industries—such as cement, fertilizer and oil refineries—were successful except the steel industry. That's why the steel sector was again included in the second five-year plan. President Park never gave up the steel industry. . . . In order to develop railways, water supply, sewerage and roads, President Park thought we needed not only cement but also steel. . . . In order to produce ordinary weapons we needed steel. President Park thought it was a must that we produce steel.[8]

Various teams of international experts told the Korean planning authorities that the scale of a plant designed simply to meet domestic demand would be too small to achieve necessary economies of scale. "The president faced severe opposition everywhere," says Kim Mahn Je, who returned from the United States in the early 1960s and quickly became an important economic adviser. "The World Bank turned it down flatly. The U.S. opposed it. Brazil had a huge steel plant and it [had] failed miserably. Understandably, because of other countries' experience, [potential lenders] were skeptical."

Although he had no money to fund his dream, Park Tae Joon went ahead and founded the Pohang Iron and Steel Company in April 1968, four months after the president had put him in charge of the nation's steel project. Park vividly remembers the frustrating wait for money. "I waited the whole year of 1968 to see if negotiations with the U.S. Exim [Bank], the IBRD [the World Bank] and KISA [Korea Iron and Steel Association] would produce any result. But nobody reported any good conclusion to me."

Finally, in February 1969, he traveled to the United States, but was given a cold shoulder by World Bank and Exim Bank representatives in Washington. Korea had demonstrated no special technological skill in metallurgy, and it did not have a trained labor force capable of running a project of this scale and complexity. Korea had, according to the experts, no comparative advantage in iron and steel-making.

At last, Park Tae Joon turned to the Japanese, who had promised to pay blood money in the form of aid and loans to compensate Korea for losses inflicted during Japanese colonization. As the price for normalizing relations with South Korea in 1965, Japan agreed to provide $500 million in loans and grants. That Korea was able to get Japanese approval to use the money for the planned steelworks was due in large part to Park Tae Joon's connections.

> Even before that time I had very sound personal relationship[s] with Japanese people. From the simple fact [that] I went to Waseda I was able to make a lot of good friends in Japan. Through those friends it was possible to approach [Yawata Steel] chairman Inayama [Yoshihiro] and [Fuji Steel president] Nagano [Shigeo]. When I went to them I [emphasized] the importance of Korean-Japanese cooperation. I tried to convince them [by] saying that the Japanese ruled Korea for 36 years. The Koreans have been deprived of many things because of Japan, so the Japanese must compensate Korea materially and psychologically.[9]

Known as "Dynamite Park," the general lived on the construction site while the Pohang works were being constructed and earned a ferocious reputation for his meticulous inspections of progress at all hours of the day and night.

He once measured a concrete footing and found it a few centimeters too thin. Furious at what he thought was the contractors' attempt to cheat Posco by skimping on cement, Park ordered the floor dynamited and rebuilt. "When dynamite was scarce, he made the managers destroy them with sledgehammers, even if it took all night."[10] This was typical of Park's passion for excellence. Although Koreans are often apt to let quality suffer in their rush to get a project done, Posco was a stunning exception. It has maintained extremely high quality standards and at the same time consistently managed to shatter international records with its rapid construction schedules.

One of the company's suppliers later described the round-the-clock efforts by Posco employees in the early days, efforts that made the Japanese seem lazy in comparison. "I recall our marketing people doing business in Japan Monday through Friday and then going over to Korea for the weekend knowing fully well that the Posco employees would be working on [Saturday and] Sunday," said Gary Livingstone, the president of Luscar, a Canadian coal supplier. "The Posco office was on the second floor of the YWCA building in Seoul and on Sunday the building was locked. The only way into the Posco office was to climb up the fire escape, go across the roof, and then enter the office through the window."

When Park decided that Posco employees should learn to play golf in order to have something to do with foreign suppliers, they went out on the golf course with the same zeal with which they tackled the steel business. Livingstone visited Posco after a week in which some of the senior managers had tried to master golf, on Park's orders. The hands of the Posco managers were so blistered that they could hardly hold the golf clubs when the day of the tournament came.[11]

Park Tae Joon has been called "the man with iron blood" and criticized for an often imperious manner.[12] "I am well aware that many of our managers and employees say that I demand too much," he once admitted to Posco managers. That he could enjoy such widespread admiration for so long in a country where big business is generally regarded with suspicion stemmed from the perception that he was a national capitalist, working for the good of the nation rather than building a family dynasty.

Until Park left in 1992, Posco was run in a fittingly militaristic manner. Assistants in identical beige uniforms rushed around its offices and steelworks, and many of the famous photos of Korean workers in military formation were taken at Posco. This was the imprint of a man whose life was his work. "Work is my only hobby," he told one interviewer.

This obsession with work has, not surprisingly, taken a toll on Park Tae Joon's personal life, as it has on that of many Korean men. On graduating from college, Park's eldest daughter wrote her father a letter saying, "I leave home wondering what kind of man my father is," and complaining that because her father spent all his time in Pohang he had missed her childhood and could have no idea who she was.[13] In a revealing response, Park wrote that the Roman Empire had been great because Romans left home and hearth to strike out, "while Koreans were content living an honest but humble life in their small thatched huts." He went on to criticize the extended Confucian family, "in which everyone from the grandfather to the youngest child lived in one house," as a reason for Korea's long history of economic stagnation.[14]

At few companies has hard work paid more dividends than at Posco. Posco initially had an annual steel production capacity of 1.03 million metric tons. The Japanese designers who had helped set up Posco envisioned a facility with an eventual capacity of 2.3 million to 3 million tons.

But even before the first bulldozer drove onto the construction site, Park was thinking big. He demanded that the Japanese revise the plan to allow a 9 million-ton plant. During the 1970s and early 1980s Posco kept expanding until the plant reached this 9 million tons of rated capacity, turning the fishing village of Pohang into the world's single largest steel production site by the mid-1980s.

Tellingly, because Posco managed its facilities so well, actual production was more than 100 percent of rated capacity many years. This well-executed military approach to business paid big dividends in an industry like steel.

Park and his Posco men were willing to invest heavily in the most modern production equipment, and successive administrations made sure they had the necessary funds. The long depression in the world steel-making industry also meant that foreign equipment suppliers were willing to provide extremely generous financing and extensive technical support. Capital spending on computers was also heavy; Posco was one of the major reasons why South Korea was U.S. computer giant IBM's largest market in Asia after Japan.

Beginning in the early 1980s, Posco began planning for a second integrated ironworks, this one on the southwestern coast. In an engineering feat that topped even its success at Pohang, Posco constructed its new facility in the Kwangyang Bay on an artificial island. The plant started operating in March 1987, fifteen years after the Pohang plant. By the mid-1990s, Posco's total production capacity was more than 20 million tons a year; it was the largest steelmaker in the world after Japan's Nippon Steel.

By 1986 Posco had became powerful enough to form a 50–50 joint venture with USX, the former U.S. Steel, to modernize the U.S. company's Pittsburg, California steelworks. It soon started shipping this low-cost American steel back to Asia. Korea is now the world's seventh-largest steel producer, thanks almost exclusively to Posco. "Almost single-handedly, he created and developed Posco into one of the world's pre-eminent steel producers. Building his company into a truly first-class steel business has made Pohang and Korea a major force in the international steel arena," said David Roderick, chairman of USX.[15]

International success did not come immediately, however. Even in the 1970s, after Posco had started production, it was not taken very seriously. "I was rather enthusiastic about what I had seen and heard in Pohang on my first trip," said German steel executive F. W. Middleman. "In the seventies the bosses of the international steel industry just laughed at my remarks. They could not believe that some day a Korean company would compete with them. . . . Today they know better."[16]

This steel factory, and the other heavy industry facilities that were built subsequently, set Korea apart from the other Asian tigers, especially Singapore and Hong Kong, which largely concentrated on trading and light industry. And although Taiwan's China Steel is an impressive company, it is far smaller than Posco. Posco provides the steel to build the supertankers and passenger cars at

Hyundai's massive Ulsan complex less than an hour's drive to the south. Posco's steel goes into subway cars, rail lines and electronics products.

Still state-controlled, Posco has become one of the world's largest and most efficient producers, prompting admiration by its competitors in Japan, Germany, and the United States. Ironically, this admiration is perhaps even greater from the Chinese and Russians, who have been stunned that a state-owned steel company could be so successful.

An oft-told story has Chinese leader Deng Xiaoping on a trip to Japan asking Japanese steelmakers how to develop his country's steel industry. The reply, from Nippon Steel's Inayama Yoshihiro, was to ask if China had a Park Tae Joon.[17] Hyundai founder Chung Ju Yung, a vigorous supporter of private industry, says that "the only state-owned corporation to surpass a private enterprise in international competitiveness is Posco, not only in Korea but in the whole world."[18]

Park Tae Joon was a heroic figure as head of Posco, an image that his staff worked zealously to maintain. To commemorate Park's sixtieth birthday the company published a commemorative volume including testimonials by people who had worked with him. The titles of some of the essays, which were apparently chosen by Park's staff, sound as if they were celebrating a divine force. "A Beacon in a Very Dark World," "A Great Leader with Integrity, Foresight, and Vision," and "Oriental Giant, with Normally Uncombinable Human Qualities," are some of the more memorable titles. Hagiography aside, this sort of deification shows how Park—and, to a lesser degree, other Korean business and political leaders—have been regarded by their staff.

Samsung founder Lee Byung Chull probably came as close to the essence of Park's virtues in a myth-making essay for this commemorative volume. "When asked what his beliefs are, he answers 'steel' without hesitation. 'Blue Rock' [Park's pen name] combines the spirit and vitality of a soldier with the soul of an entrepreneur. He is a master at avoiding defeat. His soldier's spirit, the idea that any defeat is a lasting defeat, is the driving force behind his success." Lee's encomium, said to be the last document he wrote before dying, borders on hagiography, but it is a revealing glimpse into how the pre-eminent cultured entrepreneur of the Japanese generation saw the premier warrior-entrepreneur.

In retrospect it seems natural that Posco would succeed. While the first phase of Posco was under construction, though, prospects for the Korean economy seemed grim. The promised take-off of light industrial exports that was at the heart of the second five-year economic development plan (which ran from 1966 to 1971), had not materialized. Industrial labor was restive; peasants were flocking in from the countryside, and the average rate of profit for Korean companies was little better than break-even. The planners had already prepared the third five-year economic development plan (1972–76), but Park and his inner advisers felt something more dramatic was needed.

The new industrial plan suggested by Park's advisers was based on "the limited effects of light industry in the accomplishment of economic self-reliance."[19] After ten years of export-led growth, the government wanted to put maximum emphasis on self-reliance rather than integration with the international economy. The resulting Heavy and Chemical Industries (HCI) plan, which eerily echoed Kim Il Sung's *juche* policy of autarkic development for North Korea, was to alter forever the face of Korea, Inc.

Notes

1. Park Chung Hee's calligraphic rendering of this slogan hangs prominently in the administration building at the Pohang Steel Works.
2. This, at least, is Park Tae Joon's account. In fact, his family was far better off than was Park Chung Hee's.
3. Park Tae Joon, *The 'Separated' Families and Other Essays*, p. 193.
4. Ibid., p. 194. Park is a great supporter of bathing and cleanliness, which he believes are connected to quality and high standards.
5. Ibid., p. 182. His resumé says that he completed his studies at Waseda in March 1947; the course at the Korea Military Academy was completed in July 1948.
6. Ibid., p. 182.
7. Ibid., p. 39.
8. Author interview, October 1991.
9. Author interview, October 1991. The importance of "the simple fact" that Park had such "good friends" can hardly be overemphasized. Inayama and Nagano were two of the most powerful industrialists in Japan. Inayama, moreover, had been a bureaucrat in what later became the Ministry of Trade and Industry (MITI). At the time that Park approached Inayama and Nagano, they had just begun (or were just about to begin) talks that would lead in 1970 to the merger of Yawata and Fuji and the formation of Nippon Steel, the world's largest steelmaker. Interestingly, in light of the Japanese decision to support Posco, the Japanese steel industry was suffering from massive overcapacity in the late 1960s, something that the formation of Nippon was designed to cure. See Chalmers Johnson, *MITI and the Japanese Miracle*, especially pp. 87, 246, 282–83.
10. *Asian Wall Street Journal*, January 23, 1992.
11. Park Tae Joon, *'Separated' Families*, p. 408, for these two paragraphs (Sunday window entrance and golf).
12. Ibid., p. 341.
13. That Park's family chose to stay in Seoul, rather than move to Pohang, underscores the magnetic pull of the capital, where education, politics, intellectual life, and power are concentrated. Park's case is by no means unusual: Most middle and upper-level managers assigned to the provinces keep their families in Seoul if possible.
14. Thanks to John Gittlesohn for this quotation from Park's daughter, which was related to him in a 1987 interview with Park Tae Joon. Park tells a somewhat different version of the story in *'Separated' Families*, p. 12. The quotation about the Romans is from *'Separated' Families*, p. 14.
15. Ibid., p. 387.
16. Ibid., p. 405.
17. Ibid., p. 329. This is Samsung founder Lee Byung Chull's version of the story. On p. 303 of the same book Kim Ho Gil, the president of the Posco Institute of Technology, tells a different version of the story, with Deng wanting five or six Park Tae Joons.
18. Ibid., p. 349.
19. Economic Planning Board, *The Economy in 1972*, pp. 11–12.

6

Yushin

Orientals possess a mysterious, unified and harmonious spiritual culture that can scarcely be understood completely by Westerners, who have different ways of thinking and different systems of logic. Although it is risky to generalize, it is clear that Oriental cultures have a certain gentle, mild, rhythm and harmony.

—Park Chung Hee[1]

Park Chung Hee had tolerated a limited amount of press criticism and dissenting views from opposition politicians and student protesters in the 1960s, but that all changed as his first decade in power came to a close. Fears of North Korea grew when the United States reduced the number of its troops in the South. Then Park won the 1971 presidential election by only the narrowest of margins—he probably would have lost a truly fair and free election—over opposition leader Kim Dae Jung.

As a result, in the 1970s politics moved backward, to a type of brutal domestic repression that had not been seen since the crushing of the autumn 1946 uprisings. Harsh politics marched in lockstep with a ferocious push into heavy industry, the two legs of Park Chung Hee's policy of building a strong state.

The Heavy and Chemical Industries plan and the Yushin constitution, as they were known formally, together made possible a kind of economic control that produced a powerful and chilling spurt of economic growth. Says a former professor who took a senior post at the Blue House in the mid-1970s:

> Before Yushin I think the [economic] mechanism ran less smoothly because of political input. Park used to refer to that period and speak contemptuously of how businessmen used to lobby through political party bosses to affect govern-

ment policy. After Yushin there was a belief on the inside that we had succeeded in freeing economic policy-making from the pressures of politics and business, [that we had] insulated it. There was almost a belief that we were conducting our economic policies and political policies in a vacuum, dedicated to the good of the entire community. At least that was what we told ourselves.

If you agree on high growth, low inflation, industrialization, expansion of trade, then this gives you a set of parameters. The less you are subject to pressures to swerve away from those objectives the better it is. That is the assumption you inculcate yourself with. Park was confident, sure of his performance, sure of the direction. He had no doubts.[2]

It was in the 1970s that the Korean economy's characteristic features emerged—the increased reliance on big business groups and the growth of institutionalized corruption.

In 1972 a political clampdown began that lasted, except for a brief interlude, until 1987. South Korea was the most politically repressive of East Asia's fast-growing economies, and this political intolerance was intertwined with its economic growth.[3] To view either politics or economics in isolation is to see less than half the picture.

In view of the present crumbling of North Korea, it is hard to appreciate how different the situation was in the early 1970s. North Korea's obvious economic edge over the South had disappeared, but the North still had the moral high ground because it had no foreign troops on its soil and it proudly pursued *juche*, its nationalist policy of self-sufficiency. The South depended on U.S. troops and foreign capital. The North's military was still stronger than the South's and, given the apparent disengagement from Asia by the United States, there was a strong possibility that the South soon would be ripe for the taking.

It was against this backdrop of fear and foreboding that Park in 1972 declared martial law, railroaded a new Yushin ("Revitalizing") constitution through the government-controlled legislature, and had himself re-elected president for a six-year term. Park's constitution was a notoriously repressive document, one that prohibited any sort of criticism—even of the constitution itself.[4] "Groundless rumors" were a crime and unexplained absences from school theoretically could be punished with the death penalty.

Many Koreans say that if Park had retired before Yushin, he would have gone down in history as the Korean George Washington. But Park Chung Hee did not, perhaps could not, give up power. Instead, he gave up the fiction of democracy and left it to his aides to justify his increasingly harsh rule-for-life. "Just as a household economy is more likely to remain solid and prosper under an octogenarian mother-in-law than under a young daughter-in-law, it is a felicity for the nation that His Excellency will rule until the year 2000," said one top assistant.[5]

The United States Pulls Back, Korea Cracks Down

If one had to pick a turning point for Park's move toward autocracy, it would be March 26, 1970. That was the day U.S. Ambassador William Porter went to the Blue House and told Park that the United States was pulling out one division of troops, about 20,000 men, nearly a third of the total U.S. forces on the peninsula. This was part of the so-called Nixon Doctrine, or Guam doctrine, which told U.S. allies that they had better be prepared to assume more of the military burden.

Park bitterly resisted the withdrawal. "Park was more than displeased," according to congressional aide Robert Boettcher, who talked to many U.S. officials involved with the decision.

> He was intransigent. The South Korean president told Porter that he would not allow the American troops to leave Korea. The United States government had no right to take them out, he insisted, so he simply would not permit it to happen. Porter had expected displeasure, but he was hardly prepared for an outright refusal Park had no authority to make. . . . Porter returned to the embassy shaken but undeterred. Give him time, he thought. Let him absorb the initial shock."[6]

Park had good reason to be afraid. Shortly after the last time U.S. forces had pulled out of Korea, in 1949, Kim Il Sung had attacked. Even after the Korean War cease-fire was signed in 1953, North Korea remained provocative. In January 1968 a thirty-one-man North Korean commando team infiltrated the country and got within a few hundred yards of the Blue House before most of its agents were killed in a gunfight. Two days later, the U.S.S. *Pueblo* was captured by North Korea. In 1969, in one of the first crises of the Nixon administration, a U.S. spy plane was shot down in international waters by the North, killing all thirty-one crew members. Park understandably thought that a U.S. pullback would send the wrong message to Kim Il Sung.

Prime Minister Chung Il Kwon told Porter that he would lay down on the airport tarmac to prevent planes from leaving. Porter joked in response: "Do that, my good friend, but let me take a picture before the planes begin to roll." Still, the Koreans kept protesting the withdrawal. At a meeting in Hawaii in July, Defense Minister Chong Nae Hyok told his U.S. counterpart, David Packard, that his orders were to prevent any withdrawal of U.S. forces. Chong tearfully told Packard a story from Korean history about an envoy who was forced to commit suicide because he failed his mission.[7]

Finally, in exasperation the White House sent Vice President Spiro Agnew to Seoul in late August 1970. Agnew was there as Richard Nixon's personal emissary, a fellow hawk reassuring Park Chung Hee that the military drawdown did not mean the United States was abandoning its commitment to defend South Korea in case of an attack.

Park was buying none of this. In a meeting that started at ten o'clock and was scheduled to last one hour, Park and Agnew went at it for a full six hours. There were no breaks for coffee, lunch, or even to go to the toilet. Agnew's aide, General John Dunn, later described the grueling session as "brutal and absolutely offensive" and described Park's behavior as "a performance by a head of state unlike any I had ever seen."[8]

A U.S. official involved with security affairs who worked closely with the Koreans during the early- and mid-1970s remembers the city as a capital on the edge.

> When I came, people were still talking about the Blue House raid of 1968 and the seizure of the *Pueblo*. The first [North Korean infiltration] tunnels were discovered while I was here. There was a tremendous sense of the looming military threat of the North. There were commando raids from the North, and at night there were metal poles stuck on golf fairways to keep AN–3s [a light Soviet-designed plane] from landing. The North Koreans were known to have a mockup of downtown Seoul and the war games that we fought still had the North able to take Seoul in a matter of days. There was a real threat.[9]

Relations between the United States and the South Korean military were not always good, particularly because South Korea clandestinely tried to develop nuclear weapons capability during these years. Says this official:

> The military relationship between the U.S. and South Korea was OK on the surface but brittle underneath. The Koreans had a lot of things going on in terms of weapons procurement and contingency plans. The nuclear program surfaced at that point and there was a lot of secret planning on the part of the South. . . . Privately, I think [Park Chung Hee] was very contemptuous of the fact that we had not stayed and won in Vietnam, and I think he had some qualms about our reliability, which is why he authorized the start of the nuclear program.

Security forces in Seoul were extremely jumpy. In October 1976 a Northwest Airlines cargo plane taking off from Seoul's Kimpo airport on a flight to Japan veered off course and flew over the Blue House. Following a policy of shooting first and asking questions later, troops protecting the presidential compound fired antiaircraft shells at the jet. The pilot doused all the plane's lights, went into a steep dive, and flew safely on to Tokyo, but one person was killed and twenty injured from the falling antiaircraft shells.

Government critics say that Park cynically used the threat from the North to justify his harsh rule. While even those who worked closely with the former president concede that he let his fears get the better of him in the late 1970s, they insist that his concern about North Korea was both genuine and well-founded.

Nam Duck Woo, the deputy prime minister for economic affairs from 1974 until 1978, was one of Park's inner circle of economic advisers during much of the Yushin period. Although not directly involved in politics, Nam saw the president's concern with the threat from the North.

I don't deny that [Park and the KCIA] used the threat of national threat as a means of controlling society. It does not follow that there was not a real threat. No one can deny that North Koreans were committed to the ideology of unification by revolution.

I'm really annoyed by arguments that the national security threat was a fiction to justify national security authoritarian rule. It's nonsense. We really had it. Peace is not guaranteed by any foreign country. There was really a sense of urgency on national security matters. Every day, every ministry was working out what should be done in case North Korea [were to] undertake another gamble. . . . The threat was real. We had a real sense of urgency.[10]

Park almost certainly would have favored heavy industry even without the specter of North Korea looming over Seoul, but the military threat prompted him to direct more resources into defense-related production. "Park was driven by this belief that we had to take care of ourselves on defense," says a senior official who worked closely with the president on national security issues in the 1970s. After Agnew came to announce the troop withdrawal, Park:

drew the conclusion that the U.S. would go home when the U.S. wanted to. Hence, dependence on the U.S. was precarious and eventually we would have to defend ourself. Then came Carter to reconfirm and strengthen Park's belief [with the announcement that he would withdraw all U.S. ground forces by the end of the 1970s. Park then] accelerated the defense program. This defense buildup had a distorting effect on the overall economic policy. It sucked resources away from where they would have been more efficient.

The KCIA Brings the One-Party State to Korea

The May 1961 revolutionaries had formed their own secret police almost immediately after the coup. On June 10, 1961, the new organization was born with 3,000 employees. By 1964, it had an estimated 370,000.[11] Unlike the U.S. CIA, whose name it consciously borrowed, the Korean CIA was explicitly designed to spy on its own citizens, to conduct both foreign and domestic operations. "It was Januslike," said the U.S. official. "It looked in and it looked out. There was no separation between the two, but its real power was on the inward face. We were here to help them on North Korea, but they didn't know much about North Korea."

From the beginning, the KCIA was controversial. Headed by Kim Jong Pil, one of the colonels who had been instrumental in Park's coup, the agency was criticized for its subterranean role in elite politics, criticism that underscored the relative openness of politics in the 1960s. The *Korea Handbook*, a semi-official annual, devoted substantial space in its first edition, published in 1964, to attacking the KCIA. It charged that the Supreme Council for National Reconstruction:

was merely a figurehead to put approving stamps and make official announcements of policies already formed by Park Chung Hee in consultation with someone outside the Council. For this reason it was generally recognized that Kim Jong Pil, head of the CIA, was the number two man of the military junta, although he was holding a position which, theoretically, was beneath the Supreme Council.[12]

The handbook goes on to charge that the chairman of the standing committee on economic and financial affairs of the Supreme Council for National Reconstruction was not even informed in advance of the disastrous June 1962 currency reform.[13]

Kim Jong Pil, Park Chung Hee's nephew and close associate, spent much of the early 1960s trying to build a one-party state along Communist (or Taiwanese) lines. He used the KCIA to try to amass the money he needed for this enterprise. Kim was implicated in several celebrated scandals in the early 1960s, including stock market manipulation and abuse of foreign exchange privileges in connection with the construction of the Walker Hill hotel casino in Seoul and automobile imports.

The KCIA and local police had a network of informers throughout private companies, as well as on campuses, in political organizations, and in the media. Almost no Korean was beyond the reach—literally—of the KCIA. One dramatic illustration of the agency's long grasp came in 1967 when a group of seventeen antigovernment students was kidnapped in West Germany and brought back to Korea.

In the United States, the KCIA harassed antigovernment Koreans. Opposition leader Kim Dae Jung was kidnapped from a Tokyo hotel in 1973. Shortly before Park was assassinated in 1979, the former head of the KCIA, Kim Hyung Wook, disappeared in Paris, presumably murdered by South Korean agents.

A more mundane example of the KCIA's ability to keep tabs on people came in 1970. Cho Sung Il, the son of a leading opposition political leader, was asked by the Blue House to return from the United States, where he had a fellowship at Harvard's Center for International Affairs. Although Cho had been an interpreter for UN commander-in-chief Charles Bonesteel and his contacts with the U.S. military provided him with a measure of protection, he feared retribution from the Korean authorities because of his father's opposition activities.

I asked Bonesteel to help me go to the U.S. Bonesteel wrote to Kissinger, and I got the fellowship. I wanted to stay for good in the U.S., but Park Chung Hee wrote me a letter and asked me to come work for the Korean government.

I left my family in Boston. I wanted to make a reconnaissance by myself. My father was the number two opposition leader after Yun Po Sun, and he wanted me to go visit Yun Po Sun. I didn't want to go because I knew the intelligence agents would pick that up but I couldn't disobey my father. So I went to see Yun at night at his house in Anguk-dong. He asked me to contact Kim Eung Soo and Kang Young Hoon [two prominent Koreans who were living in the U.S.] and see if they would join the opposition. [In spite of the precautions], the KCIA found out about the meeting and so I was not allowed to work at the Blue House.[14]

After the harsh Yushin measures were declared in 1972, the KCIA under its hard-line chief Lee Hu Rak was even less interested in genuine intelligence about the North Korean threat. Ironically, Yushin was declared only three months after secret North-South contacts had produced a historic seven-point communiqué, issued on July 4, in which the two sides pledged to end their quarter-century of hostility and work together. Next, at the end of August, Red Cross representatives from North and South Korea held an unprecedented meeting in Pyongyang. Then on October 12, only five days before Park stunned the nation by imposing martial law, Lee Hu Rak met the North Korean deputy prime minister at the truce village of Panmunjom and inaugurated the South-North Coordinating Committee.

But the contacts with the North, rather than easing tensions, spooked the South into harsh measures against any sign of domestic dissent, real or imagined. The U.S. official, whose work brought him into close contact with the KCIA during this period, was chilled by what he saw:

> Once I met Lee Hu Rak [shortly after he had been to North Korea for talks]. I tried to raise a neutral topic. "You recently went to North Korea," I said. "How did that make you feel?" "Very strong," he said, referring to the North Koreans, gesturing with his thumb up. "One-man rule. Quite a guy." It was an admiring reaction toward Kim Il Sung.
> The South got a look at the North and, instead of saying "we've won the economic competition," they said, "if we're going to talk to these guys we've got to tighten up." That led to Yushin and martial law. There was a sense that any turbulence in the South needed to be tamped down because the North would take advantage of this. I think that was a misreading of the situation.[15]

Park encouraged competition among the different security agencies, which included the KCIA, the Capitol Garrison Command, the Defense Security Command, the Presidential Protective Force, and the intelligence bureau of the Korean National Police. Their power was extraordinary. It was no exaggeration when a KCIA officer told Shin In Ryong, a Christian activist and law school graduate who was arrested and tortured: "The KCIA is the top policy-making body of the government. We are not regulated by any law. We can kill any traitor like you. . . . We can set free any criminal."[16]

It was, as two of the president's critics pointed out after his death, a society permeated by fear.

> The impression that Park's domain was infested with his intelligence agents permeated every nook and cranny of the society. A sense of the immediacy of his governance pervaded the whole country. Bureaucrats, politicians, judges, military men, diplomats, businessmen, journalists, professors and scholars—

not to mention his minions and sycophants—all performed for a one-man audience, "the personage on high." When it was necessary to refer to him in private conversation, even his critics resorted to hushed euphemisms.[17]

The economy developed quite literally under the gaze of the president, whose picture hung on the wall of every government or private office. Koreans did not need any prodding to put up the president's picture. But one Swiss businessman, who found the growing personality cult of Park Chung Hee repugnant, received a visit from the KCIA asking him to put up the president's picture. It was a visit that showed both the scope of this personality cult and the ease with which a foreigner could bluff in Korea.

> It was in 1977 or 1978. We were in the Daewoo Building, at the time the largest office building in Seoul. They came to me and said we should put up a picture of Park Chung Hee. I told them that I would be happy to but that, under the Swiss Constitution, if we put up a picture of a foreign head of state we would have to put up a picture of our president too. Of course our constitution doesn't say this. But I told them that I was concerned about what the staff might think because we would have to change the picture on the first of January every year when we change presidents. The KCIA man said that the agency would discuss this internally. I never heard from him again.[18]

The agency kept a tight watch over business. One morning the manager of a foreign bank branch in Seoul came into his office to find several garbled telexes. He asked his Korean secretary to notify the senders to resend the messages. She told her foreign boss that it would be easier simply to contact the KCIA, which kept copies of all incoming messages. She did, and a few hours later the bewildered manager received copies of his telexes, along with a card stating that these had been provided with the compliments of the KCIA.

Politics was a life-and-death affair for many companies. No one wanted to cross the government, which controlled so much of the economy. The government forced the independent *Dong-A Ilbo* newspaper to purge its staff in 1975 by ordering advertisers to boycott the newspaper. Any firm in the country could have been brought down if the government had told the state-owned banks to shut off their credit lines.

Before he disappeared, former KCIA director Kim Hyung Wook told the U.S. congressional committee investigating the Koreagate scandal that Park Chung Hee "imposed severe pressures and sanctions on businessmen who did not give him their undivided loyalty. In many cases, charges were fabricated and these individuals were sent to jail. In addition to imprisonment, the businesses of these individuals were often confiscated."

Kim claimed that these companies included Yonhap Steel, Shinjin Automobile, Chungang Industries and Construction, Tongkwang Business, Koryo Deep Sea Fishing, Koryo Shipbuilding, Kwang Myong Printing, Koryo Foods,

Kyungnam Business, Taehan Transportation, and Cheju Bank.[19] Of course, it was often difficult to separate personal or political motivations on the part of the president from sensible economics. Shinjin Automobile, according to scholars Leroy Jones and Sakong Il, had "one of the worst performance records of any major Korean enterprise."[20] There may have been political motivations, but there certainly were ample economic ones.

Agents were everywhere. The Swiss businessman remembers visiting a British bank in Seoul and surprising a KCIA agent, who regularly and openly visited the Swiss businessman's office to look for intelligence tidbits, disguised as a window cleaner. The agent circulated through the bank branch looking for information.[21]

It was not only the KCIA that kept close tabs on businessmen. The Seoul city police department had an intelligence unit overlapping the KCIA's. This businessman was once summoned to the Seoul Station police headquarters, next to the Daewoo building to receive an unsolicited award for good corporate behavior.

> I went to the top floor and was shown into a large office. There was a huge desk with a lot of telephones on it. In the middle of the desk was my file, a big file, two or three inches thick, bound with cardboard. On the front cover my name was written in English in large black letters. It was like a scene from Kafka. My file was the only thing on the desk besides the telephones. Then the brass came in and they handed over the citation to me, with the five-star head of the police on one side of me and several four-stars on the other side, and took photos. Nobody said a thing about the file and I left. Two or three months later my office manager came and said, "you received this citation and now the police are going on a picnic and it would be nice if we gave them 200,000 won for their picnic."

Park's control over society was nearly absolute. People did not dare to talk in restaurants or *kisaeng* houses, because waitresses reported to the KCIA or the police. A prominent professor at Seoul National University got a vivid demonstration of just how wide a net Park's intelligence agents cast. "One day in the mid-1970s I withdrew five million won (about $10,000) from the bank. The next day I was visited by the KCIA. They wanted to know what the money was for. They asked if the money was for the opposition, for a countercoup or for the Communists. They immediately found out when money changed hands."[22]

This network meant that Park had so much information that he could blackmail or ruin virtually anyone in the elite. Periodically, he did just that. Intermittent anticorruption campaigns designed to "purify" society resulted in the dismissal of hundreds of civil servants at a time. Even those in the innermost circles of power were not immune. Kim Sung Gon, founder of the Ssangyong group and a member of the gang of four (Kim Jong Pil, Lee Hu Rak, and Kim Hyung Wook were the others) who were closest to Park in the 1960s, fell afoul of KCIA head Lee Hu Rak in the early 1970s. Kim, who at the time was a powerful member of the National Assembly, had his mustache pulled out one hair at a time by KCIA agents.

The KCIA was, in the words of former U.S. diplomat and Korea scholar Gregory Henderson, "a state within a state, a vast shadowy world of . . . bureaucrats, intellectuals, agents and thugs."[23] By the 1970s its targets included nearly everyone in the country. They were particularly concerned about Kim Dae Jung, one of the few people who dared to speak out against Park Chung Hee.

Kim Dae Jung had just finished lunch with opposition politician Yang Il Dong in Room 2211 at the Tokyo Grand Hotel, and he was saying good-bye. It was a Wednesday afternoon, August 8, 1973; he had been in Japan for almost a month after returning from the United States, where he had spoken out against the Yushin regime. Kim, South Korea's only effective opposition politician at the time, bid farewell to Yang and stepped out into the corridor. He was immediately attacked by six men.

"One clapped his hand over my mouth, shoved me into the room next to Mr. Yang, punched me and kicked me and put a cloth with anesthesia over my face." Four of the men dragged him into an elevator and took him down to the hotel basement. They shoved him into a car and drove for about five hours toward Osaka, in central Japan. First he was taken to a house on a beach, then he was put on a small motorboat and then onto a more powerful sea-going vessel. The crew tied weights onto Kim's arms and legs, and he heard the crew talking about ensuring that his body did not surface.

Kim Dae Jung, who had narrowly lost the 1971 election to Park Chung Hee, had emerged as the most eloquent critic to Yushin. Prohibited from speaking out at home, he had taken his message abroad, lashing out at the president's decision to outlaw dissent under the guise of national security.

Kim Dae Jung knew that the arm of the KCIA stretched abroad. After arriving in Japan on July 11, Kim moved discreetly in Tokyo, changing hotels every few days and registering under false Japanese names in an attempt to throw the KCIA agents off track. "Friends around me warned of some kind of plot against my life," he said. There was a plot, and it was organized by KCIA head Lee Hu Rak, almost certainly with the approval of Park Chung Hee himself.

"There was growing anger when Kim Dae Jung criticized Park Chung Hee abroad," said a U.S. official who was involved in the effort to save Kim's life. "It's one thing to criticize your boss at home, it's another thing to do it abroad. [U.S. Ambassador] Phil Habib sensed it had been done by the [South] Koreans. He told everybody in the embassy to turn up their hearing aids. By pooling everything it became clear within twenty-four or forty-eight hours that he was in the hands of the South Koreans."

Two days after his abduction, Kim lay manacled and blindfolded in the boat, praying for his life to be spared. As the crew discussed the details of Kim's planned killing, a brilliant flash pierced his blindfold. A plane overhead—Kim believes it was the U.S. CIA—had dropped a flare, a light that signaled the beginning of the end of his nightmare. The crew took off Kim's blindfold, offered him some orange juice and helped him smoke a cigarette.

U.S. pressure and an uproar in Japan, where the government was deeply embarrassed by his abduction on Japanese soil, apparently persuaded Park Chung Hee and Lee Hu Rak that they had more to lose by killing Kim Dae Jung than keeping him alive. He was brought back to South Korea, held in a house near Seoul, and then dumped out on a street near his house in the capital. Five days after he disappeared, a dazed and disoriented Kim Dae Jung stumbled through the front door of his modest house and into his wife's arms.[24]

Koreagate: Exporting the Korean System

Park Chung Hee feared two things, according to former KCIA director Kim Hyung Wook: Kim Dae Jung and the U.S. Congress. The 1973 kidnapping of Kim showed how far Park was willing to go to silence his most eloquent critic. The Koreagate scandal showed the lengths to which Park would go to try to influence the U.S. Congress.

In his heart, Park Chung Hee would have liked to do without the United States. But U.S. troops acted as a tripwire along the front lines and subsidized U.S. grain made up for a shortfall of domestic rice. Making sure that the troops stayed and that the military and economic aid spigot kept gushing led to Koreagate, the infamous and clumsy influence-buying scandal in Washington.

The Koreagate affair was at its heart an attempt to export the Korean style of domestic politics to Washington. White envelopes stuffed with crisp hundred-dollar bills were supposed to help ease open the doors of powerful members of Congress and White House officials. The scandal was a tale of factional infighting, bullying, and rake-offs of cash by the Koreans involved, who were often more interested in lining their own pockets than using the money to buy friends and silence enemies in the United States. It was the sort of export Korea could have done without. For however lax the political standards of Washington were in the early 1970s, the crude attempt by Koreans to buy congressional support eventually caught up with Tongsun Park, the KCIA, and the motley assortment of Korean operatives who were involved.

Koreagate started with Tongsun Park, the glib, garrulous son of an affluent family in Seoul. Park liked to entertain lavishly in Washington, where he had gone to study. "While some people like movie actors or actresses," he said, "I always enjoy the company of political figures."[25] He threw parties he could not afford and let on that he was related to Park Chung Hee—until the KCIA put an end to that bit of fictitious genealogy by summoning him back to Seoul and putting him through an overnight interrogation.

Tongsun Park, however, did not scare easily. He was persistent, he was charming, and he was a shrewd manipulator. Park first used his Washington political connections to win the lucrative business as the sole selling agent for huge shipments of rice from California and Louisiana to feed a Korea whose farmers could not produce enough grain. He did this by shrewdly playing up his connections in Korea—primarily a poker-playing friendship with Prime Minister Chung Il Kwon, the man who threatened to lie down on the tarmac to prevent U.S. troops from leaving Korea—and his acquaintance with Representative Richard Hanna. Tongsun Park was a master at convincing people that he was more important than he really was and at turning the most casual acquaintance to his advantage. He was a quintessential hustler who thrived by acting as a bridge between Koreans and Americans who knew little about one another. A former employee of Tongsun Park's—who later was duped out of about $60,000 by Park in a real estate deal that went bad—describes a visit to Seoul by his boss in the early 1970s:

> He had brought back this photo album from Washington with all these people, with congressmen, senators and White House staff, high government officials, posing with him at the parties he threw.
> He would try to get people who were important [in Seoul] to look at these. He was playing the smoke-and-mirrors game to show that he was important in Washington. He wanted to enlist support on this end so that he could use his contacts in Washington.
> People think that he met with Park Chung Hee and that he was supposed to go lobby on behalf of the Korean government. He never met Park Chung Hee one time face to face, although he badly wanted to.[26]

Tongsun Park, it seems, wanted to meet everyone, and few people were immune to his hustle. One exception was U.S. Ambassador to South Korea Philip Habib, who told the embassy staff in Seoul in the early 1970s that the one man they were not permitted to meet was Tongsun Park.

Rice was so profitable because it was bought at subsidized prices, but sold in Korea at four times the world price. Tongsun Park received over $9 million in commissions for his rice monopoly, and about $850,000 of that went to members of the U.S. Congress.[27] Even that was not enough money to finance Park's lavish lifestyle and he frequently borrowed money from Richard Hanna.

The Koreagate scandal illuminated the way money and politics were mixed together in South Korea, with Park Chung Hee and his cronies playing by a completely different set of rules than the rest of the country. Former KCIA head-turned-government-critic Kim Hyung Wook told the U.S. Congress that he had helped Tongsun Park get the rice agent monopoly and had deposited $3 million of Korean government funds at a U.S. bank in order to help Park get a loan. As if that were not enough, the KCIA, on Kim's orders, had changed $100,000 on the black market in Seoul for Park and smuggled the money to Washington in a diplomatic pouch. This happened, said Kim, simply because Tongsun

Park was an acquaintance of the prime minister and because he promised to use his influence with Congress to win support for Korea—especially military support. But most of the money, said Kim, apparently went to support Park's expensive lifestyle. "While he stated that he was distributing money to the U.S. congressmen, I think much of the money he pocketed by himself."[28]

Tongsun organized tours for visiting congressional delegations, in the hopes that officials in Seoul could impress upon them the nature of the North Korean threat and win their support for continued military assistance. Lobbying Congress is not, of course, illegal. Giving congressmen and their wives large, unreported cash donations, as the Koreans did, is.

Tongsun Park did not spearhead a well-coordinated lobbying effort. Instead, it was a rather free-floating affair where the Koreans used whomever they could—and where those with access to cash managed to skim off some for themselves. Congressional investigators believe that some of the money Tongsun Park received may have been passed on to his protector and poker partner Chung Il Kwon and perhaps the ruling party—although there were complaints that Park was keeping too much money for himself. Korea got cheap rice, and the commissions went to pay for a lifestyle Park could not otherwise afford in Washington.

Tongsun Park's lobbying effort was largely self-generated and he acted more as a freelancer, albeit one who tried to advance Korean government interests, than as a full-fledged Korean agent. But, as is often the case in Korea, it is impossible to draw a clear line between government and private initiatives.

Just how that line should be drawn was never tested in court. Although Tongsun Park was indicted on August 26, 1977, on thirty-six counts including bribery, illegal campaign contributions, mail fraud, racketeering, and failing to register as a Korean agent, he had fled the country long before. Later, after bilking investors in a land scandal in Seoul in the early 1980s, he fled again, settling in the Dominican Republic.

The Koreans seemed to think that they could just buy their way out of any problem with the U.S. Congress or administration. This attitude was remarkably unsubtle, with little attempt made to find out who might be most susceptible to donations and who might reject them—who might be effective and who would be a waste of money.

Richard Nixon's special assistant, John Nidecker, went to Korea to represent the United States at a prayer breakfast in May 1974. Nidecker was stunned to be given a white envelope stuffed with $10,000 in crisp hundred-dollar bills just before he left the Chosun Hotel for Kimpo airport. On the envelope was written, "Bon Voyage—Park Chong Kyu." Park Chong Kyu, nicknamed "Pistol Park," was the director of the presidential security force.

As criticism of Yushin grew in the United States, and $93 million in foreign aid to Korea was cut from the U.S. budget at the end of 1974 because of human rights violations, South Korean activities in the United States became more sinister.

In 1974 and 1975, Park Chung Hee personally directed Operation White Snow, a KCIA scheme to prevent congressional criticism of human rights violations. Hancho Kim, a Korean-American living in the Washington area, received $600,000 from the KCIA to buy off members of Congress. Kim was supposed to pay the money to five members of the House Foreign Affairs Committee. However, he had nothing like the influence he claimed. For him, the money was simply a windfall. He used most of it to buy a new Cadillac and pay off his debts to banks, furniture stores, and department stores. Some of the money went to pay his children's tuition and $10,000 was donated to Findlay College in Ohio, where he had attended school for one semester. The school gave him an honorary degree and established the Hancho Kim Far Eastern Center.[29]

The KCIA harassed Korean-Americans in the United States in an attempt to squelch criticism of an increasingly repressive regime. Symptomatic of how close the regime was to total implosion, the KCIA even had to threaten and harass former officials, such as former KCIA director Kim Hyung Wook and Kim Ki Wan, a former KCIA agent who had been involved in the Kim Dae Jung kidnapping but later emigrated to Los Angeles.

The most damaging single blow to the Park Chung Hee administration was a congressional appearance by Kim Hyung Wook on June 22, 1977. Kim had been a military academy classmate of Park's and took part in the May 1961 coup. He headed the KCIA for six-and-a-half years, from March 1963 until October 1969.

Kim was also notoriously corrupt. His testimony was motivated less by an attack of conscience than a desire to extract revenge after losing out in a struggle for power with Lee Hu Rak. A congressional investigator remembers Kim as a thug:

> In all the many hours of interviewing Kim Hyung Wook, I came to the conclusion that this man was a caricature of a gangster. . . . Considering that he was one of the two or three most powerful people in the country for six or seven years, one has to conclude that either Park Chung Hee was an idiot or he was condoning outrageous criminal behavior. Whether Park was putting money in his pocket or not, he knew he was heading a criminal enterprise.[30]

In a desperate, last-ditch attempt to prevent Kim from testifying, Park Chung Hee dispatched a loyal aide, Min Byung Kwon, to Kim's house near New York City. Min, a minister without portfolio and member of the National Assembly, told Kim that he should not testify. Instead, Kim should return to Seoul or move to a third country. The government would take care of all his expenses—a figure of $1 million was repeatedly mentioned.

Kim rebuffed Min, and early the next morning slipped out of his house to go to Washington several days before his scheduled congressional appearance. Min, angered by Kim's disappearance, threatened Kim's wife. "From now on, you won't be able to live in the States, and don't consider coming back to Korea. Call your husband and tell him not to testify. Then you can live quietly."

Kim Hyung Wook was well aware that his life was in danger. He told congressional investigators in June 1977, after he talked to a reporter: "Mr. Min [Byung Kwon] told me that when *The New York Times* interview was first published, President Park called the chief of the KCIA and said to kidnap me, bring me back, and that he was going to kill me. That is why the rumors were circulated consistently before my testimony that I would be killed."[31]

Despite the threat, Kim testified in Washington, but his days were numbered. He disappeared in Paris in October 1979, shortly before Park Chung Hee was assassinated, and is presumed to have been murdered.

Kim Hyung Wook's disappearance has been the subject of intense speculation. There is a popular version of the story, which has it that Kim was lured to Paris by someone he had known for many years—who was later rewarded with an ambassador's post. He was kidnapped in Paris and brought back to Seoul. Taken to the basement of the Blue House, he was supposedly confronted by Park Chung Hee, along with KCIA head Kim Jae Kyu and presidential aide Cha Chi Chol.

The story goes that Park accused Kim of betraying the country. Kim angered the president by shouting back: "You are the betrayer. You betrayed the nation." Park lost his temper, grabbed Cha Chi Chol's pistol, and killed Kim.

The truth may never be known, as all of those supposedly involved in the incident are dead. But this much is clear: The May revolution was devouring itself.

Corruption: The "J-Factor"

Park Chung Hee took power with spectacular show trials and public spectacles intended to destroy so-called parasites and profiteers. His laments about the evils of corruption were loud and persistent. But the reality of the Park years was the construction of an elaborate edifice of corruption.

Park presided over a country in which the art of corruption was refined to a breathtaking extent, one in which much of the money extorted from businesses was simply recycled into political campaigns, and most of the balance used to pad the salaries of government officials.

Much of Park's anticorruption rhetoric was a cynical political ploy, for the issue was a useful way of dislodging those in power when Park and his colleagues staged their 1961 coup. But it was also an authentic expression of the contempt and anger that these peasants' sons felt for the city slickers who had made it big in politics or business.

Park and the younger colonels who were the muscle in the coup had seen in the army how corruption could sap an institution. After the Korean War, many officers were shamelessly corrupt—sometimes, during the Syngman Rhee years, so venal that they sold food and gasoline on the black market. Troops went hungry, or were forced to walk long distances, because their supplies had been sold by their commanders. Officers pocketed U.S. money earmarked to hire construction workers and surreptitiously forced their men to work through the night, even between full days of training. "Koreans had always known corruption, but its extreme form, its more prehensile pattern, arose inside the Korean Army and at this time," wrote Gregory Henderson, in his classic work on Korean politics.[32]

As one general put it to Park Chung Hee some months before the coup: "Everyone is in it. Privates steal on foot. Officers steal in jeeps. Generals steal by trucks."[33] However, it was not just the military. Anyone with government connections could easily exploit them for profit during the 1950s.

For all their rhetoric, the new military leaders were more concerned with controlling and channeling corruption than with eliminating it. Kim Jong Pil, the young colonel who along with Park was the most important of the coup leaders, was intent on building a strong party that could control the government.

Kim was exiled from the country for a period of time in the mid-1960s after he was accused of irregularly importing *pachinko* machines (a pinball game popular in Korea and Japan); running up share prices on the stock market in order to reap profits for the ruling party; reselling imported cars (which were bought with scarce foreign exchange) at windfall profits, and diverting foreign exchange to build a hotel and casino at the Walker Hill resort complex on the outskirts of Seoul, which would generate profits for Kim and the ruling party. The Japanese provided everything for this operation, right down to the poker chips.[34] The Walker Hill hotel complex is controlled by the Sunkyong group, one of the six largest conglomerates in the country and one that was later linked by marriage to President Roh Tae Woo.

In three of these four scandals, privileged access to foreign exchange was used for schemes that could in no way be considered part of Park Chung Hee's grand nation-building enterprise. Gambling in particular was precisely the sort of zero-sum activity that Park Chung Hee's economic authoritarianism was allegedly designed to eliminate.

Japanese businesses provided two-thirds of the Korean ruling party's budget from 1961 through 1965, according to a secret estimate by the U.S. CIA. The CIA estimated that six firms paid a total of $66 million, with one contribution as high as $20 million.[35] The bribes presumably were paid in return for preferential business treatment.

Favored companies enjoyed easy access to loans when the foreign currency spigot was turned on in the late 1960s. In turn, they kicked back some of the money to the ruling party. Ssangyong, owned by Park crony Kim Sung Gon, got more than $100 million in foreign loans in the late 1960s, and Korea Explosives received $67 million. Jung-en Woo notes caustically that "a massive influx of foreign capital in the late 1960s financed half of the nation's total investment, and tumbling after it was an avalanche of a particular kind of corruption that presented the regime with electoral victories and impressive influence over the nation's business."[36]

Because the system was at its heart corrupt, virtually everyone was vulnerable to punishment. Cho Choong Kun (known as Charlie Cho), at the time a vice president of Korean Airlines, was arrested in 1974 and jailed for twenty days for violating foreign exchange regulations. The garrulous Cho, whose machine-gun style of speaking English is a legacy of the time he spent doing business in Vietnam with the U.S. military, now is the vice-chairman of the airline, which is the core company of the huge Hanjin group.

Although Cho does not like to talk publicly about the case, a source familiar with his version of the story has it that he gave out large quantities of foreign currency—around $100,000—in the year before he was arrested as gifts to Korean politicians who were taking trips abroad. These kinds of donations were not unusual—some of the money would go to finance shopping sprees in New York or Tokyo, and some of it would be passed on to juniors whom they met on the trip as "encouragement money," a token of friendship and a lubricant to ensure continued smooth relations.

"Every time someone like a minister or the prime minister went to the States [or another foreign country] it was customary to give them some money, usually one or two thousand dollars," said an airline executive many years later. "It wasn't a bribe, it was just our customary way of doing things." The gesture was no doubt appreciated. Even those who were privileged to have a passport—and passports were not freely available until 1989—faced strict limitations on the amount of foreign exchange they could buy.

Charlie Cho's problems arose when the time came to replenish his company's foreign exchange holdings in Korea, because the money had been taken from domestic hard currency ticket sales. Cho asked his Tokyo office to help him make up the shortfall by slashing operating expenses and bringing $100,000 into Korea. However, the two executives who were bringing the cash in were arrested by customs agents. When Cho refused to provide the prosecutor with the names of the politicians who had received money from him, he was imprisoned for almost three weeks, until Park Chung Hee himself intervened.[37]

Park did not hesitate to make an example of people who had crossed him; he seemed to delight in periodic anticorruption campaigns staged against businessmen (and their free-spending sons), bureaucrats, military officers, and politicians. In a well-publicized 1975 case, South Korean police barged into the bedroom of thirty-one-year-old Park Tong Myong early one morning and arrested him on charges of smuggling $250,000 abroad. Police made much of the fact that the son of a Christian clergyman spent his money in the United States chasing Playboy bunnies, buying silk shirts and expensive neckties, and the he owned a Mercedes.[38] In the "Seven Little Princes" scandal around the same time, a public campaign was launched against the sons of several chaebol founders who were deemed to be living too extravagantly.

Park wanted to channel corrupt funds, just as he wanted to control bank loans, for the maximum political advantage. It was not a matter of eliminating corruption but of controlling it. During the 1960s, it was foreign firms that apparently coughed up most of the cash. In addition to Japanese contributions, two large

U.S. companies, Gulf Oil and Caltex, each made multimillion-dollar contributions to fund the ruling party. Gulf gave $3 million to the Democratic Republican
Party for the 1971 election and thus materially helped Park Chung Hee narrowly
beat Kim Dae Jung in the presidential contest. Gulf chairman Bob Dorsey, who
told a U.S. congressional committee that the money may have won the election
for Park, said in Gulf's defense that the company had bargained its contribution
to the ruling party down from the original asking price of $10 million.

Foreign businessmen in Seoul called the money that Park and his cronies
demanded "juice," and they factored the "J-factor" into their business calcula-
tions. The government could be remarkably unabashed about squeezing juice out
of businesses, be they foreign or domestic. In mid-1975 the senior vice president
of General Motors Korea, Herbert Telshaw, gave Prime Minister Kim Jong Pil a
check for 50 million won ($104,000) as part of a "voluntary" contribution to
national defense. The campaign was started in 1973 and, by the time of
Telshaw's gift, $31 million had been collected, most of it after Saigon fell to the
Vietnamese Communists in April 1975.

Telshaw said the chairman of Daewoo Motors, who was Korean, wanted to
donate eight times as much, even though the venture was barely breaking even.
Applications for bank loans, new business licenses, and permission for foreign
companies to repatriate foreign earnings would not be guaranteed to donors. But
foreign businessmen in Seoul believed that not to donate generously to causes
such as the defense fund was to invite trouble from the government.[39]

Banks, securities firms, and insurance companies donated $2.1 million to the
fund through the Bank of Korea. The construction association, the spinners and
weavers association, and Samsung Moolsan Industrial Company each donated
$417,000, suggesting that these so-called donations were a matter of following
government orders. Typically, the Blue House decided how much money was to
be collected and would give the orders to the major business organizations, the
Federation of Korean Industries, the Korean Traders Association, and the Korea
Chamber of Commerce and Industry. The leaders of these organizations would
meet with the heads of companies and associations and set quotas for donations.
These generally would be parceled out on the basis of a company's ability to
pay. There was no accountability for these funds after they were collected.

After Park's death, about half a million dollars was found in his personal
office safe. In Park's defense, it is worth noting that at least most of the money
stayed in Korea. "The people who are corrupt [in South Korea] put their money
into the country," Washington SyCip, a management consultant in the Philippines and the chairman of the Asian Institute of Management, told a group in
Seoul in 1991, to nervous titters. "It still creates jobs, the same as any other
money. If Mrs. Marcos puts her money into Swiss bank accounts, it does not
create jobs [in the Philippines]."

Moreover, Park genuinely believed in national development. Unlike the elite,
snobbish rulers of Vietnam, Park understood the degradation of poverty and was

imbued with the passion to eliminate it. But the corrupt political system he created, whose parallels with Japan are obvious, continues to impede Korea's aspirations for open, representative government and to hobble its economic growth.

End of the Thatched Roof Era

As a peasant's son, Park was acutely conscious of the problems farmers faced and he was determined not to leave the countryside behind as he pursued his forced-march development campaign. But in the late 1960s, and especially after the completion of the expressway linking Seoul and the southeastern port of Pusan in 1970, urban squatters' settlements grew alarmingly. Park realized that more needed to be done for the country's rural poor.

In 1971 Park inaugurated the Saemaul Undong (New Village movement), a plan to do for the countryside what was being done for factory areas: impose discipline and order in an attempt to generate economic growth. Saemaul has been held up as a model community development program, catapulting a generation of Korean peasants out of their enduring poverty trap. Certainly, that is part of the story.

Saemaul was an important milestone in the economic development of Korea. "Until then we had been basically an agriculturally oriented society and economy," said Park You Kwang, who was a young official at the Economic Planning Board when Saemaul began. "Most farmers were very lazy and gambling and drinking was an everyday thing, especially during the winter. They had lived that way for thousands of years."[40]

Saemaul taught them to stand tall. Park Chung Hee, talking about the benefits of Saemaul, said:

> Never again will the man from the city, the man from the government, *any* man, be able to push the country-man around against his will. Before Saemaul, it was the farmer who rushed to bow to the township chief; now, with Saemaul, it is the township chief who rushes to bow to the farmer. And what has been done in this respect in the countryside will come about in the nation itself.[41]

Certainly, Saemaul raised living standards and spurred villagers to become more self-reliant. But Park had no interest in seeing farmers really stand up against the government. Much later, in 1990, diplomats at the newly opened Polish embassy in Seoul looked into the possibility of using a Saemaul-type program to invigorate rural development. The conclusion, as recounted by the Polish ambassador: Saemaul was too similar to the discredited Communist system that had left Poland economically ruined.

Saemaul was a product of the military reformist spirit that animated Park and the men around him. Away went the thatched roof huts that had dotted the countryside for centuries. Park considered these roofs too primitive for a would-be developed country, so he ordered their replacement with corrugated metal roofs and, later, concrete tiles. The fact that straw was a far more effective insulator against the bitter winters and steaming summers of Korea did not trouble Park. Metal was modern, and straw was not. For those villagers who protested, Park offered a sop: the Korean Folk Village was built near Suwon, a walled city south of Seoul, where traditional houses were preserved for future generations. Peasants who refused to re-roof their houses had their traditional roofs destroyed by zealous local officials.

Between 1972 and 1979, according to the country's all-seeing statisticians, a total of 2,450,000 houses had their thatched roofs replaced. That works out to about half of all the houses in the country, excluding the two major cities of Seoul and Pusan. Whole villages went from thatch to metal in a few years, changing forever the face of the Korean countryside.

The rural development statistics, which government officials and the state-controlled press trumpeted, certainly were impressive enough. Nearly 2.8 million homes were electrified. Electrification to rural households was subsidized as a matter of deliberate policy, so that peasants could install televisions, which would bring them into contact with the modern world. Bridges, roads, irrigation canals, dikes, and small reservoirs were built, using almost exclusively unpaid village labor. The government supplied expert assistance and some of the materials, such as cement, although villagers always had to pay part of the costs to ensure that the program would not simply degenerate into an expensive handout in which the community had no incentive for success.

There was a strong element of coercion in the Saemaul movement. This bullying was not limited to peasants who wanted to keep thatched roofs, but included village property owners. Park decreed that all facades on main streets in towns and villages should be straight. Untidy, rounded corners were, in Park's mind, a sign of a disorderly past that he wanted to do away with. Even today, the false facades that were built to comply with this military-style directive are visible in many rural areas.

There was even a saccharine Saemaul song, supposedly—and perhaps really—written by Park Chung Hee himself in May 1972, which ran: "You and I get up! Let us turn our efforts to build our Saemaul and the good life to come!"

There was a Saemaul pledge, which came in the form of loud speeches blaring from ubiquitous loudspeakers every morning. The green-and-yellow Saemaul flag fluttered in villages throughout the country. The movement did not, at least during its early years, deteriorate into a sterile propaganda campaign. Instead, Saemaul was regarded by many international experts as a model rural development program. Critics, however, feared that the country was on its way to becoming one big boot camp, shining its shoes and making its bed in accordance with the Great Commander's orders.

Much as it might seem to outsiders like a quasi-religious cult, Saemaul did have some important payoffs. A U.S. adviser, Michael Adler, was stunned to notice the changes that had occurred in Korean villages between his first visits in the 1950s and his trips in the 1970s.

> My recollection of the people in the villages in those [early] days still can haunt me. I didn't see a village that was anything other than a wreck. The overwhelming majority of the children I saw in the rural areas suffered from malnutrition, scabies and other illnesses. When I went back and took a look at the same areas in 1971 and 1972 I was amazed at the change in the appearance of the rural areas, and the people. The villages were clean and orderly. The people, particularly the children, looked healthy. Although some of them may have been scantily clad, they were clean; their clothes were simple, but clean and in good condition.... I believe that most of the credit goes to Koreans themselves. They are extremely hard-working people. The average Korean farmer is an amazing individual. He works all day and half the night and leaves nothing undone that possibly can be done.[42]

If this account is to be believed, the laziness, gambling, and drunkenness that the Economic Planning Board's Park You Kwang said typified the Korean farmer were erased with remarkable speed and thoroughness. No doubt both Park's and Adler's accounts are exaggerations, but it is undeniable that the countryside was reshaped remarkably.

The three goals of Saemaul were to improve living standards, raise incomes, and promote "spiritual enlightenment." However, as the 1970s came to a close, the rhetoric of the New Village movement became more important than its actual accomplishments. Social control took precedence over raising rural incomes. The Saemaul movement was extended to urban areas and factories in an effort to tame the hundreds of thousands of villagers who were streaming into urban areas in search of new jobs. Saemaul taught them how to arrange flowers and bow correctly, an ironic coda to Park Chung Hee's pledge that the farmer would never again have to bow to the official.

Saemaul also became increasingly distant from the needs of farmers. In 1972 peasants had ample time available for the voluntary labor on which Saemaul depended. But by 1979 the impact of cash crops, part-time employment, and increased access to towns and cities left them few free hours for building dikes and bridges. Moreover, from 1975 on there was more or less full employment in Korea for the first time in its history. By the latter years of the 1970s there was even a labor shortage at harvest time, which lured poor urban laborers back to their villages, where they could earn more as day laborers than they could in the city.

Saemaul was, in spite of its many shortcomings, largely successful in promoting rural development, allowing Park and his economic team to concentrate most of their attention on industrial development, especially the Heavy and Chemical Industries Plan. But it was also part of Park's strategy of trying to control every aspect of development from the top. Rhetoric aside, he was suspicious of any sort of local, grass-roots activity.[43]

Death of a Lady

On the day the first subway line opened in Seoul, August 15, 1974, Park Chung Hee lost his wife. Park was presiding over Liberation Day ceremonies at the National Theater on the northeastern edge of Namsan Mountain, not far from the city center. A singularly inept pro–North Korean resident of Japan was dispatched to Seoul to assassinate the president. The would-be killer accidentally fired a bullet into his own left thigh as he pulled out the .38 caliber Smith and Wesson pistol with which he hoped to kill Park. One of his wild shots hit Park's wife, Yook Young Soo, who sat at the rear of the stage as her husband gave his Liberation Day speech.

Park dropped to the floor during the shooting, but got up as police dragged the assassin away and his wife was rushed to the hospital. "Ladies and gentlemen, I will continue my speech," he said, and he did. After he had finished the speech, Park noted that his wife's handbag and shoes were still lying on the floor. He picked them up and left.[44]

For all Park's bluster, he was an introverted, withdrawn man, more at ease in his Blue House office monitoring economic performance than out making speeches. His wife had been a balancing influence, keeping him from becoming too removed from the cares of ordinary Koreans and too influenced by hard-line advisers like Lee Hu Rak and Cha Chi Chol. When he met opposition leader Kim Young Sam after his wife's death, Park sobbed that "since my wife died this large presidential palace seems like an empty Buddhist monastery."[45] A few months after Park's wife was killed, a U.S. official was at a small dinner with Park Chung Hee and several senior American and Korean officials.

> Everyone sat there like tin soldiers. To get the conversation going I asked Park if he ever compared himself to Kemal Ataturk. "I would like to do for Korea what he did for Turkey, to leave Korea economically strong and militarily protected," he replied. But, he said, "I'm not going to stay in office indefinitely. Some people told me that I should not have run for office again, and if I listened to them perhaps my wife would have been alive."[46]

By the end of the 1970s, Park had withdrawn almost completely. Koreans are always eager to please their bosses, often to the point of sycophancy, but a cold, raw atmosphere of fear and paranoia seeped into even the top ranks of Blue House officials during those years. *Washington Post* reporter William Chapman captured this atmosphere in a 1979 article:

> Even his loyal aides were often terrified. Early this year, a foreign reporter was chatting with one of Park's more sophisticated executives. He is a man of broad learning and considerable detachment, regarded by outsiders as one of the few in Park's government who enjoyed a sense of personal security.
>
> Suddenly the special telephone linking his office with the president's rang on a desk 15 feet across the room. The official bounded to his feet and raced

like a frightened rabbit to grab the phone before it stopped ringing. Throughout the conversation that followed, he stood stiffly at attention.[47]

During the late 1970s, and continuing for a decade, windows on buildings any-where near the Blue House had to be taped up so that it was impossible even to look toward the compound from a distance. Picture-taking was prohibited from the top of Namsan Mountain, in downtown Seoul, or from most buildings until the late 1980s. When Park met visitors, they had to be seated an hour before his arrival.

In the 1970s Park was increasingly concerned about what he thought was a growing threat from the North, and he was determined to counter it with his own military and industrial build-up. Koreagate, Saemaul, and a more ferocious KCIA were the political faces of this concern. But there was an economic side as well. The 1970s saw a decision to dive into heavy industry. It was a plunge that has had far-reaching consequences for the Korean economy. Twenty years later the economy is still defined by these choices Park made in the 1970s.

Notes

1. Park Chung Hee, *To Build a Nation*, p. 187.
2. These quotations are from an author interview conducted in January 1991. This scholar-mandarin, like many other high officials, refused to be identified. "It's still too close," he said by way of explanation, reflecting the sense that the wounds of the Park and Chun years still have not completely healed.
3. For comparative analysis see World Bank, *The East Asian Miracle: Economic Growth and Public Policy*.
4. The Chinese characters for this were the same as those used for Japan's Meiji restoration, which laid the groundwork for that country's economic expansion at the end of the nineteenth century.
5. Quoted in Kim Suk Jo and Edward J. Baker, "The Politics of Transition: Korea After Park," pp. 3–4.
6. Nixon received a decision memorandum containing three options for troop with-drawals in South Korea: remove both divisions, remove one division, or leave just a few brigades. Nixon was supposed to choose only one option. Instead, he checked all three. Acting on his own, White House aide Alexander Haig unilaterally decided to remove one division, making one of the most significant changes in U.S. policy since the Korean War. Robert Boettcher, *Gifts of Deceit*, p. 89.
7. Chong lost his job the next month but did quite nicely for himself, remaining active in politics until the mid-1980s, capping his career as the speaker of the National Assembly from 1981 to 1983 and chairman of the ruling Democratic Justice Party in 1983–84. The quotation by Prime Minister Chung is from ibid., p. 91.
8. The account of Porter is from ibid., p. 90. Dunn is quoted on p. 95. This section relies heavily on Boettcher's account of the withdrawal negotiations, pp. 90–96.
9. All comments from this former official come from an October 1991 author interview.
10. Author interview, December 1991. Almost no one would argue that the threat from the North was a "fiction." It was the exaggeration of this threat, the government's monopoly on the debate, and the cynical manipulation of the danger for domestic political purposes that were at issue.

11. Joungwon Alexander Kim, *Divided Korea: The Politics of Development, 1945–1972*, p. 234.

12. *Korea Annual*, 1964, p. 124.

13. Ibid. The discussion of the KCIA is scattered throughout pp. 117–28.

14. Cho says he was slated to become protocol secretary and interpreter for Park at the Blue House. He was not, however, disqualified from working in the government because of his opposition lineage. Instead he went to work for the prime minister, at the National Security Council, then moved to the Construction Ministry, where he was a protégé of Kim Jae Kyu—the KCIA head who later killed Park. Cho rose to the powerful position of director general of the national physical planning bureau at the Construction Ministry before he was purged in 1980. Author interview, January 1991.

15. Author interview with former U.S. official, October 1991.

16. Quoted by Kim and Baker, "The Politics of Transition," p. 7.

17. Ibid., p. 2.

18. Author interview, October 1991.

19. Kim Hyung Wook, p. 11 of U.S. Congress, House, *Hearing before the Subcommittee on International Organizations of the Committee on International Relations.* 95th Congress, 1st sess., part 1. June 22, 1977, p. 24 (cited as Kim Hyung Wook testimony).

20. Leroy P. Jones and Sakong Il, *Government, Business and Entrepreneurship in Economic Development: The Korean Case*, p. 132.

21. The KCIA agents were sometimes efficient and sometimes bumbling. But the important thing is that they were always there. By one estimate, the agency employed 300,000 people in the 1970s on a full-time or casual basis, about one out of every hundred people. "We had regular visits from the KCIA," said the Swiss businessman. "They wanted money and to know how the business was and whether we had any problem with the staff. They had to do something so they could fill out a report, but the main purpose was to get something in addition to their salary."

This businessman once found that an employee suspected of being a KCIA agent had a tape recorder in his desk to record conversations with employees. "It's hard to say what he really looked for," the businessman remembers. "ninety-five percent of what he reported must have been absolute nonsense." But it was nonetheless intimidating. This employee was fired only because he was caught cheating the company. "The final end was the guy came back to try to extract a better settlement. He showed me his papers and said, 'I am a colonel in the KCIA and I only did my job.' "

22. The quotation is from an author interview in June 1987.

23. Quoted in *Newsweek*, November 19, 1979.

24. Kim believes that he was saved by a U.S. surveillance plane. His book *Prison Writings*, p. ix in a chronology of Kim's life, says that "American aircraft spot the KCIA boat and keep it under surveillance, preventing the assassination." However, a U.S. official involved with the effort to save Kim maintains that it was not a U.S. plane that dropped the flare and that the United States did not know where Kim was at the time. Author interview with U.S. official, October 1991. Much of this account is drawn from *The New York Times*, August 15, 1973.

25. This quotation is from a press conference he held in Seoul in which he defended his activities and said, "I don't think I should be penalized for pursuing my avocation." *Far Eastern Economic Review*, September 9, 1977.

26. Author interview, October 1991.

27. Boettcher, *Gifts of Deceit*, p. 70.

28. Kim Hyung Wook testimony, p. 24.

29. Ibid., pp. 31–4. Also see Boettcher, *Gifts of Deceit*, pp. 277–78.

30. Author interview with Ed Baker, February 1992.

31. Congress, House, *Hearing before the Subcommittee on International Organizations of the Committee on International Relations*, 95th Congress, staff interview on July 11, 1977, p. 67.

32. Gregory Henderson, *Korea, The Politics of the Vortex*, pp. 345–50, for these and other examples of corruption in the military. The quotation is from p. 347.

33. Michael Keon, *Korean Phoenix*, p. 58.

34. Quoted in Woo Jung-en, *Race to the Swift*, p. 107. Other sources that mention these incidents include the *Korea Annual* (1964, pp. 125, 132, 133) and *Far Eastern Economic Review* (March 21, 1963, p. 611).

35. Woo Jung-en, *Race to the Swift*, p. 107.

36. Ibid., pp. 107–8.

37. This information comes from an author interview, November 1991. A different version of this story appeared in *The New York Times*, September 22, 1974. According to this account, the police said that Cho was being investigated on charges of diverting $330,000 of the airline's overseas earnings to buy property in Los Angeles and Tokyo (for use by the ground crews), rather than remitting the money to Seoul.

38. The *New York Times*, June 30, 1975.

39. The *New York Times*, June 10, 1975.

40. Author interview, October 1991.

41. Keon, *Korean Phoenix*, p. 224.

42. Michael Adler, an official with the U.S. Agency for International Development, testimony in *Hearings before the Subcommittee on International Organizations of the Committee on International Relations*, House of Representatives, 95th Congress, 2nd session, Part 6, Hearings July 19 and August 2, 1978, p. 100.

43. Kim and Baker, *The Politics of Transition*, pp. 11–12, write: "The petitions of puny farmers' organizations over some bungling of local agricultural policy—for example, distribution of rotten sweet potato seeds—have been quickly escalated into grave public order problems. A minuscule credit union formed by poor working girls inspired by the Urban Industrial Mission was subject to, among other things, a most rigorous tax investigation. Another group of women workers, who were trying to elect representatives of their own choosing rather than those nominated by the government-dominated National Textile Workers Union, were set upon by goons, beaten and smeared with human excrement while police officers looked on in amusement. One hundred twenty-six of them were fired and their pictures were circulated nationally lest an unwary employer hire any of them."

44. Keon, *Korean Phoenix*, p. 199.

45. Quoted in Kim and Baker, *The Politics of Transition*, p. 9. This is Kim Young Sam's version. At this meeting, Park bought, bullied, or cajoled Kim Young Sam into silence.

46. Author interview, October 1991.

47. *Washington Post*, November 3, 1979.

7

The Big Push

National strength is based on the nation's economic strength. The fundamental element for self-reliant national defense and in laying the foundation for unification is the national potential to achieve a completely self-sufficient economy; and exports constitute the leading element for the completion of a self-reliant economy.

—Park Chung Hee[1]

On July 3, 1973, a triumphant Park Chung Hee and Park Tae Joon gripped a long, flaming rod and thrust it into the blast furnace at Pohang Iron and Steel, igniting the steel age in South Korea and realizing a big part of their heavy-metal dream.

This Posco complex was only one of many heavy industrial projects. A few months earlier, just south of Posco along Korea's eastern coast, Hyundai started building ships before the concrete in its dry dock had even dried. This would soon be the world's largest shipyard and one of the biggest users of Posco's steel. Later in the 1970s, ground was broken for what was billed as the largest machinery complex in Asia. Throughout the decade large chemical facilities were built in a country that seemed to have no possible need for them.

Park Chung Hee placed his biggest bets on heavy industry. With this roll of the dice he forever changed the nature of Korea, Inc. He not only cajoled and browbeat companies, but deliberately distorted prices—got prices "wrong," in the words of scholar Alice Amsden—in order to encourage investment in heavy industry.[2]

During the 1970s economic growth became Park's excuse for his increasingly repressive rule. The bold push into heavy industry was both a way of economic leapfrogging and a way of building up the country's military against any threat from the North. Ironically, the result, at least during the 1970s, was to make South Korea a lot more like the North.

Park, like his North Korean rival Kim Il Sung, was fond of slogans designed to whip up enthusiasm among workers, businessmen, and bureaucrats. Nineteen sixty-six was the "Year of Hard Work" while 1967 was the "Year of Progress." In 1968 Koreans were told to "Fight While Working, Work While Fighting." The message was always the same: Only by building a strong, prosperous economy could the nation's survival be guaranteed. But nations are not built on slogans alone.

Park's own long-standing bias in favor of heavy industries was buttressed by the belief that only in this way could Korea escape from its chronic trade deficits with more developed countries. Park and his advisers were also concerned about being undercut by lower-cost challengers from other up-and-coming Asian countries.

In the early 1970s, the drawdown of U.S. troops coupled with the imposition of textile quotas by the United States convinced Park that he had to do something dramatic, that he needed to make a developmental leap. The troop withdrawal "left him no choice but to fall back on his old ideas," remembers Ssangyong chairman Kim Suk Won, the son of one-time Park Chung Hee ally and company founder Kim Sung Gon. "Lots of guys said to him, 'We have no alternative [if we want] to survive.' "[3]

The Heavy and Chemical Industries (HCI) program, which Park publicly inaugurated in January 1973, was bound up with the need to build up a defense industry. Its plants were located for the most part in the extreme southeast, as far from North Korea as possible.

The president's announcement of what would become known as the Big Push occurred at a time of political and economic turmoil. The notorious Yushin constitution had been announced only a few months earlier. Park was also under siege on the economic battlefront. Following a huge increase in foreign debt during the late 1960s, South Korea had been forced to turn to the International Monetary Fund (IMF) for help in 1971. Then, in August 1972, as businesses groaned under crushing debt burdens, Park had annulled curb market loans in an effort to keep troubled companies afloat and punish allegedly usurious money-lenders. What he succeeded in doing instead was cutting off credit for thousands of companies that relied on the curb market for money that the state-run banking system could not provide.

Curbing the Curb Market

Although the economy had grown at a rapid clip during the 1960s, danger signs started flashing as the decade drew to a close. Businesses had been suffering as a result of huge debts, which they had taken on with Park's approval as foreign borrowing soared during the late 1960s. Debt as a percentage of equity doubled from 56 percent in 1965 to 113 percent in 1968.[4] Many of the loans went to politically well-connected companies, and a substantial percentage (an estimated 5–10 percent) was recycled to the ruling political party in the form of "commissions" and kickbacks. By 1969, South Korean companies were in danger of suffocating from the debt load that they had piled on their tiny capital base. The government took over thirty firms in 1969, all of them foreign loan recipients; ninety more firms teetered on the brink of bankruptcy.

By 1971 the number of bankruptcies of firms receiving foreign loans had climbed to two hundred and South Korea faced its first foreign debt crisis. The IMF stepped in for the only time in South Korea and administered the bitter medicine of devaluation—which raised debt-service costs but helped exports—and imposed strict limits on new foreign borrowing. Businesses howled in pain. Significantly, however, South Korea refused to bow to IMF pressure to end its export subsidies.[5]

Park Chung Hee decided to help business by cracking down on the curb market. This was like trying to make water flow uphill. Nam Duck Woo, who was finance minister at the time, explains the thinking behind the president's decision.

> Korean companies were faced with a structural problem. There had been no long-term credit facilities whatsoever. The maturity of bank loans did not exceed one year [but] there had been very vigorous investment activities in the past ten years. The companies had to borrow short-term money for long-term investment. It was very natural for them to have a credit crunch.
>
> The business community was crying for some measures to relieve their credit difficulties. FKI chairman Kim Yong Wan appealed directly to President Park, saying that the curb market was the source of all trouble, and that the government should do something to correct this situation. Neither of them were economists and they did not fully understand that this could happen [because] the curb market is really a real money market. [But] President Park gave his instructions to his aides in the Blue House to work out some measures.[6]

On August 3, 1972, the government froze all private loans. The measures echoed Park's rash and disastrous 1962 currency confiscation. Because the financial system was so repressed, the curb market was an important safety valve for those who needed funds but did not have sufficient clout to get them through the banking system. It was also an important means of saving. Koreans, like many Asians, lend money through informal associations, in order to get higher interest rates. In Korea, these are known as *kye*, and they are usually (but not always) controlled by women who are either related or know each other through a school tie.

The size of the curb market was huge—more than one-third the size of the official loan market. After Park's decree, some 350 billion won in curb market borrowing was declared, equal to 34 percent of the credit in the banking system.[7] The actual amount was certainly larger, although it is impossible to say how much larger.

A total of 209,896 people registered as creditors. About 70 percent of them were small lenders with less than 1 million won in assets ($2,889 at official exchange rates). They were told that they would have to endure a three-year moratorium on repayments of both principal and interest. After that, interest rates would be limited to 18 percent a year. That was a far cry from the monthly market rates of 2 to 4 percent when Park froze the market. The interest rate subsidy was a massive boon to business, which would enjoy negative real interest rates for the rest of the 1970s on much of its borrowing.

Nam had no real say in Park's decision to slam the lid on the curb market but, as an economist, he could try to steer it in a more rational direction. He figured that he could use Park's decision to modernize the Korean financial system by introducing new financial institutions to bridge the gap between the curb market and the repressed official financial system, and that he might be able to wean Koreans of their habit of investing through the *kye*.

> I thought it was necessary to make the people aware that the curb market was not a good thing. The *kye* was a very outmoded way of financing. [I thought] perhaps it might help modernize Korean banking culture, credit culture. After all, since President Park was determined to carry it out I had no choice.
>
> Freezing the curb market alone would make no sense. It would create controversy and upset economic stability. I thought I could take advantage of this situation to introduce pervasive financial reform in this country, including the short-term money market, mutual trust funds, credit unions plus national investment funds. Very few people appreciate the other measures but in retrospect I think the other measures were more important in Korea's financial development.

Nam's measures were one of the few attempts to inject market forces into the financial system. But they have had relatively less long-term impact than he could have hoped at the time, and they were overshadowed by the measures to control the curb market.

There are not many countries, especially those that claim to believe in market forces, that simply erase the assets of nonbank savers with a presidential decree. But Park was never one to let theory or consistency get in the way of his orders. For the pragmatic president, the August 1972 freeze on the curb market was simply a bold way to try to get out of the economic dead-end that Park thought the country faced.

Metal-Bashing: The Heavy and Chemical Industries Plan

At the beginning of 1973, without even bothering to consult his economic ministers, Park with great fanfare launched the so-called Heavy and Chemical Industries plan designed to build up these capital-intensive industries and distract the public from the political situation. He also set a goal of $10 billion in exports and a per capita GNP of $1,000 by 1980. This target looked absurdly optimistic. Total exports in 1972 had been only $1.62 billion and per capita GNP just $318. Exports would have to sextuple and per capita income triple in eight years to meet Park's ambitions.[8]

Because of the resistance to this plan that Park knew existed in the senior ranks of many ministries and other important areas of the economy, he created a special Heavy and Chemical Industry committee in the Blue House. This committee took priority over the rest of the government, bypassing the Economic Planning Board and giving orders directly to the Ministry of Finance, the banks, and the Ministry of Commerce and Industry. The committee drew up the plans for shipyards, heavy engineering plants, power generation equipment plants, chemical plants, and a range of other industries. Its officials negotiated with senior industrialists to build and operate these plants, and provided the finances and the import licenses to equip them.

Kim Chong Yom was Park Chung Hee's senior adviser for economic affairs and a key player in this industrial build-up. While Lee Hu Rak and other unsavory persons repressed domestic politics, Kim took charge of economic affairs. Kim, remembers an official who worked at the Blue House during the 1970s, "was like a computer on two legs. He could spin out all these facts and figures at any moment. How many kilometers of highway had been added last year and this year, how many tons of rice had been harvested, and how many had been bought by the government. He had the budget in his head all the time."

Kim and a handful of other men were the brains of Korea, Inc. The policies of the 1970s were essentially dreamed up by this small circle of people. Their plans were complex, requiring billions of dollars of fixed investments, the import of foreign know-how, and armies of highly skilled workers. That it worked as well as it did is testimony to the quality of Korea's workers and, above all, to the power to mobilize society that existed in this authoritarian country.

This ten-year master plan included detailed government plans for five industries: shipbuilding, machinery, chemicals, steel, and nonferrous metals. Interestingly, the list of favored industries did not originally include automobiles. Electronics, although not formally part of the plan, in fact received similar preferential treatment.

The government decided where plants would be built, what their capacity would be, and which companies would build them. It remade the face of Korea by bulldozing vast areas where the industrial estates would stand. Changwon, a spit of land near the southeastern city of Masan and as far from North Korea as it was physically possible to go on the Korean peninsula, housed the machinery complex that would be the cornerstone of Korea's arms industry. Posco and Ulsan, the site of Hyundai's massive shipyard and auto factory, were a bit further up the coast.[9] In the southwest was a new chemical complex at Yeochon.

The HCI plan was a watershed in Korean development. The decision to build up heavy industries such as shipbuilding, autos, military goods, and capital equipment set Korea on a course forever different from its rivals in Hong Kong, Singapore, and, to a lesser extent, Taiwan.

Although this development gave Korea manufacturing capabilities its competitors will never possess, it did not make intuitive economic sense, as economist and former Deputy Prime Minister Nam Duck Woo recognized.

> It was very obvious to everybody that we wouldn't have any advantage in chemical industry. I was a bit embarrassed. Financing those ambitious projects was going to fall upon me. President Park knew that I was rather skeptical but he persuaded me that building up heavy industry was the right choice for the long-term interests of the country.
>
> He said national industrial power rested on heavy industry. It was a rather nationalistic view. Then came Vietnam, talk of domino theories, and the Nixon Doctrine. He had a real sense of urgency on national security and he was determined to develop the defense industry. I think these two considerations [underpinned the HCI program].
>
> As a finance minister I worried about how to finance these ambitious projects. He knew that I was reluctant and he once told me, "Mr. Nam I know you are worried about financing problems and are afraid of these projects. Japan once fought the whole world and lost and their country [found itself in] a miserable situation. But they recovered and their economy is moving so fast. It will become one of the major economic powers in the world. Japanese people had guts, enough to fight the whole world. I'm not going to fight the whole world, I'm just trying to build up some heavy industry for the long-term interests of this country."

Nam was only one of the most prominent of a group of foreign-educated technocrats who attempted to balance the populist, nationalist, heroic economic ambitions of Park with neoclassical macroeconomics. Their role was limited to carrying out the president's ideas in the most economically rational fashion.

> What I tried to do was reconcile his request with the economic rationale. I created the NIF [National Investment Fund]. People don't understand why I did it. The most obvious [purpose] was to finance petrochemical industries. The second hidden purpose was that I had a device by which to say no. People didn't understand that. We pooled funds from various sources of a public nature. Government employers pension fund, other similar funds plus some contributions from the commercial banks. I knew very well that tapping resources by mandate is against the rules of the market economy, I know that, but I had to do [it], because President Park wouldn't give it up.

The thinking behind the HCI plan was not as irrational as many of its harsher critics have suggested. Kim Jae Ik, a prominent technocrat until his death in 1983, was fond of pointing out that the capital cost per job created in shipyards was actually quite low. Shipyards required massive numbers of workers—an important consideration at a time when about half a million workers a year were entering the work force—as well as vast quantities of steel (produced at the nearby Posco mill). These industrial behemoths also stimulated the acquisition of managerial and technical skills.

Lee Suk Chae, a government official who was initially skeptical about the plan, says that there were five key economic factors—in addition to the political ones—that prompted the government to adopt the heavy industry strategy. Korea had a large, cheap, well-educated work force; as Posco demonstrated, it could acquire state-of-the-art facilities, which would give it a leg up over its more established competitors; it could borrow money from abroad for investment; a protected domestic market provided a captive customer base; and its businessmen and government officials were used to international market pressures and could readily develop export markets.

> In addition to these favorable economic conditions, Korea had the benefit of the Japanese model, which could serve as a rationale for the HCI Plan in many respects. As a latecomer, Japan had relied heavily on foreign technology and equipment in its HCI development efforts. . . . [This strategy] enabled Japan to become a fully developed nation. Therefore, in order for Korea to catapult into the ranks of advanced nations, the government felt that development of HCI was the only available choice, and that there was little reason why Korea could not repeat the Japanese success.[10]

The creation of Korea, Inc. was a by-product of these ambitions. The president needed the economic growth that only business could provide, and businessmen needed the business licenses and access to cheap loans that only the government could grant. Reliance on heavy industry, which required about $10 billion in investment, ensured that this government-business alliance would continue. Business has been unusually dependent on government and, even today, still counts on government for both subsidies and, in some cases, specific guidance.[11]

As the government cajoled business to invest in heavy industry, the face of Korea, Inc. changed. Bigger became better. Big companies were more than ever dependent on the government for cheap funds. But the HCI program also laid the foundation for the emergence of gargantuan business groups, which by the late 1980s could challenge political leaders. It was a delicate balancing act, one that became more unstable in the 1970s as the government pushed companies into capital-intensive heavy industries and their borrowing increased.

"Park was proud of the business types," says one of the mandarin officials who worked in the Blue House for most of the 1970s and whose condescension toward business reflects that traditional view. "They were his children, his creations. They made Koreans go somewhere."

The relationship between business and the president was ambiguous, but the president clearly had the upper hand. "Park had them trembling with fear," remembers this official, pressing his thumb down. The president could—and sometimes did—crush businessmen like insects. But, mostly, the 1970s were a time of tremendous success, of big plans being made and, somehow, against all the odds, being fulfilled.

Joel Bernstein, a U.S. AID adviser, remembers visiting the Chungju Fertilizer Plant, which had been criticized (by both Koreans and the U.S. General Accounting Office) for cost overruns and inefficiency when it was built with U.S. help in the mid- to late-1950s. Koreans, who ran the plant on their own by the time Bernstein visited, showed him a production chart. Although this plant predated the Big Push, in its operation it was typical of the Korean tendency to run flat out.

> They showed me this chart and it was level with slight jigglings all the way across the top, and the level was at 108 or 110 percent of capacity. So I asked them about it. I had never seen a petrochemical plant with that kind of operation. Well, they had figured out a way to piece-by-piece take the major units down without stopping the operation.[12]

Other major industrial plants, including steelmaker Posco, also consistently exceeded their rated capacity, with some running at 110 percent or 115 percent of their theoretical maximum, year after year. The military-style push to produce more would serve Korea well throughout the 1970s.

Park and the chaebol were determined to burst onto the world industrial stage with a flourish. Says Jung-en Woo: "Every new plant had to be one of the best and the largest in the world and boasted of as such, the quickest ever built, or the most efficient ever operated, almost as if the program jostled for a place in the Guiness Book of World Records."[13] That Korea was able to get technical assistance and favorable financial terms from foreign suppliers to build these modern factories reflected its position as one of the few buyers of new industrial capacity during the sluggish 1970s.

Alan Plumb, a British merchant banker who went to work in Korea in the mid-1970s, remembers that the scale of the projects seemed out of step with the realities of daily life in Seoul.

> The massive scale of industrial activity didn't seem real. One time I went to Ulsan, to Hyundai Heavy Industries, and drove down inside this huge dry dock that you could hardly see out of. It was incredible, but it seemed more so when they told us that it wasn't just here in Ulsan where Hyundai was building ships and cars, but that in Okpo Daewoo was building another shipyard almost as large and that just up the coast Pohang was constructing a massive steelworks.[14]

A senior executive at the Hyundai group says that to most of the world projects like the Ulsan shipyard looked preposterous. But for Hyundai chairman Chung Ju Yung they were just the normal way of doing business. Said the executive:

> It may have seemed audacious. But to Chung a ship was just a metal vessel filled with instruments, and he was confident that his construction experience taught him how to build metal vessels. A dry dock was simply a big hole in the

ground lined with cement. Most of the holes he built were round or square, the dry dock was a big rectangle. Hyundai spent $250 million on that shipyard; [Daewoo's] Okpo cost $1 billion, and it was a smaller shipyard.[15]

Even as Hyundai workers were building the dry dock, Chung was out selling his ships. He showed prospective buyers the picture of a beautiful sandy beach and assured them that this would be the site of his shipyard. When Hong Kong shipping magnate C. Y. Tung asked Chung if Korea had any experience building boats, the Hyundai founder pulled out a Korean 500-won note. Pointing at the picture of Admiral Yi Sun Sin's sixteenth-century iron-clad turtle boats, he confidently assured Tung that Korea had been making high-quality boats for almost four hundred years.[16]

Korea was simply not on the map for most foreign investors. They might have had dim memories of it as a divided, war-ravaged country, but the notion of it becoming a developed nation seemed implausible. Says banker Alan Plumb:

> In order to attract outside investors to Korea you really had to do an educational job. You had to say where it was, where it had come from, how it was going to get there, how it was different from other developing countries. Most people's immediate reaction was, "It can't last, there must be something wrong, they don't count like we do." I kept coming back to this nebulous reason Korea will succeed, the will of the people. I could hear my visitors mumbling under their breath, "He's no good, he's eaten too much of that rice, he's become like those funny people with fat faces."

Shrugging Off the Oil Shock

Even after the 1973 oil shock, which saw oil prices quadruple, Park Chung Hee remained steadfast in his determination to drive ahead with the HCI plan. Most countries suffered an economic setback, and one would have expected that South Korea, which was tying its future to energy-intensive heavy industry, might pause. But Park kept pouring in funds, with only minor modifications.

"This ambitious Heavy and Chemical Industry plan once faced severe challenge due to last year's oil shock and consequent world inflation," Park said in June 1974. "Some of us suggested that the HCI plan should be modified substantially considering [the] new economic environments caused by the oil shock. The government, however, continued to implement the Heavy and Chemical Industry plan with its basic framework intact, and this began to bear fruit."[17]

Korea and Taiwan responded completely differently to the first oil shock. Taiwan kept its currency fixed, in order to keep the oil bill down, and curbed other imports and deflated the local economy. Korea, by contrast, devalued the won and absorbed the oil price increases, even though prices shot up. Foreign currency holdings were run down, and more money was borrowed abroad. Park was simply unwilling to slow down the HCI build-up. Woo chronicles Korea's response:

> Rather than curtail investments in basic and defense-related industries, Seoul simply bulldozed ahead on its course of expansion, slashing its currency to push exports, and amassing debts to finance the imports needed to sustain production and investment. Instead of alternatives to petroleum [the Koreans] recycled petrodollars.[18]

Park was too optimistic. There were, as a result, some delays in the fourth five-year plan. Finalized at the end of 1976, it designated only machinery, steel, and shipbuilding as worthy of continued support. By that time it became clear that the world steel market was likely to remain depressed for some time. It was also evident that Korea really did not have any comparative advantage in nonferrous metals, fertilizer, and pulp. The scheduled completion of Posco's fourth-phase expansion (which represented a sevenfold increase over its original 1-million-ton annual capacity) was delayed one year, to 1982. The size of a planned copper smelter was cut by 20 percent, and an aluminum smelter was canceled. The number of new shipyards was cut from nine to two and the scale of three fertilizer plants and a pulp plant were cut. But by any measure, the scale of the industrial expansion was still immense, practically unprecedented in history except in wartime economies.

For all his talk about self-sufficiency and economic nationalism, Park was supremely pragmatic. He knew that the country needed foreign technology and capital and he brought it in. Jung-en Woo notes that foreign investment in chemicals and petroleum refining accounted for almost 40 percent of total foreign investment and was pivotal in building up the domestic industry. "Chemicals was an industry that could not do without foreign equity participation and technical assistance. Not a single fertilizer plant, not a single petrochemical complex was a product solely of Korean capital and know-how." Companies such as Gulf, Caltex, Union Oil, Mitsui, Bechtel, Dow, British Petroleum, and Aramco have helped build what has become a substantial oil and petrochemical industry.[19]

This was not simply a case of importing foreign technicians and learning from them, for Park also helped engineer an extremely unusual reverse brain drain. Thousands of Koreans had emigrated to the United States, or had gone for graduate training and simply not returned. A master list let Park know where they all were. When he decided that more scientists were needed, he lured them back to the motherland with attractive packages. They wanted housing, cars, schools, and salaries competitive with what they were making overseas. Park saw that they got all of what they asked for. This is how the Korea Institute of Science and Technology was built in the 1970s and how Postech was built in the 1980s. The top ranks of South Korean industry are filled with men who studied—and often worked—abroad, at some of the best universities and biggest corporations in the United States.

By the late 1970s, thanks in part to the skills that these returning Korean scientists brought, Park was confident enough of the country's technical capacities that he began cutting back on foreign investment. The concessions of the 1960s and early 1970s, such as tax holidays and subsidized loans for foreign investors, were scaled back. Foreigners usually could not invest unless they pledged to export most of their production or transfer technology to a local partner. Among the top fifty exporters in 1978, there were only three foreign companies, Motorola, Signetics, and Fairchild. Together they accounted for only 1.7 percent of total Korean exports. Daewoo Industrial alone accounted for 5.5 percent of exports that year. Park and his bureaucrats were willing to borrow heavily, but they wanted to keep ownership of—and as much control as possible over—their industries. This strategy, which was quite similar to the Japanese one, paid handsome dividends during the 1980s as Korean companies reaped the benefits of their international competitiveness.

Foreign borrowing, as opposed to foreign investment, remained extremely important through the mid-1980s. This reflected Korea's decision to take more risk—in the form of debt—rather than giving away equity to foreigners.

The emphasis on keeping direct foreign investment in check and channeling funds to domestic companies had a profound impact. The 1970s were the heroic years of the Korean economy, years when the chaebol grew from little specks in the international business scene to quite sizable organizations and sprawled across scores of different companies in virtually every industry.[20]

The HCI plan gave the chaebol heads who were involved in building heavy industrial projects regular, direct access to the president and his immediate staff. Money to fund expansion flowed freely at subsidized interest rates. The roads and ports and rail lines they needed were all built by the government. The business licenses needed to set up other projects were handed out easily to those who were favorites. Permission to acquire companies—sometimes even rivals— was granted to those with the right connections to the Blue House. They were the go-go years for Korea's up-and-comers, the *munobal* ("octopus") conglomerates whose tentacles were grasping everything within reach.

Notes

1. Park Chung Hee, *The Road to National Survival*, p. 52.
2. Alice H. Amsden, *Asia's Next Giant*, has the most extended analysis of this deliberate distortion.
3. Author interview, November 1990.
4. Lee-Jay Cho and Yoon Hyung Kim (eds.). *Korea's Political Economy: An Institutional Perspective*.
5. Jung-en Woo, *Race to the Swift*, pp. 109–10.
6. Author interview. December 1991. All quotations from Nam in this chapter are from this interview.
7. The preceding figures are from Wan-Soon Kim, in Cho and Kim (eds.), *Economic Development in the Republic of Korea*, p. 168. The following figures are from Woo, *Race to the Swift*, pp. 113–15.
8. This data is from Suk-Chae Lee, "The Heavy and Chemical Industries Promotion

Plan," in Cho and Kim, *Economic Development in the Republic of Korea*. A good discussion of the background and consequences of the policy is in Yoo Jung-ho, *The Industrial Policy of the 1970s and the Evolution of the Manufacturing Sector in Korea*.

9. Most of Hyundai's operations were concentrated in Ulsan, on the southeastern coast of the Korean peninsula. After the Korean War, Ulsan had been one of the many fishing villages dotting the coast along the Sea of Japan. The waters off this coast were cold and deep, superb for the fish that were one of the few sources of protein in Korea's preindustrial diet. The deep port also made Ulsan ideal as an industrial center. The Japanese had built a major fuel oil storage site at Onsan, just south of Ulsan, but this had been largely destroyed by the U.S. Military Government in 1946 and 1947. The United States apparently thought that leveling Korea's skeletal industrial base was appropriate punishment for Japanese aggression in World War II.

10. Suk-Chae Lee, in Cho and Kim, *Economic Development in the Republic of Korea*, p. 439.

11. The HCI plan, which was released in June 1973, planned for total investments of $9.6 billion between 1973 and 1981. Ibid., p. 432.

12. U.S. Congress, House, *Hearings before the Subcommittee on International Organization of the Committee on International Relations*, 95th Congress, 2nd session, Part 6, Hearings July 19 and August 2, 1978, p. 56.

13. Woo, *Race to the Swift*, p. 131.

14. Author interview, March 1991 was the source for Plumb's remarks in this chapter.

15. Author interview, March 1991.

16. The anecdote is told widely in Seoul. This version comes from a former senior Hyundai executive.

17. Office of the President, Republic of Korea, 1974, quoted in Suk-Chae Lee, "The Heavy and Chemical Industries Promotion Plan," in Cho and Kim, *Economic Development in the Republic of Korea*, p. 435.

18. Woo, *Race to the Swift*, pp. 127–28.

19. Ibid., pp. 138–39.

20. Yoo Jung-ho, *The Industrial Policy of the 1970s and the Evolution of the Manufacturing Sector in Korea*, provides a statistical glimpse into how Korea's firms burst onto the international scene in the 1970s. In 1970 total Korean exports of heavy and chemical products (including iron and steel, machinery, and so forth) accounted for only .07 percent of the world export total. By 1980 they had grown more than tenfold to .80 percent. Three years later they had doubled again, to 1.60 percent. Growth in light industrial products, such as textiles and footwear, was also strong, soaring from 1.83 percent of the world export market to 5.27 percent in 1980. See his table on p. 90.

8

Chaebol

The government tells you it's your duty and you have to do it, even
if there's no profit. Maybe, after the year 2000, Korean businessmen
will be able to put their companies' interests ahead of those of the
government or of society.

—Daewoo Chairman Kim Woo Choong[1]

"I shall go to Korea," Dwight Eisenhower promised U.S. voters as he stumped
for votes during the 1952 campaign. Hyundai's Chung Ju Yung was one of those
who benefited most directly from the fulfillment of that campaign pledge, for he
had a contract to see that the barren cemetery Eisenhower would visit had a
lawn. Figuring Eisenhower would not notice, Chung cut corners by transplanting
barley shoots and walked away with windfall profits.[2] It was a characteristic
gamble for Chung, a brash peasant's son who had run away from home as a
teenager. By the 1970s he had moved on to bigger things than barley shoots—
ships and cars.

Key business groups, particularly Hyundai and Daewoo, were favored by
Park during the 1970s because of their willingness to invest in heavy industry.
The founders of these two groups, Chung Ju Yung and Kim Woo Choong, were
particular favorites of President Park because of their commitment to growth and
their eagerness to charge into risky ventures. But they were not alone.

"The government asked [the chaebol] to invest in key industries," remembers
Kim Suk Won, chairman of the Ssangyong group, whose father's alliance with
Park Chung Hee vaulted the company's small textile business into the ranks of
the largest chaebol. During the 1970s Ssangyong built a massive oil refinery,
expanded capacity at its cement factory, and, at Park's behest, took over a

113

money-losing operation making marine diesel engines. "Whether businesses liked it or not, they had to do it," said Kim of the investments in heavy industry.[3]

This forced-investment policy boosted big businesses' share in the economy. In 1974, sales of the ten biggest business groups were equivalent to 15 percent of the GNP. By 1980, the figure was nearly half, and by 1984 it was more than two-thirds. In 1984, sales of the two largest chaebol, Hyundai and Samsung, alone equaled 24 percent of GNP. This increased share occurred at a time when the economy itself was growing extremely rapidly, so these figures actually understate the relative growth of these firms.[4]

Because capital was scarce, what mattered was whom a businessman knew. It was sometimes more important to be a good lobbyist than a good businessman. What counted most in the dynamic Korean economy was access to capital and getting the government go-ahead for new businesses. Access to capital required a nod of approval from someone in power.

Only favored businessmen got the funds and the coveted business licenses they needed to grow. Kim Suk Won, who took over the Ssangyong group at the very junior age of thirty in 1975 when his father died, says that his biggest business difficulty was trying to establish rapport with this circle of political-economic decisionmakers—men who for the most part were a generation older than he—who controlled the money and the licenses.

"My late father had a personal relationship with President Park, Park's cabinet, and influential government officers. Other chairmen had their own relationships. I had no human relationship. My father's fame gave me a lot of favor [but] I had to be very diligent. My biggest handicap was creating new human relationships."[5]

Anything was possible for those businessmen who were singled out for favored treatment. "Tax policy, trade policy, and credit and interest rate policies were all mobilized to promote the development of the heavy and chemical industries," says scholar Yoo Jung-ho.[6] The government shoveled credit to the favored industries. The share of so-called policy loans, or loans explicitly directed by the government, increased from 47 percent in 1970 to 60 percent in 1978. That means $60 of every $100 in loans was explicitly sanctioned by a government committee and subject to preferential terms. The other $40 was largely doled out according to less visible patterns of favoritism on the part of government officials or bank managers.

In a typical year about half the policy loans went to heavy industry; the rest went to agriculture, trade promotion, and other government programs. Interest rates on the policy loans were also substantially lower than rates on commercial loans, and access to otherwise scarce capital was nearly automatic. In 1976, 74 percent of all manufacturing investment went to heavy industries; a government study in 1979 estimated that the figure was on its way to 82 percent that year.[7]

Control over the financial system, always tight, was further strengthened in the 1970s. The savings rate was forced up, as consumers and other businesses found their funds diverted to lending for heavy industry. Inflation rose, and borrowing costs for businesses allowed to borrow from banks were negative. Industries covered by the HCI plan enjoyed even greater benefits—borrowing costs that were 25 percent less than for other businesses.[8] Tax polices and import protection were also arranged to benefit big groups in the plan. The government guaranteed that it would make good on bad loans.

"It made credit decisions very easy," said British merchant banker Alan Plumb. "No company would come to you if it was not a good credit. There was no credit assessment. . . . There were no corporate collapses in those days."[9]

Hyundai

Chung Ju Yung, who had come to Seoul as a teenager to seek his fortune in the 1930s, first worked on the docks at the nearby port of Inchon. Then he found a job as an errand boy at a rice mill in Seoul, where his first few nights were supposedly spent secretly learning to ride the shop's delivery bicycle. Chung bought an auto repair shop in Seoul in 1940. After World War II, with the help of a younger brother who spoke English, he befriended the U.S. military forces that occupied the southern half of the peninsula. He parlayed these contacts and an appetite for work into construction contracts with the U.S. military and, later, the Syngman Rhee government.

Chung ingratiated himself with Park Chung Hee by bidding a token one won to rebuild the original Han River bridge, which was still in ruins in the mid-1960s. He lost money, of course, but he got what he wanted: Park's attention for finishing the job ahead of schedule.

Chung took on increasingly ambitious construction projects and expanded abroad as early as 1966, when Hyundai won contracts from the U.S. military for highway construction in Thailand and dredging in Vietnam. It was Hyundai that was tapped to build the lion's share of the 424-kilometer highway linking Seoul with the southeastern port of Pusan, the country's second largest city, during the late 1960s.

The highway was another of those unpredicted successes that international experts said was economically infeasible. After a World Bank study team spent many months and about $1 million studying the project, it recommended against the project. Park then plotted the road's course, which not coincidentally went through both his and his wife's home towns.

The three other contractors who were invited to bid could not come up with an estimate, while Chung came in below what the government expected to pay. Park liked Chung, a rough-and-ready go-getter who often slept on the site with his men. Once, when Park paid a surprise inspection visit by helicopter to the work site at dawn, Chung was already up working with the construction crew, confirming Park's view that Chung had the same dynamic, driving desire to build his company that the president had to build the nation. It was during the construction of the Seoul-Pusan highway that Park made Chung the informal construction minister, and the two men often dined together on Thursday evenings in the private second-floor quarters of the presidential Blue House. These were informal affairs, with the men drinking the traditional fermented rice drink, *makkolli*, and wearing open-necked shirts—an anomaly in buttoned down, suit-and-tie South Korea.

A curious and fertile mixing of the traditional and the modern was embodied in both of these economic warriors. "Both men believed in the power of human will," says another guest at these dinners. "They believed that Korean economic development must be built on that work ethos, but both of them also believed in using Western technology."[10] Both also shared the traditional Korean penchant for frugality and a belief that the agricultural base must remain intact.

When Park decided that South Korea needed a large-scale shipyard, he chose Hyundai to build it. In the early 1970s Hyundai constructed the world's largest shipyard at the eastern port of Ulsan, booking orders even before the shipyard was completed. Chung was initially refused financing by British, Swiss, and French bankers. It was not hard to see why. Hyundai itself had no shipbuilding experience, and no Korean firm had ever built a vessel larger than 10,000 tons, yet Chung wanted a $60-million loan to build a shipyard that could produce 260,000-ton crude oil carriers.

Even the Korea Shipbuilding Industry Association refused to back Chung, telling prospective lenders that the project was impossible. "Don't you know that the person who thinks a job is possible is the one who is going to get it done?" Chung remembers telling the British bankers. It was a quintessential expression of his dogged, driven character.

When Chung had trouble arranging financing overseas, Park told him to try harder, implicitly threatening him that Hyundai would receive no more government favors if it could not deliver what the president wanted.[11] International lending agencies believed that Korea had no chance of making a success of shipbuilding, just what they had said about Korea's ability to make steel profitably when they turned down Posco's loan request. Hyundai eventually got its loan from the British and almost simultaneously received an order from a Greek ship owner for two large oil tankers that were to be identical copies of existing vessels produced at the Scotlithgow shipyard in Scotland. Through a technical transfer agreement, Hyundai obtained the designs and built the ships. The first ship was constructed even as the shipyard was being built around it.

The keel was laid down before the walls of the dry dock had even been built. The cement floor had just been laid and had not even cured. In typical Korean fashion, Hyundai laid the keel and spot-welded it together, then brought in international ship certifiers and took pictures so that it could receive a progress payment. After the visitors had come and gone, it did the final welding work.

Hyundai was obligated by the terms of its contract to copy every procedure of the Scotlithgow design. It was forced to build the ships in separate halves, because that was how Scotlithgow did it, even though its dry docks were large enough to build the ship in one piece. Try as it might to copy the designs, however, Hyundai's inexperience was apparent when the time came to assemble the two halves of the ship and the internal fittings and pipes did not match. The skepticism of the international bankers and buyers appeared to be right on target, for only after much re-jigging did the ship fit together.[12]

Delays continued to haunt the company and postpone delivery. Then the world shipping industry plunged into a recession triggered by the October 1973 oil shock. The Greek ship owner refused to take delivery of the first ship. A Japanese buyer also refused to take delivery of another two oil tankers, and a Hong Kong line declined to take its ship. Desperate, Hyundai asked for help from the U.S. embassy. John Bennett, who headed the embassy's economic section at the time, remembers getting an unusual call from one of Chung Ju Yung's top aides, who said that the chairman wanted to have lunch with him.

> I was ushered in and 32 of the company's top executives were sitting in the chairman's office. We made small talk for an hour; we had lunch and made small talk over the meal. Chung asked if he could make a call on me at the embassy the next day. I said yes. I couldn't figure out what it was all about. Well, I got the visit from Chung the next day. It seems that he had a VLCC [oil tanker] that a Greek ship owner had refused to take delivery on. He asked if Gulf would take it and could I do anything about this.
>
> I got in touch with the Gulf guy here in Seoul and introduced the two guys [from Gulf and Hyundai]. I wasn't involved anymore but thought I would be a hero. Six months later I was called in by an assistant minister of MCI [the Ministry of Commerce and Industry] who read me the riot act and said what rats the Americans were because Gulf didn't take the ship. Gulf here in Seoul had agreed, but the finance people in Pittsburgh did not see the need for another ship so they said no.[13]

In the end, Gulf took the ship and formed a joint venture with Hyundai, if for no other reason than as an insurance policy to protect its interests in Korea. The incident is a useful illustration of how closely government and business are tied together in Korea, as well as the activist role that the U.S. embassy could play.

Its shipbuilding activities alone would have been enough to keep most companies busy. But at the same time Hyundai was expanding its overseas construction activities at the insistence of Chung Ju Yung, and despite the opposition of his younger brother, Chung In Yung. The younger Chung had been in charge of highway projects in Thailand and Indonesia. The Indonesian project had been a disaster, with the firm losing $56 million on a $50 million contract to build a highway from Jakarta to Bogor, and Chung In Yung was reluctant to go into the Middle East. "His older brother, knowing nothing about the details, said, 'Go,' " remembers a former Hyundai official. The decision split executives in the company into two camps, depending on which brother they were loyal to, and the brothers stopped speaking. Then, shortly after the 1973 oil shock, Chung Ju Yung expelled his brother from the company.[14]

The sharp rise in oil prices and Korea's complete dependence on petroleum imports hammered the economy. The government pushed Hyundai and other Korean construction companies to look to the Middle East for new business. In 1976 alone Hyundai won a staggering $1.4 billion in Middle East construction contracts, including a $931 million industrial port at Jubail, Saudi Arabia.[15] From 1977 through 1979 nearly 300,000 Korean workers went to the Middle East, equivalent to more than a quarter of the entire male manufacturing work force back in Korea.[16]

Not surprisingly, Chung could be ruthless. He worked hard and he expected his employees to do the same. But sometimes Hyundai's militaristic culture pressed men beyond the bounds of endurance. During the mid-1970s, workers at one of Hyundai's massive construction sites in Saudi Arabia revolted, killing two managers and destroying $48 million in capital equipment. A subsequent investigation revealed that the company had been forcing the laborers to work fifteen-hour days in hundred-degree-plus heat.

The Hyundai founder gave his competitors little quarter, as Ssangyong's Kim Suk Won found out. The young second-generation chairman went to see Chung in the late 1970s to try to persuade Hyundai not to expand its investment in marine diesel engines and not to thwart Ssangyong's investment in turbochargers for the engines.

> I told the chairman that investment from Ssangyong alone was enough for the domestic market. Investment by two companies would be unnecessary over-investment. The chairman said he would think about it. A couple of days later I heard that the moment I left the chairman's office he called the director of the section in charge [of this project and said] "Whatever method you use, don't let Ssangyong become involved in this." Losing is death [for the chaebol founders]. . . . I felt like I'd been stabbed in my back.[17]

Daewoo

Daewoo became another favored company during this heroic heavy industry phase. The older generation of chaebol chairman had often begun working in rice mills, sometimes owned by their families and sometimes not, and gradually moved into different domestic businesses.[18] Daewoo founder Kim Woo Choong grew up in a different generation, at a time when there were many more opportunities for a young, aggressive man—particularly one whose father had been Park Chung Hee's teacher many years earlier.

Kim was oriented toward the international market almost from the start. He began his business career working in a trading company that imported yarn and cloth. On a trip to Southeast Asia he picked up samples of fabric in Hong Kong and Saigon. But by the time the ebullient Kim arrived in Singapore he was telling buyers that the samples were produced in Korea. He took $300,000 in orders for fabric and headed for home, where he had the goods copied and delivered.

In 1967, at the age of thirty, Kim invested a borrowed $5,000 to start a new trading company, Daewoo ("Great Universe"). Even at that young age he had had seven years of experience in the import-export business, as much as almost anyone else in the country. "There were only five of us in a small corner room in someone else's building when I founded Daewoo," Kim said later. In spite of his background, however, Kim was too junior to assume the title of president in age-obsessed Korea. Instead, he appointed a colleague several years older to head the company, and Daewoo exported knitwear made by small Korean manufacturers to Singapore, where the goods were shipped on to markets in Indonesia and Africa. In his first year in business, Daewoo exported $580,000 worth of textiles; by its third year exports had soared to $4 million. Daewoo opened its first textile factory in the southeastern port city of Pusan in 1968 and by 1972 had five factories. Marketing offices in Singapore, London, and New York opened in 1969.

Daewoo's international network combined with its high-quality mass production facilities in South Korea won it business from major U.S. retailers. To get a big order from Sears, Daewoo made an exact copy of the U.S. company's garment-testing facility at one of its factories in Korea. In 1970, Daewoo's exports doubled to $8 million. Kim Woo Choong had the foresight to see that the United States was likely to establish quotas on textiles and garments. "The news of impending quotas came as a jolt," Kim said later. "I began seeking out government officials and other businessmen in the domestic industry and suggested that Korea devise a common strategy to cope with the situation. Everyone only demanded data and documents, however, and I found no one to cooperate with."[19]

So Kim went it alone, increasing Daewoo's exports as rapidly as possible. When quotas were in fact established in 1972, Daewoo's quota was nearly a third of the Korean total. "Daewoo alone, as a company, received even larger quotas than some entire nations could get," Kim said proudly.[20] His foresight in anticipating what the impact of quotas would be, and how the Korean government would allocate them on the basis of existing market share, shows entrepreneurial talent at work in the restricted Korean context. After the quotas were handed out, Daewoo took advantage of the system to raise its prices, and, later, to sell off part of its allotment to other companies. This was quintessential political capitalism, trading on knowledge and contacts for advantage.

Kim Woo Choong also excelled at acquiring existing companies, exploiting another way that entrepreneurship worked within the confines of Korea, Inc. In the nine years after Daewoo Industrial was founded in 1967, Kim Woo Choong acquired eleven firms. There was no business plan here, only a desire to seize opportunities. These companies were scattered across the business landscape. They included firms in textiles, finance, machinery, and cosmetics. These acquisitions were funded both by bank loans and through the country's embryonic stock market. Kim Woo Choong was one of the first Korean chaebol founders to take his company public on the stock exchange. He did this at a time when most chaebol owners were more concerned with keeping control of their companies than raising equity capital.

In 1975, only eight years after it was founded, the Daewoo empire included 23 companies, 30 overseas branches, 35,000 employees, and annual sales of nearly $250 million. By 1976, Daewoo's exports were more than $300 million, equal to more than 4 percent of Korea's total. By the end of 1989, Kim claimed to be the forty-seventh-largest business venture in the world, one that had accounted for 8 percent of total Korean exports since the company's start in 1967.[21]

Although Daewoo had started as a textile company, Kim Woo Choong's success in building an empire attracted President Park's attention and the group was pulled into heavy industry. In 1976, Daewoo took a fateful step when it acquired the Korean Machinery Manufacturing Corporation (Hankuk Machinery) from the Shinjin group. This poorly run, under-capitalized company had been founded under the Japanese in 1937 (it originally made submarines for the Japanese navy); it was turned over to the government after independence and run at various times by the Ministry of National Defense and the Ministry of Commerce and Industry. It was finally given to Shinjin Automobile Manufacturing Company in 1968, but because of its precarious financial position was supervised by the Korea Development Bank's Special Administration Division.

In spite of debt forgiveness and interest-rate cuts, Shinjin was unable to turn Hankuk Machinery around. The government, faced with the choice of renationalizing the firm or finding another chaebol to take it over, shopped the company around. Several other groups refused to have anything to do with Hankuk Machinery, pleading that they were already overextended.

Eventually, Daewoo agreed to take the company. In accepting an offer it probably could not have refused, Daewoo's character was forever altered. No longer would Daewoo be a nimble trading, finance, and light industrial company. Instead, its future was melded to metal-bashing industries. Before the decade was over, Daewoo was to take over an auto manufacturing operation and one of the world's largest shipyards.[22]

By turning over his other businesses to his brother and devoting all his energies to Hankuk Machinery, Kim Woo Choong managed to turn the company around and even made a small profit in 1977. He merged the company with the small Daewoo Heavy Machinery Company and renamed the new company Daewoo Heavy Industries. It remained a listed company in which the Korea Development Bank had a large share, with commercial banks and individual investors holding most of the rest of the shares. Daewoo itself had only a minority stake although the Daewoo group controlled the company.

At the end of 1976, Kim Woo Choong turned forty, an age at which he could start to be taken seriously as a company president. Moreover, as a graduate of the prestigious Yonsei University, Kim could draw on help from his classmates who were now occupying increasingly important positions in the government, banks, and other companies. Kim's success at making a go of Daewoo Heavy Industries thrust him into a public role as the representative of a new, younger generation of Korean chaebol leaders. Kim happily became the spokesman for the new chaebol, and he reveled in his role as a brash newcomer whose demeanor contrasted with the rigid style of senior executives at Samsung, Hyundai, and Lucky-Goldstar. He bragged about his ability to turn battered companies around by working alongside his employees.[23]

The older business leaders might have disliked this style, but in the new Korea success based on hard work was admirable. Unlike many business leaders, who were fond of whiskey and women, Kim Woo Choong seemed to have no vice but work. A teetotaler, Kim drank barley tea at the bibulous parties and receptions that lubricate Korean business. The energetic Kim boasted that he worked every day of the year and got by on five ("four, according to my wife") hours of sleep a night.[24] The first time Kim Woo Choong took a complete day off was after his son was killed in a November 1990 auto accident.

"Hard work is the mother of fortune," says the Daewoo chairman, whose devoted employees call him *tosa*, a term of respect used for a scholar with supernatural powers. "Work is both our love and our greatest interest."

Daewoo's wages were well above average, and in return Kim expected total dedication. Until the mid-1980s, employees were expected to work seven days a week, often twelve hours or more a day, to help meet export targets. "I believe my generation must continue to make sacrifices so that the next generation will be the first of Korea as an advanced nation."[25] Because Kim did not play golf or have any hobbies outside work, his employees were expected to follow suit.

Kim's close relationship with President Park was cemented by the fact that Kim Woo Chong's father, a schoolteacher who was killed during the Korean War, had taught the young Park in Taegu. The student-teacher bond in Korea is sacred, and Park, who had briefly been a teacher, passed it on to the next generation.[26]

Buoyed by his success at Hankuk Machinery, Kim Woo Choong turned his attention to the auto industry. Shinjin had failed to save itself by transferring Hankuk Machinery to Daewoo. U.S. diplomat John Bennett found himself involved in trying to rehabilitate the limping auto venture at General Motors's request.

> [The owner of Shinjin] had pledged stock in the company as security for loans with the KDB [Korea Development Bank]. I talked to the president of KDB and said, "Wouldn't it be nice if you could get this guy out of GM because he's spoiling the development of the company because he doesn't have money to

put in [for needed investments]." I was astonished. KDB actually took his stock and he lost the company. The government simply appointed a retired general as president of GM Korea.

General Motors was desperate to find another partner. GM executives told the government that they wanted someone else. In response, the government informed the Detroit automaker that Daewoo would be its new partner.

Six weeks later I got this panicked phone call from GM saying, "We're being sold into servitude to Daewoo." The GM people were outraged. Once they heard that they were going to get Daewoo as a partner they wrestled around for a week. I don't know how he did it, but Kim Woo Choong went and talked to the chairman in Detroit and the attitude changed.[27]

Daewoo was now seen in the Blue House as the company that could fix any government blunder, however big. After the Hankuk Machinery and the GM venture came a shipyard. Kim Woo Choong was first invited and then—he claims—ordered to take over the giant Okpo shipyard project. The shipyard, which was part of the HCI plan, had originally been assigned to the Korea Shipbuilding and Engineering Corporation (KSEC). But the massive project had smothered the company and Okpo had been taken over by a government-owned shipbuilding corporation. By 1978, it was only one-fourth completed and drowning in debt.

Convinced that only Kim Woo Choong could succeed in rescuing the Okpo shipyard, President Park personally asked him to take over. Kim, according to his account, politely refused. But the chairman of Korea, Inc., would not take no for an answer. While Kim Woo Choong was overseas on a business trip, on August 31, 1978, the government announced that the management of Okpo shipyard was being transferred to Kim Woo Choong's Daewoo group, along with 51 percent of the shares. Korea Development Bank took the other 49 percent by converting loans into equity.

In his decision to give the Okpo shipyard to Daewoo, Park was playing the role of nation-builder and investment banker, with scant regard for anything so cumbersome as legal procedures. If KSEC did not like the decision, as it doubtless did not, there was no one to complain to. The press was muzzled and the judiciary under the control of the Blue House. Critics often complain that badly managed chaebol are never called to account, but Daewoo's rise was founded on just such punishment. The difficulties at Shinjin and KSEC shaped the Daewoo of the 1980s.

Kim Woo Choong was above all a salesman, a man who believed in his ability to tackle any project, whatever the odds. Unfortunately for Daewoo, its move into heavy industry at the end of the 1970s was disastrously timed. It came just as inflation was accelerating and the world economy was about to receive its second oil price shock. Export growth slowed, and the chaebol were under attack for their increasing dominance of the economy. Daewoo was the most vulnerable of the group. By 1978, after it had taken over the Okpo shipyard, debts at Daewoo Heavy Industries alone were twice as large as the entire group's equity. There was a price to pay for dancing with the president and entertaining his dreams.[28]

Why Big Is Beautiful

The chaebol have been vilified by Koreans, but it is important to understand the context in which these huge, if often poorly managed, groups developed. The desire on the part of Korean entrepreneurs to form groups of businesses, often in completely unrelated areas, was already established before Park took power in 1961. In the 1950s, business groups such as Hwashin, Samsung, and Lucky were already relatively large. They were controlled by a single owner-manager and had several different business lines.

The Japanese zaibatsu of the 1930s provided the pattern on which Korean companies modeled themselves. In a society in which business opportunities were almost unlimited but access to capital and government licenses was diffi-cult to obtain, groups often had an advantage over their smaller competitors. Companies formed during the 1960s and 1970s followed the pattern set by the first generation of Korean business groups.[29]

Size meant strength, and allowed the chaebol to cross-subsidize new activi-ties. Without a minimum amount of capital, managerial resources, and business skills, the chaebol could not have gone into a wide range of new areas, let alone become internationally competitive. Size allowed companies to be able to afford to make the inevitable "donations" to the government for causes ranging from flood relief to political campaigns. Groups also had a greater ability to deal with the extraordinary bureaucracy of a government that was, after all, involved in virtually every part of the economy.

In the late 1970s as many as 120 different documents were needed to export a product, according to an Economic Planning Board study. In an export-led econ-omy this might seem mind-boggling, but it was an everyday fact of life. More-over, at one point Korea had 221 different targeted credit programs.[30] What seemed inscrutable and opaque to foreign businessmen was not simple for their Korean counterparts either. "Foreign companies have a lot of complaints about laws and regulations, but remember, we are living with it," says Ssangyong chairman Kim Suk Won.

The requirements of the Confucian-inspired state bureaucracy meant that every successful company had an unusual structure in which the general affairs department loomed large. This department, while it might have some financial control function, essentially existed to deal with the bureaucracy.

The entrepreneurs would race ahead, and the men in general affairs would sweep up the mess behind, file the documents, and negotiate or pay fines for infringements of regulations. It was the general affairs staff who would talk with officials over a drink to determine how a proposed course of action could be deemed legal, or to decide which rules and regulations were truly important and which could be ignored safely. The same department usually decided which payments could be cleared legally through the audited books, and which would have to be handled in some other way. In short, the general affairs staff helped keep the company's facade looking clean for the economic police, who included tax authorities, industry associations, and relevant ministries. Although Korean companies did not have an exact equivalent to the *yogore-yaku* ("executive in charge of filth") found in some Japanese companies, the dirty work in Korea was done by the general affairs department.

To have a general affairs staff required a certain minimum size. In a very small company, the owner could handle affairs with the help of one lieutenant and a bookkeeper. But for small and medium industries the heavy government regulation and intervention was a serious handicap. For larger companies it ceased to be as much of a problem because their staff had a multitude of school and family ties. By the 1970s, medium and large companies had deliberate policies to try to recruit graduates of Kyonggi High School and Seoul National University, the most prestigious combination, who would bring the best connections of their generation. In the 1960s this had been difficult, because that educational elite had wanted to enter government service, but in the 1970s it became easier (and in the 1980s the preferred course), as business attracted increasing numbers of top-flight graduates.

By the late 1970s there were more than twenty chaebol, but the difference in size was tremendous. Daewoo, the fourth-largest group, was only half the size of Samsung and Hyundai in terms of sales, while Korea Explosives and Hyosung (the eighth- and ninth-largest groups) were only one-eighth the size of Samsung. Lotte, the fourteenth largest, had assets in Korea that were only one-sixteenth the size of Samsung's and Hyundai's. Yet the group was still large enough to include a hotel, a construction company, a major confectionery company (the founding company), an electronics company, a machinery company, and a trading company with a monopoly on exports of red ginseng.

Because of this rapid growth, there was a chaotic aspect to corporate life. "Business could be haphazard at best," remembers Alan Plumb. "Three days before we were to sign the contract for our merchant banking joint venture, two of our shareholders found that they were not allowed to invest in unlisted companies so they had to drop their planned investment. But everyone was thinking like a chaebol, trying to expand wherever he could." It was this impulse toward growth at any cost that defined Korean companies and the Korean economy during the 1970s.

The economy became intensely concentrated. Between 1966 and 1976 the number of firms grew 10 percent while the average size of the firms grew 180 percent. By contrast, in Taiwan, the number of firms increased by 150 percent but the average size of firms grew only 29 percent. The value-added of the top ten conglomerates in Korea more than doubled from 5 percent in 1973 to 10.9 percent in 1978. By 1978, the top ten conglomerates had 22 percent of manufacturing sales, a figure that peaked at 30.2 percent in 1982.[31]

The direct intervention of the president, the HCI plan, the bureaucratic system, and the perpetually tight credit situation all helped big business groups grow bigger. It was much easier to expand into a new field for a group with an effective organization for dealing with the bureaucracy, and a profitable mother company from which cash could be generated, than it would be for an entrepreneur to start out on his own. Moreover, larger companies could also enlist allies in the bureaucracy to strangle vulnerable companies with bureaucratic interference and by shutting off credit. Tales of this sort of back-stabbing frequently surfaced.

Because the government did not allow large firms to go out of business, companies could often grow by taking control of weaker firms, as Daewoo and others did. For example, when the Yulsan group went bust, the Saehan Merchant Bank found that its $5 million loan to Yulsan Aluminum had been converted— by the government—to $5 million in equity, representing a two-thirds stake in the company. Nothing happened for the better part of a year, but the company was then transferred to the Hyosung group, which took over the loan. The banks just wrote the checks to finance a game played by government and business.

The president, his HCI committee, the bureaucracy, and least of all the technocracy, did not sit down together to grow one company or another. They were building a nation, and they picked out industries they wanted Korean companies to be leaders in. Given the capital needs of the push into heavy industry, and the structure of Korea's young economy, they necessarily interfered with businesses in what by Western standards was an extraordinary fashion. There was a heavy cost, but in many senses the policy worked. It allowed a latecomer to close the gap with the industrial world.

By the end of the 1970s, Park's obsession with industrial growth was reaching the point where the costs were starting to outweigh the benefits. Yet Park increasingly looked like Korea's Captain Ahab in his relentless pursuit of economic growth and industrial might. "He wouldn't take even one year off to restructure the economy," says Kim Mahn Je, who was president of the prestigious Korea Development Institute from 1971 until 1982 and who subsequently served as minister of finance and deputy prime minister under Chun. During his last months in office, however, Park was apparently beginning to see how much damage his emphasis on heavy industry was wreaking on the economy.

Notes

1. *Financial Times*, October 31, 1984.
2. In fact, Eisenhower did notice the barley shoots: Luckily for Chung, he liked the effect. In the end, Chung walked away with three times what he had bid for the project.

The strategy of bidding low, winning the contract, and hoping to raise the price as time went on became a hallmark of Korean contractors. This account comes from unpublished material provided to the author by Hyundai.

3. Kim Suk Won, press luncheon at the Seoul Foreign Correspondents' Club, October, 1990.

4. Quoted in Alice Amsden, *Asia's Next Giant*, p. 116. The companies do not themselves account for this large a share of GNP, which measures value-added rather than sales, but it is a useful indication of economic concentration.

5. Author interview, November 1990.

6. Yoo Jung-ho, *The Industrial Policy of the 1970s and the Evolution of the Manufacturing Sector in Korea*, p. 34.

7. Ibid., pp. 42–44. The estimate is from an early 1979 government study.

8. Suk-Chae Lee, "The Heavy and Chemical Industries Promotion Plan," in Lee-Jay Cho and Yoon Hyung Kim (eds.), *Economic Development in the Republic of Korea*, p. 443.

9. Author interview, March 1991. "Nothing was written down," adds Plumb. "You talked a lot on the phone and commitments were made without written documents. Koreans were very non-legal, very trusting. The level to which commitments were made verbally was astonishing. People would make verbal commitments to lend $5 million or $10 million."

10. Author interview with Chung Hoon Mok, a former Hyundai executive who attended some of these dinners, October 1993.

11. Leroy P. Jones and Sakong Il, *Government, Business and Entrepreneurship in Economic Development: The Korean Case*, p. 119. Another version of the story, which comes from a former senior Hyundai executive, has it that Chung, after being turned down by Japanese shipbuilders worried that they would be "feeding the tiger," got a commitment from a Norwegian shipyard to provide technical assistance. "Based on this half-baked commitment he got Park Chung Hee to back the shipyard." At a time when the average cost of bulk carriers was only $3 million to $5 million, it was hard to write a business plan that could do much more than pay the interest on the loans.

12. This recounting of the incident is based on an expatriate shipbuilding source intimately familiar with Hyundai's yard, who maintains that the problems Hyundai experienced in fitting together the vessel were not unusual. Amsden, in *Asia's Next Giant*, p. 278, tells a racier version of the story, which implies that the entire shipbuilding venture was at risk.

13. Author interview, September 1991.

14. This account is based on an author interview with a former senior Hyundai executive in October 1993.

15. Jones and Sakong, *Government, Business and Entrepreneurship in Economic Development*, p. 357.

16. Amsden, *Asia's Next Giant*, p. 100, using Labor Ministry figures of 292,600 male workers equaling almost 27 percent of the male manufacturing work force. The percentage is somewhat misleading, of course, because Middle East labor data represent a cumulative figure over a period of three years while the manufacturing work force figure is for a single point in time.

17. Author interview, November 1990.

18. Hyundai's Chung had been an errand boy in a rice mill and Samsung's Lee Byung Chull established his own mill using inherited money. The Koo family, one of the two founding families of what became the Lucky-Goldstar group, also started in rice milling.

19. Kim Woo Choong, speech at Small Business Conference, Seoul, September 17, 1990. Other sources are a November 1988 author interview; articles in *Fortune* (August 20, 1984); *Financial Times* (October 31, 1984); and a profile in Jones and Sakong, *Government, Business and Entrepreneurship in Economic Development*, pp. 361–64.

20. Kim Woo Choong, speech at Small Business Conference, Seoul, September 17, 1990.

21. Ibid. Regarding employees, etc., Jones and Sakong, *Government, Business and Entrepreneurship in Economic Development*, pp. 361–64.

22. Jones and Sakong, *Government, Business and Entrepreneurship in Economic Development*, pp. 127–32 on Hankuk Machinery; *Fortune*, August 20, 1984.

23. Jones and Sakong, *Government, Business and Entrepreneurship in Economic Development*, pp. 127–32, 361–64.

24. *Asian Finance*, November 15, 1985.

25. Kim Woo Choong, speech at Small Business Conference, Seoul, September 17, 1990.

26. *Fortune*, August 20, 1984, regarding Kyunggi and Kim's father's death. That his father was Park Chung Hee's teacher comes from a personal communication from a Daewoo executive, in February 1988. More cynical observers think that without this personal connection with Park Chung Hee, Daewoo would not, could not, have thrived. That would be to overlook Kim's extraordinary energy and deny Kim his very real accomplishments.

27. Author interview, September 1991.

28. By the mid-1980s, when it became clear that Okpo was in danger of dragging down the entire group, the legend of how the firm ended up in Daewoo's hands was firmly entrenched in the group's mythology. One foreign banker who knows Kim well and whose firm has been a major lender to Daewoo believes that Kim badly wanted Okpo. His view is widely shared in Seoul.

29. See Carter J. Eckert, *Offspring of Empire*, for a detailed discussion of this point. Eckert argues that the development of capitalism in Korea was quite different from that in Japan during the Meiji period; the Korean experience naturally reflected the stresses of colonial occupation. Significantly, businessmen's accommodation to authoritarianism is an important characteristic of Korea's political and economic structure and a legacy of the Japanese era.

30. World Bank, *World Development Report 1989*.

31. *Economist*, Third World Survey, September 23, 1989, p. 39; Suk-Chae Lee, "The Heavy and Chemical Industries Promotion Plan," in Cho and Kim, *Economic Development in the Republic of Korea*, p. 465; see also Jones and Sakong, *Government, Business and Entrepreneurship in Economic Development*, pp. 260–69.

9

Slowdown

We have no alternative . . . but to slow down.
—Deputy Prime Minister Shin Hyon Hwak[1]

In a political campaign in the late 1960s, Prime Minister Kim Jong Pil had won over a potentially hostile crowd of peasants by pouring water into a cup. Even after the cup was full, he continued to pour, and the water spilled over. Kim declared, "The cup I am holding here can be compared to what the country absolutely needs for such things as national defense, economic development and so forth. If our economy continues to expand at the present rate and produces more wealth than absolutely needed, then wealth will begin to spill over the cup and fill your pocket. We all have to tighten up our belts and work hard to fill the cup."[2]

By the late 1970s, the cup had begun to run over. The average Korean family in 1979 was still poor, but it often had enough money left over for a radio and a black-and-white television, sometimes even a refrigerator, and a few other consumer goods. Consumption of rice, fruit, fresh vegetables and, above all, meat, shot up. Demand for basic goods like toothpaste and toilet paper also increased. Moreover, the embryonic middle class wanted color television broadcasting and more university places for its children.

By 1978, a surge in consumer demand coupled with continuing investments in heavy industry fueled inflation that was over 20 percent a year and climbing. This boom in spending, which was underpinned by massive remittances sent home by Korean construction workers in the Middle East, not only caused economic problems but provoked a crisis in Korea's ethos of enforced austerity.

From September 1974 to December 1978, economic policy was led by Nam Duck Woo, the country's longest-serving deputy prime minister. Nam was known in some circles as "Dr. Inflation" for his unwillingness to sacrifice economic growth to an austere anti-inflation policy. He was generally supported in this view by a president who wanted things to be done, by businesses that could invest at negative real interest rates thanks to government-directed loans, and by those workers whose wages were growing faster than inflation. But as inflation accelerated in the late 1970s, spurred in part by substantial overseas earnings, which prompted South Korea's first current account surplus in 1977, there was increasing grumbling about the direction of economic policy.[3]

Political repression and unequal growth produced instability and a distorted, overheated economy. While most Koreans thought of themselves as middle-class beneficiaries of hyperactive development, there were dangerous pockets of discontent. Although nominal wages rose quickly, rising inflation prompted labor to keep ratcheting up its demands.[4] The rural sector, in spite of Saemaul's contribution, still lagged behind the city. There was also a large underclass of the urban poor eking out a precarious existence. Although the reported unemployment rate was low, it masked widespread underemployment, because anyone who worked even one hour a week was regarded as employed.

Even more threatening to the government was the restiveness of the middle class, the group that had benefited most from development. The rapid growth of the country had created a large class that had never existed before, what the Koreans (like the Japanese) call "salarymen," the middle- and upper-level managers of major companies. This group, trying to save for its future and its children's future, found itself threatened by the instability of prices during 1976, 1977, and 1978.

Park's record of spurring economic growth during the 1960s and 1970s was extraordinary, putting Korea in the ranks of the world's fastest-growing nations. But by the end of the 1970s Park was living on borrowed time, both literally and figuratively. Economic growth had been bought at the cost of political repression, social dislocation, and a destabilizing bout of inflation.

A key group of technocrats seized the initiative and convinced the president that he had to radically shift his approach and put the brakes on the economy. Not since the 1965 interest-rate reform and the 1970 foreign exchange crisis had Park Chung Hee been forced seriously to consider orthodox economic policies. For most of Park's tenure, growth had triumphed over stability, and the president's dreams of rapid industrial expansion had triumphed over his economists' pleas for stable growth. Park's economic house was shaken to its foundation in the late 1970s. But an elite group of technocrats saved the economy from lurching out of control and laid the groundwork for far-reaching changes in the 1980s.

The Cult of Austerity

In 1978 Seoul was a drab capital city of 8 million people. Its broad boulevards had plenty of room for the handful of cars in which government officials and senior businessmen were chauffeured about town. Cars were black, and television was black-and-white.

A strict midnight curfew kept nightlife to a minimum and ensured that people were ready to work the sixty- or even eighty-hour workweeks that were common. The color televisions, imported autos, chocolates, and cigarettes that eased life for the ruling elites throughout much of Asia, Latin America, and Africa were not easily available in Korea. This was part of Park's enforced social contract. Koreans would suffer as one; later, he promised, they would eat the fruits of development together. Says banker Alan Plumb of Seoul of the 1970s:

> There wasn't any neon. [It was illegal.] There were black cars, no shop lights, very dingy street lights and traffic lights. The midnight curfew really ordered people's lives. If you lived in the suburbs of Seoul and you hadn't caught a cab by 10:30 you wouldn't get home.
>
> The whole scale was quite different. You didn't see many vehicles. To drive your own car was an extremely exotic thing to do. Somewhere else in Korea these apparently twenty-first-century plants were being constructed. But it was hard to tie the village nature of Seoul to the development of the economy through these plants. In Seoul there were mostly one-story factories, often typical sweatshops.[5]

Park's cult of austerity stemmed partly from the traditional Confucian value that disapproved of flashy displays of wealth, a creed exemplified by Park himself. The president's undershirts had holes in them, and Park was fond of saying that he had not bought a new suit in ten years because there was nothing wrong with the ones he had. "I always thought of him as a Japanese soldier living in the Meiji era," says Kim Mahn Je, who at the time headed the Korea Development Institute. "He maintained a very simple lifestyle. . . . Other than industrial growth and the military [Park] was very reluctant to spend money on anything else, like sports. He just hated to 'waste' resources on these things."[6]

The only color broadcasts were on the U.S. military's Armed Forces Korea Network (AFKN) aimed at the 40,000 or so U.S. troops in the country. Korean television broadcasts were exclusively in black and white, ostensibly because color televisions used more electricity, but also because color was seen as an unnecessary extravagance. Relatives from the United States hand-carried modern consumer goods on return trips and bribed their way through customs but, publicly at least, well-off Koreans downplayed their wealth. South Korea had one of the lowest per capita ownership rates of automobiles in the world, a situation encouraged by high tax rates on car purchases and gasoline. Those cars that existed were domestically produced, and almost uniformly black; the government did not even allow the production of red cars until the mid-1980s because they were deemed too ostentatious.

Park decreed that only domestically produced consumption goods should be sold in Korea. Korea thus was a mix of outward-looking exporters, tailoring their products to the world markets, and domestic monopolies and oligopolies that were protected by the country's import-substitution policy and strict licensing procedures. In many cases, the two kinds of companies existed within the same firm, or at least within the same business group. In the postwar period, only Japan and Taiwan have had comparable hybrid systems that are partly shut off from the world yet respond to competitive international pressures and take advantage of global economic growth.

The president believed fervently that the rich and middle classes must save in order to provide the funds needed to invest in increased industrial output. He also was savvy enough to realize that Koreans would tolerate the rigors of his forced-march industrialization only if they felt that everyone was sacrificing more or less equally.

Park's ability to convince most Koreans that they were sacrificing for the good of the country was an important aspect of Korea's success. Although Park's system was at its core corrupt, he was a master at show trials and of making an example of a corrupt official who had crossed him. This was good theater and good politics. In 1974, for example, two ministers and other government officials were forced to resign as a result of a diamond smuggling scandal involving some of their wives.[7] But by the end of the 1970s, a larger middle class was starting to demand higher living standards and it did not want to be put on trial for indulging itself occasionally.

Macro-Mistakes

The rapid growth of the domestic market created immense macroeconomic problems for the Korean economy, which was geared to channel finance into the export sectors and deny industries producing solely for Korean consumers access to capital. As a result it was difficult for domestic industries to expand their factories to keep pace with demand. If they did, it was typically by raising prices to generate more profit.

The shortage of consumer goods was more acute because the HCI committee had grossly underestimated the cost of financing the build-up of heavy industry. The shipyards, refineries, chemical plants, steel mills, and auto factories that the chaebol were building gobbled up vast amounts of capital that otherwise could have been invested in housing or producing consumer goods. Former U.S. diplomat John Bennett sums up the problems facing the Koreans, problems that were magnified by the big push into heavy industry.

> It was clear that the Heavy and Chemical Industry program was a disaster. A, you had a world recession. B, you had severe economic problems here [in Korea]—crop failure, an exchange rate [that was] out of line, political uncertainty, inflation, [heavy] borrowing abroad, trade unions, and the energy crisis [from the second oil shock], which raised energy prices and caused the world recession.[8]

Those companies that were producing for export could easily accommodate the rise in domestic demand. As exports slowed, these firms simply started selling to domestic consumers—at higher prices, thanks to the lack of competition. Such businesses, especially those making consumer electronics, made substantial profits. But those firms producing purely for the domestic market had been systematically starved of capital. Such companies could only hope to raise prices faster than inflation and use the additional profits to expand production.

However, for many items this was impossible because the government dictated the price. The prices of 148 items were controlled because no more than three manufacturers for these products existed in Korea, and no imports were permitted. These wide-ranging price controls were another reminder of the long reach of the supreme logistics commander Park Chung Hee and his obsession with managing the economy.

By the late 1970s, middle-class consumers who were priced out of the housing market started spending more on consumer items, causing shortages and pushing up inflation. With almost all imports of consumer goods prohibited in order to save foreign exchange, products simply disappeared from the shelves as consumers returned to their wartime habit of hoarding. In 1977 and early 1978 basic goods such as toilet paper, toothpaste, and electric fans vanished from stores as demand outstripped supply in a rash of panic buying, stoking a sense of crisis.

But rising property prices were most unsettling of all. The surges in real estate prices during the latter part of the 1970s reflected problems associated with the high-growth, high-inflation policy and the lack of investment alternatives. Bank savings were penalized by low interest rates, especially during a time of high inflation. Restrictions on overseas investments and the tiny size of the domestic stock market meant that would-be savers had few outlets for their money other than hard assets, such as gold (whose import was limited) and property.

Property transactions also had the benefit of being harder for tax and intelligence authorities to monitor, an advantage in a country with an often punitive tax system. Real estate development was also extremely limited because Park wanted to channel scarce capital into industrial development, especially at a time of heavy spending on heavy and chemical industries. If the Korea Housing Bank needed to be looted for industrial investment, as it occasionally was, then less housing was built.

Between 1977 and 1978 alone land prices doubled. The Federation of Korean Industries said that between 1965 and 1978 house values had gone up 30 times and that prices for residential land had increased 79 times.

For the emerging middle class, the increase in apartment prices hit hardest. Apartments had not existed until the early 1970s and originally were introduced as low-income housing units to re-house squatters. In the mid-1970s, upper-middle-class apartment complexes began to spring up in newly fashionable districts south of the Han River. By the late 1970s the demand vastly exceeded supply, and many would-be buyers found themselves priced out of the market. While dreams of apartments were a middle-class ideal, the rise in house rents affected every level of society. Renters had difficulty keeping up with the increase in *chonsei* payments.[9]

Surging property prices were only one of the most visible—and politically explosive—consequences of running the economy too hard, of pushing for an unsustainable growth rate. Between 1974 and 1980, wholesale prices nearly tripled, rising an average of 22.7 percent annually.[10] Consumer prices rose almost as quickly. Nominal wage growth was also steep, averaging a stunning 30.9 percent a year. This had an extremely corrosive effect on economic behavior, forcing companies and workers into a mad scramble to push up wages and raise prices in an attempt to beat inflation.

While the domestic market roared ahead, however, exports began to slow. In terms of volume, exports rose less than 5 percent in 1978 and actually fell in 1979. Park's policy of sacrificing the domestic economy for exports, and of tolerating inflation in order to keep the economy on a fast-growth track, seemed to be failing.

As inflation mounted, policymakers began considering emergency measures. A small group, which included Kim Jae Ik, Kang Kyong Shik, Kim Mahn Je, Park You Kwang, and, later, Kim Ki Hwan, began discussing measures to restructure the economy in late 1978. This was politically risky. Many businessmen and bureaucrats opposed the changes called for in the HCI program because they threatened their way of doing business.

Slowing the Growth Machine

As a result of mounting dissatisfaction with sputtering exports and rising inflation, Deputy Prime Minister Nam Duck Woo was deposed in December 1978. His replacement was a man who was willing to sacrifice growth for stability. Shin Hyon Hwak had already served in several ministerial posts as far back as 1957. He had been minister for reconstruction (the precursor to the Economic Planning Board) in the late 1950s during a period of U.S.-inspired price stabilization and zero economic growth.

Shin had for some time tried to promote a stability-oriented economic policy, and after taking office he immediately announced that he would pursue a monetarist approach. That meant curbing the growth in money supply, even at the cost of an economic slowdown. Upon taking office, Shin quickly joined forces with a group of key technocrats who were secretly working to liberalize the economy. Park You Kwang, at the time director of the planning bureau at the Economic Planning Board, the technocratic nerve center of the economy, was one of those working on the liberalization plans.

> The HCI gestation period was very long. We worried that the economy had already reached a level of complexity where a limited number of government

officers could not handle it, so that it had to be done by the market. Due to the Middle East construction boom, the economy was hot, really hot. Land speculation had started and something had to be done.[11]

This sort of thinking was heretical in the go-go years of the late 1970s. Business, or at least big business, had no great quarrel with inflation. Because the chaebol were borrowing from banks at preferential interest rates, inflation meant that the favored companies actually enjoyed a negative real interest rate of about 7 to 15 percent. Says Park You Kwang:

> It was President Park's very strong conviction to build up production capacity of [heavy and] military goods. For us, as semi-economists, it was silly to pursue for a long time, because the methodology was "government-led." Somebody in the Blue House or the MCI [the Ministry of Commerce and Industry] drew pictures of the machinery industry and set up special funds and then selected companies to be in the program, allocated funds, and made targets. It was not a market-oriented program. When they were building the factories they did not know how much they could sell to foreign buyers, although their facilities were marvelous.
>
> Nobody was saying it, but companies were also competing to be in the program, because it automatically meant they could expand their operations [by allowing them to get business licenses for expansion]. Discretionary financing was overwhelming, and this exacerbated the funding shortage in light industry.
>
> During the latter part of 1978 Kang Kyong Shik thought we ought to change the policy direction. The economy was so distorted. The central core [of the EPB planning elite] wanted to move in market orientation. [But the Blue House and even most of the EPB did not.]
>
> We started to prepare something quite different from the ordinary. We criticized agricultural policy, the export credit program and the financial policy [especially preferential lending policies], the HCI plan, the rural housing program, direct price controls and financial policies. These policies were the cornerstone of Park Chung Hee's program.[12]

Park You Kwang was at a critical level, near the pinnacle of the working-level officials in the bureau. He had joined the EPB in 1966, right after graduation from Seoul National University. In becoming a public servant, he had followed his father, who had been a Seoul city official until he disappeared, presumably killed by the invaders, during the North Korean invasion of the capital in June 1950. Park had worked throughout the EPB, had received a master's degree in public policy at the Maxwell School at Syracuse University, and had served at the Korean consulate in Chicago for three years. His background was not atypical of the technocrats who were rising to positions of prominence in the government.

Shin Hyon Hwak accepted the preliminary recommendations by the technocrats for economic restructuring after he took over as deputy prime minister in December. On January 11, 1979, he outlined a radical liberalization policy to

Park Chung Hee. "It was a revolutionary action," says Park You Kwang. "The study did not just criticize the targets but criticized the [systemic] distortions [caused by the Heavy and Chemical Industries plan]. Mr. Shin particularly emphasized the importance of the liberalization of the financial sector. We thought that if we were to move toward market orientation that the financial sector must take the place of the government in allocating funds."

Park told Shin to let the group continue its study. The team made the risky decision to work as much as possible in secret, often ducking down the street from their offices near the U.S. embassy to hole up in the Koreana Hotel, where they could escape the scrutiny of other officials and the local reporters who cover government ministries in lemming-like press pools. They went back to the president and won his grudging approval in March.

Reflecting the consensus-building necessary in Korea for a policy change initiated from below, the group commissioned dozens of studies—a total of thirteen on macroeconomic issues and thirty-one on sectoral issues. Most of the work was done by the EPB, which prepared twenty-nine studies. Park Chung Hee commissioned the EPB to come up with a policy package, which was adopted in April 1979. However, Park was not altogether convinced that the economy was in such bad shape, and the president's ambivalence strengthened hard-liners in business and the bureaucracy who wanted to preserve privileges such as export subsidies and import liberalization and resist a cutback in rural building programs.

Interestingly, the program included a contradictory and anomalous proposal to increase public relief spending. This relief scheme was inserted at the insistence of the KCIA, which believed that social problems in the slums were a political danger, especially as the economy slowed down and put people out of work. The KCIA, of course, was not simply being soft-hearted. Its job, after all, was not merely to spy on students and political dissidents but to watch for signs of widespread social discontent. Unrest would give agents of North Korea a chance to promote a degree of social disorder in the South in order to make external defense impossible—or threaten Park Chung Hee's absolute power.

In March the KCIA had warned that a slowdown in the economy would cause further discontent among the less well-to-do who were being left behind by inflation. Employment began to drop noticeably in the middle of 1979, as inventories lengthened and payments were not made. Companies did not replace workers who left, and many small companies collapsed, as did one large one, the Yulsan group.

Dictatorship in Decline

As the economy started to slow, Park's political authority began to fray. The opposition narrowly edged out the ruling party in National Assembly elections in December 1978, although a rigged proportional representation system allowed the government party to continue controlling the legislature. Then on May 30, 1979, at the opposition New Democratic Party (NDP) convention, Kim Young Sam engineered a surprising upset of party leader Lee Chul Seung. Lee had kept the New Democratic Party a quiet opposition for most of the 1970s, prompting many Koreans to suspect that he was paid off by the government. The radio announcement of Kim's victory brought spontaneous cheers in bars, tearooms, and buses, for he was a politician that younger Koreans could support.

The consequences of the economic slowdown became apparent as increasing numbers of companies were unable to pay wages. Desperate workers began to protest. In a celebrated case in August, women workers at the Y. H. Trading Company, a wig manufacturing company that had gone bankrupt, took refuge at the opposition New Democratic Party headquarters. The women protesters wanted back pay owed them, and they counted on finding safety at the party's offices. However, at two o'clock in the morning on August 11, 1,000 riot police stormed the building in an operation code-named "Entebbe," trampling and beating opposition politicians who were camped out on the first floor to provide symbolic protection for the workers. At least forty people were hospitalized and, in the confusion, one of the young women was pushed or jumped to her death from the fourth floor.

A government report contended that it was the protesters who were to blame. The report claimed that the workers were driven to suicidal despair as a result of a "hypnotic trance" induced by the "fanatic slogans and songs" of the activists. The most "impure" (that is, Communist) slogan the government could cite was, "Better to gain through struggle than to take ten handouts."

The Y. H. affair, as it was called, glaringly displayed all that was wrong with the Yushin system. The opposition, playing on public sympathy for the young, innocent women, used the incident to attack Park's legitimacy. The government reacted by trying to depose Kim Young Sam as the New Democratic Party's head. On September 8, the Seoul District Court suspended Kim as party leader, and on October 4 the National Assembly voted to expel Kim from the legislature. Nine days later, sixty-nine opposition lawmakers tendered their resignations. Then riots broke out in the southern industrial cities of Pusan and Masan. The solid facade of the Yushin order was cracking. Soon it would be smashed by the death of the president.

Notes

1. Statement of April 17, 1979.
2. *Monthly Review of Korean Affairs*, vol. 1, no. 1 (May 1979). I am grateful to Tony Michell for this reference.
3. Alice H. Amsden, *Asia's Next Giant*, p. 100, cites an average inflation figure of 17.3 percent from 1962 to 1969 and 19.2 percent from 1970 to 1979.
4. Ibid., p. 102, claims that real wages increased rapidly during the late 1970s for manufacturing workers. Real increases in manufacturing wages averaged 18–20 percent per year from 1976 through 1979.

5. Author interview, January 1991.

6. Author interview, November 1990.

7. *Dong-A Ilbo*, September 16, 1974, cited in Leroy P. Jones and Sakong Il, *Government, Business and Entrepreneurship in Economic Development: The Korean Case*, p. 118.

8. Author interview, September 1991.

9. *Chonsei* is the practice of putting down large rental deposits; tenants pay no further rent and receive all the money back when they leave the apartment; the landlord's profit from investing the money makes up the rental return. The practice reflects the acute shortage of credit in the Korean economy.

10. Kim Kihwan, *The Korean Economy: Past Performance, Current Reforms, and Future Prospects*, pp. 44–45.

11. Author interview, October 1991.

12. Ibid.

10

The Assassination

The heavens trembled and the earth shook, nature seemed to wither and the people were stricken by fright and grief.
—Acting President Choi Kyu Hah

Dishes of roasted mushrooms, sliced beef, kimchi, and seasoned greens were laid out for what would be Park Chung Hee's last supper. The president and three of his most senior aides sat on the floor in a traditional Korean room in a KCIA building just outside the presidential Blue House compound. Two women, a model and a singer, served the meal and poured whiskey from a bottle of Chivas Regal, one of the many luxury imports prohibited in Korea. The singer was famous for a romantic ballad, "That Day, That Man."

The men watched the evening news on the state-owned broadcasting network. The president complained that coverage of a dedication ceremony for a new sea dike that he had attended that day was skimpy. The men drank more. They smoked Sun cigarettes. Then they quarreled. This much we know with some certainty. Just what happened next is unclear. But a few minutes later Park Chung Hee was dead.

The trouble apparently started after President Park accused Kim Jae Kyu, his KCIA chief, of failing to keep protests in Pusan and Masan under control. On October 16 students from Pusan's two major universities had taken to the streets in protest, joined by a large number of ordinary citizens. Police stations and tax offices were burned in an otherwise orderly demonstration, and martial law had been declared in Pusan as of midnight October 18. The nearby cities of Masan and Changwon, where Hyundai International had a huge industrial complex, erupted in antigovernment demonstrations the next morning, prompting the im-

138

position of garrison decree, just one step removed from martial law. More violence and destruction of property took place than at any time since Park had taken power. Even more worrying were signs that students and workers were forming an alliance, something that had always been one of Park's nightmares.

In April 1960, riots in Pusan and Masan had preceded the fall of Syngman Rhee. Moreover, Pusan was opposition leader Kim Young Sam's constituency and a stronghold of antigovernment forces. Yet while everyone was aware of the parallels between 1960 and 1979, no one seriously considered that Park's rule was endangered. This looked like one of the periodic crises in Korean political life that flare up and then burn out with few traces. Indeed, less than a week before Park was assassinated, William Chapman of the *Washington Post* wrote that Park Chung Hee seemed "to be as firmly in command as at any time during his 18-year rule."[1]

As the men dined that evening, Kim Jae Kyu warned Park that the government would have to be prepared to kill 3,000 people to restore order. Park said he was ready to kill 30,000 protesters. Cha Chi Chol, a ferocious ex-paratrooper who had risen to become Park's closest adviser, chimed in to support tougher measures against the protesters and chided Kim Jae Kyu for failing to keep order. Then the KCIA head left the room and came back with a hidden pistol.

"Your Excellency, how can you run a government with an insect like this," sneered Kim, gesturing at Cha. The KCIA chief pulled out his pistol and shot the president's adviser. Cha fled, fatally wounded, into an adjacent toilet. Next, Kim shot the president himself at point-blank range.

"Are you all right, Your Excellency?" asked one of the women. "I am all right" he grimly replied, slumping forward. Those were his last words. Park Chung Hee died where he sat, blood pooling around him on the smooth floor. When reporters visited the room five days later for a grisly re-enactment of the crime, a pool of the president's dried blood was caked on the floor.

Kim rushed out of the room in his stocking feet to a nearby dining room in the KCIA compound and pulled the military chief of staff, Chung Seung Hwa, into a car. "Big things have happened," said Kim. Big things indeed. In the confusion, Kim Jae Kyu's subordinates shot and killed several presidential guards. Park's aide Kim Kye Won, the fourth man at the dinner, was left to clean up the mess and move the bodies to a nearby army hospital.

With those few bullets on the evening of October 26, 1979, Kim Jae Kyu ended an era. The ruthless nation-building days of Park Chung Hee were finished in a few quick squeezes of the trigger. There is much about that night that will never be known, including the degree to which Park's assassination was premeditated and the extent to which Kim Jae Kyu enjoyed—or thought he enjoyed—support for his attempted putsch among other officials. Many Koreans believed that Chung Seung Hwa's presence nearby meant that he was part of the conspiracy, but it is just as plausible that the chief of staff was lured there by Kim Jae Kyu to provide the appearance of support. In any event, Kim apparently was convinced that the government could survive only by eliminating Cha Chi Chol and, apparently, Park Chung Hee as well. Says a U.S. intelligence analyst:

> His failure to take any aggressive action to follow up supports the notion that he had no intention to take power. He was using an old weapon, his personal pistol, which probably had not been used for a long time [before the killing] and which misfired several times. The choice of weapons did not look like someone out to take over the government.[2]

Martial law was declared just after midnight, with the explanation that the president was indisposed. It was not until 7:30 the next morning that Park's death was announced. He had been killed in an accident, Koreans were told. More complete—and often contradictory—versions of the killing were released over the following weeks.

According to the government account, Kim Jae Kyu was engaged in a plot to overthrow the president and seize power. Initial reports indicated that Kim Jae Kyu acted on his own, while later ones said that he had support from several officers, including Chung Seung Hwa. All these accounts are suspect, however, for investigators were less interested in establishing the truth than in jockeying for power in the post-Park period.

Violence was almost the only path for political change. Under Park, politics had offered no avenue for reform, because the president had neutered the political process in order to concentrate his energies single-mindedly on national development. With Yushin he had effectively installed himself as dictator-for-life. Yet like all dictators, it was only a matter of time before Park lost touch with reality.

Says a U.S. official who knew Park:

> The tragic thing about Park is that if he had only retired as president he would have been regarded as Korea's greatest living hero and Korea would be much further along on the road toward democracy. After his wife's death he became isolated and overly influenced by Cha Chi Chol. He withdrew and accepted the canard that he was the only man who could lead Korea.[3]

The tremendous economic growth of the 1970s had carried a heavy social cost, a cost made apparent by the riots in Pusan and Masan. The KCIA's job was to protect not only the president but the country, and Kim Jae Kyu feared that the system had become so brittle that it might crack. Better to do away with the president, Kim Jae Kyu apparently believed, than to risk the ruling elite's hold on power—and the economic progress that had been made—by allowing Park to continue his dictatorial rule indefinitely.

Cha Chi Chol's emergence as the president's most trusted adviser worried many of the ruling elite. Cha was hated by many of those who had been closest to Park, and there was fear that the president was falling under the influence of a

Korean Rasputin. The most charitable explanation for Park's assassination is that Kim Jae Kyu genuinely believed that the ideals of the May 1961 revolution had been betrayed and that the only way to open up the political debate about Korea's future was to do away with the president. We will never know what Kim's motives were, for he was executed following a speedy trial and despite, it emerged many years later, reservations on the part of several Supreme Court justices.

Before the debate on the new Korea could begin, the former president had to be mourned and buried. By the government's count, 9.5 million Koreans, one out of every four people in the country, streamed to the four-tiered funeral altar in downtown Seoul to pay their respects to the slain president. Mourners bowed and lit incense in front of the large photo of Park draped in black ribbon and surrounded by vases of chrysanthemums. There were scenes of near-hysteria as the mourners streamed past the altar. One man sliced his finger open and wrote condolences in his own blood before collapsing.

The funeral was a fitting memorial to gigantism and Park Chung Hee's personality cult. The service began on the plaza in front of the old Japanese colonial administration building at Kwanghwamun, as more than 2,000 foreign and Korean dignitaries had the weird experience of listening to Park's voice boom out one last time, as tapes of his speeches urging the preservation of traditional culture, national unity, and vigilance against North Korea were played. Although it was not played, Park's speech from the opening of the Seoul-Pusan expressway was one of the final contenders for this bizarre funeral oration by the deceased himself. On the plaza festooned with tens of thousands of chrysanthemum and asparagus flowers, mourners listened to volleys of gun salutes, Beethoven's *Eroica*, and acting President Choi Kyu Hah's lament that "the heavens trembled and the earth shook, nature seemed to wither and the people were stricken by fright and grief" when the president was killed.

The coffin was trundled into a bus custom-made by Saehan Motors, the Daewoo–General Motors joint venture. A large picture of Park, draped with black ribbon, rode on the roof of the big black Buick that headed the cortege. Behind it came one hundred Korea Military Academy cadets in dress uniform who pulled the hearse that, covered with 72,500 white and yellow chrysanthemums, looked like a parade float. Through the hearse's large picture windows the crowd of 2 million mourners lining the streets of Seoul could see the closed coffin draped with the Korean national flag and illuminated with fluorescent lights.

The funeral cortege drove slowly down the broad Sejong Boulevard in front of Kwanghwamun, a boulevard flanked by government ministries and the U.S. embassy. The procession headed through the heart of Seoul, past the colonial-era rail terminal and south, across the Han River to the National Cemetery, which nestled in the foothills on its far shore.[4]

Large crowds thronged the route to pay their respects to the president. But after the procession had passed, the crowd surged into the streets in an unparalleled display of unruliness that showed the regimentation of the Yushin era was over. Although acting President Choi may have felt the heavens tremble and the earth shake, critics of Yushin saw people step more lightly in the streets of Seoul when they heard the news of the president's death.

From November 1, 1979, until May 16, 1980, Korea moved in contradictory and ultimately conflicting directions. In these brief six months, Korean democracy blossomed and then was crushed. The student movement rose and was brutally brought down. Korean labor briefly, exuberantly, broke free of government control. Technocrats, freed from the political pressure on top, began to chart a new and more rational economic policy for Korea as they built on the economic restructuring plan that had been under discussion since the end of 1978. The political opposition, with a brief chance to take power, fractured along factional lines. During those heady months businessmen also scrambled to build ties with the new economic team in the wake of their patron's death.

These groups were ultimately unable to control the country's future. Once again, the military stepped in and thwarted democracy. Officers of the Korea Military Academy's eleventh class, the first truly professional academy graduates, rose up against the older generation of generals in an odd creeping coup d'état that began on December 12, 1979, and finished with the imposition of martial law on May 16, 1980. In the process, the army crushed the Seoul spring, arresting the movement for democratic change that had been spurred by Park Chung Hee's assassination.

Each power group in society had its own view of the future, but not all could prevail. For six months the different groups worked to realize their conflicting goals with just enough success to stoke the sense of crisis that foreshadowed the forcible end of this democratic experiment. Some compromised with the victorious side, while others laid aside the struggle for another day, a day that would not come until 1987.

Notes

1. *Washington Post*, October 22, 1979.
2. Author interview, January 1994.
3. Author interview, October 1991.
4. Imelda Marcos, who could have designed this procession, missed most of the extravaganza because her plane was delayed by fog. She caught up with the procession at the National Cemetery in time to hug Park's children in consolation.

11

Democracy Denied

The East's Confucian culture emphasizes harmony and the Golden Mean, rather than confrontation. Based on agrarian culture, it features moderation, reconciliation and harmony while human relations are shaped by traditional ethics rather than rights under the law.
                                                        —Chun Doo Hwan[1]

There were not many cars in Seoul at the end of 1979, and just about everyone who had one enjoyed the luxury of having a chauffeur, for autos were expensive and drivers were not. Foreign diplomats out for a Sunday drive remember gawkers attracted by the odd sight of someone actually driving his own car. Seoul's traffic congestion, now chronic, was just a dream for Hyundai's Chung family and other automakers.

It was unusual, then, when on the evening of December 12, 1979, traffic was snarled south of the city center between the Namsan tunnel and the Han River bridge. This peculiar traffic jam was the beginning of what later became known as the 12–12 incident, and it marked the start of Chun Doo Hwan's grab for power.

Two groups of soldiers were engaged first in a stand-off and then in a gun battle near an official compound that was home to the foreign minister, the defense minister, and the martial law commander. The military vehicles spilling onto a main street backed up traffic. Later that night, as most of the city slept, a brief but brutal barrage of firepower accompanied an assault on the Ministry of Defense, located on the edge of the U.S. military base. The firefight ended with the arrest of the defense minister.

But when the city awoke the next morning it was as if nothing had happened. That day, military officials announced that martial law commander Chung Seung Hwa and Defense Minister Noh Jae Hyun had been arrested in connection with the investigation into Park Chung Hee's assassination. The military assured Koreans that this was simply an internal affair of the armed forces. For several months the military indeed seemed to stay out of politics as the country exuberantly lunged toward democracy. But five months later the cabinet was dissolved, martial law was declared, and a brutal crackdown began. December 12, 1979, the night of the generals, was the first act in a tragedy that saw Korea's hopes for political liberalization shattered.

Like all dictators, Park had left behind a vacuum. The country had come so far in the eighteen years of Park's rule and suddenly, at a time of economic and political turbulence, he was gone. Never was the fragility of the Korean economy more nakedly displayed, and never did the gnawing fear that the fragile shoots of growth would wither seem more likely than at the end of 1979. In fact, 1980 was the first year the Korean economy contracted since before Park took power. Modern Korea had no precedent for a successful peaceful transfer of power, and Park had groomed no obvious successor. Indeed, he had deliberately weakened anyone who was a potential threat to his one-man rule. For nearly two decades the force of one man's personality had driven the country along the harsh road of modernization. After his death, the economic gains that had been so painfully won under Park's rule threatened to disintegrate under the twin forces of world recession and domestic political chaos. Now would come the true test of Korea, Inc.

Night of the Generals

Martial law commander Chung Seung Hwa had put on his mufti and was about to go to his nephew's engagement ceremony, but first he wanted to watch the beginning of the seven o'clock news. As he sat downstairs with his family, two officers arrived at the house and asked to see him. Chung was in a hurry, but he grudgingly went upstairs to find out what his unannounced visitors wanted of him. They told the general that they wanted to take him in for questioning.

The intruders were from Chun Doo Hwan's Defense Security Command and they had come to arrest Chung at his official residence in Hannam-dong, about three miles southeast of the presidential Blue House. The official compound straddles a hilltop just north of the Han River, near the heavily traveled Han River bridge.

Chung's guards tried to protect him, and a scuffle broke out. Shots were fired. Defense Minister Noh Jae Hyun, who lived in a nearby house in the official compound, happened to be home. Hearing the shots, Noh fled, slipping out of the compound, across the campus of Dankook University, and onto a street on the far side of the university. He flagged down a taxi and fled for the relative safety of the U.S. base at Yongsan, a bit more than a mile to the east of his house.

Minister Noh was soon joined at the U.S. bunker by the head of the Korean joint chiefs of staff. "They didn't know anything," says a U.S. adviser who was at Yongsan that evening. "All they knew was that there had been gunfire at the martial law commander's house and then they ran like hell. We had these guys sitting in our bunker and all they knew was that they had heard gunshots. Nobody could get through to [President] Choi [Kyu Hah]. The Blue House was incommunicado. We didn't know that Chun [was behind this], that in fact he was probably at the Blue House at the time. All we knew is that we couldn't get hold of the president."

Chun Doo Hwan, meanwhile, was stymied by a president who refused to sign the arrest warrant for martial law commander Chung Seung Hwa until it was countersigned by Defense Minister Noh Jae Hyun. Chun was looking for Noh, who was hiding out in the U.S. bunker at Yongsan. It was like a deadly Marx Brothers routine.

A loyalist to martial law commander Chung sent out an armed party from the Capital Garrison Command to find out what was happening at the compound of official residences in Hannam-dong. These troops trapped the members of the Defense Security Command in their armored personnel carriers —with Chung inside one of the vehicles—on the steep, narrow streets leading up to the official compound. A firefight broke out between the two groups and turned what Chun had hoped would be a simple arrest into a much more serious incident as two of the most elite units in the South Korean army battled it out on the streets of the capital.

Meanwhile, Chun was in a huge secret underground bunker near Kwanghwamun with a core group of seven co-conspirators, including Roh Tae Woo, the man who would follow him as president. They knew that they were in trouble. Chun's gamble in arresting Chung Seung Hwa was looking like a losing bet. If he failed, Chun would almost certainly face execution. He needed more troops. The only two sources of nearby firepower were the Capital Garrison Command and the Special Warfare Command. Both were commanded by older men, who could not be counted on to support him, and might in fact oppose his attempt to arrest Chung and wrest power from their generation.

Chun and his gang then took an all-or-nothing gamble and pulled South Korean troops down from the Demilitarized Zone, where they were facing North Korea. Roh ordered some of the troops from his Ninth Division, as well as some tanks from a nearby unit not under his command, to leave their positions on the front lines and head for the capital. Chun and his fellow coupmakers also needed to make sure that other units did not start moving against them, so they put out a series of telephone calls to their classmates and juniors who commanded units north of the capital and who were in a position to actually move troops in support of one side or the other.

The decision to pull troops off the North Korean border reflected Chun's desperation. Commandeering front-line troops for help in an internecine battle

146 • TROUBLED TIGER

was risky, because it weakened the South's defenses and could have encouraged the North Koreans to take advantage of the confusion. The move angered U.S. commander John Wickham, who should have been notified but was not, and made him an implacable foe of Chun. Wickham later said that if a U.S. general had done something similar he would have been executed.

Chung Seung Hwa later condemned the incident as "an unpardonable coup d'état staged under a premeditated plan drawn up by ringleader Chun Doo Hwan and a handful of politically ambitious soldiers bent on grabbing power. Such a mutiny is clearly punishable by death under the military criminal code."[2] But the gamble paid off.

Chun was able to take power successfully thanks to his position as one of the leaders of a secret military class fraternity, one that is popularly called Hanahoe, the "One Way Association." These sorts of affinity groups are common among classmates in Korea, but Hanahoe played an unusually important role in influencing not only Chun and Roh's Class 11 but younger generations of Korea Military Academy graduates as well. These ties were never more crucial than on the night of December 12, 1979. The colonels and one-star generals who commanded troops north of the capital simply held their positions and faced north, with the important exception of the troops and tanks that Roh Tae Woo had moved into the capital to support Chun. "A [Korean] friend of mine received a call that night," remembers the American analyst. "The caller said, 'General, you're a corps commander on the DMZ. We want you to face north tonight and do your job and that's all.' And that's what he did." The bonds of a new generation that wanted power were tested and held.

A hagiography of Chun describes his calling his family together hours before the coup started and asking them, "Would you let yourself be swept away in a big stream which you do not think is flowing in the right direction, or would you try to make the stream flow in a direction you think is right even if you have to risk your own life doing that?"[3] Chun told the Korean people what he told his family: that Chung Seung Hwa was implicated in the murder of Park Chung Hee and could not be allowed to escape unpunished. In fact, Chun could have little illusion that he was mounting a putsch to grab power from an older generation of generals, a generation of men that KMA Class 11 officers regarded as corrupt and undependable.

As Chung Seung Hwa succinctly put it in his testimony to the National Assembly nine years later: "To kidnap the martial law commander. . . . at the risk of their lives was an obvious military rebellion and a coup designed to grasp power."[4] Kim Bok Dong, Chun Doo Hwan's rival as Class 11 leader (and Roh Tae Woo's brother-in-law), who was not involved in the coup, believes that Chun and Roh acted impulsively. "They didn't plan to take power. They did it to save their careers. But after that, they could not turn back."[5]

In fact, the events of December 12 did constitute a coup, although it took almost five months for Chun to consolidate his power. The move by Chun and his military academy classmates and their juniors was prompted by reports that Chun would be transferred out of Seoul to the isolated east coast city of Kangnung. Obviously, this would remove Chun himself from the center of power. Moreover, in combination with other transfers and promotions it signaled an attempt by the older generation to retain its grip on power.

Although several soldiers had been killed in the brief firefights that broke out at Hannam-dong and a handful of other locations around the city, little seemed to have changed on the following day. Those who ventured into downtown Seoul on the morning of December 13 saw the main government ministry building by Kwanghwamun gate surrounded by armored vehicles and troops. Some other major government buildings were also under military supervision.

But the Ministry of Finance and the Economic Planning Board, which were only about two hundred yards away from the capitol building, had only their small, routine security presence. What had happened the night before seemingly was an affair of the generals, one that did not appear to affect the economic mandarins. Throughout the day, the elite sought information from anyone who might have it. Even an official as highly placed as Deputy Prime Minister Shin Hyon Hwak resorted to sending his special adviser Kim Ki Hwan to foreign embassies in an effort to find out what was happening—or what the foreign diplomats thought was happening.

No statement was issued by the military, and no proclamation made. Later that day, the minister of defense simply announced that General Chung Seung Hwa had been arrested for questioning. (He was charged on December 24.) Over the next few days, the troops faded away, and the general public assumed that the country was still inching toward democracy. A new cabinet was appointed on December 14, with no apparent interference from the military, and Defense Ministry officials insisted that the incident was purely a military affair. New defense minister Choo Young Bok told a *Newsweek* correspondent:

> There are many rumors and misunderstandings. Just look at me and believe me. It was simply an effort to arrest, on solid grounds, a general suspected of being implicated in President Park's assassination. . . . The military did not change the cabinet, the president or any policies. If it had been a coup, it would have been different. . . . [The military's] basic principle is anti-Communism. Aside from that we are positively neutral in political matters. I am convinced the military cannot and should not interfere in politics.[6]

During his lifetime, Park Chung Hee had ensured that the military would not be a threat to him. Competition among the KCIA, the Defense Security Command, the Presidential Security Force, and the Capital Garrison Command was constant. Most notably, in the spring of 1973 KCIA head Lee Hu Rak uncovered a coup allegedly planned by Yun Pil Yong, the commander of the Capitol Garrison, which resulted in the purging of many members of Class 11 from the military.[7]

The members of KMA Class 11, the first four-year class and the leaders of a more professional generation of military men, had long been closely scrutinized by Park Chung Hee, who feared them as the leaders of a new generation of officers. Park tried to seduce them by rotating them through positions of power on the Presidential Security Force, the South Korean equivalent of the U.S. Secret Service, and the Capitol Garrison Command. They also had his ear: during the 1970s, Chun Doo Hwan was one of less than half a dozen people in the country who could immediately get an appointment with Park. Nonetheless, Park discriminated against Class 11 in promotions. Part of that was because there simply was no room for them at the top. The men who had quickly risen to the rank of general during the Korean War were allowed to serve indefinitely, as retirement regulations were bent to accommodate them. Says the U.S. adviser:

> With the rapid expansion of the Korean Army in the Korean War anyone who had served in the Japanese army as a sergeant or spoke 10 words of English went from second lieutenant to general in three years. They made their careers not as officers but as generals. . . . The result was abject discrimination against the KMA [Class 11] boys because they had no experience in [the Korean] War. I remember tracking their promotion patterns and shaking my head in disbelief at the discrimination these KMA graduates were suffering.
>
> KMA graduates [beginning with Class 11] had the best education anyone could get in Korea in those days. It was a four-year curriculum put together by Americans and sometimes taught by Americans, based on the West Point curriculum. They were taught everything from modern warfare to modern economic principles and there were American advisers all the way down to the battalion level. The American way was throughout the Army. KMA Class 11 was only important because it was the first [four-year class].

By 1979, Class 11 officers were impatient. A round of changes that occurred between Park's assassination and the December 12 incident suggested that the older generation—nominally led by Defense Minister Noh Jae Hyun and Chung Seung Hwa—was intent on keeping control of the military. Two new corps commanders were named, and neither was from the ranks of KMA Class 11. Says the U.S. adviser:

> I believe it was a KMA Class 17 officer [most likely Colonel Huh Hwa Pyung] who went to Chun and said, "If you don't move against them first they're going to move against you." I think that was the basic motivation for 12–12. I don't think Chun meant to take power directly and immediately.

That may be too charitable an interpretation, for Chun Doo Hwan seemed to think that he was cut out for great things. An unwittingly revealing official biography provides some useful glimpses into Chun as he wanted to appear— and is a telling example of the sort of sycophancy that Korean leaders, in both the North and South, tolerate and even encourage.

Chun Doo Hwan

The first sentence of Chun Doo Hwan's authorized biography, *Man of Destiny*, is a curious lie, laying out Chun's fundamental insecurity. His biographer, following the lead of his government handlers, claimed that Chun was born in January 1931. In fact, Chun had advanced his age by a year to make himself seem older—and thus more legitimate—to Koreans. In February 1981, shortly before he was sworn in as president (he had been acting president since September), Chun's aides ordered local officials to change his birth records.[8]

With an opening like this, there is little reason to take altogether literally what follows in one of the few biographies of Chun. The myth spun out in this book is of an incorruptible, generous, honest man, never afraid to fight for what he believes is right. Born, like his hero Abe Lincoln, in humble surroundings, Chun nonetheless was said to have a bit of royal blood, with his father's side claiming to trace its ancestry back to a general loyal to the founder of the Paekche kingdom and his mother's side alleging descent from a Shilla king.

Reality was more mundane. The Chuns were from a dirt-poor family in the southeastern village of Hapchon, where his father was a tenant farmer with a smattering of classical Chinese education. His mother gave birth to five boys and five girls, three of whom died at an early age.

Three years before Chun Doo Hwan was born, so the story goes, his mother had an unusual dream. She was desperate to bear a son who survived, for her first two sons had died in accidents, and her husband was threatening to leave her if she did not bear another son. (That a government-sanctioned biographer would record this threat by Chun's father testifies to the obsession Koreans have with producing a male heir.)

Chun's mother dreamed that three men and a woman walked out of a rainbow and called her "mother." In the dream, the first man had a dark face and wore royal blue robes. The second had broad shoulders and a majestic face, and bore a crown on his head. The third man also looked very strong and masculine. Finally, there was a woman wearing a red velvet gown.

Chun's oldest brother, Ki Hwan, was born shortly after the dream. He went on to become a policeman—a man in blue—earning the nickname "godfather of Yongsan" for the power he had over this Seoul district during his brother's presidency. Then came the future president, the one in the dream with the crown. A third son, Kyung Hwan, survived birth and grew up to become a manly karate teacher, thug, and convicted felon. Chun's mother then gave birth to two daughters, one of whom died in infancy, fulfilling the prophetic dream of three men, a woman, and a rainbow.

This intimation of greatness seemingly was confirmed when Chun Doo Hwan was just over one year old. An itinerant Buddhist monk begging for barley thought he saw great things destined for the Chun household. Being a novice, he was reluctant to come out with his prophecy, but when Chun's mother insisted he said, "Your physiognomy indicates you are going to be the mother of a great man, but your protruding front teeth may get in the way." Chun's mother decided she would get rid of her buck teeth.

> She asked a neighbor, who always had been a good helping hand in the village, to pull her teeth with a pair of pincers. His attempt, however, failed because he did not have the guts to watch her stand the tremendous pain. After he left, she tied herself to one of the log pillars in the house and struck it hard with her buck teeth saying to herself, "I'll do anything for my children, no matter what!"[9]

She got rid of her buck teeth, but it took Chun's mother two-and-a-half months to recover from her self-inflicted wound. This story epitomizes the Korean mother who will sacrifice anything for her sons. Mythical or not, it is not far from the truth. Nor would the superstition of Chun's mother seem out of place even in today's Seoul, where parents force most prospective couples to submit to a fortune-teller, who decides whether or not to bless the marriage.[10]

Chun's family had been driven from its home village in southeastern Korea, to Japanese Manchuria before finally settling in Taegu in impoverished circumstances. His father, who had lost his government job, worked as a herb doctor. While his younger brother, Kyung Hwan, slept swaddled on the future president's back, Chun Doo Hwan studied from a book that was suspended from the ceiling with string. In Taegu, he walked ten kilometers to school and ten kilometers back during his high school years. He developed a dislike of Communists after the liberation, which he demonstrated by standing up to leftists who encouraged a school boycott.

When the Korean War broke out, Chun signed up for the military. His mother, however, would have none of it, but she did allow him to apply for the first four-year class of the Korea Military Academy. His roommates there included Roh Tae Woo and Kim Bok Dong. His grades were mediocre, but he was a good athlete.

In 1959, four years after graduating from the military academy, Chun married the daughter of an officer who had been assigned to the KMA while he was a cadet. Chun supposedly protested that he was too poor to marry, but Lee Soon Ja said that she would take care of the money. That she did—with a ruthlessness and single-mindedness that would haunt Chun after he became president. Shortly after he married, Chun was sent to the United States to study psychological warfare training at the Special Warfare School in Fort Black, North Carolina. The following year he underwent Ranger and Airborne training in the United States. He was well on his way to becoming a modern military man in the American mold.

In 1961 Chun, as a prominent member of Class 11, was instrumental in throwing the support of KMA cadets behind Park Chung Hee's coup.[11] For forty-eight hours the fate of Park's coup hung in the balance, as the United States tried to rally support for the elected civilian government. KMA cadets helped tip the balance in favor of Park. In 1962, as a reward, Chun briefly served with the new KCIA and was promoted to major. He moved smartly up the ranks, commanding the Capital Garrison Command in the late 1960s. In Vietnam Chun commanded a regiment in the same Ninth Division that would provide critical support on the night of December 12, 1979.

Chun won his first general's star in 1973, and in 1976 he served on the Presidential Security Force. He won his second star in 1977. In 1978, he had the good luck to be commanding the First Division when it discovered an infiltration tunnel built by North Korea under the DMZ. At least partly as a result, he was named to head the Defense Security Command in March, only seven months before Park Chung Hee was assassinated. The assassination fortuitously left Chun as one of the most powerful men in the country at a time when the supreme leader had been eliminated. Perhaps his mother's dream had been right, and Chun Doo Hwan was indeed a man of destiny. Destiny, however, still awaited a few more rough pushes before Chun emerged on top of the heap.

The Seoul Spring

The first few months after Park's death were a time of euphoria. With the restraints of the Yushin era crumbling, anything seemed possible. Choi Kyu Hah, the figurehead prime minister who had become acting president when Park was killed, was formally elected president on December 6 by the country's electoral college. For his inauguration two weeks later, on December 21, the platform that Choi stood on was brought down from the 4.3 meters customary under Park Chung Hee to 3 meters, in order to make the new president less imposing. In another gesture designed to show that Choi's was to be a less imperious presidency, the choir that sang "Hail to the President" was cut from 230 members to 120.[12]

Choi was a tall, self-effacing bureaucrat, a man who found himself thrust into a job beyond his leadership capabilities. He was so cautious, said one Korean analyst, that he "would tap a stone bridge three times before deciding to cross it." He was a bureaucrat, not a leader, and as a result the military was once again able to move.

Choi cautiously began to dismantle the Yushin system. The day after he was formally elected president, Choi repealed Emergency Decree Number 9, the infamous 1975 edict that had banned virtually any antigovernment activity. This was the law that made it illegal even to criticize the Yushin Constitution or the Emergency Decrees themselves. Sixty-eight political prisoners who had violated Decree Number 9 were immediately released.

Tellingly, however, the government did not release ninety-six people who had been arrested on November 26 by the Martial Law Command at a rally calling for the immediate abolition of the Yushin Constitution. Because of the restrictions on political gatherings, the group had tried to disguise its rally as a wedding presided over by the distinguished Quaker theologian and dissident Hahm Sok Hon. Although this putative wedding party was tiny compared with the hundreds of thousands of people who attended antigovernment rallies the following spring, the government was nervous about the possibility that dissidents and human rights activists might mount a sustained challenge at a time of extraordinary political flux. The arrests and torture of the detainees, which antigovernment critics claimed was severe even by Yushin standards, did in fact succeed in blunting the development of an organized political opposition for several months.

During the 1970s, Christian activists had formed a key part of the antigovernment movement. About a fifth of the country regarded itself as Christian, the largest percentage in Asia after the Philippines, and religious activists took an increasingly prominent role as opposition political parties were stripped of any power. Many activist church members had fought consistently for human rights and, through groups like the Urban Industrial Mission, for workers' rights. After Park's assassination these older dissidents and younger university students formed one pole of the opposition movement. Opposition politicians, most of whom were grouped around Kim Dae Jung or Kim Young Sam, formed the other pole.

In October 1979, the parliamentary opposition had been caught off guard by Park's assassination. But when the moment to take power came, the contenders started a self-destructive process of bickering, one that the government encouraged with tactics aimed at splitting the opposition.

Despite opposition leader Kim Young Sam's strong showing in the months before Park's death, he did little to capitalize on the new freedom the opposition enjoyed. Kim Young Sam's energies were devoted to fighting a challenge for leadership of the opposition mounted by his long-time rival, Kim Dae Jung. Kim Dae Jung had narrowly beaten Kim Young Sam to clinch the nomination as opposition candidate in the 1971 presidential election. Kim Young Sam, who had been so confident of winning the nomination that he had his acceptance speech ready in his pocket, never forgot the humiliation he had suffered at Kim Dae Jung's hands, and the rivalry between the two resurfaced in early 1980.

Labor and students were also growing increasingly militant. In the spring of 1980 a sharp rise in labor activism threatened the alternately paternal and brutal control of labor that had been a hallmark of the Park years. At the same time, the student movement began to gather momentum after years of repression.

On February 29 President Choi restored the civil rights of important opposition figures, including former President Yun Po Sun, Kim Dae Jung (who had been banned from politics since 1973, when the KCIA had kidnapped and nearly killed him), theologian Hahm Sok Hon, and 684 other people. In retrospect this marked the high point in the democratization process. It was also the apogee of the liberal wing of the Christian church in the Korean opposition. The student movement that emerged in the 1980s was far more radical than the human rights movement of the 1970s had been. The human rights activists were largely displaced by students who talked of anti-imperialism, U.S. withdrawal, and solidarity with farmers and workers.

Throughout the Yushin period the student movement had been extremely weak. Protesters were instantly arrested. Consistent political opponents were locked away for months or years at a time. That changed dramatically when a new school year began in March 1980 after the long winter break. The anti-government protests gathered momentum after the April 19 anniversary of the 1960 student revolution. The streets of Korean cities witnessed daily demonstrations calling for the end of martial law, speedy democratization under a new constitution and the removal of Chun Doo Hwan—who in mid-April became head of the KCIA—and Prime Minister Shin Hyon Hwak. Protesters also wanted the end of compulsory military training for students and the re-admittance of students who had been expelled from universities for political activities.

Although many conservative Koreans were unsettled by the demonstrations, Korea had a time-honored tradition of student protest against unjust rule. In Confucian society students and scholars were supposed to be the conscience of the nation, risking their careers, even their lives, when protest against an illegitimate ruler became necessary. The earliest student protests in Korea took place as far back as the sixteenth century. More recently, students had been important in anti-Japanese protests and pivotal in overthrowing Syngman Rhee in 1960. One reason that every Korean government takes student protests so seriously is that Korean students do have the moral right to try to overthrow governments—and sometimes they succeed.

Some measure of student protest was acceptable, but the Korean elite was alarmed by the emergence of labor unrest. Workers, to the upper-class way of thinking, were uneducated people who had no business meddling in politics.

At the beginning of the Yushin period, Park Chung Hee had asked for advice on how to handle labor affairs in the 1970s. One of those asked was Professor Tak Hee Jun, who had reminded Park that the country that had oppressed workers the most in the past—Russia—had ended with the capitalists' losing everything. Only an industrial democracy could prevent long-term problems during industrialization, Tak warned. If workers were oppressed they would revolt. Park replied that, while he sympathized with this view, he felt that in its condition Korea could not afford a labor movement for at least the next ten years. Instead, Park's Yushin system prohibited both strikes and collective bargaining.

With the Yushin system in ruins, workers eagerly awaited the annual spring campaign for wage increases. (Most Korean companies negotiate pay hikes with their workers during March and April.) During the early months of 1980, union members began to vote out the corrupt leaders and timid time-servers who dominated the organized labor movement. Throughout the country, workers began to complain of abuses and to express their grievances through strikes. In a sign of the confusion in the government, the Office of Labor urged collective bargaining at the same time that other officials continued to insist that the laws prohibiting collective bargaining and collective action were still in effect.

Three incidents embodied the pent-up passions of the labor movement. On April 21, about 700 coal miners in the eastern mountain town of Sabuk seized control of the town and the coal mine that dominated it. As in many other countries, Korea's coal miners had a long history of militance. In Sabuk, they had been kept in check for years with the help of a company-sponsored union leader. The company paid the union leader's salary—standard practice in Korea—and did not require him to work in the mine. But the sweetheart contract he agreed to sign in the spring of 1980 was intolerable to the miners. They went on a hunt for the union leader. Unable to find him, they captured his wife instead.

Stripped half-naked, she was put on public display in the center of Sabuk and held hostage for four days, while workers kept government troops at bay. This was a horrible, brutal incident, but it was one that was fully in keeping with the sort of brutality and indignity regularly inflicted on workers. A government that allowed nonviolent women strikers to be smeared with human feces while policemen chuckled, one in which police regularly beat workers and in which physical and emotional abuse was common, should not have been surprised to find that workers could give as good as they got.

An eyewitness sympathetic to the miners described workers stoning riot police and destroying a police station in Sabuk:

> At dusk huge bonfires blazed on the grounds of the company offices, fed by furniture, documents and equipment from the offices. Four officers for the company came to the church and asked to. . . . stay the night. All officers' families went into hiding. All that night there was looting. The officers' residences were wrecked. TV sets, refrigerators, radios were destroyed; buses and trucks belonging to the company were smashed.

The nightmare of the nation's rulers seemed to be coming true as workers blindly lashed out. The government seized on the situation to justify the harsher measures that followed. "The Sabuk incident. . . . added to political, economic and social chaos," a government report said in justifying the subsequent crackdown. "North Korea, which was looking for an opportunity to invade the south, was encouraged to move armored forces closer to the Demilitarized Zone on a large scale."[13] This part about the North Koreans was absolutely untrue, at least according to U.S. military sources (who provided the South Koreans with their most useful military intelligence), but the propaganda served its purpose.

While unsettled by the violence, public opinion was generally favorable to the demands of the unionists. An editorial in the conservative *Chosun Ilbo* newspaper complained that:

> would-be aristocrats among the labor management have put the miscalculated and weakened labor union organization to improper uses and have patronized

industry in their quest for personal gain and luxury. This exploitation of the workers is the exceedingly sorry state of affairs created by such developments.[14]

The second important strike was at the Tongmyong Timber Company. Here, as in the earlier Y. H. affair that preceded Park's assassination, the problem was bad management. Tongmyong was going bankrupt, and its owners, themselves locked in private feuds, failed to realize the perilous state of the company's finances. They attempted to divert funds to other subsidiaries and failed to pay either back wages or severance pay to workers. Out of desperation, workers finally occupied the premises and threatened the family of one of the owners with violence.

Tongmyong represented the most common type of labor-management conflict in 1980. Of the 719 labor disputes registered from January through April (seven times the number in all of 1979), 534 were over unpaid wages. Another 25 were sit-ins to prevent plant closures. Disputes reflected not only the giddy experience of political freedom but the bigger problem of a slowing economy. The economic contraction threatened to destroy whole sections of the export industry.

The third important strike was in the ironically named "Peace Market" area near Seoul's East Gate. This warren of sweatshops was the center of the domestic garment industry. Not surprisingly, for an industry that depended above all on cheap wages, some of the country's worst working conditions were found there. Moreover, the Peace Market had a long history of labor activism. In the early 1970s, a young union activist had burned himself to death there in a dramatic act of protest. Chun Tae Il's suicide had awakened intellectuals to the sacrifices endured by the country's workers in the course of industrialization and had galvanized the country's embryonic labor movement. As the government's labor policy disintegrated in the spring of 1980, a flurry of sit-ins and work disputes spread through many of the small apparel factories in the market. Although there was no violence, the prolonged work stoppages alarmed many Koreans.

To conservative Koreans this combination of student and labor unrest provoked panic. Among those old enough to remember the Korean War, the chaos seemed eerily reminiscent of the late 1940s, when rival politicians and a radical labor movement vied for power after the U.S. occupation troops pulled out in 1949. That period of political chaos had, of course, been violently cut short by the North Korean invasion in June 1950. Little more than a decade later, the Second Republic dissolved in demonstrations and disorder before Park Chung Hee took power in 1961.

In 1980, the hard-line camp in the government was strengthened by Chun's self-appointment as acting director of the KCIA on April 14. Chun had previously shunned public roles, but by the spring he had solidified his position enough that he felt confident with this high-profile job, although he still headed the secretive Defense Security Command. The control of both military and civilian forces was in his hands. Chun's holding of two jobs was unconstitutional, since a military officer was not supposed to hold a civilian post, but even in the best of times those who hold power in Korea are rarely checked on constitutional grounds.

Even civilians inside the government claim not to have known that the Seoul spring of democracy was doomed even before the blossoms opened on the capital's forsythia bushes and cherry trees. "We didn't see the nature of [the December 12] incident," says Lee Hahn Been, who at the time was deputy prime minister for economic affairs. "In fact, until General Chun combined that post [as head of the Defense Security Command] with the CIA there was no indication whatsoever that the military had any intention or capacity to intervene into policy-making on economic affairs."

In a speech in San Francisco on February 15, 1980, Lee alluded to the "unfortunate incident of December 12" and said, "The important point is not that the incident occurred but that its occurrence did not affect the political and economic progress of Korea. Given the highly professional character of the present military leadership. . . . an incident of this sort is most unlikely to recur in the future."[15]

Lee's high-profile trip to the United States was seen at the time as a message of support from the U.S. government for the South Korean civilian government and a warning to the military to keep its hands off civilian politics. Certainly, Lee could not have predicted the ferocity of the government's purges in the summer of 1980 nor the brutality of its troops in Kwangju, but in retrospect the technocrats seem naive. Apparently, they thought that they could make an alliance with the military, and that the military would allow them to run the economy and society pretty much as they liked. They did not especially like the military, but they thought they could work with it.

Protests continued to gather momentum as April rolled into May. The demonstrations of 1960–61 had been made up of only a few thousand people, but in May 1980 tens of thousands of people took to the streets.

The demonstrations were capped with a huge rally on May 15 when fifty thousand students gathered in front of Seoul Station. Then they marched toward the city center. Journalist Ron Richardson described what in retrospect was a fateful demonstration:

> As soon as they began to move, human barriers of riot police were drawn up in their path; streets were cleared of traffic; sirens screaming, more than 50 armed personnel carriers roared into position around government buildings, and several companies of troops in battle dress set up roadblocks.
>
> In the fight that followed between the student vanguard and the front lines of police, the police held their ground despite everything the students hurled at them, including six commandeered city buses which were driven or rolled through their lines, killing one young officer and seriously injuring three others. With teargas, batons and a wall of shields, the police contained the demonstrators so they got nowhere near the soldiers. After two-and-a-half hours of confrontation, students and police had battled to a standstill, and could be seen shaking hands and exchanging greetings.[16]

Both the opposition and conservative political leaders worried that the situation was getting out of control and that continued confrontation could give the military a pretext for seizing complete control. Opposition figures and dissident leaders asked the students to halt the demonstrations. In exchange, on May 16 Kim Jong Pil publicly called for an end to martial law. Because he controlled the government faction in the National Assembly, the local press trumpeted this as a major breakthrough. The end of Yushin, which had been stalled in parliamentary bickering, was set for the end of May. Legislators would meet on May 20 to formally end martial law. Choi Kyu Hah cut short a trip to the Middle East and he was expected to announce the end of martial law on his return. But Chun ended the illusion that civilian politicians would take control of Korea's future.

Bloodshed in Kwangju

On May 17 one of the most extraordinary cabinet meetings in the nation's history took place at the capitol building behind Kwanghwamun. Arriving at the cabinet meeting, ministers were startled to find that Chun had stationed armed troops inside the halls of the building, in stiff formal positions, rifles at the ready.

There was no other coercion, for none was needed. The presence of the soldiers told those cabinet members what was coming. The entire cabinet meeting lasted just a few minutes, as Chun simply told the cabinet members that they were to acquiesce in his decision to impose martial law and that they would then resign.

Martial law began at midnight. However, just before eleven o'clock in the evening, in pre-emptive strikes an hour before the crackdown legally began, security agents raided the homes of ten men, including Kim Dae Jung, Kim Jong Pil, Lee Hu Rak, "Pistol" Park Chong Kyu, and Kim Chi Yol, the hard-line justice minister from the end of the Park regime. Kim Young Sam was, for some reason, not picked up, although he was put under house arrest.

All political activity was banned. Hundreds of activists around the country were rounded up by the military and security forces. All colleges and universities were closed, and newspapers, radio broadcasts, and other publications were censored.[17]

Radical students had prepared contingency plans in case of a military clampdown. Their plans included calls for protest rallies. Not surprisingly, when it became clear that the military was playing for keeps, most of these demonstrations on May 18 were poorly attended. Those would-be demonstrators who showed up were simply arrested as they assembled. In one city, however, demonstrators did manage to assemble in considerable numbers.

That city was Kwangju in South Cholla Province, and the events that followed left a permanent scar on Chun's Fifth Republic. The southwest had a long history of rebellion. As early as the seventh-century unification of Korea, Cholla was the center of the rival kingdom of Paekche, which triumphant Shilla forces subjugated with the help of Chinese troops. During the Japanese period it was the rice basket of Korea, and its fertile paddies supplied cheap grain to the Japanese urban poor through the port of Mokpo. In the 1940s and 1950s South Cholla was generally regarded as more radical than most of South Korea. The Communist military mutiny in 1948 in which Park Chung Hee took part started in the Cholla port town of Yosu, although government troops killed people throughout the province. The last Communist partisans in South Korea were captured on Mt. Chiri (straddling the Cholla-Kyongsang border) only in 1961, eight years after the armistice halted the Korean war.

South Cholla had been largely bypassed in the push to industrialize Korea during the 1960s and 1970s. The main Japanese-built rail line ran between Seoul and Pusan, in the southeast, as did the main highway that Hyundai built in the 1960s. In 1980 a diplomat who visited Mokpo described it with little exaggeration as the only Korean city that looked exactly as it had the day the Japanese left in 1945.

The neighboring province of South Kyongsang, by contrast, had been the center of the projects that had created a coastal crescent of industrialization running from the southeastern city of Pohang down along the coast to Masan. From the Posco steelworks to the massive Hyundai shipbuilding, auto, and engineering facilities in Ulsan to the bustling port of Pusan, to the Changwon industrial complex near Masan, and the city's Japanese-dominated free export zone, the southeast was a place of industry.

The people of South Cholla not surprisingly felt they had been discriminated against. This feeling was not simply paranoia. Throughout Korea there was a general mistrust of people from Cholla dating back for centuries. Cholla natives were said to be cleverer than most Koreans, but untrustworthy.

"Whenever we have a maid from Cholla, she will always steal something, no matter how small," said a woman office worker in Seoul in a characteristic remark. Said another woman, from the neighboring South Chungchong Province: "My brother said that if I married a man from Cholla no one from the family would go to the wedding but our mother. He also says that of every ten people who cheat him in business, nine are from Cholla." This regionalism is surprisingly common and casual even among well-educated Koreans. Samsung Chairman Lee Byung Chull made it a company policy for many years that no one from Cholla should be hired. Like Samsung, many other large chaebol had their origins in Kyongsang, while few businesses from Cholla joined the ranks of the largest groups.

Chun and the clique of Korea Military Academy officers who had seized power with him were not out to punish Cholla, but they decided to teach the country the dangers of defying martial law. The demonstrations in Kwangju were the first test for the military rulers, and they were dealt with ruthlessly. Chun shifted Special Warfare troops into the city. These were tough, elite soldiers who were trained to slip behind enemy lines and kill silently.

"It was a stupid policy to take guys who are trained to eat snakes and put them in charge of crowd control," a U.S. military analyst said later. These were the same units that had been used to brutally attack the demonstrators in Pusan and Masan, the attack that helped spur the fatal argument between Park Chung Hee and Kim Jae Kyu. The task of these special forces was not legitimate crowd control but intimidation. It went tragically wrong in Kwangju.

On Sunday and Monday several violent confrontations occurred between the troops and demonstrators. Reports of deaths spread, although most of the killings actually took place on Tuesday as troops withdrew. As darkness fell on Monday, demonstrators converged on television broadcasting offices in protest against false reports minimizing the extent of the confrontation and blaming demonstrators for the violence that had occurred. That evening the Munhwa Broadcasting Corporation (MBC) building was burned, and the next morning the state-owned Korea Broadcasting Service (KBS) office was also incinerated.

It was on Tuesday that things got really rough. Around two o'clock on May 20 about 300 paratroopers guarding the South Cholla provincial government building fired M–16s at demonstrators who tried to storm the building in a hijacked armored personnel carrier.

Journalist Shim Jae Hoon remembers that one of his sources in Kwangju had urged him by telephone to come down, saying that the situation was indescribable and that he had to see for himself. "Koreans always say that kind of thing, so I didn't think it was necessary to go down. But then I tried calling him the next day and the telephone lines were cut. You don't just cut the telephone lines unless something really serious is happening. So I rented a car and went to Kwangju."

What Shim saw was carnage of a sort that the country had not witnessed since the Korean War. Doctors and nurses said they had treated people who had died of bayonet wounds. A middle-aged government worker, who said he escaped a beating by troops only when he produced his identification papers, claimed to have seen a soldier rip open a young woman's blouse and slash her chest with a bayonet.

> A demonstrator who rammed his vehicle into the line killed or wounded seven soldiers. Whether it was before or after this assault that troops began firing on demonstrators is not clear, but scores of Kwangju citizens lay dead on the street as panicky soldiers shot their way clear of the crowd. After the paratroopers fled the city center, enraged demonstrators armed themselves with wooden staves, iron bars and pitchforks and raided the city's police station.[18]

Seventy buses were taken from the Kwangju Express bus company. A coal mine was raided, and dynamite stolen. Demonstrators commandeered armored personnel carriers, jeeps, and trucks from the Asia Motor Company. At 3:30 A.M. on May 27, after rebels controlled the city for a week, troops moved to retake Kwangju.

Following the crackle of gunfire and the heavy thud of mortar shells, the troops took control of the center of the rebellion. As the assault began, a young woman militant grabbed a loudspeaker and repeatedly shouted into the night, "All citizens and students of Kwangju, let's stand up and protect our lives and property." There was a crackle of M–16s and her voice was stilled. That ended the 10-day rebellion of Kwangju.[19]

After the siege ended, the city was shell-shocked, stunned that its own government had savagely turned on the people of the city, killing innocents like a middle-school boy who was on his way home from a bathhouse. Wrote Shim: "The streets remained empty with shaken citizens peering out of windows. Nothing like it had happened since the 1950–53 war. Burned vehicles lying by the roadside, and combat-ready troops everywhere told of the price Kwangju had paid for its antigovernment outburst."

Chun's violent path to power, capped by the bloody Kwangju incident, left a stain on the new administration, one that remained for the eight years of the Fifth Republic. It denied the country's new leader the popular legitimacy that he craved, and it helped push dissidents down an uncharted road of radicalism. No longer were antigovernment protesters mostly drawn from the ranks of university-educated civil rights advocates, as they had been in the 1970s. Liberalism and human rights had less appeal for a generation whose friends, colleagues, and comrades had been beaten, bayoneted, shot, and clubbed by their own government. The dissidents in the 1980s veered toward the socialist, nationalist, class-based struggle that the country's leaders had always feared. In trying to suppress dissent, Chun succeeded in creating a bitter cadre of radicals who would bedevil the government long after he left office.[20]

Notes

1. *Far Eastern Economic Review*, January 30, 1981.

2. He made the comment in testimony at the National Assembly on November 30, 1988.

3. Cheon Kum Sung, *Chun Doo Hwan, Man of Destiny*, p. 104.

4. National Assembly testimony, November 30, 1988.

5. He made this remark in a 1988 interview with John Gittlesohn, to whom I am grateful for passing it along.

6. *Newsweek*, January 21, 1980.

7. This paragraph is based on Kim Suk Jo and Edward J. Baker, "The Politics of Transition: Korea After Park," p. 6. Kim and Baker note that the head of the Defense Security Command, Kang Chang Song, was ousted shortly afterward. Lee Hu Rak himself fled to the Bahamas after being shot at, apparently by Park Chong Kyu, head of the Presidential Protective Service. By the late 1980s, however, he had returned to Seoul.

8. *Dong-A Ilbo*, November 2, 1988.

9. Cheon Kum Sung, *Chun Doo Hwan*, p. 5.

10. Korean superstition is not limited to family matters, for even high government and business officials regularly consult fortune-tellers. "It's not unusual for me to do a lot of detailed work on a client proposal and then have the client go and consult a fortune-teller," says a Western lawyer who has worked for many years in Seoul. "He will always take the fortune-teller's advice over mine."

11. Cheon Kum Sung, *Chun Doo Hwan*, pp. 56–66, on Chun's support for Park's coup.

12. *Far Eastern Economic Review*, January 14, 1980.

13. Cited in Donald Clark, ed., *The Kwangju Uprising*, p. 83, "Report on the Kwangju Incident to the National Assembly National Defense Committee, June 7, 1985," as reprinted from *Korea Herald*, June 9, 1985.

14. *Chosun Ilbo*, April 26, 1980.

15. *Far Eastern Economic Review*, February 29, 1980 and author inverview, February 1991.

16. *Far Eastern Economic Review*, May 23, 1980.

17. *Korea Annual*, 1981, p. 8.

18. *Far Eastern Economic Review*, May 30, 1980.

19. Ibid.

20. Sources for this chapter also include a series of articles in the *Far Eastern Economic Review* by John McBeth, January 12, 1989. Other sources are National Assembly testimony in November 1988, a U.S. State Department report on the incident published in 1989 and Clark, *The Kwangju Uprising*, as well as author interviews with U.S. officials and material provided by John Gittlesohn based on his interviews with numerous Korean officials.

12

Purification

Because of the phenomenal expansion of our society, traditional virtues, manners and moral dignity have faded away to be replaced by
rampant materialism resulting in irregularities, injustice, corruption
and mistrust. Unless these evils are erased, we cannot attain our true
integrity as a nation. . . . The current social reforms must be seen as
ground leveling, the first step in the construction of a society of
justice. A society of justice then would represent the revival of traditional values and the achievement of a moral ethic for a new age.
                                                    —Chun Doo Hwan[1]

For Park Kwon Sang, the 1980s looked as if they would be a decided improvement
over the repressive Yushin years. In 1973, government pressure had forced him out
as managing editor of the nation's most prestigious newspaper, *Dong-A Ilbo*. During
the political thaw that followed President Park Chung Hee's assassination, Park
Kwon Sang was rehabilitated, and he reached the pinnacle of Korean journalism
when he was named *Dong-A*'s editor-in-chief on January 1, 1980.

With Park Chung Hee dead, thousands of other intellectuals and politicians
who had been banned—or simply silent—during the 1970s were also able to
start speaking out, writing freely and engaging in political activities. It was a
heady time, a breath of fresh air after the dreary and dangerous Yushin years.
The night of the generals on December 12 had been unsettling, but the process of
political change was still moving forward.

By August, however, Park Kwon Sang was out of a job. "Chun came in and
kicked 717 journalists out," he remembers. Park was thrown into a political void
that even six years later left him unable to deliver a paper on the British parlia-

162

mentary system to a local meeting of the Korean-British Society out of fear that the subject was too politically charged.[2] What happened to Park Kwon Sang was replayed thousands of times across the country as former government officials and intellectuals were left to pick up the pieces of lives that were shattered by the military takeover.

For Chun and his band of rebels, as the spring of 1980 gave way to the summer monsoon season, there could be no turning back. The tragi-comic events of the December 12 incident, the imposition of martial law as events slipped out of control in the spring of 1980 and, finally, the bloodshed at Kwangju left Chun no choice but to push forward on the road to dictatorship. A misstep could have meant his ouster and, perhaps, his execution.

Chun faced a dilemma. To survive in power demanded nearly absolute political control, yet in order to strengthen his legitimacy as a ruler he needed to present himself as a revolutionary. He had to make at least a show of sweeping away the bitter remains of the Park era and reforming society and the economy.

In the immediate aftermath of the Kwangju killings, Chun and those around him groped for a way to legitimize their precarious political position. They were uncertain about what relationship they should pursue with the nominal head of state, President Choi Kyu Hah, and unsure how to reach an accommodation with the constituent power groups of Korea, Inc.—the bureaucrats, businessmen, and technocrats who ran the economy.

There were striking parallels with Park Chung Hee's May 16, 1961 coup. In 1961, President Yun Po Sun had remained in power for several months after the coup, but real authority had passed to a Supreme Council for National Reconstruction three days after the coup.

Chun followed a similar pattern of allowing a civilian president to retain nominal authority for a time while he quietly controlled most important policy decisions. Chun became acting president only in September 1980. Like Park, he also set up a quasi-revolutionary body to bypass the normal bureaucracy during this period. On May 31, 1980, Chun formed the Special Committee for National Security Measures (SCNSM). The committee's ostensible role was to act as an advisory body to President Choi and to coordinate policies between civilian and military agencies. Although the committee included twenty-six members (nine civilians and seventeen military), real power rested with a thirty-man standing committee made up of eighteen military officers and twelve government officials. To signal the special committee's importance, Chun stepped down from his controversial post as head of the KCIA to devote himself full-time to this new body.

By early 1980 Korea was a society in turmoil, one in which the old constraints of the Park era were breaking down. Chun's imposition of martial law in May ended political debate, but it had done nothing to win him legitimacy. So he turned to that old twisted standby: purification.

The purification ritual that Chun undertook during the summer of 1980 was partly a clever public relations campaign capitalizing on the Korean public's disaffection for politicians and bureaucrats, and partly an expression of genuine hatred on the part of the young colonels around Chun for those they perceived to be corrupt voluptuaries. Purges, as any good Confucian rebel knows, are the easiest way to eliminate one's seniors. The young officers, many of them from the country, could neatly do away with opponents of all stripes. For all the talk about corruption, the main victims were teachers, journalists, students, labor activists, and church leaders. "The purges were a way of shifting power to a new generation, but they were also about class," says Park Kwon Sang. "Who was Park Chung Hee? Who was Chun Doo Hwan? They were not only from poor families, but the poorest. In England officers are from rich families. In this country, [they come from poor backgrounds and] even generals inherently resent rich people."

Purge

On June 13, the Special Committee inaugurated its purification campaign with a nine-point guideline promising to "purge impure elements," "rectify amoral business activities," and "purify the nation by rooting out various social vices." Students of Chinese purges, from both the pre-Communist and Communist periods, will find the tone of this extraordinary document familiar. The June purification measures were an atavistic response to the tumult of rapid social and economic development. Part exhortation, part morality play, they reflected Korea's inability to develop new ways of dealing with the tensions inherent in its own hyperactive development process.

Purification started in earnest with an attack on corrupt officials. On June 18, the martial law commander charged that nine politicians and former government officials, including Park Chung Hee ally Kim Jong Pil, had illegally amassed almost $150 million (85 billion won) while in office. Even for cynical Koreans, the seized assets represented an incredible amount. KCIA founder and former Prime Minister Kim Jong Pil was said to have more than $36 million in real estate, including a 5,000-acre tangerine orchard on the southern island of Cheju, a 2,100-head dairy farm in the central province of Chungchong, and a newspaper company in Seoul. Kim also had over $7 million in thirty-four secret bank accounts in Seoul and a stash of antiques and jewelry that contained a 1.1 kilogram gold sword. Kim also purportedly confessed to collecting $2.5 million in political donations and "cooperation fees" from forty-one companies over the previous seventeen years.

Former KCIA head Lee Hu Rak allegedly had $32 million in assets, garnered from various contributions and leveraged with a good deal of successful real estate speculation—much of it apparently trading on inside knowledge. Former army chief of staff Lee Se Ho had a $18.5 million fortune, some of it gained through embezzling government funds while he commanded South Korean troops in Vietnam.

The martial law commander's anticorruption announcement listing the guilty was a who's who of the well-connected. Former Deputy Speaker of the National Assembly Kim Chin Man had $17 million in assets; Kim Jong Pil's brother (Kim Jong Nak), $15 million; presidential bodyguard "Pistol" Park Chong Kyu (who would later be implicated in an apparent multimillion-dollar payoff by Northrop), $12.8 million; a former prime ministerial aide, Lee Pyong Hi, $4 million; presidential economic secretary Oh Won Chol, $3.5 million; and Chang Tong Un, the director of the government housing corporation, $1.8 million. The government said that in exchange for not going to jail the men had agreed to turn their assets over to the state.[3]

The antigraft announcements implicated men at the top of the government. Three subsequent purges in July affected the entire government and spilled over into part of the private sector. First, on July 9, 232 senior officials—12 percent of the top echelon—were sacked. On July 15, 4,760 lower-ranking officials were dismissed. One week later, on July 22, 1,819 officials from banks and state-run corporations were fired.[4] The toll included one cabinet minister, six deputy ministers, five administrators, and three provincial governors. Determined to outdo Park Chung Hee's 1961 cleansing, the government billed the extravaganza as the biggest purge since the founding of the country in 1948. The first government body to fire employees was the KCIA, which shed 300 members for "incompetence, corruption, a lethargic attitude and tendency to promote personal greed."[5] Lawyers, pharmacists, and accountants were also purged in the same period, with those who were ousted derided as persons of status who had abused their positions in the constellation of Korean society.

Like many of the events of the early Chun years, the impact of this brutal housecleaning was mixed. The good, the bad, and the unlucky were tossed together in the upheaval. Some of those purged were notoriously corrupt, others were political opponents of the regime, and yet others were unfortunate enough to be fingered for minor breaches of social codes such as the one prohibiting luxurious weddings.

The randomness of the process sent shivers through the bureaucracy. "Today, in the economic planning, finance, commerce and industry and other ministries, officials can be seen nervously sifting through papers, intent only on knowing who is leaving and who is staying," journalist Shim Jae Hoon noted during that dismal, confusing summer.

One of those caught up in the purge was Cho Sung Il. Cho, who was director general of the national physical planning bureau at the Ministry of Construction, one of the most powerful officials in the country. "I could decide that a factory should go here"—he gestures with his finger—"or there and I controlled the population of Seoul." Cho, who was posted to the National War College when Chun took power, knew "something fishy" was up when he was asked to come to the ministry and submit his resignation.

> The Minister of Construction wanted to see me. Everyone had submitted a resignation to give him a free hand. I asked if my name was on the list and was told it was. I had a personal enemy in the bureaucracy [who was competing

166 • TROUBLED TIGER

with me to become minister]. He thought that if I were promoted it would hurt his chances. He put my name in with his own handwriting. At first, I got my name removed from the list [of purged people]. The martial law command intervened [because of my contacts there] and it was canceled. I had been an instructor at Fort Benning [Georgia] for Korean officers and I had many influential friends. Then my enemy intervened again and insisted that if an exception were made for me that the whole [purge] would fail.[6]

In one ministry, junior officials wrote protests against the dismissal of a colleague for a minor breach of the wedding code, stating that they had all committed the same offense and should all be dismissed. A ban on luxurious weddings had been imposed by Park Chung Hee in an attempt to reduce conspicuous consumption, but it was generally disregarded by the affluent, the very people at whom it was aimed. The Family Code, as it was called, forbade weddings in hotels, wedding gifts, engraved wedding invitations, and even traditional Korean ceremonies. Typically, these sorts of minor transgressions were used as a stick when it came time to mete out punishment for one campaign or another. This practice of having numerous laws on the book but enforcing them only rarely or punitively is characteristic of a country in which the rule of law had virtually no meaning.[7]

Some organizations caught in the purges found themselves up against quotas. In one research institute the director reportedly decided to purge one of his brightest young staff members. The man was single and talented and thus, the director told him, would be able to find another job easily. This arbitrary weeding-out process naturally unnerved and demoralized bureaucrats.

The campaign was intense enough that the World Bank worried about the purge's effect on government competence. The bank estimated that 10 percent of Korea's senior and 5,000 junior civil servants had been weeded out. A confidential report fretted that "the state bureaucracy has lost a sizable fraction of its most experienced decision-makers and the gap created may not be effectively filled from below . . . [while] . . . thousands of discharged officials could covertly feed public resentment of authoritarianism and military rule."[8]

On July 24, 1980, the SCNSM promoted all officials handling civil petitions and doubled their pay. A hiring freeze that had been put in place was lifted, and all agencies dealing with the public received permission to hire the staff they needed.

Six days later the Special Committee, stretching the definition of national security, prohibited cram classes for students trying to pass the university entrance exam. The competition to pass this exam was extremely intense, and tutoring naturally favored the wealthy. This prohibition on private tutoring is one of the best examples of Chun's attempts to pander to the reflexive egalitarianism that periodically appears in Korean politics. The effect was simply to increase the price of tutoring by driving it underground.

Universities were at the same time allowed to increase the number of admissions by 30 percent, opening up more entrance places. For the first time, however, universities also were required to fail 30 percent of students. Until 1980, entering university had required day-and-night study for months or even years. But, it was almost unheard of for a student once accepted not to graduate, unless dismissed for political activism.

In August, a more insidious phase of the purification campaign began, one that targeted dissidents and labor activists. On August 4, the Special Committee announced its Special Measures to Eliminate Social Evils as part of "a pan-national social purification movement." The measures were, in the words of the committee, intended "to root out all social evils at their sources and reshape the consciousness of the people so as to help build up a bright and just society in the belief that such a just society cannot be built without eliminating the cancerous elements in our society."[9]

It was a campaign that left another dark stain on the legacy of Chun's Fifth Republic, for many of those rounded up were put in brutal re-education camps, where at least fifty people died. After Chun left office in 1988, the Defense Ministry released documents acknowledging that the dead included thirteen victims of "sudden external shock." A provincial reporter told of being held in a dark cell the size of a rice basket for two days after he complained about the camp. He also wrote of seeing an inmate killed by army officers after being tied to the back of a jeep and dragged around the camp compound.

In all, 57,561 offenders were picked up for martial law scrutiny as part of the August purification drive. Of those, 3,052 were brought to trial at a military court, 38,259 were sent to purification camps, and the rest set free with warnings.[10]

The media was also purged and pruned in what was termed, in typical Confucian style, "self-renovation." In reality, this attack on the press was little more than a way of destroying one of the few remaining sources of opposition to the heavy-handed control Chun and his military colleagues were imposing on the country. At the beginning of August, the Special Committee announced that it had canceled the registration of 172 weekly and monthly publications because they were "obscene, vulgar, [or] instigating social confusion and creating a mood of class consciousness."[11] In November, the number of newspapers was cut, as publications were forced to close or merge. New restrictions forbid Seoul-based papers from stationing correspondents in the provinces or provincial ones from putting correspondents in the capital. About eighty magazines were closed down. The two major news agency services, Hapdong News Agency and Orient Press, were merged into the Yonhap News Agency, and this agency absorbed five minor news agencies to form a single wire service controlled by the government.[12] About all that was left of Korea's press were sports and women's papers and magazines.

The military administration was even more ruthless in its neutering of the electronic media. Dong-A Broadcasting, a private commercial radio station owned by the *Dong-A Ilbo* newspaper, was merged with the state broadcasting station. The influential Christian Broadcasting Station was forced to limit itself to religious broadcasting and refrain from news or other commentary.

Samsung founder Lee Byung Chull was ordered to give up his Tongyang Broadcasting Corporation (TBC) television network. He received only token compensation. Shareholders in the third television network, Munhwa Broadcasting Corporation (MBC), also had to surrender their shares to the state for only a token payment. These confiscations gave the government complete control over all television broadcasting.

Kim Dae Jung's Trial

Kim Dae Jung still walks with a limp, a reminder of a head-on collision when a truck smashed into his car during the 1971 presidential campaign. That, Kim believes, was the first government attempt to kill him. His 1973 abduction from a Tokyo hotel described earlier was the second. A Catholic, Kim has a martyr's fatalistic certainty that what he is doing is right. He had outlived Park Chung Hee, but in 1980 he had another brush with death at the hands of the government.

Like Park Chung Hee, Chun and his cronies worried more about Kim Dae Jung than any other opponent. Arrested an hour before martial law went into effect in May, Kim was charged on trumped-up national security charges in August. Some of the charges dated back to his activities in Japan in 1973, where he allegedly founded an antistate organization before he was abducted and nearly killed by the KCIA. The government also charged Kim with sedition, claiming he had organized the Kwangju uprising. This charge was a bit baffling considering that Kim was safely in the hands of the KCIA at the time, but that did not stop the government from hauling him into court after more than two months of confinement.

Shim Jae Hoon reported on the trial:

> Kim's usual verve and self-confidence were missing. Nearly three months of detention by the martial law authorities had exacted a toll. He appeared emaciated, and his cheekbones stood out on his pallid face. His eyes were sunken. Kim appeared so weak that he was allowed to testify seated, contrary to Korean custom. Two armed military policemen flanked him constantly.[13]

Kim, who claimed that he was stripped and tortured during his two months in detention, delivered a credible defense but was nonetheless sentenced to death after this show trial. However, if Chun thought that he could do away with Kim easily, he miscalculated. Protests came in from not only the United States and Japan, but governments and human rights organizations around the world. Spain, Greece, Australia, West Germany, and Sweden all condemned the sentence. Formal protests came from countries accounting for more than 70 percent of Korea's export markets, a more potent form of pressure than the United States—with its extensive security commitments—could muster alone. Shim Jae Hoon caustically noted that "the sentence has, within weeks, earned Chun a reputation as an oppressor which it took the late Park Chung Hee more than 10 years to acquire."[14]

It was not an idle threat to kill Kim. More than ten years later, Kim Dae Jung said—and U.S. officials involved with his case agree—that the military was deadly serious about doing away with its most dangerous opponent. "At that time, the generals thought it would be impossible for them to stay in power while keeping me alive," he contended. "They were intent on killing me." Kim said he was visited three times in the KCIA jail by a Chun subordinate, Lee Hak Bong (later a legislator in the National Assembly), who was also heading the sensitive investigation into Park Chung Hee's murder. "He said, 'You must cooperate with us or we will kill you. If you cooperate with us you can have anything you want except the presidency. If you refuse we will have no alternative but to eliminate you.' "[15]

But the protests had their effect. U.S. warnings that North Korea was readying a major propaganda offensive to take advantage of Kim's execution helped convince Chun to relent. But in the end, the United States traded a Washington visit for Chun Doo Hwan for Kim Dae Jung's life. Chun was the first head of state to meet Ronald Reagan after the new U.S. president took office in 1981. The new Korean president used the visit for maximum domestic political advantage, demonstrating to Koreans that he had the solid backing of Washington. This willingness to bolster Chun's standing at home would come back to haunt the United States.

Chun and South Korea would need all the support they could get, for 1980 was not only a tumultuous political year, it was also an economic disaster. The problems of domestic inflation and overinvestment were exacerbated by a world economy plunging into recession. Chun's first year of power would be the first time since before Park Chung Hee had taken power that the economy contracted. Korea's businessmen, bureaucrats, and generals would have their collective wits tested by an unprecedented economic downturn.

Notes

1. Quoted in *Asian Wall Street Journal*, August 26, 1980.
2. Harassment by the police prevented Park from giving his speech as scheduled in the spring of 1987; only in March 1988, after Roh Tae Woo took office, was Park able to discuss the mechanism of British parliamentary democracy. His remarks in this chapter come from a November 1991 author interview.
3. *Far Eastern Economic Review*, July 4, 1980, is the source for all data except the size of the tangerine orchard and the number of cattle, which are from an interview with Kim Jong Pil that appeared in *Newsweek*, December 17, 1979.
4. *Far Eastern Economic Review*, July 9, July 22, August 1, 1980.
5. *Korea Herald*, June 21, 1980; *Asian Wall Street Journal*, August 5, 1980, says about 8,667 government officials were dismissed.
6. Cho claims that he was "a very clean official. I wanted to stay clean until I became minister. After I became minister, well . . ." After Chun's downfall, Cho waged a success-

ful campaign to win an apology and compensation from the government for those who had been purged. Cho's story is based primarily on a January 1992 author interview.

7. A more recent example came in 1992, when an acquaintance's father died. Following local custom, the family paid to put a death notice in one of the country's largest newspapers, which every day runs scores of similar advertisements. The newspaper accepted the money and ran the notice. A few weeks later the family was contacted by the police, who informed them that the advertisement was illegal because it contravened the Family Code, and that they would have to pay a fine of several hundred dollars, negotiable according to the family's means. The family paid. The newspaper kept running the advertisements. And the police presumably kept shaking down the bereaved.

8. *Asian Wall Street Journal*, December 12, 1980.

9. *Korea Annual* 1981, p. 26.

10. Ibid.; also *Far Eastern Economic Review*, October 26, 1988. These numbers are slightly different from those released by the Ministry of National Defense, on September 30, 1988, and published in local newspapers on October 1, 1988.

11. *Asian Wall Street Journal*, August 2, 1980.

12. *Asian Wall Street Journal*, November 15, 1980; *Korea Annual* 1981, pp. 36–38.

13. *Far Eastern Economic Review*, August 29, 1980, pp. 15–16.

14. *Far Eastern Economic Review*, September 26, 1980.

15. Author interview, December 1991.

13

The Crunch

> The dilemma for [foreign] investors is that opportunity knocks now—but no one really knows whether the place is going to go down the tubes or not.
>
> —Anonymous U.S. businessman[1]

The year 1979 had not been a good one for bankers sitting in New York, London, Washington, and Tokyo. Park Chung Hee's October assassination had preceded the seizure of the U.S. embassy in Iran by only a few days. In Nicaragua, the Somoza family had been unseated by a popular revolution just a few months earlier. A putsch by young officers heightened the tension in neighboring El Salvador. Jittery lenders naturally worried that a tide of retribution and revolution was going to sweep away some of their biggest clients. Odd though it seems now, South Korea was high on their worry list. Deputy Prime Minister Lee Hahn Been conceded that bankers feared that South Korea "would become another Iran without Ayatollah Khomeini."[2]

The U.S. Federal Reserve sounded the warning bells on January 25, 1980, at a luncheon meeting attended by senior staff and major U.S. bankers. The Fed, although concerned about third world debt in general, singled out Korea as a country where bankers should tread cautiously. The Fed cited Korea's current account deficit, which was expected to widen to $5 billion in 1980, its dim prospects for exports, and the risk of increased domestic political instability as reasons for urging bankers to be wary of making new loans. The U.S. central bank also noted that a recent CIA report had warned that some sort of North Korean provocation was possible, given the uncertain domestic political situation after Park's death.

"You questioned Korea," remembers banker Alan Plumb. "You didn't have anything to fall back on. It was the first time industrialization had faltered. If there had been an economic downturn and Park Chung Hee was still running the place it would have been different, but you had political turmoil and the economic downturn. All you could fall back on was talk about the Korean people and their will to survive."[3]

The slain president's recipe of high growth, high inflation, and political repression would be tested in the aftermath of his death, as the ties that bound Korea, Inc. unraveled. His assassination came at the worst time for policymakers, just as they were trying to implement a stabilization program designed to right the excesses of the big push into heavy industry.

In the immediate aftermath of Park's death, as the country's political future remained uncertain, economic policy drifted. However, even as Chun Doo Hwan and Roh Tae Woo were plotting their December 12 takeover, a civilian cabinet was formed that, in its brief five-month tenure, would put a tremendous imprint on the economy. But if Park's death gave the new cabinet more freedom to act, the increasing skittishness of international bankers and the International Monetary Fund made it imperative that they move boldly.

In January 1980, less than three months after Park's assassination, Korea's mandarins adopted a form of textbook economic shock therapy. Alarmed by surging trade deficits and soaring inflation, they responded by holding down money supply growth and jacking up interest rates.

The shock policies started under interim President Choi Kyu Hah. When Chun Doo Hwan took power and dismissed the civilian cabinet later that year, he continued these orthodox economic policies. While economic development was not on Chun's original agenda, a series of intensive economic tutoring sessions convinced Chun that if he squandered Park's legacy of economic growth he would not survive. But rather than attempting to copy the grandiose forced-march development of the Park years, Kim Jae Ik and Chun's other economic advisers persuaded the new president that he had to restructure the economy. The excesses of the high-growth, high-inflation 1970s would be squeezed out and the foundation laid for what advisers called "the second take-off."

However, although the economic record of his administration was in many respects laudable, Chun never won the legitimacy he sought through economic growth. Because of his bloody seizure of power, as well as his inability to make a clean break when it came time for him to step down, Chun could rule only by increasing coercion to levels that ultimately proved unacceptable to business, labor, and the country as a whole. Although the policies pursued under Chun's Fifth Republic were very different from those under Park, and Chun gave the technocrats far more control than Park had, this tension between economic growth and political legitimacy remained.

The Bulletproof Cabinet

On December 14, 1979, only two days after the 12–12 incident, a new cabinet was appointed. Koreans called it the "bulletproof cabinet," a sardonic reference to the ministers' ability to survive the young generals' assault. Unwittingly or not, the new ministers served to camouflage Chun's consolidation of power in the spring of 1980 by boldly restructuring the economy without any overt interference from the military. Made up of respected technocrats, this cabinet, and the ones that followed it, were to have far more say over economic policy than their peers had enjoyed under Park Chung Hee. Such freedom reflected Chun's recognition of his own ignorance as well as the need for a buffer against jittery international creditors.

In terms of economic policy, this cabinet was one of the most knowledgeable ever assembled in Korea. Incoming Prime Minister Shin Hyon Hwak, who had tried to slow the economy down after he was named deputy prime minister for economic affairs at the end of 1978, had first been appointed to the cabinet in 1959. Experienced enough to command authority, he was nonetheless willing to listen to the young Turk technocrats at the Economic Planning Board.

The new deputy prime minister, replacing Shin Hyon Hwak, was Lee Hahn Been, head of the Aju Technical Institute. In 1951 Lee had been the first Korean to graduate from Harvard's MBA program. Having served under Syngman Rhee, Chang Myon, and Park Chung Hee, Lee was also the first bureaucrat to work his way up from the very bottom of the civil service ranks to become its chief economic policymaker. To foreigners, he was one of the best-known of the new, Western-educated technocrats whom U.S. advisers and expatriate businessmen were so fond of.

A scholar, Lee had studied the development of the Korean bureaucracy in his book *Korea: Time, Change and Administration*. Thus the deputy prime minister's post was a particularly apt appointment for the balding man with round black glasses who looked more like a professor than a powerful economic official. The new minister of trade and industry was Chong Chae Sok, formerly president of the Korea International Economic Institute, a government think tank specializing in luring overseas Korean academics back home and slotting them into influential positions in government or business. The extremely able Kim Won Gie, formerly governor of the Korea Development Bank, remained as minister of finance. Kim Ok Kil, president of the prestigious Ewha Women's University, became minister of education. She was only the third woman ever named a minister in Korea, and the first since the 1940s. Although Kim had little power, she helped confirm the general public impression that this was a cabinet whose members had solid credentials and were well-trained in their fields.[4]

The new cabinet also made a nod in the direction of Korea's sizable Christian community. "Mr. Shin approached Kim Ok Kil and me at the same time," Lee

Hahn Been said in an interview eleven years later. "He told me that the coopera-tion of the two of us was of the highest importance from his point of view. We were both in academia. We were both from the Protestant Christian Church. It seems that [this combination of scholarship and Christianity] was recognized as an important source of support for the civilian government."[5]

Ironically, Shin's approaches to Lee Hahn Been and Kim Ok Kil took place only hours before Chun's coup began.

> This so-called 12–12 incident occurred during the formation of the Cabinet. I was approached on the afternoon of the twelfth. I didn't know, [Prime Minister Shin] didn't know, and Kim Ok Kil didn't know [that the military was plotting a takeover]. This was a bona fide civilian offer given by Prime Minister Shin and President Choi. The two had to wrestle with that 12–12 problem while forming the cabinet. On their part it must have been very painful. They were very well-meaning people, trying to form a genuinely civilian cabinet. . . . We didn't see the nature of that incident. In fact, until General Chun combined that post with the CIA there was no indication whatsoever that the military had any intention or capacity to intervene into policy-making on economic affairs.[6]

The separation of civilian and military power, the naïveté of the civilians, and the ultimate ability of the technocrats to work with the military are all characteristic of the internal dynamics of the Korean state.[7] So, too, was the unwillingness or inability of most Koreans to confront the military, to imagine that a coup could fail, or to boycott a military-dominated government.

The new cabinet had the unenviable job of restoring the country's credibility among international lenders by squeezing the excesses out of an economy that had grown fat on inflation and an overvalued currency.

The new cabinet quickly set to work pulling together an economic shock package at the end of 1979 and the beginning of 1980. The policies announced beginning January 12, 1980, were a radical challenge to business as usual. Bank interest rates rose five to six percentage points. The interest rate for ordinary bank loans, for example, jumped from 19 percent to 25 percent. Petroleum prices increased 60 percent, on top of a 50 percent increase the previous summer. The won was sharply devalued by nearly 20 percent, to 580 won to the dollar. It was the first devaluation since 1975, in spite of inflation that consistently ran over 20 percent a year.[8]

Everyone could see that the exchange rate of the won had been out of touch with reality and that Korea was pricing itself out of export markets. No one had dared to raise this issue with the late president, because Park Chung Hee increas-ingly had equated a strong won with a strong Korea. Devaluing the won would be a sign of weakness, Park thought, even if it reflected competitive realities.

Deputy Prime Minister Lee Hahn Been and his economic team set up a system to allow the currency to float, although it remained loosely pegged to the dollar. This exchange rate was set every day by a small committee in the Bank of

Korea using a basket of currencies as a guide. This apparently technical set of adjustments was to have a dramatic impact on Korea's exports as the decade progressed, permitting Korea to adjust to the shocks of the 1980s very successfully. Maintaining a link to the dollar was also critical in powering Korean exports in the second half of the decade as the dollar slumped against the Japanese yen.

The new cabinet had, however, no unified view on interest rates, the second major policy dilemma. Those who had supported the tight money, monetarist approach in 1979 now insisted that the interest rate structure be overhauled. They argued that a combination of high inflation and controlled domestic interest rates discouraged savers. The real interest rate, after accounting for inflation, was often negative, so potential savers were more inclined to spend their money than to put it in the bank, where it could be channeled to industrial growth.[9] Although credit was always tight, for businesses that could get loans this was a great system because it allowed them to borrow money cheaply. Favored businesses could simply keep expanding. Profits, never of overriding importance in Korea, could remain firmly subservient to growth.

The combination of floating exchange rates and the substantial jump in interest rates was the most radical economic measure since Park had tried to do away with the curb market in 1972. Borrowers, who had counted on inflation to allow them to raise prices and make their interest payments, were hit hard. Foreign borrowing costs rose because of the won devaluation. Domestic borrowing costs rose as a result of the interest rate reform.

"It was as radical as any [reform programs] we hear about these days, the Polish one or anything else," said Lee Hahn Been.

> I became very unpopular in the National Assembly, [questioned] nightly by television networks and tormented by businessmen and housewives for having raised the exchange rate, wiped out fertilizer subsidies, raised the gasoline price, coal prices, and bank interest rates. The only place I got approbation was at the IMF and the IBRD [World Bank].[10]

This was not simply an academic exercise, for South Korea badly needed money to span the widening gap between imports and exports as well as to pay interest on existing loans. The political uncertainty following Park's assassination and the December 12 putsch simply heightened international lenders' nervousness.

In mid-February, Lee Hahn Been took his show on the road, stumping U.S. financial centers in an effort to generate support for a $300 million loan by the state-owned Korea Exchange Bank. Reporting on Lee's trip, a correspondent in Washington, who had apparently been briefed by U.S. Export-Import Bank officials, said that political stability in Korea was the key to continued borrowing.

> Burned by the unforeseen events in Iran, bankers are now keenly aware of how political events can overwhelm economic factors. Should the present crop of Army officers be overthrown in yet another coup, private bank money to South Korea would quickly dry up unless some stability asserted itself.[11]

In Seoul, Alan Plumb remembers how chastened the Koreans were by the way the economy had turned against them. "What I remember about 1980 was the way that people who had started to show some arrogance in the late 1970s became much more humble. They adjusted to the true economic position. They needed foreign investment, foreign capital."[12]

Business reaction to the shock therapy was hostile. Every company faced a steep rise in interest rates, higher oil prices, and increased expenses for any imported goods. Korean companies had always relied on extremely rapid growth to keep their heavily leveraged companies from being crushed by the burden of interest rates. It was, for most Korean companies, like riding a bicycle. If they could not keep moving forward, they would topple over. Daewoo, for example, did not pay many of its managers their salaries for months on end. When it came time to pay out regular bonuses—which are a set part of the salary structure—the company handed out vouchers that could be used to buy Daewoo-manufactured television sets and other appliances instead of cash.

Clearly, an economic contraction, or even a severe slowdown, could bring many of these over-leveraged multibillion-dollar organizations crashing down. However, Lee Hahn Been and his team were willing to take that risk. Devaluation, higher fuel prices, and higher interest rates meant, as Lee said, that "we were tripling their burden at one stroke."[13]

These radical policies were possible only because of an unusual convergence of personalities. After taking over as deputy prime minister in December 1978, Shin Hyon Hwak had forged close bonds with some leading younger policymakers and technocrats. Prime among them were Kim Jae Ik and Kang Kyong Shik at the Economic Planning Board and Kim Mahn Je, who headed the Korea Development Institute.

These younger officials had mostly been insiders during the period of rapid expansion in the 1970s. They were all professionally trained, and they were aware of the promise and the perils of the high-growth, heavy industrial strategy. They also knew what needed to be done at this time of crisis, and they had the backing of Shin Hyon Hwak, Lee Hahn Been, and, through them, President Choi, to take whatever action was necessary.

Lee Hahn Been viewed this combination of old boy network and professional expertise as the key to carrying Korea through this time of crisis.

> This is the beauty of the Korean technocracy. This pool of wisdom was there [throughout the government], headed by a few principals who appreciated them and who, out of academic or professional background, shared a community of views. At the political level and the bureaucratic level there was a convergence. . . . This tight professional consensus between Deputy Prime Minister, Prime Minister, and major staff, [most of whom had worked together before], as well as the nature of the crisis, helped us. Unless there was a crisis the business community and the parliament would not have gone along with it.[14]

Although companies initially suffered because of higher repayment costs for overseas and domestic loans, the best of them made up the difference—and much more—in terms of increased exports. Devaluation was particularly helpful to textile companies and light industrial manufacturers of products such as shoes and toys that had lost their international competitiveness in the late 1970s. The change in currency value encouraged companies to pay more attention to exports again. The results were dramatic.

In 1979, Hyundai Corporation had total exports of $493 million, yet in the otherwise depressed year of 1980 Hyundai's exports more than doubled to $1.028 billion. Samsung's exports surged from $772 million to $1.23 billion. State-owned steelmaker Posco, which was not even among the country's top 100 exporters in 1979, became the sixth-largest exporter in 1980. Total exports rose 16 percent in 1980, but large groups took a disproportionate share of the gains. The automatic access to export finance enjoyed by their general trading companies helped immeasurably in the tight credit environment.

The January package marked a significant milestone in the development of Korea's economy. The economic shock therapy signaled the independence of the technocrats and bureaucrats in setting macroeconomic policy. "I had no political ambition or intention to run for election," said Lee Hahn Been later. "I was merely acting as a professional technocrat. . . . Had I been a politician I would not have dared." Whatever political interference there might be in micro-matters, the fundamental macroeconomic decisions were now in the hands of professionals. This was to be a key feature for much of the Fifth Republic, often to the dismay of business.

The bulletproof cabinet proved not to be so. Cowed by the rifle muzzles leveled at them as they walked into one of Korea's shortest cabinet meetings, ministers heard without protest Chun Doo Hwan's statement that they would submit their resignations and that martial law would be imposed at midnight on May 17, 1980. No threats were made, but none were needed. It was, as one of the ministers dryly put it, "intimidating atmospherics."[15]

Turning to the Economists

Early in 1980 Kim Jae Ik, the director general of the Economic Planning Board's planning bureau, was summoned to the Yonhui-dong residence of Chun Doo Hwan. He went with some trepidation, but an invitation from the two-star head of the Defense Security Command was not one that he could have refused. This meeting was the start of an extraordinary alliance between a technocrat and a general, one that was to have a powerful impact on the direction of the Korean economy in the 1980s.

Kim Jae Ik's widow, Lee Soon Ja, remembers when the invitation was extended to her husband:

I was so scared. The military was not popular. We were afraid and we were so scared that those people might do something terrible to the country. They were so powerful. If you said "no," you didn't know what they would do.

We didn't know who Chun was. We hadn't seen him before. We saw generals at big government receptions or government gatherings. But Chun as an intelligence officer didn't appear at those kinds of public things.

[We don't know how Chun found my husband.] He was lecturing to the generals' and colonels' seminars as the [Economic Planning Board's] planning director before Park's assassination. Maybe some of the young generals recommended to Chun Doo Hwan that Kim Jae Ik was the right person to consult on economic affairs. We don't have any connection to the military. We don't have any friends who are in the military.[16]

Kim Jae Ik had been born into a family of wealthy landowners in 1938. The youngest of nine children, he spent part of his childhood on his family's estate near Chonan, in South Chungchong Province, in the central part of what is now South Korea. It was a fertile area of the peninsula, and the Kims lived well, for they had owned large tracts of land there for generations. Kim Jae Ik's father had attended university in Japan, and he made sure that his children—his three daughters as well as his six sons—had access to the best schools in Korea. The family had a second home in Seoul, where Jae Ik, his mother, and his siblings spent most of their time.

Even the family's wealth and privilege could not protect it from the violent upheavals that followed the liberation, an upheaval that left almost no family untouched. Kim Jae Ik was in the sixth grade when the North invaded. His father was in Chonan and disappeared, probably murdered by the North for the "crime" of being a landowner. Three of his older brothers—one a teacher at Seoul National University and the other two students there—also vanished during the invasion. His family had already seen its wealth pared by the 1949 land reform. The war took almost everything that remained. Two of Kim's sisters, who had converted to Catholicism in the late 1940s, entered a convent; another became a social worker in New York City. His two surviving brothers went into business but with little success.

As a student, Kim Jae Ik wanted to become a scientist, but he was color-blind and thus, under South Korea's whimsical standards, was prohibited from studying natural science. Instead he went to Seoul National University's department of political science, one of the most prestigious in the country.[17]

After graduation, Kim Jae Ik finished first in the Bank of Korea's entrance exam, a notable accomplishment at a time when the brightest graduates in the country vied to join the government. He joined the research department at the Bank of Korea, which was also the government planning agency, and helped draft what became the first of Korea's five-year economic plans. Worried that he did not know enough to do proper economic analysis, he wanted to study abroad. But he could not afford even the $380 boat passage to the United States, much less schooling costs. In 1966, he won a fellowship to the East-West Center at the University of Hawaii, then moved on to Stanford, where he earned a Ph.D. in econometrics with work in simultaneous equation models.

Returning to Korea, he worked at the Blue House and then at the Economic Planning Board during the 1970s. As director general of economic planning, Kim had the unenviable job of overseeing the implementation of the fourth five-year plan, which stressed heavy industry. Although this plan was out of step with the free market gospel that Kim had learned in the United States, Park Chung Hee and his Blue House advisers were marching to a different drummer. In early 1979, near the end of Park's reign, Kim was a key member of the stabilization team that tried to lower monetary growth, suspend new projects in the heavy and chemical industry sector, lift price controls, and liberalize imports. The oil shock that year, which nearly doubled Korea's oil bill in the following twelve months, threatened these attempts at reform. Park's death simply erased them from the policy agenda.

When he met Chun for the first time, Kim Jae Ik had held his position as director general of the economic planning bureau of the Economic Planning Board for three years. The bureau was a key one in the government's most important economic ministry, and Kim, as director general, occupied the senior working-level position. During his stint as head of the planning bureau, his office had become the primary port of call for all manner of foreigners, from World Bank officials to businessmen of every caliber.

Foreigners liked Kim Jae Ik because of his clear-headed, no-nonsense approach to the Korean economy. Kim, after his return from Stanford, applied his considerable analytical abilities to simplifying economic issues in a way that surprised his contemporaries. Kim was fond of analyzing issues simply in terms of supply and demand, a concept that did not fit well with the visionary projects of Park Chung Hee and his nation-building enterprises of the 1960s and 1970s.

Kim's approach allowed him to arrive at solutions that were elegant and economically efficient. He prepared a flow chart of the Korean economy, which he used to illustrate points to foreign visitors. The points he stressed were ones that foreigners were often receptive to hearing.

For example, Korea Aluminum was an energy-intensive company that received enormous amounts of subsidized electricity from the state-owned electricity monopoly. Korea had to squander precious foreign currency to build electrical power stations for a high-cost aluminum producer that sold its output onto the local market at four times the world price. To Kim Jae Ik, Korea Aluminum was an example of economic irrationality that should be shut down. There was no talk from him of infant industries or the Korean need for self-reliance. Kim was even bold enough to talk privately of importing rice and letting the country's agricultural sector wither away, a policy that was anathema to the professed ideology of support for the rural sector. Such talk was refreshing, even if it did not lead to action under Park.

To Westerners, Kim embodied the dynamic technocracy that had been key to Korea's success. Among Koreans, however, he was not universally well-regarded. "Many people thought he was a traitor," remembers his widow, thanks to Kim's insistence that imports would be good for the economy because companies would be forced to improve their competitiveness. "Policymakers always thought that buying things from outside was a crime. They said we must [only] sell things." At the time, the country was so insular that his wife was not even allowed to accompany him on official trips abroad because of restrictions on travel designed to save foreign currency.

Park's assassination and the political uncertainty that followed left Kim adrift. The early months of 1980 found Kim Jae Ik "weary and demoralized," remembers his colleague Kim Ki Hwan. "In his view, not only had the stabilization program failed, but the political instability that followed President Park's assassination in 1979 threatened to undo the gains of almost two decades of hard-earned growth in the Korean economy."[18]

No one knew what would come next, politically or economically. Kim Ki Hwan remembers the uncertainty, coupled with fear that the Korean military could end up pursuing inward-looking policies as Burma's generals had done. "We thought the country could really go wrong," he said later.

This period was one of the most discouraging times of Kim Jae Ik's life, remembers Lee Soon Ja.

> After Park's assassination [Kim and the officials he worked with] were really confused. There were so many reforms they were planning to do. They didn't know what would come next. President Choi, if he had personal charisma, or personal power, or if he were smart, then our whole history would have been very different. He was so mediocre. No one thought he was president. He didn't do anything. He just sat there and didn't move.
>
> They all were so confused in the government because the president was so weak. Bureaucracy in Korea is so political. Bureaucracies in Japan or France are so strong that they are self-sustaining. [But here] it is so political. It just depends on who the president is. It was a vacuum.
>
> By [January] my husband was quite frustrated. He almost gave up being an economic planner and he was considering getting out of government and going to KDI [Korea Development Institute] or back to college to pursue his college career.

Then came the summons from Chun. This allowed Kim Jae Ik the chance that few economists ever have: to see his ideas translated into action, thanks to backing from a powerful political leader. His initial skepticism about Chun was quickly overcome. Lee Soon Ja explains:

> After he talked to Chun a few times, he decided to take on the challenge. When I asked him how Chun was, he said something like "it could have been worse." Chun was personally naive and admitted that he knew nothing about economics. [My husband] said [Chun] would follow his ideas.

He called him over to Yonhui-dong, to his private house, for informal consultations. For a couple of months my husband went to see Chun early in the morning, at 6 A.M. They had economic consultations; that is what they called the tutoring sessions. He went three or four times a week [until martial law was declared in May.]

It is hard to overstate the impact that the technocrats had on Chun, for they, along with the young colonels who helped him come to power and a handful of other advisers, convinced the new president to make economic success a corner-stone of his tenure. As result, Chun took an intense interest in the economy, engaging first Kim Jae Ik and later several other technocrats as tutors. Kim Ki Hwan was the most frequent tutor, but Sakong Il (later finance minister) and Suh Sang Chul (later energy minister) were also engaged for tutoring sessions. Kim Ki Hwan remembers Chun as a diligent student.

Considering his job, he was a rather serious student. In order to make the session productive I would prepare lecture notes. I would have the lecture notes printed in a hurry. I would send the lecture notes in the day before the session. Most of the sessions were early in the morning at 7 or 8. I would arrive at 7 or 7:30. We would start with a coffee. For most of the sessions he would have read the notes the night before.[19]

The technocrats had two themes they wanted to get across to Chun: price stability and market liberalization. They tried to keep things as simple as possible, remembers Kim Ki Hwan, an economics professor who had studied and taught at the University of California at Berkeley before returning to Korea in the mid-1970s.

We would try to make the concepts as simple as possible. To make the idea of market incentives understandable we would say, for example, "People waste things if they are given freely." He would jump in and say, "That was what I saw in the military. Soldiers waste supplies if they are simply given out." . . .
How did we convince him that stabilization was good? We used the experi-ence of Germany after World War I and the experience of the nationalist Chinese government during the end of World War II. We said that if you want [to maintain] political power you shouldn't have any inflation. Income distri-bution will deteriorate and if inflation continues the people who suffer the most will be those without the money to hedge against inflation. That argu-ment was very effective.[20]

A man who worked as a senior official at the Blue House under both Chun and Park remembers watching the new president struggling with economics.

What you had there was a raw mind if there ever was one, a *tabula rasa*. You don't expect a general who has been running a field army to know anything about economics. One thing that can be said for him is that he worked hard. He wanted to learn economics. He wanted to know what it was all about. "What is this M1? And you also have M2?" he would ask. "What is the difference?" He was a hard worker. He would take a lot of material with him when he went upstairs to his living area [at the Blue House]. It was quite obvious to us when he came back down the next day that he had read it all, almost like a student preparing for a final exam. The pace was really frantic. On the one hand you had to run the government and on the other you had to tutor the president. To Kim Jae Ik and to Kim Ki Hwan we really owe the economic success of the Chun era.[21]

Kim Jae Ik also reassured nervous foreign investors and lenders that the new Chun government would pursue reasonable economic policies. In the early 1980s, South Korea's $40 billion in foreign debt put it behind only Brazil, Mexico, and Argentina among the world's debtor nations. A foreign banker accompanying the bank's top executives on a visit to the Blue House shortly after Chun took office told a reporter, "When we walked in, we were surprised to see Kim Jae Ik. . . . We were delighted to see him there and we all relaxed."[22]

Chun gave Kim Jae Ik and the technocrats extraordinary freedom. After he became president, Chun told Kim Jae Ik, "You are the president of economic affairs." Because there was effectively no opposition, the technocrats could do what they wanted. While this allowed them to implement harsh policies without worrying too much about political resistance, this style of governing carried its costs. The government tried to convince people that its policies were correct, but this was another example of the sort of top-down evangelizing that ordinary Koreans were coming to distrust.

Kim Jae Ik and the economic team of the early Chun years had three basic goals. They wanted to cut the government deficit, limit monetary growth, and slow wage hikes. A budget freeze in 1983 succeeded in cutting the total government deficit as a percentage of GNP from 4.7 percent in 1981 to 1.4 percent in 1984. This was done largely by cutting subsidies to the country's dozens of state-invested corporations and reducing outlays for farmers and for the National Investment Fund (which supported the Heavy and Chemical Industries plan). As a result of these policies, by the late 1980s the government budget was comfortably in surplus.

Monetary policy was also tightened and interest rates raised. Broad monetary growth (M2) was squeezed from a lax 26.9 percent in 1980 to an extremely tight 7.7 percent in 1984. Companies that had depended on easy credit to finance their operations howled in pain.

The government also slammed the brakes on wage growth. Unions were effectively banned—a policy the technocrats let the security authorities carry out—and employers were pressured to keep wages low. Nominal wages grew 22.7 percent in 1980 (after growing more than 30 percent a year from 1976 to 1978), but that rate decelerated quickly. From 1984 through 1986 wages rose less than 10 percent a year, the only three years of single-digit wage growth since before Park Chung Hee had taken power.

Popular as he was, Kim Jae Ik nonetheless had many enemies in the chaebol, among bureaucrats, and in the ranks of property owners. He was derided as a theoretical economist, a man so devoted to his free market ideology that he had no feeling for the pain that his policies caused. In opposition to Kim Jae Ik and the technocrats were the self-styled proponents of the "real economy," more comfortable with cozy backroom deals than the impersonal forces of the marketplace.

From early 1979 until late 1983 Kim Jae Ik and the technocrats mounted the only sustained internal attack on the traditional rules of Korea, Inc. since its foundation in 1961. Kim pursued his mission with a theological certainty that free markets would mean more prosperity for his country. His model, remembers former U.S. diplomat John Bennett, was Switzerland, a small country that used its comparative advantage to great benefit.

In the end, his challenge to the accepted conventions of Korea, Inc. was stillborn. In Rangoon, in October 1983, Kim, like his father and brothers, was to have his life snuffed out by the North Koreans.

Colonels Versus Technocrats

Although Chun gave Kim Jae Ik and the technocrats a free hand in running the economy, there was resistance among some of the key colonels who had helped Chun come to power. The colonels were interested primarily in consolidating their power through their purification drive. They saw this task in terms of getting rid of corruption, crime, laziness, and moral laxity—and, above all, neutering or eliminating political opponents. The technocrats, who did not want to dirty their hands with politics, were interested simply in rationalizing and reforming an economy that they thought had gone off track.

The Blue House advisers split into two groups on economic policy. One believed in high growth to help the country solve its problems. This represented a return to business as usual for Korea, Inc. The other group, smaller in number, wanted to bring down inflation. They thought the pain that a slowdown in inflation—and growth—would entail was something the country had to endure in order to improve its long-term prospects. Inflation, the technocrats believed, was a cancer eating away at the body politic, and radical treatment was necessary to eliminate it. Inflation, as Kim Jae Ik used to remind everyone in the circle of Blue House advisers, distorted resource allocation. People or companies who had access to bank loans found it easy to borrow and let inflation reduce the value of their repayments.

A Blue House political official remembers the bitter debate over economic policy in the early days of Chun's rule:

> At one internal discussion I remember [Kim Jae Ik] getting very angry. [Usually] he was not an emotional type at all. He was very calm. He said to the growth people, "If we suppress the official interest rate—they were arguing for

a negative [real] interest rate—you will take money from maids who are saving 20,000 won a month and turn it over to the chaebol. I will not be a party to that." It was a fierce emotional struggle internally.

From that experience I learned something. I am not an economist but I learned that economic policy-making is not value-free. It is a question of power. Nothing comes cost-free. It is one thing to say we are all in favor of low price inflation. The question is, is the leadership prepared to pay the price to keep inflation down?[23]

The answer, it turned out, was that Chun was willing to pay that price. And in the Korea of 1980, his was the only voice that mattered. Chun's control over society allowed the technocrats to do what they said needed to be done.

A prominent scholar and later a senior minister, who was a confidant of Kim Jae Ik's, remembers "very, very serious disagreements between the technocrats and the colonels. Kim Jae Ik was terribly harassed by Huh Hwa Pyung," Chun's closest military adviser. The technocrats were concerned primarily with rationalizing the economy, bringing down inflation, reducing and eliminating costly agricultural and export subsidies, and outlawing the use of aliases in stock and real estate dealing so that a fair tax system could be introduced.

The colonels, on the other hand, were more politically minded. "They didn't want the president to be overly influenced by these 'naive' economic policymakers who had won him over," says the confidante. "They also didn't like the fact that with these major economic policies the president would be dependent on someone who had nothing to do with grabbing power. There was such jealousy involved. The colonels would attack Kim Jae Ik because they wanted to drive him out."

Kim Ki Hwan thinks that the colonels, having tasted power, simply did not want to surrender it.

There was a deep philosophical difference. These colonels, in the beginning they didn't know the implications of the policy lines that the reformers were pushing forward. Then they learned later on that implementing these reforms would mean less power. They were against the real name requirements [which would have outlawed the use of aliases in banking and stock trading].

The reason so much conflict occurred between the technocrats and the colonels over non-interference in the market [is that] business people began to know the colonels and they got specific requests from companies. They acted as spokesmen for industries.[24]

This military elite thought it alone had the discipline and the zeal to lead the country. For their part, the technocrats thought their specialized knowledge gave them the right to make policy. It was a split between country boys who had made good (such as the Korea Military Academy graduates) and the genteel academics (usually from Seoul) who had been born to wealth and often educated abroad, as was the case with many of the technocrats. This tension nurtured the development of an elite faction that developed among people raised in or near the southern city of Taegu, in North Kyongsang (or Kyongbuk) Province. This became the so-called T-K (Taegu-Kyongbuk) faction, which became increasingly important in the 1980s. It included Chun, his successor Roh Tae Woo, and large numbers of senior officials in both of their administrations. Along with the Kwangju incident, which deepened the bitterness of residents of the neighboring Cholla region, the T-K faction had the unfortunate effect of inflaming regional tensions in Korea throughout the 1980s and into the 1990s.[25]

Putting the Pieces Together Again

In July the two most powerful corporate board members of Korea, Inc., were summoned to the office of Shin Byong Hyun, the minister of commerce and industry. Hyundai's earthy founder, Chung Ju Yung, and Daewoo's hustling chairman, Kim Woo Choong, had enjoyed the favors that went with being Park Chung Hee's favorite businessmen. Unfortunately for Chung and Kim, with Park dead and the economy sliding, corporate restructuring was in vogue.

Shin, following a script laid out by the Special Committee for National Security Measures, told Chung and Kim that the auto and power generation industries were the government's two priorities for consolidation. Hyundai and Daewoo competed head-on in both of these fields, but Shin ordered them to shuffle their empires in order to eliminate this competition. At stake were assets worth well over $1 billion.

Shin ordered Chung to take the power business and gave autos to Daewoo's Kim. Chung said that he would go along with the plan, provided that GM agreed. GM did not agree and the plan went awry. The government still took away the power generation business from Hyundai—without proper compensation—and gave it to Daewoo, which could not afford it.

The colonels and the technocrats both agreed that the economy needed to be restructured and, in spite of their differences, they managed to find some common ground. The young officers around Chun wanted a wholesome economy, whatever this might mean. Just as they were purging the social sphere, they thought they could sweep out all that was "impure" in business. The SCNSM, which had been set up at the end of May, was their institutional vehicle for change.

There were two key subcommittees as far as business was concerned. One was the economics subcommittee, headed by Kim Jae Ik. The other was the commerce and industry subcommittee, headed by Kum Jin Ho. Kum was the brother-in-law of Roh Tae Woo, whose troops had allowed Chun to pull off the December 12 coup. His other brother-in-law was Kim Bok Dong, who had alternated with Chun as leader of the Korea Military Academy's Class 11.[26]

The committee's first target was the troubled heavy industrial sector. Park's attempt to build up this sector during the 1970s was based mainly on security concerns, fear of protectionism, and his desire to jump-start the development process. Now the new team, taking a closer look at heavy industry, was using more rigorous economic criteria. After Park's death and the removal of former Blue House economic officials, such as Heavy and Chemical Industries plan cheerleader Oh Won Chol, they also found out that the investment in heavy industry had distorted the economy far more than they had thought. For example, funds had been surreptitiously siphoned from the Korea Housing Bank to fund investment in new manufacturing plants.

Moreover, there was likely to be no market for many of the products that these factories were to make. A World Bank study noted that even if Hyundai International's Changwon complex received every single order for South Korea's new power plants it would still be operating at only half its rated capacity. The plant would need to get a staggering 50 percent of all new business in fourteen developing nations to make economic sense.[27]

As a result, the Special Committee found that "excessive investment, inefficient management and substandard productivity of the [heavy and chemical industry] sector all combined to seriously threaten the wholesome development of the Korean economy."[28] While investment funds going to the heavy and chemical industries had been reduced to 60 percent of the nation's total loans, the Special Committee decided to take more drastic action by merging competing companies and eliminating some excess industrial capacity. This was very much an ad hoc plan, but with a dangerous average debt-equity ratio of 4:1 in a stagnant economy it was clear that something dramatic needed to be done.[29]

During the summer of 1980 the government ordered twenty-two companies in six industries to merge or consolidate their operations. This showed the pragmatism of Korea, Inc. at a time of crisis, as any talk of the free market was jettisoned.

Chung was probably delighted to slough off Hyundai International's Changwon facility, into which some $700 million was in the process of being invested at his younger brother's initiative, onto Daewoo. Hyundai faced a cash squeeze because Saudi Arabia was withholding $90 million in payments to Hyundai Construction, the group's cash cow, because of an alleged bribery scandal. (A high-ranking official at the Construction Ministry at the time maintains that the dispute arose because Chung Ju Yung welshed on paying an agreed "commission" and that the Saudis punished him in return.)

Daewoo did not do well in the deal. At the end of 1979 it already had just over $1 billion in debt, a staggering nine times as much in debt as equity. In the previous two years it had invested $237 million in the unfinished Okpo shipyard, which it had taken over at Park's request in 1978. Piling on more debt to take over businesses that had little prospect of finding customers did not make much economic sense. As a Daewoo executive told a reporter, "We are prepared to manage the industry if that is what the government wants. But they are the ones who will have to find the finance. We do not have the $700 million to buy out the joint Hyundai Heavy Industry interest."[30] In the end, Daewoo simply managed the Changwon machinery complex for several months before it was taken over by the government.

Daewoo won a Pyrrhic victory when it managed to keep its auto venture through skillful lobbying by its foreign partner, General Motors. The government had ordered Saehan Motor (owned half by Daewoo and half by General Motors) to merge with Hyundai Motor. Hyundai's Chung wanted to force Daewoo out of autos, essentially giving Hyundai a monopoly leaving Daewoo with its troubled Okpo project as well as the Hyundai International complex at Changwon. However, Hyundai's insistence on a controlling share of the auto venture, and General Motors' refusal to back down, eventually scuttled the deal and allowed the Daewoo–General Motors company to remain intact. Chun's critics enjoyed the story that a vice president of General Motors had said that his company was bigger than South Korea and that Chun would regret forcing the Detroit automaker to accept a deal it did not like.[31]

The chaebol were powerful enough that restructuring was not a matter of simply ordering them to change. Every company fought with all its lobbying power; the result, sometimes described as a triumph of state power, looks more like a demonstration of the art of resistance. However, in some cases the haggling cast a blight over companies for several years, during which investment ceased and managers were distracted from business. The technocrats had little patience for businesses' arguments. Men like Kim Ki Hwan thought that it was high time for business to wake up to the realities of the marketplace and stop relying on government help.

> All the chaebol were in serious financial difficulties. In order for them to get better what they [wanted] was more subsidies, more help from the government. They were not market-oriented, they were not independent. Their thinking was very much like the bureaucrats.[32]

The most extreme case was the former Hyundai International, which became the state-owned Korea Heavy Industries and Construction (KHIC). Founded by Chung Ju Yung's younger brother, Chung In Yung, Hyundai International had split from the rest of the Hyundai group in the late 1970s, apparently because the elder Chung worried about the possible damage that the huge project might do to his firm. (The younger Chung, for his part, had opposed the move into overseas construction.) It was a wise decision.

"The scale of the plant exceeded even his wildest dream," said Shin Byong Hyun, who became deputy prime minister in late 1980. "The heavy industry plant in Changwon is so enormous that it can meet domestic demand and then some. Even so, three more such plants were on the drawing board."[33] In the midst of this, Chung In Young was hauled in by prosecutors for questioning on charges that he had illegally diverted 8.5 billion won. Meanwhile, equipment was rusting in the sea air at the huge Changwon complex, as machinery that had been ordered months or years earlier kept arriving.

Daewoo could not handle the company, and divested it only a few months later. Late in 1980, the troubled capital equipment producer ended up in the hands of the Korea Electric Power Company (Kepco), the state electricity monopoly. Kepco ran it as a fiefdom of the ruling Democratic Justice Party during the 1980s, and it racked up losses of more than $1 billion. The contrast with the state-owned steelmaker Posco could not have been sharper.

A foreign businessman who used KHIC as a contractor from the early days believes that this mismanagement cost Korea the chance to become a major player in the world capital goods market during the 1980s.

> It started out with a crippled order book, a crippled reputation and a crippled management. Worst of all it had a horrible deficit because the jerk-around had raised construction costs. The reason they were given to Kepco for control is because of the idea that the only thing they were capable of producing was electrical power generating equipment. It was totally political. It had nothing to do with Kepco's ability to understand, administer, and manage the technical or commercial marketing requirements of the company.[34]

The government would have had a hard time doing anything positive with Hyundai International. The company had a staggering debt load almost ten times as large as its equity. But it could not simply be shut down because it had already spent huge sums on capital equipment. "The choice before us was whether to scrap the whole deal or to intervene to save the project at a considerable expense to the government," said Shin Byong Hyun. Unfortunately, 300 billion won was poured on top of the 300 billion won that had already been invested, and the cash was not accompanied by a vigorous management team. That decision would cost Korea dearly.

Daewoo managed to keep its auto venture and avoid being stuck with the Hyundai International machinery venture for long. But it nonetheless was the hardest hit by the about-face in industrial policy. Kim Woo Choong claimed he had taken over the troubled Okpo shipyard, at President Park's insistence, with the promise that the Korea Development Bank would inject 250 billion won in new equity to help finish the project. But after Park's assassination, the bank, no longer under pressure from the Blue House to help Kim, refused to put any more money into the shipyard. Daewoo muddled through, finally completing the project several years later. But the huge debt overhang and the slowness with which the shipyard was put into service crippled the operation. At the end of the 1980s, the mishandling of Okpo came back to haunt both Daewoo and the government as debt payments once again threatened to bring the entire group down.

The companies fought the restructuring as best they could. Ssangyong chairman Kim Suk Won describes it as a bargaining process, saying that he "had to get rid of something . . . to satisfy the government officers." As a result he gave

Ssangyong's high-voltage transformer business, which fell into the electrical power business category, to Hyosung.[35]

Many mid-sized chaebol were forced to take drastic action simply to survive. The Kumho group had started out with two taxicabs in Kwangju in 1946. By the late 1970s it ran a large bus company, a major tire manufacturer, and a chemicals operation. It had expanded into overseas construction, steel-making, and even consumer electronics. As a result of the contraction in lending growth the company was forced to undergo radical surgery. It spent most of the early 1980s shedding peripheral businesses, just as the technocrats hoped that many chaebol would be forced to do.

This restructuring was, fittingly enough, presided over by a technocrat, a Yale-educated economist who previously had worked in the Blue House under Park Chung Hee and taught at Sogang University. But even Park Seong Yawng counts this restructuring—necessary though it was—as one of the hardest things he has had to do. "It was very hard to decide which ones to give up [and] which ones to keep." For companies addicted to growth, shrinkage was painful and, in image-conscious Korea, a humiliating loss of face.

If one looks at the Korean economy as a single sprawling conglomerate, sort of a chaebol out of control, then what occurred in 1980 was a massive corporate restructuring. Competing and overlapping product lines were eliminated, sometimes because of superior efficiency and sometimes because of better lobbying. Different managers were appointed to run lagging enterprises, such as the Changwon complex, in a major management shake-up. As in any organization, there were fierce internal turf fights.

The restructuring of the industrial sector took place against a dramatic worsening of the economy. By June 1980 it was already clear that whatever long-term measures were taken, fairly drastic short-term measures were also required. The most dramatic news was that the population of Masan, the city next to the giant Changwon industrial complex, had dropped by 26,000 since the beginning of the year and that workers were returning to the countryside at the rate of 700 per day. Construction work stalled, and orders for the Masan free export zone continued to drop.

The Korean economy, which had ushered in an era of full employment in 1976, was now clearly running backward. As the demographic time bomb kept ticking, unemployment was a serious specter. The economy had to provide jobs for about a half-million new workers every year. This actuarial imperative had spooked economic planners in the 1960s and had spurred many of them to argue against the capital-intensive HCI plan. Their worst nightmares were coming true: Heavy industrial projects remained unfinished, and the economy stagnated.

Reflecting the bitter battles with the Blue House, the government responded with a poorly thought-out plan to stimulate the economy. Interest rates were cut, although not to the levels before the January shock plan had been introduced. The scheme was a reversal from January's austerity plan. These stimulatory measures would be repudiated before the end of the year.

In the end, 1980 had the singular distinction of being the only year from the end of the Korean War until the present in which the economy contracted. The gross national product fell 5.2 percent even while inflation raged. Consumer prices soared 29 percent, and wholesale prices leaped 39 percent.[36]

Yet Chun adopted a sanguine tone. At the beginning of 1981, in his first New Year's address to the nation as president, Chun regretted that the economic difficulties could not be eliminated "with a single sweep of the hand or the pressing of a button." This statement reflected Kim Jae Ik's view that the erratic policy changes that had been a hallmark of the Park years would be eliminated. Chun also said that "stability is the key to economic progress," promising the country that his administration would be different from the permanent economic crisis state of the 1970s.

The early 1980s were a sobering time for the chaebol, which had thrived during the heady years of the late 1970s. Businesses, like government, typically drew up five-year plans that they expected to exceed. In 1980 through 1982 actual performance fell far short of the targets. During the early 1980s many companies did not revise their plans. "The object of business now," one industry representative told a reporter, "is simply to survive."[37] The high-growth, high-inflation years of Park Chung Hee's Yushin regime were finished, but companies did not know what to do next.

After its 5.2 percent drop in 1980, economic growth was a relatively low 6.2 percent in 1981, bringing the economy just above where it had been at the end of 1979. For two years, one of the world's fastest-growing economies had stagnated. Scandal was to follow stagnation.

Notes

1. *Asian Wall Street Journal*, August 22, 1980.
2. *Asian Wall Street Journal*, April 26, 1980.
3. Author interview, January 1991.
4. Prime Minister Shin and Deputy Prime Minister Lee had worked together during a similar period of crisis two decades earlier in the chaos that accompanied Syngman Rhee's ouster, the short Yun Po Sun–Chang Myon civilian government, and Park's military takeover. "This was to me intellectually and professionally not jumping onto new ground but managing at a higher level of responsibility in a situation which was not dissimilar to the one I had been exposed to in 1960–61," Lee said in a February 1991 interview with the author.
5. Author interview, February 1991.
6. Author interview, February 1991.
7. Kim Ki Hwan, one of Chun's technocrat advisers, was one of many people who underlined this separation between the world of the civilians and that of the military. In a February 1992 interview he said, "Park had not allowed the military and civilians to interact very much. Park kept them separate. An ordinary person would not even know the names of [even important] generals."
8. The best account of this is "The Comprehensive Stabilization Program," by Nam Sang-Woo, in Lee-Jay Cho and Yoon Hyung Kim (eds.), *Economic Development in the Republic of Korea*.

9. Korea's enviable savings rate, which increased from less than 10% in the 1960s to nearly 40% in the late 1980s, accounted for much of its economic success. There is, however, little or no demonstrated relationship between real interest rates and savings rates in Korea. High savings rates probably reflected lack of a social safety net, lack of consumer credit and the general policy of discouraging consumption.

10. Although this was a sweeping program, it was not as radical as the subsequent programs adopted in Eastern Europe after the fall of communism, for it left the fundamental state-corporate alliance largely untouched and many critical administrative controls in place, notably those dealing with the financial and industrial sectors.

For similar remarks by Lee, see also *Asian Wall Street Journal*, August 22, 1980.

11. *Far Eastern Economic Review,* February 29, 1980. This also has an account of the Federal Reserve luncheon meeting. At the time, Korea was the largest Eximbank client, with more than $3 billion in loans and guarantees.

12. Author interview, March 1991.

13. Author interview, February 1991.

14. Author interview, February 1991.

15. Note on the chronology: May 17 was a Saturday and martial law began at midnight. Cabinet resignations were officially submitted on May 20. The SCNSM was inaugurated on May 31. Chun became president in September.

16. The material on Kim Jae Ik's life is based on an October 1991 interview with Lee Soon Ja (who, confusingly, has the same name as Chun's wife) as well as Kim Kihwan's unpublished manuscript, "Kim Jae-Ik: His Life and Contributions," and his section in Lawrence B. Krause and Kim Kihwan, eds., *Liberalization in the Process of Economic Development.*

17. Many of his fourteen classmates in the international relations department (class of 1960) later became prominent figures in Seoul—professors, journalists, executives, and government officials. Tragically, this small group included two others who were killed in the same North Korean terrorist incident that was later to take Kim Jae Ik's life: Suh Suk Joon (deputy prime minister) and Lee Kee Wook (deputy minister of finance). Kim Kihwan, " Kim Jae-Ik."

18. Ibid., p. 18.

19. Author interview, February 1992.

20. Author interview, February 1992.

21. Author interview, January 1991.

22. *Asian Wall Street Journal*, August 24, 1983. This was also used as source material for some other Kim Jae Ik anecdotes.

23. Author interview, January 1991.

24. Author interview, February 1992.

The colonels could be foolish in their heavy-handed attempts to run the economy. One example of this, which was related to the author by a British diplomat in 1989, occurred in 1980 when the commercial secretary of the British embassy in Seoul paid a courtesy call on the colonel who had just assumed a senior position at the Seoul subway authority. The diplomat emphasized how eager Britain was to complete the sale of some equipment for the subway system and said that financing had been arranged under the Export Credit Guarantee Department (ECGD). Eventually, the colonel smashed his hand down on the table and demanded to know what the ECGD was, and whether it was the actual seller or a broker. The colonels were looking for brokers—whom they saw as middlemen skimming off profits—everywhere.

25. The issue of the T-K faction's ascendancy during the Chun and Roh administrations is extremely complicated; the cleavages are not as neat as this shorthand summary suggests.

26. The Ministry of Trade and Commerce was the precursor to the Ministry of Trade and Industry, which in 1993 became the Ministry of Trade, Industry and Energy. In 1983, Kum was appointed minister of trade and industry. Later, during Roh Tae Woo's administration, he was widely regarded as one of the most influential powers behind the throne and his backing was key for many ministerial appointments.

27. *Far Eastern Economic Review*, September 5, 1980. See also *Far Eastern Economic Review*, June 5, 1981.

The restructuring meant that Hyundai International was the country's sole supplier of power generating equipment, construction equipment, and other heavy machinery. Daewoo, Samsung, and the original Hyundai were limited to cars, shipbuilding, and industrial boilers.

Kia was merged with Dong-Ah Motor and forced out of the passenger car business until 1987; it made trucks and specialized vehicles. Its motorcycle business was divided between Daelim and Hyosung Heavy Industries.

28. *Korea Annual* 1981, pp. 29–30.

29. The figure is from *Far Eastern Economic Review*, June 27, 1980, citing a World Bank study that says that by 1979 this was the debt-equity ratio.

30. *Far Eastern Economic Review*, September 5, 1980.

31. Although this story sounds apocryphal, a senior GM official in South Korea (who was not involved in the events of 1980) said that he thought the tale was true. Given GM's record of heavy-handedness in South Korea—which is discussed at greater length elsewhere—the story may be based on an accurate account.

32. Author interview, February 1992.

33. These quotations drawn from an interview with Shin that appeared in *Far Eastern Economic Review*, May 15, 1981, and an article on Changwon in *Far Eastern Economic Review*, June 5, 1981. The latter article has information about debt-equity ratio. Vice President Kim Chong Joo said that Hyundai International collapsed because of a staggering debt-equity ratio of almost 25:1. Kim said the company had $730 million in assets and $32 million in equity.

34. Author interview, March 1991.

35. Kim Suk Won delights in telling how he extracted revenge of a sort from Hyosung a few years later. When Hyosung teetered on the edge of bankruptcy he acquired its floundering securities company. The renamed Ssangyong Securities became immensely profitable in the late 1980s on the back of Korea's stock market boom. Author interview, November 1990.

36. All data is from the Bank of Korea. There are some minor differences in data depending on the base year used.

37. *Far Eastern Economic Review*, November 28, 1980.

14

From Reform to Scandal

All forms of corruption must be cleaned up and the old social order must be reformed to eliminate a sense of incongruity. . . . Many irregularities sprang up as a by-product of rapid economic growth in recent decades. A typical case in point is the abuse of political power to accumulate illegitimate wealth. How can the nation sanction the building of fortunes of billions and tens of billions of won through the influence of office?

—Chun Doo Hwan[1]

That Lee Soon Ja could not do much about her most obvious fault was hardly to be blamed, for Chun Doo Hwan's wife had an extremely strong chin, a sign, according to Korean physiognomy, that she was forceful, aggressive, and unsympathetic. Koreans privately called her *chukoktok* ("rice spatula chin"), in reference to her broad, flat jaw that resembled the wooden spatula Koreans use to serve rice.

Koreans take physical features extremely seriously and, at least in the case of Chun's wife, they were right to. Lee Soon Ja started off her reign as First Lady badly by appearing at her husband's March 1981 inauguration sporting a smock of a type worn only by the royalty of the Yi dynasty.[2] The symbolism was not lost on much of the nationwide television audience. She became a woman the Korean public loved to hate and the subject of endless rumors, many, but not all of them, groundless. There was no major new building anywhere in the city that a taxi driver might not hint was hers—and hers through some illegal deal at that.

Certainly, Lee Soon Ja was pushy, and she had dabbled in speculative money-making activities when her husband was an officer. It was military wives who typically took the white envelopes stuffed with cash from those of lower rank hoping to ingratiate themselves with their superiors and improve their chances of promotion, and it was the wives who ran the *kye*, the immensely profitable curb market lending circles. She was also known as a real estate speculator of some skill. Although Lee Soon Ja was greedy, she was no different than her peers. "She was a typical army wife of her generation," says a U.S. military analyst.

A biography oozing with praise for Chun describes the courtship between him as a young military cadet and Lee Soon Ja, the daughter of a Korea Military Academy instructor. After he was commissioned, Chun wrote Soon Ja a letter, saying that he could not marry her because he was too poor. She visited him and told Chun they would be married the following week. "Let me take care of this money stuff and you just keep your mind on your duty as an army officer!" she told Chun. She had apparently done quite a good job indeed taking care of the money, managing to buy a house in Yonhui-dong, in northwestern Seoul, in spite of Chun's meager army pay.[3]

The tales of wrongdoing by the First Lady and her relatives gained credence with an announcement by the Public Prosecutor's Office on May 7, 1982, that it had arrested a couple who were related to Lee Soon Ja. The charges against Lee Chol Hi and his wife, Chang Yong Ja, were simply technical violations of possessing U.S. dollars in their house. (Under the Foreign Exchange Control Law it was, until 1989, illegal for a Korean citizen to fail to deposit foreign currency in an authorized bank account.) Next, against a backdrop of conflicting government announcements and frenetic rumors of high-level complicity, the outline of one of the biggest scandals in postwar Korea emerged.

Scandal was to follow scandal for the president's extended family. While Chun's technocrats pushed reforms, trying to free up an economy that had been cossetted by government intervention for decades, many of the president's relatives had a simpler agenda: making money by trading on their family name. Thanks to his coup and the bloody siege in Kwangju, Chun had never enjoyed legitimacy. He hoped to earn it the hard way: through economic reforms, through fulfilling his repeated promise to step down after one term, and by successfully preparing for the 1988 Seoul Olympics. Corruption and scandal, which eventually reached into the First Family, made that task impossible and ultimately contributed to Chun's downfall.

"Madame" Chang

When Chang Yong Ja, a vivacious thirty-eight-year-old socialite known for her large parties and good political connections, married a former high-ranking intelligence official in early 1982, some 200 bankers, government officials, and businessmen attended the event. As the largest scandal in modern Korea unfolded a few months later, most of them wished they had not.

"Madame" Chang and "General" Lee, as they were known to Koreans, had shamelessly traded on their connections with the Blue House to build a pyramid loan scheme. They approached companies that had decent reputations but needed cash. In Korea's chronically cash-starved economy, where bank loans were limited largely to companies investing in government-approved projects, most companies always needed more funds. Even the biggest firms in the country sometimes turned to the curb market to meet funding shortages.

In outward appearances, Chang and Lee were no different from the majority of private money lenders. The duo lent money to companies and took security in the form of promissory notes worth more than the loan. This was a primitive form of securing the loan, one used by many curb market lenders. These notes were usually redeemed by companies before their due date, although there was also a secondary market of sorts because they could be discounted at banks and through money brokers.

Companies trusted the couple, who boasted of their connections to the Blue House and threw lavish parties. However, Chang and Lee, who had promised simply to hold the promissory notes as security, in fact sold them on the curb market to cover their mounting losses on the stock exchange. Although they had sold the notes, they nonetheless took repayments from the companies. Over a fifteen-month period, which started in early 1981, the duo sold promissory notes with a face value of nearly $1 billion. The scheme widened as Chang and Lee bribed officials at the Cho Hung Bank to make loans to the half-dozen companies they lent to. Alternatively, they borrowed money from banks by playing up their Blue House connections, and then lent the money, at higher rates, to companies that could not borrow from banks because they did not have enough clout.

The scale of the scandal was tremendous. The total curb market was roughly estimated at 3 trillion won; Chang and Lee were controlling nearly one-quarter of the market. To put this in perspective, the value of promissory notes Chang and Lee floated was equivalent to 13 percent of the total currency in circulation (M1) and almost equal to the entire value of issued securities on the Korea Stock Exchange. Chang and Lee, in other words, were no bit players, but two of the legendary "big hands" who controlled Korean financial markets until the late 1980s.[4]

The scheme collapsed when a company with a small amount of promissory notes outstanding complained to authorities that its promissory notes were still in circulation although it had repaid its loan from Chang and Lee. The fraud bankrupted two companies that had borrowed from the couple and required an emergency rescue of four other firms. The damage to Korea's fragile financial system would have been far worse had the government not acted quickly to pump in emergency loans to banks and securities companies. Distorting the curb market as Chang and Lee had done threatened to disrupt the entire business community, and not merely the borrowing activities of the six major corporate victims.

The Madame Chang affair, as it was called, underscored just how primitive Korea's financial system was and how easily it could be manipulated. Decades of financial repression had left smaller companies starved for the capital they needed to grow and had opened up profitable opportunities for anyone with money to lend. Financial repression was an invitation for fraud, because anyone who could extract money from banks at below-market interest rates, as Chang and Lee did, was guaranteed a profit.

The possibility of fraud throughout the financial system was amplified because of the common use of aliases in real estate, securities, and bank transactions. This practice, which reflected the need to hide wealth in a country that nominally frowned on riches and which often used tax audits as a political tool, was not outlawed until 1993 because so many powerful people benefited from the secrecy that the practice encouraged.

It was a political disaster for Chun that the public now associated corruption with his Fifth Republic and his wife's relatives. While no public accusations were ever made that Chun or his wife were involved, conspiracy-prone Koreans, encouraged by General Lee's earlier hints of high-level protection, were convinced of a Blue House connection. Journalist Shim Jae Hoon wrote:

> Dealers on the curb market and stock exchange appear convinced that she had political clout. "How else could you summon a bank president to your office in a matter of minutes?" asked one source, who saw the Chohung Bank president (one of those now dismissed) making his way to her office on the 18th floor of Seoul's Lotte Hotel.[5]

When prosecutors raided her two-story mansion south of the Han River—in a compound surrounded by barbed wire—they found all the resources of a primitive bank, which was, in effect, what Chang claimed to be running. The find included $400,000 in cash, 37 kilograms of gold bullion, 1.3 billion won worth of jewelry, a 1,500-piece antique collection, and three Mercedes-Benzes. She also was said to own 600 pieces of property worth 32 billion won, scattered across the country.[6]

A former government official echoes the views of many people in Seoul, when he says that the scandal brought out into the open what many in the country's elite had long known.

> When the Chang incident took place it was there for everybody to see. Chun's younger and elder brothers [who were also engaged in corruption] were small fry compared with the operators in the Lee [Soon Ja] family. Other people put up with [Chun's brothers] and kowtowed and expanded their greed. But Lee's in-laws were operators in their own capacity.[7]

Seoul's rumor mill had it that Chang and Lee got their start using political funds from the Blue House. Politics under Chun, just as under Park, required huge quantities of cash, because even Korea's authoritarian rulers needed money to buy meals and token gifts for millions of ordinary voters during election campaigns.

Chun's purge on taking office had disgorged a reported $142 million in illicit funds from nine key officials of the Park years. Chun was also rumored to have taken control of Park's political funds as part of his investigation into the president's death; gossip in Seoul had it that some $4 billion was recovered from a Swiss bank account where it had been stashed by Park. (Although there almost certainly were some political funds, it seems unlikely that they amounted to anywhere even near $1 billion, given the diligence with which Chun's aides later worked to raise a paltry—by comparison—$100 million for what was to become the scandal-ridden Ilhae Foundation.)

Many stock market insiders in Seoul believe that Chang and Lee had received their initial stake from one of these sources of cash, although no evidence has ever emerged to support these rumors. Others thought that the money might have resulted from a liaison Chang allegedly had with Park Chung Hee. All that is certain is that Chang traded on her political connections to perpetrate a massive fraud that threatened the stability of the country's rickety financial system.

The scandal took a heavy toll, as Madame Chang brought down a smorgasbord of relatives, acquaintances, bank presidents, and cabinet members with her. Those who fell included Chang's husband, Lee Chol Hi (a former deputy director of the KCIA and member of the National Assembly), her brother-in-law, Lee Kyu Kwang (who was the uncle of the First Lady), the presidents of the Chohung Bank and the Commercial Bank of Korea, and fifteen others.

"General" Lee was a foul-tempered man fond of boasting of his Blue House connections. Once, on an official trip to the Middle East in his position as head of the Korea Mining Corporation, he ordered all official receptions canceled. He responded to suggestions by Korean diplomats that this was not acceptable by reminding them to whom he was related.

Lee was one of the few relics of the Park Chung Hee era who had escaped being purged by Chun. That Lee Chol Hi could escape Chun's purification process showed just how cynical the operation had been. According to former KCIA head Kim Hyung Wook, Lee Chol Hi had been a key figure in the Kim Dae Jung kidnapping. He allegedly acted as a go-between for KCIA director Lee Hu Rak and KCIA operatives in Tokyo and subsequently paid hush money to one of the key agents involved in the kidnapping.[8]

The scandal became very much a family affair. First Lady Lee Soon Ja's uncle was charged with bribery in the case. Her seventy-two-year-old father thought the scandal sufficiently serious to step down from his position as head of the Korean Senior Citizens Association. The president's younger brother, Chun Kyung Hwan, also resigned from one of his minor posts as part of a cosmetic effort to remove relatives from influential positions.

Accepting moral responsibility, the director and deputy director of the Office of Bank Supervision and Examination resigned. As the scandal grew, the entire cabinet tendered its resignation, and several members of the ruling Democratic

Justice Party also offered to quit. Chun accepted eleven of the twenty-four resignations offered to him.

The resignations, not just of the family members but of so many mid- and upper-level bureaucrats, were an interesting admission of collective guilt. Many of those who were caught up in the aftermath of the scandal had no doubt heard rumors of what Madame Chang and General Lee were up to, but whether because of fear or simply inertia, none wanted to put a halt to patently illegal and disruptive behavior. This was the bureaucracy's first demonstration that it had to fight harder against pressure from the top or be prepared to face a reckoning someday. As one member of the budget team said shortly after the scandal, "Every time I get a phone call from the Blue House to increase a particular budget item, I cut it in half." The events of 1987 through 1989 were to vindicate those who adopted a less sycophantic posture.

Certainly, the structure of Korean society made it easier for scandals like this to occur. There was—and still is—an unwillingness to question orders said to come down from the presidential Blue House. In the early 1980s, for example, a con artist made off with more than $100,000 from the Bank of Korea's Pusan branch after presenting a forged request from the Blue House for U.S. dollars and Japanese yen for use in a "secret operation."

In another case around the same time, the state-owned MBC television network was prepared to take a female comedienne off the air because of purported pressure from a senior official at the Blue House. It was only by chance that an MBC television producer had gone to school with the Blue House official who was supposedly applying the pressure and discovered that the call was a hoax.

Madame Chang knew how to take advantage of her position, but her act also contained a good deal of bluster. "I had a friend who was a bank president," remembers a former Blue House official. "I was out of the country at the time, but when I came back I asked my friend how he had managed to stay out of it. He told me that one day Madame Chang had come in and deposited an enormous amount of money at the bank and then asked to see the president. The staff was trembling at the amount of money she deposited and showed her to the president's office. She introduced herself, they talked, and she asked if she could use the telephone. She appeared to speak to someone at the Blue House. Then she said that she would be using this bank frequently in the future.

"Shortly after that first visit she came in and asked for an enormous loan. My friend was suspicious, and his instinct played a good role. He figured that if the Blue House were involved, as Madame Chang said, that there would have been a visit from someone at the Blue House. So he said no. That was the end." But Koreans were too often afraid to say no.[9]

The Madame Chang affair was capable of such destructive force because the government controlled funds tightly in an attempt to channel money into productive investment. The only way a loan could be given for working capital (rather than fixed investment), which companies needed to finance everyday operations such as maintaining inventories, was by pledging land as security. Instead, working capital was supposed to come from the original investors' capital or from profits.

Inevitably these funds were inadequate to cover any disruptions in cash flow, let alone finance expansion in Korea's dynamic economy. Moreover, income did not always match the seasonal strains of expenditure, especially in a country where large parts of salary are paid as regular bonuses.

Without a private money market to recirculate funds and supplement the banking system, Korea's economy would shrivel. Twice during Park's tenure, in 1961 and 1973, the government had frozen all outstanding curb market loans and attempted to convert them into government bonds in an effort to lower funding costs for businesses and do away with usurious moneylenders. In both instances, the economy had been brought almost to a standstill.

Most corporations are constantly scrambling for short-term loans, rather than attempting to issue bonds or other instruments. Bonds are of short duration—typically one year—and underwriting costs are much higher than in countries with a developed financial market. Although the bond market developed in the late 1980s, there was still a wide gap between the government-set bond rate and curb market rates. Many private lenders preferred to forego the safety of the official bond market for the higher returns on the curb market. In 1979 and 1980, and at other times of crisis, the rate on the curb market could reach 5 percent per month, while a monthly rate of 1.8 percent to 2.5 percent was still considered normal in the early 1990s.

The major money dealers performed a very important broking function between lenders and borrowers of short-term funds and this semi-official credit market touched all levels of the economy. Housewives and others, including army wives such as the young Lee Soon Ja, did the same job on a smaller scale, running credit circles that lent to retail stores and other businesses as well as to individuals. This private money market was as important to parts of some chaebol as to small businesses, since even in the mid-1990s some of the biggest business groups sometimes have to turn to the curb market.

Ironically, only a month before the Madame Chang scandal broke, Chun had launched a new attack on corruption in an attempt to resuscitate his image as a reformer. The scandal completely destroyed this campaign, and the embarrassment over the Madame Chang affair ensured that Chun would never again initiate any purification or anticorruption movements.

Chun's political problems were compounded by bad luck. In many people's minds the Madame Chang scandal merged with the case of a deranged policeman who killed fifty-five people in a provincial town, and the death of ten people in a subway construction accident. This sudden swing in popular public opinion—as opposed to the elites who had never fully accepted Chun—was a warning for the ruling group that unexpected accidents could bring down the government.[10]

Collapse of a New Chaebol

Korea's financial troubles did not end with the curb market scandal. The following summer a high-flying new chaebol, the Myungsung ("Bright Star") group collapsed in bankruptcy after its chairman was indicted for embezzling $142 million. Kim Chul Ho was another of Korea's dynamic political capitalists whose dreams were limited only by their access to bank loans. In 1981, Kim had announced that he would build the world's largest church, a mountaintop cathedral designed to hold half a million people. He also planned a floating sixty-two-story hotel near Inchon. Shortly before Myungsung went bust, Kim announced his grandest plan of all, building a Korean leisure complex fifteen times larger than California's Disneyland.

A dreamer, Kim was also a Christian who said that his goal was to revitalize Korean culture using Christian love. "The profits one makes and the wealth that accrues therefrom, in fact, do not belong to the individual but to the society where one belongs."

Apparently Kim interpreted this philosophy to mean that he could use borrowed money any way he liked. He borrowed $150 million through the curb market in a complicated scheme that laundered the money through the Commercial Bank of Korea as if the funds were normal loans. A mid-level bank employee was said to have used an astounding 1,720 different false name bank accounts to shuffle the money to Myungsung.

Kim apparently received the backing of Lee Soon Ja's father, retired general Lee Kyu Dong. Between December 1981 and May 1982, Kim donated $140,000 to the National Elderly People's Association, which Lee chaired. Kim also spread the word that Myungsung had General Lee's backing, although it is uncertain whether Lee was really backing Myungsung or Kim was "playing the common but risky game of implying a powerful backing where there was none."[11]

In any event, on August 17, 1983, Myungsung chairman Kim Chol Ho was arrested on charges of large-scale tax evasion and embezzlement. On August 29, the prosecutor arrested the former minister of transportation, who had served from March 1981 to May 1982 and was responsible for all tourist and hotel matters, along with fifteen other men on charges of influence-peddling and accepting bribes. The minister, Yoon Ja Joong, was a general who became head of the Korean Air Force after the December 12, 1979 coup and had subsequently served as a member of the Special Committee on National Security Measures (SCNSM).

Later that summer, another scandal emerged after two companies—with the help of employees at the Cho Hung Bank—forged credit guarantees. The president of the bank was charged with accepting 200 million won in bribes from the head of Yongdong Development Promotion in return for extending large loans and credit guarantees. Eighteen lower-ranking employees at the bank were also arrested in the case.[12]

There was a common thread running through these scandals: the curb market. The difficulty in getting bank loans and the huge difference between interest rates charged on bank loans and on the curb market fueled instability in the financial system. It spawned a huge, unregulated financial market that was subject to periodic panics.[13]

What was left of the Fifth Republic's moral superiority, which in Confucian thinking confers the divine right to rule, died in the curb market scandals of May 1982. The Madame Chang scandal was a turning point for the Fifth Republic. It was in this incident that what Koreans regard as fatal weaknesses in Chun's character emerged, a blindness and a hubris that would eventually bring him down. Said former Deputy Prime Minister Lee Hahn Been:

> On the positive side, he listened to the technocratic pool. That gave him the stability that was bound to follow from his package of reform. Another credit comes from his military background which loves fanfare and [as a result] the choice of the Olympics as a governmental program.
>
> Basically, as a person he was not prepared . . . to be a comprehensive reformer. In terms of character, background, Weltanschauung, we had the misfortune to have at the helm of state [a man] whose character was not prepared. It seemed to me, as an outsider, that he was very callous about some of these misdeeds which followed from wrong connections, wrong appointments. There was an aspect of hubris. Kwangju was one example, the Madame Chang case another.
>
> As a ruler they belong to different classes. Park was a ruthless man but a very intelligent, rational, consistent man. President Chun, except as he listened to the good staff that he inherited from earlier periods, I don't think had other positive instincts.[14]

It was not only influential technocrats like Lee who were beginning to have doubts about Chun. Even some of his closet advisers turned away from the president. The most important defection was by Huh Hwa Pyung, who took a fellowship at the conservative Heritage Foundation in Washington, D.C., paid for by a generous donation from the Federation of Korean Industries.

Although the administration was riven by disputes at its most senior levels, on June 24, 1982, the third cabinet reshuffle in five weeks brought in an economic team of exceptional ability and probity.

The new prime minister, a surprise appointment, was Kim Sang Hyup, the respected president of Korea University, which his family had founded, and a member of the board of directors of the influential *Dong-A Ilbo* newspaper. Kim had been considered a possible presidential candidate in the past, although he never sought the post. He was born to money, and most Koreans considered him above corruption. Chun, afraid that the backlash against the Madame Chang scandal could even topple the government, brought in Kim as a legitimizing force.

However, Chun appointed Kim Sang Hyup, his senior by more than ten years, in the arrogant, imperious fashion that was his hallmark—and in doing so further alienated the country's established elite, who already regarded him as an arri-viste. Chief presidential secretary Chang Se Dong simply called Kim one day, shortly before he was to leave on an overseas trip, and told him that a car would pick him up and bring him to the Blue House. He was brought to Chun's office, where the president informed Kim that he was to become prime minister. "There was no room for hesitation, no time to think about it," remembers a confidant of Kim.[15] "From the day he took the job he tried to leave it, but, of course, in a way that would not anger Chun." Kim would get his wish, but only after one of the most bizarre and tragic events in modern Korean history.

Notes

1. *Asian Wall Street Journal*, August 26, 1980.
2. Chun was elected interim president in August and was inaugurated on September 1, 1980; he was then re-elected as president the following February and had another inauguration on March 3. I am grateful to Shim Jae Hoon for the anecdote about the smock.
3. Cheon Kum Sung, *Chun Doo Hwan, Man of Destiny*, p. 48, has the money quotation; p. 70, the reference to the Yonhui-dong house.
4. *Asian Wall Street Journal*, and Bank of Korea *Economic Statistics Yearbook* (1984) for monetary data.
5. *Far Eastern Economic Review*, May 21, 1982. Shim also wrote:

> She also impressed her friends with the scale of her operations. Meeting a prospective borrower in her office one day, she first intimidated him by mentioning his tax problem—information which, sources said, could have been obtained only from official sources. "It is our job to help a good but struggling company like yours."
>
> When a borrower became suspicious of her financial capacity or her political connections, Chang indicated that her money was "linked to important national causes." [Note the deliberate vagueness, which works quite well in the Korean language.] Borrowers were under strict orders not to reveal the source of the money lest it cause political embarrassment.

6. Ibid.
7. Author interview, January 1991.
8. This is according to the testimony of former KCIA head Kim Hyung Wook to the U.S. Congress. Kim testified under oath in 1977 that Lee Chol Hi, who at the time of the kidnapping was assistant director of the KCIA, "was to be the contact between the director of the KCIA [Lee Hu Rak] and those in Japan." His contact in Japan was Kim Ki Wan, a KCIA operative whose cover job was minister at the Korean embassy in Tokyo, where he used the alias Kim Jae Won (p. 40). Kim later left the agency and emigrated to the United States. Kim Hyung Wook (pp. 64–65) describes a payment allegedly made by Lee Chol Hi (who by that time was deputy director) to Kim Ki Wan in Los Angeles to buy his silence. U.S. Congress, House, *Hearing Before the Subcommittee on International Organizations of the Committee on International Relations*, 95th Congress.
9. The anecdotes about the Bank of Korea scam, the MBC hoax, and the bank president were related by the Blue House official cited earlier. The money was said to be "much more" than tens of thousands of dollars. It was, however, recovered.
10. *Asian Wall Street Journal*, May 13, 17, 18, 19, 20, 21, 24, 1982, for articles on the Madame Chang scandal.

11. *Asian Wall Street Journal*, August 19–20, 1983. See also *Asian Wall Street Journal*, August 30, 1983.

12. *Asian Wall Street Journal*, September 27, 1983; and *Asian Wall Street Journal*, October 17, 1983.

13. Not all the scandals were related to the curb market, however. One of the more poignant occurred in the summer of 1984, when the chairman of the ruling Democratic Justice Party was forced to resign after a political rival mailed a 148-page report detailing his extensive property holdings to three local newspapers. The government's immediate response was to investigate not only Jung Nae Hiuk but to look into charging his political rival (who had grown up in the same village as Jung) with libel, as if Jung were simply the innocent victim of a defamation campaign. An official of the National Security Planning Agency had helped direct the smear campaign against Jung. *Far Eastern Economic Review*, July 19, 1984.

14. Author interview, February 1991.

15. Author interview, September 1990.

15

To Die in Rangoon

History would suggest increasing paranoia and repression. Let's
hope it doesn't happen like that.

—Anonymous Western diplomat[1]

On October 9, 1983, the South Korean ambassador to Burma arrived at
Rangoon's Martyrs Mausoleum at the head of a motorcade. A bugler mistook the
ambassador for Chun Doo Hwan, who had been delayed by traffic, and blew the
first notes to start a memorial ceremony. That was the signal a squad of North
Korean commandos hidden nearby had been waiting for. They instantly deto-
nated a powerful remote-controlled bomb, which blew the mausoleum apart,
killing seventeen Koreans and four Burmese. The blast shook buildings a mile
away as a hail of metal and tile showered down from the ceiling, where the bomb
had been placed, on the South Korean presidential party. Panicked survivors,
many of them wounded, ran from the mausoleum as huge plumes of smoke rose
into the air.

Besides Chun, only four members of the sixteen-man official South Korean
delegation survived the bombing. Among the dead were some of Chun's most
talented advisers: Presidential Secretary for Economic Affairs Kim Jae Ik, Deputy Prime Minister and Minister of the Economic Planning Board So Sok Jun,
Minister of Energy Suh Sang Chul, Minister of Commerce and Industry Kim
Dong Whie, Presidential Secretary and former Ambassador to the United States
Hahm Pyong Choon, and Minister of Foreign Affairs Lee Bum Suk. These men
died while the intended target, Chun, escaped unhurt. A cruel, sardonic saying
became popular among some Koreans: "They killed those whom we could not
spare, and spared the one we could have done without."

A Burmese inquiry found that three North Korean terrorist commandos had slipped off a North Korean boat anchored in Rangoon in late September. They stayed at a North Korean diplomatic residence in Rangoon, where they received bomb material, including liquid incendiary bombs, TNT powder, and liquid fuel. On October 7, two days before the blast, the commandos installed two remote controlled Claymore mines between the false ceiling and the roof of the mausoleum. The mines consisted of explosive packed behind 700 metal ball bearings, which, along with the shards from the ceiling, rained their deadly hail onto the South Korean party.

The three North Koreans, who were caught separately in the days after the explosion, tried to escape arrest by blowing themselves up with hand grenades. One of the commandos was killed; another killed three Burmese soldiers before being arrested.[2]

In addition to hand grenades, the North Korean commandos carried booby-trapped fountain pens and the wireless transmitter used to set off the powerful explosion. Burma, long a prominent member of the nonaligned movement, quickly broke off relations with North Korea. But the bombing had done its damage to the South Korean technocratic elite, with consequences quite different from those intended by North Korea.

The Rangoon bombing followed by little more than a month the downing of KAL flight 007 by a Soviet fighter plane, killing all 269 people aboard, a tragedy that heightened South Korea's feeling of international vulnerability. As it turned out, the bomb blast in Rangoon killed not only men but the hopes of far-reaching economic reforms. It understandably fueled Chun's paranoia about North Korea and drove him further along an insular, self-destructive path.[3]

Triumph of the Technocrats

Ironically, the bomb blast came just as many of the policies put in place by the technocrats were starting to pay off. The credit crunch of the early 1980s had stopped inflation dead in its tracks. But now the economy was picking up again. Moreover, a cabinet shakeup in the wake of the Madame Chang scandal in May had confirmed the ascendancy of the technocrats. Finance Minister Rha Woong Bae, although he was largely blameless in the curb market scandal, nonetheless was replaced by the ambitious, aggressive, and highly capable Kang Kyong Shik. With Suh Sang Chul appointed as minister of energy and resources, the cabinet had acquired a strong technocratic and bureaucratic bias.

The rise of the technocrats was completed when So Sok Jun joined the cabinet in July 1983 as deputy prime minister and head of the Economic Planning Board. The U.S.-educated So had worked at the Economic Planning Board, the Blue House, and the Ministry of Trade and Industry, where he had been minister from September 1980 until May 1982. His return marked the ascendancy of a technocratic triumvirate that had first joined forces in the late 1970s, when So, Kang

Kyong Shik, and Kim Jae Ik had all worked together at the Economic Planning Board. With these three reunited at the top of the economic policy-making ladder (Kim Jae Ik remained senior secretary to the president for economic affairs), the time had come to push through the economic reforms that EPB technocrats had been urging since 1977.

Essentially, So and his team wanted to move quickly toward a free, competitive economy—and this time it looked like it might really happen. The favors to the chaebol, the price controls, the thicket of import restrictions, and the other barriers to market forces were all targets of the reformers. These reform measures had been proposed in the 1970s but were largely blocked by President Park, who, as an economic nationalist, could make no sense of them. In 1980, as Chun was consolidating his power, similar measures had been blocked by a failing economy and political upheaval. In 1983 there were no longer any obstacles standing in the way of the technocracy. Business, labor, and farmers—all of whom had an interest in preserving the current situation—were firmly under control. The press was muzzled, and the president was willing to trust his economic advisers to a degree that would have been unimaginable under Park.

Moreover, the task of stabilization that the economic technocrats had set themselves was largely complete. Consumer price inflation plummeted from 29 percent in 1980 to 7 percent in 1982 and 3 percent in 1983. Import growth was slow, so that there was a dramatic reduction in the current account deficit, in spite of lower export growth than predicted. This improving macroeconomic picture gave the technocrats room for their reforms.

Deputy Prime Minister So first of all took the unprecedented step of calling for a rapid review of the fifth five-year plan. Not since 1963 had a five-year plan been revised officially. This brief stock-taking measure was intended to permit a full appraisal of the steps needed for thorough economic liberalization.

The new ministers called for a top-to-bottom reappraisal of the plan within nine months. The reformers singled out two targets for dismantling: industrial controls administered by the Ministry of Trade and Industry (MTI) and the financial controls supervised by the Ministry of Finance (MoF).

To the working-level MTI bureaucrats, as opposed to the academically trained technocrats, this new policy direction had a chilling effect. "What will there be left for us to do?" a group of MTI directors complained in a conversation in September 1983. If we cannot control investment and we cannot control imports and we cannot control licenses, these key working-level officials wondered, what was the purpose of their ministry? The bureaucrats were concerned because they could see that this was not the sort of ritual public relations exercise that the government goes through to make a good impression on foreign trading partners, but that their seniors were serious about pushing through radical changes.

Directors, who usually range in age from their late thirties to mid-forties, oversee the day-to-day implementation of policy from their desks, which are always placed as far from the door as possible in a Korean office. They are usually the most senior officials in the large, open-plan offices where the bureaucracy's work gets done—the highest-ranking officials without an office of their own. Directors have tremendous discretion in speeding up or slowing down anything that crosses their desks. In the Korea of the early 1980s, nearly everything that touched on the economy had to cross the desks of at least one, and often many more, director's desk.

The same MTI directors arranged a series of interviews with the triumvirate of So Sok Jun, Kang Kyong Shik, and Kim Jae Ik to try to discover what they were really thinking. Kim Jae Ik was highly optimistic. What had surprised him was the speed of the economic turnaround. What he wanted most to discuss in one of the last interviews before leaving for Rangoon were the problems experienced by the North Korean economy, and the trade-offs between social welfare and free enterprise.[4] His widow remembers it as a time of great satisfaction.

> By the end of 1983 he was quite happy. His main projects were on the right track. He told me and his friends that he was very lucky, that many economists only struggle and don't see things work but that he would actually see many things work before the end of President Chun's term.[5]

Financial reforms could be adopted most quickly. It was up to the Ministry of Finance to revise tariffs, remove indirect and direct import restrictions, and to change foreign investment patterns. In the past, the Ministry of Finance had been less important than the Ministry of Trade and Industry and the Economic Planning Board in controlling foreign investment, although legally the Finance Ministry had greater authority. Finance Minister Kang Kyong Shik announced that, in the future, the Ministry of Finance would make the actual decisions about matters such as imports and foreign investment in an attempt to bring law and practice more into line.

The most immediate hurdle facing financial reform was the low quality and skill of banking executives, who had done little more than process government orders for the previous two decades. As Minister Kang Kyong Shik said, "Those who work in the banking industry as well as business and people in the government are so accustomed to some sort of nationalized banking operations and allocation that it's not so easy to change the way of doing things."[6]

Minor changes had occurred in 1982, when the government nominally privatized two commercial banks and ruled the chaebol ineligible for many kinds of subsidized loans. In June 1983, two new commercial banks opened their doors, the first new banks since the late 1960s. KorAm Bank, a joint venture between Bank of America and twelve Korean companies led by Daewoo, was headed by Kim Mahn Je, an influential technocrat who had been president of the Korea Development Institute. Shinhan Bank was financed by Korean residents in Japan. These banks were supposed to have a leavening effect on the local industry by introducing new banking techniques that, it was hoped, would pressure Korean bankers to become more innovative.

It did not work out quite as intended. KorAm (also known as HanMi) and Shinhan have been handsomely profitable but, as of the early 1990s, they have not yet spurred local banks to become more innovative. Part of the problem was that existing local banks were, even after reform began, still forced to make government-directed loans. KorAm and Shinhan were largely, but not completely, immune to the pressure to make policy loans.

Kim Mahn Je became minister of finance in October 1983 and later served as deputy prime minister and head of the Economic Planning Board. In retrospect, he says that the government made a mistake in trying to pursue rigorous anti-inflation policies and financial reform at the same time. "The two didn't combine," Kim said in an interview later. "Banking liberalization contradicted stabilization. It squeezed credit and it made newly funded financial institutions very vulnerable to financial crises."[7]

Shakedown

The Rangoon bombing in October 1983, coupled with the downing of KAL flight 007 the previous month, created a sense of siege in South Korea. While both Chun and Park often cynically used the North Korean threat to justify their authoritarian rule, the bloody blast at the Martyrs Memorial in Rangoon showed South Koreans that the danger from their brother-enemy in the North was real. The murder of 17 senior officials, in an attack meant to kill Chun himself, pushed the president to rely even more on his small circle of hard-line military advisers and often corrupt relatives. As a result, the delicate balance that governed Korea, Inc. was disrupted, as greed increasingly marred Chun's administration.

It was apparently as the survivors of the Rangoon massacre numbly huddled in the jet taking them back to Seoul that someone suggested setting up a foundation for the widows and children of the victims. From this charitable impulse came one of the great scandals of the Fifth Republic.

The foundation was named Ilhae, the pen name of Chun Doo Hwan, and it eventually collected almost 60 billion won in donations from businesses.[8] Chun used Chang Se Dong, his chief secretary, to collect these "contributions," which in many cases amounted to millions of dollars from a single company. The requests for money came at a difficult time, when the chaebol were already reeling from the government's tight credit policy.

Ilhae was only the largest of dozens of official foundations and government projects that relied on donations from businesses. These contributions were, in many cases, just a half-step up from outright extortion. They were the price of doing business in a country where the government could destroy companies or, as was commonly the case, rescue them from their own mistakes.

Because most of this fund-raising was secret, it is difficult to know with any certainty the total amount of business contributions. But a conservative estimate suggests that forced donations—both reported and unreported—totaled some $4 billion to $5 billion during Chun's eight years in power.[9]

These billions of dollars were given in the form of what Koreans call quasi-taxes, requests for donations from the government that companies were in no position to refuse. These included regular fund-raising efforts for such causes as Saemaul Undong, for defense spending, for needy families, for veterans groups, and for aging independence fighters. Irregular requests came from the government as well. Corporations were expected to donate generously after floods, for example, or for provincial sports meets.

These quasi-taxes allowed the government to run large, off-budget organizations, a sort of parallel state. The quasi-taxes allowed the government to make expenditures for projects that would not have to suffer even the minimal scrutiny of the National Assembly and would not have to be explained to international economists. Unfortunately, these off-budget quasi-tax collections were often a form of racketeering, one that reflected the government's mistrust of businessmen (think of Park Chung Hee's assault on "illicit profiteers" after he took power) and its inability to set up a broad, comprehensive tax system. Quasi-taxes reflected the brute power of the Korean state as well as the immaturity of Korea's tax and financial institutions.

Although subject to the predations of quasi-taxes, the chaebol and the rich could largely evade normal taxes by legally using aliases in the stock market and hiding behind a veil of nominee names in their real estate dealings. Only those unlucky enough to be caught up in one of the periodic purification campaigns, or unfortunate enough to be singled out for political retribution, paid any substantial taxes on money made through stocks or real estate. Although the country's tax system was extremely underdeveloped, partly because policymakers did not want to encourage capital flight, there was nonetheless a strong feeling that those with resources should make donations for the common good. This sentiment is part of the ideal of national capitalism in Korea, as it is in neighboring Japan and Taiwan.

Given the Korean concept of *minjok* ("race" or "people"), a businessman who was seen to embody the naked self-interest of a Western entrepreneur would be a target for destruction. Chung Ju Yung might literally work his construction workers to death, but if he was doing it for national development, not simply his personal profit, it would be accepted by many Koreans. In fact, the very concept of profit is hardly understood in Korea. Those with resources, especially corporations, are expected to donate generously to those with less, even if this is done at the expense of corporate investment for the future. Given this kind of ethos, it was virtually impossible for companies to turn down fund-raising requests, especially when they came from people in power who allegedly had charitable goals.

Ilhae was the clearest and largest case of a quasi-tax, a forced donation for semi-governmental purposes. "At the beginning, I thought it was a very pure and good idea," remembers Kim Suk Won, the young chairman of Ssangyong who was one of the businessmen who helped Ilhae get started. Kim's sentiments were echoed by many other business leaders, who wanted to help the families of those killed in Rangoon. But under pressure from the Blue House the project quickly drifted away from its original idea of helping the families, who in the end received almost no money. "Every time we met, the foundation was going into a new field," says Kim.[10]

The way that Ilhae raised money resembled an intelligence operation more than a charitable foundation. "When I arrived at Chong Wa Dae [the presidential Blue House] at the request of Chang [Se Dong, the president's security adviser], there were about seven to eight businessmen in a conference room of the security force office," said Yang Chung Mo, the head of Kukje, in describing the first Ilhae meeting. "Chung Soo Chang, president of the Korea Chamber of Commerce and Industry, said the fund-raising program of the foundation would collect 10 billion won in the first year of operation and another 20 billion won in the next two years to bring the total to 30 billion won. I got the strong impression that Chung . . . [had received] prior instructions from higher authorities on matters of fund-raising and other important projects. . . . [Later, after] I promised to give 500 million won . . . I went to an undercover housing unit located near Chong Wa Dae to deliver the sum to Cho Sun Hee, then a military colonel, on May 3."[11]

Virtually every major business group donated funds to Ilhae. The biggest groups, Hyundai and Samsung, and the state-owned steelmaker, Posco, each gave 4.5 billion won. Hyundai also contributed a plot of land worth an estimated 650 million won. Daewoo and Lucky Goldstar each chipped in 3 billion won, as did three second-tier chaebol, Sunkyong, Lotte, and Hanjin (the owner of Korean Air).

Shinhan Bank, which had recently been formed with funding from Korean residents of Japan, also donated 3 billion won. In all, forty-nine domestic business groups and three Japanese-invested companies contributed a total of 57.85 billion won.[12] The foundation raised money with the help of the three major business organizations, the Federation of Korean Industries, the Korea Chamber of Commerce and Industry and the Korean Foreign Trade Association.

Some flavor of just how all this money was raised emerged after Chun left office. An opposition lawmaker claimed in parliamentary hearings that the chairman of Korean Air, Cho Choong Hoon, was bullied by Chun into raising his donation to Ilhae. When Chun saw that Cho had written down "200 million" as his donation, Chun allegedly said, "I hear that you have hidden foreign currency abroad." Cho then quickly added a 2, bringing his initial donation to 2.2 billion won.[13]

Combined with the Madame Chang scandal, the strong-arm fund-raising tactics at Ilhae cost Chun whatever goodwill toward him still remained among the business and scholarly elite. A top adviser to Chun in the Blue House, who came from an academic rather than a military background, later tried to analyze where Chun had taken a wrong turn.

"Ilhae started out innocently enough, then it snowballed. He didn't have the right advisers," says this former assistant. This theme is a familiar one in Korean history, of the good but slightly dimwitted king led astray by treacherous courtiers.

> In the first two years of office Chun was concentrating on doing a good job. He was the new boy in town and he wanted to do his best. We would tell him that he would go down in history as the first president who walked out of the Blue House peacefully. We told him he couldn't compete with Park in economic policy but that he shouldn't go down in history as the guy who let Park's legacy be destroyed.
>
> He took all this stuff seriously. That was my impression. But by the midpoint of his term he began to think about post-presidential life. He probably came to the stark realization that if he just left the Blue House he would have nothing left. He would feel insecure, vulnerable. He couldn't go back to being a general. He didn't have social status prior to the presidency. He didn't have rich friends among his close friends. He comes from a different family background. He didn't move among the rich and powerful. He felt vulnerable without the protection of official power. He began to think he needed some resources, as a means of purchasing some influence, political or otherwise.[14]

Ilhae was the result. Its public face was a respectable think tank, headed by the well-regarded technocrat and Chun's former economic tutor, Kim Ki Hwan. Ilhae had joint seminars and research projects with the Brookings Institution and other prestigious international academic bodies. Participants at its seminars included political figures, such as former Japanese Prime Minister Nakasone Yasuhiro, former U.S. President Gerald Ford, former U.S. Secretary of State Henry Kissinger, and former U.S. National Security Adviser Zbigniew Brzezinski as well as respected academics. In this endeavor to appear respectable by surrounding itself with good company, Ilhae was acting out a typical Korean fantasy. Think of the Moonies (or, as the members of the Unification Church like to call themselves now, the Unificationists) with their lavish seminars. Just as Moon Sun Myung's followers lined up well-known, but often unwitting, international figures to give their organizations credibility, Ilhae used the cloak of respectability that institutions like Brookings and well-regarded scholars like Kim Ki Hwan brought to provide it with cover.

The institute presented itself as a modest collection of buildings hidden from a main road in Songnam, on the outskirts of Seoul. Built in an undeveloped rural area on the southern side of the hills that ring the capital, on land that was donated by Hyundai founder Chung Ju Yung, Ilhae looked very much like the research institute that it claimed to be, albeit one with tighter security than the average think tank. Barbed wire surrounded the huge compound and 42 of the foundation's 170 staff members were from Chun's presidential security force.[15]

A guest house intended for state visitors, and perhaps for Chun himself, was built at some distance from the research facility. The opposition made much of this imperial retreat when it was discovered after Chun left office. However, the real damage was done in the way the vast amounts of money were extorted from corporations and then put to use building a retirement home for Chun, rather than helping the relatives of those killed in Rangoon.

Ilhae was only the most egregious of the cash-rich fiefdoms Chun and his relatives were building. His wife, Lee Soon Ja, started the Saesaedae ("New Generation") Foundation and other ostensibly charitable organizations. She collected 42.2 billion won from these foundations, most of it in money handed over to her personally. Her aides pressured the wives of chaebol executives to donate freely, increasing the resentment that many of the elite already felt toward her as a brash parvenu.

Lee only made matters worse by pressing to invest much of the money she collected in real estate in Kangnam, an affluent and booming area of Seoul south of the Han River. Moreover, in a bizarre twist on the concept of quasi-taxes, which were intended to supplement regular government funds, she even forced the government itself to donate money to her pet causes. She received 1 billion won from government coffers in the form of donations by the Interior Ministry and the Ministry of Health and Social Affairs.[16]

At the same time, other relatives were peddling their alleged Blue House influence, even for matters as petty as securing permission to build new golf courses. Because Koreans are so intimidated by presidential power and so accustomed to paying bribes to secure permission for businesses, many of these claims passed unchallenged. Distant, and usually powerless, relatives pocketed windfalls by pretending to have Chun's ear.

Although there may have been instances of quiet resistance, most businessmen simply decided to play it safe and go along with requests for favors and money. Chun Ki Hwan, Chun's older brother, had been an ordinary policeman before his sibling became president. Then, as the "godfather of Yongsan" who controlled business in a central Seoul district, the head of Daelim Industrial thought Chun important enough to give him a no-show job at a travel agency at a salary of 1.2 million won a month.

Throughout this period, the president's younger brother, Kyung Hwan, was collecting millions of dollars for his Saemaul fiefdom, which was allegedly in the business of rural improvement. Although he resigned some of his positions after the Madame Chang scandal, "Baby Chun," as the press later dubbed him, retained control of the Saemaul movement. Saemaul Undong had been almost a religious cause during the 1970s. But under Chun it was a feeding trough. Saemaul raked in 150 billion won during the Fifth Republic, and the younger Chun managed to squander much of this money.

Park Chung Hee had succeeded in carefully preserving his image as a man above personal corruption. Most important, in contrast to Chun, his family was not corrupt. Former Ilhae head Kim Ki Hwan speaks for many Koreans when he says that Chun's inability to keep his family in check was the most obvious cause of his downfall.

In a way he is the victim of the Korean family system. In a large extended family, loyalty to the family is so important and when someone in the family becomes important everyone in the family looks to him for help and protection. [Chun] failed to manage his family affairs. Park Chung Hee was more resolute in that area.

Chun came from an even poorer family. Park's family at least owned enough land to farm. Chun's family didn't even have that. They were a very impoverished yangban family without land. Only desperate people went to Manchuria [as the Chuns did].[17]

The idea that businesses should arbitrarily pay tribute to government began to come under cautious attack during the 1980s. The Federation of Korean Industries (FKI) research institute studied quasi-taxes and timidly suggested that the government use only legal taxes. But the campaign had little effect, and quasi-taxes remained in the same range under Roh Tae Woo, who left office in 1992, as they had been under Chun.

The Federation of Korean Industries estimated that quasi-taxes during the Fifth Republic ranged from 0.48 percent to 0.85 percent of total annual sales at Korean companies. In 1980, quasi-taxes were at their lowest level (0.48 percent). They rose to 0.85 percent of sales in 1983 and fluctuated between 0.74 percent and 0.82 percent for the remainder of Chun's tenure.

This was a heavy burden on companies, most of whom were making only minimal profits. The average corporate expenditure on quasi-taxes in 1980 was 220 million won. The figure peaked at just over one billion won in 1986, sank and then rose again in the late 1980s. In 1989, the average corporation spent 1.4 billion won on quasi-taxes.[18]

Significantly, the FKI study on quasi-taxes did not include unreported donations. Chun would periodically call the heads of chaebol together and hint at the amount of money he needed. The FKI, the Korean Traders Association, and the Korea Chamber of Commerce and Industry would then issue quotas for individual companies, generally based on their overall sales. Not to donate the requested amount was to invite disaster.

One of the most notorious special projects during Chun's years was the so-called Peace Dam, a dam designed to stop a supposed North Korean "water bomb." The Peace Dam campaign typified the way the tenuous checks and balances of Korea, Inc. broke down during the Fifth Republic. Acting on the basis of what turned out to be faulty intelligence, the South Korean national security apparatus decided that a dam the North Koreans were building close to the border might be deliberately blown up, unleashing a wall of water that would inundate Seoul. It was a bizarre, preposterous fantasy, but one that is to some extent understandable in the tense aftermath of the Rangoon bombing. South Korea embarked on a mass mobilization campaign, and donations poured in from schoolchildren, businessmen, housewives, and the bevy of associations that formed the foundation of the Korean corporate structure.

In all, about $70 million was collected to build the prophylactic dam, but it is unclear where the money went. Construction was quietly halted shortly after Roh took office in 1988, when the project was re-evaluated and declared unnecessary. The whole notion was completely and publicly discredited after Kim Young Sam took power in 1993.

The Peace Dam project had already strained relations between Chun and Hyundai founder Chung Ju Yung. Chung's hometown was near the site of the North Korean dam, and he paid a quiet visit to the president to tell him that the South Korean fears of a "water bomb over Seoul" were unfounded. A confidant of Chung's describes this visit to the Blue House:

> He knew the terrain, he knew how the water flowed. He knew that the dam could not be 180 meters high, because of gaps in the mountains, and he knew that it would take much longer to fill than the government was saying. He went very quietly to President Chun and told him this. His advice was rejected. He felt angry and humiliated.[19]

Chun's refusal to heed his advice embittered Chung. The two men had never liked each other much, but the refusal of the younger general to listen to the counsel of the older man drove them further apart. Partly as a result of this incident, Chung stepped down in early 1987 as chairman of the FKI, which he had headed since 1977.[20]

There had been other spats between Chun and Chung. During the late 1970s Hyundai invested heavily in acquiring liquefied natural gas (LNG) terminal technology and won a contract through competitive bidding. "Then in mid-1981 Chung was called in and told to give up the contract," says a Hyundai executive. "Hanyang got it. Chun's brother, Chun Ki Hwan, was an agent for Hanyang."

The government also wanted Hyundai, the country's largest construction company, to take over some smaller bankrupt construction firms that had been ruined by their headlong expansion into the Middle East. "Chung doesn't take bankrupt companies as a matter of principle," says the Hyundai executive. "Even after the government offered him some goodies he said no on principle."[21]

Chun was, to businessmen like Chung Ju Yung and Samsung's Lee Byung Chull, an upstart, a military officer who had been thrust on the scene. They were not happy with his reliance on what they regarded as overly theoretical economic advisers, such as Kim Jae Ik. Increasingly, however, it was Chun's personal manner that grated on them. A leading businessman speaks for many businessmen and government officials in his assessment of the difference between Park and Chun.

> I went to meetings with both of them. If Park held a meeting with business leaders for three hours, he talked fifteen minutes and listened the rest of the time. Some of it was pure bullshit. He knew how to use [us]. But still he listened. In a three-hour dinner with businessmen during the Chun years, Chun may have spoken two hours and fifty minutes on business matters. It was compulsory to go [to these dinners]. If someone else had an idea in his presence, Chun didn't like that.[22]

Most of the business community's anger was directed at the political-security staff in the Blue House. But an interventionist, slow-growth economic team compounded the general sense of unhappiness with the Fifth Republic. The economic team that stepped in after the Rangoon bombing was more cautious and less reform-minded than the one that had been killed in Rangoon.

The new policymakers' first real test came in 1983, when it became clear that the economy would turn in its first year of high growth during the Fifth Republic, a solid 11 percent. Instead of hailing this as proof that the liberalization program was working, the economic ministers fussed about the dangers of inflation and stepped hard on the monetary brakes. They brought economic growth down to 8 percent in 1984, and to 5 percent in 1985, a slowdown that brought several large companies to their knees.

The government continued to exercise tremendous control over the economy. Even though many of the new ministers believed in liberalization, the critical momentum in favor of liberalization was largely lost in the traumatic transition to a new cabinet. "In 1984–85 it was basically a command economy, in spite of all the things you can say for the private sector," says a Korean businessman who was trained as an economist in the United States, where he worked for some years as a professor.

If anything, it was a more consistent command economy in 1984–85 than it had ever been, because the technocrats had a clear idea of how they wanted to restructure the economy and they had the power to do it. Says this scholar-businessman:

> In the past, the annual budget had always been fragmented. The government would balance the main budget while it was making a big hole in the other budgets. [But under Chun] the economic management team had a balanced budget on an integrated basis. How? They simply froze wages for civil servants for several years and they set up wage-price guidelines for the private sector. It was not jawboning, as you say [in the United States], it was hammering down.
>
> With the grain management fund the government decided how much rice it would purchase at what price. It was a decision made between the Economic Planning Board and the Ministry of Agriculture, with the Blue House participating. There were no street demonstrations by farmers; [there was] no screaming in the National Assembly.[23]

A forced restructuring of the shipping industry provided the clearest example of how far the new group of economic ministers was prepared to go in micromanaging the economy, no matter how much they might profess their allegiance to free market forces. Korea had forcefully built up its merchant fleet by giving subsidies for ship purchases and by restricting the operation of foreign vessels. Korean exporters usually were required to send their goods abroad in ships built, owned, and operated by Koreans. This policy had started in the mid-1970s, when Hyundai had been unable to sell the first ships it built. The merchant fleet expansion provided jobs for sailors and an outlet for shipyard production. It also ensured that most of the freight charges from the country's growing trade volume remained in Korean hands. This kept the balance of payments problem in check and reduced the amount of money Korea needed to borrow from abroad.

The huge merchant fleet turned out to be too much of a good thing by 1984. Sluggish world trade and falling shipping charges threatened to bankrupt dozens of the country's shipping companies. Rather than letting the market take its course, however, the government took matters into its own hands. After a review, the authorities forcibly reorganized the industry. Sometimes bigger companies were eager to gobble up smaller ones, but sometimes acquirers had to be cajoled into a rescue mission with the implicit promise of a later government favor. Only seventeen of sixty-seven firms remained after the restructuring was complete. As in the case of the 1980 industrial restructuring, the attempt to merge bitter rivals inevitably led to wrangling.

As usual, the mergers favored the strong companies, which were invariably part of the large chaebol. The biggest winners from the restructuring were Hanjin, the seventh-largest group in Korea and the owner of Korean Air, and Hyundai.

A similar reorganization took place in the construction industry. Dozens of construction firms had sprouted up to take advantage of the Middle East construction boom in the 1970s. But by the early 1980s the boom had turned to bust. Sometimes failed firms were attractive because they had large land banks. Many, however, had nothing to recommend them, and companies often resisted taking them over because they could not easily shed employees from the failing firms.

"These were not mergers in the true sense of the word," says the president of a major construction company. "Some of these companies had gone into bankruptcy. When the commercial banks could not carry the bankruptcy they asked another construction company to take over. Lots of companies, like [ours], resisted very strongly. When the government said, 'We want you to take over this company' we said, 'No.' Some firms, however, could not resist."[24] This sort of resistance would have been difficult to imagine during Park's administration. Soon, however, the Chun administration would send a pointed and painful reminder to business that the Blue House still had the power not only to make companies but to break them.

Notes

1. Quoted in the *Asian Wall Street Journal*, October 11, 1983, on the possible reaction of the South Korean government to the Burmese bombing.

2. This information comes from the "Burmese Report to the United Nations on the findings and measures taken in connection with the North Korean bombing attack in Rangoon." The text is reproduced in the *Korea Annual*, 1985, pp. 358–63.

Information on the Claymore mines comes from *Far Eastern Economic Review*, October 27, 1983. Author John McBeth believes the bugler mistook the ambassador for Chun.

3. Burma was Chun's first stop on a tour that was to have included India, Sri Lanka, Australia, New Zealand, and Brunei. This was Chun's fourth overseas trip, but one that seemed to have no clearly defined purpose. Kim Jae Ik's widow remembers that her husband, who had accompanied Chun on all his trips abroad, had "strangely" commented that this would be a "meaningless" trip. Author interview, October 1991.

4. Tony Michell provided the information about the MTI directors on the basis of personal experience. John Bennett spoke with Kim Jae Ik shortly before he went to Rangoon.

5. Author interview, October 1991.

6. The quotations from Kang are from an *Asian Wall Street Journal* interview, January 11, 1983.

7. Author interview, November 1990.

8. Ilhae was composed of the characters for sun and sea. It meant, in the words of a Chun aide, that the organization "shines on the world like the sun and accommodates everything like the sea." Choi Soon Dal, whose National Assembly testimony was quoted in the *Korea Herald*, November 10, 1988.

9. This rough estimate is based on the Federation of Korean Industries estimate that about 0.5 percent GNP annually went to quasi-taxes. The FKI's estimates do not include the most politically sensitive contributions or outright bribes.

10. Author interview, November 1990.

11. *Korea Herald*, November 10, 1988.

12. The figure comes from newspaper accounts of the Fifth Republic hearings. Other figures are slightly different. To my knowledge, no official figure has ever been published.

13. *Korea Herald*, November 4, 1988.

14. Author interview, January 1991.

15. The information on the security staff came from Ilhae director Kim Ki Hwan's testimony before a special National Assembly hearing in late 1988. *Korea Herald*, November 4, 1988.

Hyundai's Chung unsuccessfully tried to reclaim his increasingly valuable land after Chun left office in disgrace in 1988.

16. *Korea Herald*, November 8, 1988.

17. Author interview, February 1992.

18. This information was provided to the author by the Korea Economic Research Institute, the FKI's research wing, in April 1991.

19. Author interview, March 1991.

20. *Wall Street Journal*, March 31, 1987. The information about Chung Ju Yung's meeting with Chun Doo Hwan is from a confidant of the Hyundai founder. The government collected 77 billion won of which some 13 billion won was not properly accounted for. *The Economist*, March 13, 1994.

21. Author interview, March 1991. This strategy was very different from Daewoo's policy of growing by acquiring troubled companies. Chung Ju Yung, in his autobiography, specifically criticized Kim Woo Choong for this policy of growth by acquisition. Chung, however, sometimes bent his rule. As noted below, Hyundai benefitted from the 1985 reorganization of the shipping industry.

22. Author interview, March 1991.

23. Author interview, January 1992.

24. Ibid.

16

Dangerous Corner

The old foxes became perfunctory in dealing with Chun. They liked Park, but they feared Chun because he was unpredictable.
                                                                —Hyundai executive[1]

On the morning of February 21, 1985, the chairman of South Korea's sixth-largest conglomerate was summoned to the president's office at the Korea First Bank (Cheil Bank) and ordered to surrender his business empire. Anything else would invite trouble from politically powerful people, Kukje chairman Yang Chung Mo was told by the bank president and a senior official from the tax office. When Yang hesitated he was warned that the order to relinquish his stock came from President Chun and that people would be "hurt" if he did not cooperate. The chairman had no choice but to use his chop, his signature seal, on the documents that had already been drawn up to dissolve his group.

The Korea First Bank then sold the corporation's new headquarters building and distributed its major subsidiaries to other business groups on secret terms. There was no due process, no bidding for assets, only a multimillion-dollar takeover operation shrouded in secrecy. The Ministry of Finance and the Bank of Korea quietly told banks to roll over much of Kukje's debt at concessional rates for the new owners. This was the ugly side of Korea, Inc., and as whispers of political retribution circulated in the business world, the Kukje collapse stood as a warning to other businessmen not to flout the will of the president or his powerful aides.

The technocrats during the mid-1980s had an ambitious agenda. They wanted to restructure the chaebol, stabilize the economy, and liberalize the financial system in order to set the stage for another growth spurt. Deputy Prime Minister

218

Kim Mahn Je, like many of his fellow technocrats, disdained the sprawling, debt-burdened chaebol that were still managed by their founding families. So it came as little surprise that the economic team he led prepared to punish some of the weaker chaebol as a way of goading the others to rationalize their business lines and management structure.

This policy was one that relied not on market discipline but, rather, on government-imposed dictates. Because of the way politics and business were woven together in Korea, and because of the cloak of secrecy that obscured Kukje's dismantling, the dismembering sparked charges of political revenge and posed fundamental questions about the fairness of the Korean system. It frightened many companies, but it also forced them to redouble their efforts to become more competitive and independent of the government.

Disciplining Business: The Politics of Pain

By the beginning of 1985, Kukje's 38,000 workers were involved in everything from making jogging shoes in Pusan to planning an aluminum smelting plant in Australia. Kukje employees were steelmakers at its Yonhap Steel subsidiary and desk clerks at its Hyatt Hotel resort on Cheju Island. They worked in construction, securities, paper-making, and shipping companies. Kukje's assembly-line workers made shirts and stuffed toys, farm tools and tires.

Set up nearly forty years earlier as a rubber-shoe maker, Kukje had prospered during the Park Chung Hee years. Yang Chung Mo, son of the founder, had gone on an acquisition binge during the 1970s. From 1971 to 1979, Kukje bought or founded nineteen companies. In 1977 alone, Kukje took over seven companies, flourishing on the strength of its political connections. During the 1970s, when Park Chung Hee arrested Yonhap Steel owner Kwon Chul Hyun on tax evasion and money-laundering charges, the president also stripped him of his steel company. Kwon was forced to sell the company at only 5 percent of its nominal value. Kukje was the lucky buyer.

In spite of this breakneck expansion, Kukje had no professional management, relying instead on an uneven collection of relatives to run its sprawling corporate empire. Yang had no sons, but eight of his nine sons-in-law were among the group's senior executives. Some Koreans called Kukje the "son-in-law conglomerate," and there were publicly reported quarrels among the family managers, most of whom had few qualifications other than their status as in-laws. An executive at another business group, who had previously served in the government, says that these squabbles made the company especially vulnerable.

> It was a time when the top management should have united and put the best foot forward. But I don't think they realized the seriousness of the times. . . . Investments were not guided by opportunity but to balance the contending claims among the major factions in the management.[2]

Kukje, in short, was a classic chaebol of the worst sort. It was in debt, inefficient, and split by family feuds. Its principal strength was its size and the hope that this size would prevent its failure. Yet in spite of the company's precarious financial status it was putting up a flashy new headquarters building. Budgeted at 20 billion won, the silver-and-glass, angular tower in downtown Seoul cost three or four times that by the time it was finished. "Anyone who builds a headquarters that ugly deserves to go bankrupt," one high-ranking technocrat later scoffed. Some of the company's construction was remarkably bad: At the Hyatt Hotel it was building on the resort island of Cheju, Kukje's joint venture partner was horrified to find raw sewage backing up into the hotel's swimming pool.

Even some of Kukje's next generation of managers knew that this sort of hodge-podge empire had to be reformed or it would not survive. Efforts to improve the company's financial and management structure had begun in 1984 after thirty-five-year-old Kim Douk Young was named to head the group at the beginning of the year. Kim, who was one of Yang's sons-in-law, quickly began a process of mergers and divestitures in an effort to streamline the company, consolidating the construction company and the Kukje Corporation trading company.

"I wanted to realign the entire corporate group so that we will be specializing in the few areas where we can do best," he told an interviewer in early 1984, by way of explaining a corporate restructuring plan. "By merging we will have increased efficiency, lower overhead costs and an improved balance sheet and financial stability." In the West, these statements would have been nothing exceptional, but in Korea talk like this was a radical departure from the tradition of paying attention almost exclusively to increasing sales, assets, and employees.

Kukje did not have the time to restructure. In late 1984, the Ministry of Finance announced that a popular tool of corporate financing, known as *wonmae* bonds, would be phased out by the end of March 1985. Both Kukje and government officials knew that this policy could sound a death knell for the group, which relied heavily on the bonds, which were a cross between straight corporate debt and the informal market.

Kukje did not have access to enough long-term funding to finance its expansion. At the same time, the company consistently ran an overdraft at its prime bank, the Korea First Bank. Both the reliance on short-term borrowing and the habitual overdrafts were common corporate strategies in capital-short Korea, but Kukje was unusually exposed. Any short-term disruption in funding, any reluctance by lenders to renew loans as they matured, could spell disaster. Kukje had to hope that the government would simply decide that it was too big to allow it to fail. In fact, at the end of December, banks acting on government orders extended an emergency 240-billion-won loan to prevent the group's collapse.

The decision to formally dissolve the group on February 21 ended this period of turmoil. After a period of bank management, Hanil Synthetic Fiber acquired Kukje's footwear and trading companies. Dongkuk Steel picked up the group's steel subsidiary. These three companies accounted for about 80 percent of Kukje's sales. Both acquirers had close ties with the Blue House. Commercial bankers took over operations at some of the smaller companies in the disbanded groups.

Between 1983 and 1987, Hanil was the second-largest corporate donor to organizations such as Saesaedae and Saemaul controlled by Chun and his relatives and donated 900 million won to the Ilhae Foundation. Dongkuk Steel had even better connections to the Blue House because it was controlled by one of First Lady Lee Soon Ja's relatives. In a 1989 lawsuit, Yang Chung Mo claimed that Dongkuk had donated 60 billion won to a Blue House political fund in return for permission to take over the steel company.

Kwon Chul Hyun, founder and owner of Yonhap Steel until Kukje took it over in 1978, was livid at the transfer of Kukje's steel unit to Dongkuk. Kwon had seen the disintegration of Kukje coming and, through a relative who had been one of Chun's assistants, lobbied the Blue House in an effort to get his company back. Some of Chun's aides apparently recommended that Yonhap be returned to Kwon, but finally, on the express order of President Chun, it was transferred to Dongkuk.

There was no room for debate or discussion because few people knew the details of the operation. Kukje's borrowings totaled 1.9 trillion won. In an unpublicized rescue operation, the Ministry of Finance and the Bank of Korea told banks simply to write off 337 billion won of Kukje's debt and reschedule another 560 billion won that was incurred by Hanil and Dongkuk when they took over the two companies. In other words, more than $1 billion of debt was forgiven or lent on concessionary terms.[3]

This was, as far as the government was concerned, an internal affair, to be settled quietly and with a minimum of fuss. But Kukje had some loans outstanding to foreign banks, which the government quickly and publicly guaranteed. It was a case in which Korea, Inc. closed ranks to the outside world.

If it had merely been a case of Kukje's creditors' forcing the company to restructure, there probably would have been relatively little controversy. But because the financial system was controlled by the government, the whole affair was tinged with politics and made Kukje an archetypal example of Korea, Inc. at work. When big companies went bankrupt in Korea, it was not only because of economic problems. As critics of Chun pointed out, other large groups had financial situations every bit as bad as Kukje's. Understandably, in a country where public explanations for controversial events usually obscure the truth, political revenge was quickly presumed.

The way these companies were parceled out prompted grumbling about the growth of crony capitalism under Chun. Although Park had played favorites, the former president had managed to convince Koreans that he was above corruption. The Madame Chang curb market scandal had alerted people to the fact that Chun's relatives were intent on plunder and that the president might let them get away with it. Kukje seemed to confirm this suspicion.

Kukje's largest factories were in Pusan, and its chairman, Yang Chung Mo, supported the opposition leader and future president, Kim Young Sam. The opposition had won a moral victory in National Assembly elections held only eleven days before Kukje's dismembering, a victory that eroded the facade of political stability and passivity that had been enforced since Chun had seized power five years earlier. The newly formed opposition New Korea Democratic Party (NKDP), aided by the dramatic return from the United States of Kim Dae Jung four days before the election, managed to win 29 percent of the vote, not far behind the 35 percent polled by the ruling Democratic Justice Party (DJP). Counting the old-line Democratic Korea Party, the opposition parties took nearly 50 percent of the vote.

Yang claimed that his support of the opposition, whose candidates won in Pusan, coupled with his failure to contribute generously to Ilhae and Saemaul, prompted Chun to topple his business empire. In an emotional appearance before the National Assembly in 1988, Yang claimed that his donation of "only" 300 million won—nearly half a million dollars—to Chun Kyung Hwan's Saemaul movement, sparked opposition to him among Chun and his advisers. He also claimed that tardiness at a Blue House reception due to bad weather had angered Chun's aides and contributed to the decision to pull the company apart. Most Koreans, eager to believe the worst about the Fifth Republic, appeared to accept Yang's contention.

Whatever the truth, the message many Koreans got was that Chun and those around him wanted no opposition, either in the form of donations to opposition political parties or resistance to his demands for the clandestine tribute he was extracting from business for the Ilhae Foundation.

What appears to have happened, in fact, is that the decision to bring down Kukje was initiated by senior technocrats who subsequently won Chun's support for reasons that probably were tainted by politics.

Nearly six years after Kukje collapsed, Kim Mahn Je spoke about the decision. Kim, who became chairman of Samsung Life Insurance in early 1991 and head of Posco in 1994, freely admitted that politics—but not political revenge—were involved in bringing down Kukje. That, he said, is inevitable in Korea, where the financial system is controlled by the government. Credit is the life-blood of a corporation, and the government officials who control its flow have the power of corporate survival. "It got to be a political decision [because] financial institutions are the main instruments used by the government. The responsibility [to decide who gets credit] falls on the government. Somebody has to decide [who gets] the ration card."

This process of rationing credit is not, Kim willingly conceded, a scientific one. "It's not market forces [which decide] who will get punished. . . . Ethical questions arise [because] it's handled by men, not market forces."

Companies faced a precarious economic situation in early 1985. An overvalued exchange rate and tight monetary growth had squeezed both exports and the domestic economy. Shipping and construction companies were in deep trouble, as were large groups such as Kukje and Daewoo. "They were on the brink of financial collapse," Kim said. "I had two choices: either stop the financial squeeze—that would mean higher inflation which would disguise their weaknesses—or let them go and [be ready to accept] wholesale bankruptcies. Even in an authoritarian regime like ours I don't think the public could swallow that. So what do you do? Even though it's very messy, you do it in an administrative way.... If you don't have enough of a market system you have to constantly juggle."

Ironically, Kim argues that politics in fact slowed down the decision to dismantle Kukje. Although Yang says Chun was angry at the election results, Kim says that the technocrats wanted to act sooner but were forced to wait until after the election to bring the company down. "We should have done it earlier. We didn't have the stomach, the guts."

The technocrats who controlled the levers of financial power were very clear about what they wanted to do. They did not much like the chaebol. Their executives were "arrogant," complained Kim Mahn Je, in a comment echoed by many other senior economic officials. Management was inefficient, unfocused, irrational. The huge, sprawling chaebol were, in short, offensive to the technocrats. "We tried to show [business] a lesson," said Kim Mahn Je, who, in this 1990 interview, remained skeptical that business would learn that lesson—"unless the whole system is changed."

As for the rumors of political involvement in the process, Kim claims to know nothing. "I had no idea what the relationship between [Chun and Yang] was, because I didn't care that much. The position of the technocrats was that we didn't care that much about the political side. Perhaps we deliberately tried not to go into that area. [The political] secretaries managed that area. We were sort of pushed aside." Kim's account largely rings true, for economic policymakers in Korea are typically outside of the main political decision-making process, which tends to be jealously guarded by a few presidential assistants.[4]

Business got the message. "Big business got scared," said a Hyundai executive. "All of them [now] knew what the government could do with one blow. It was a sobering experience, particularly for the owners. I could think of other groups which were in worse situations than Kukje financially. If this could happen to Kukje it could happen to many others."[5]

Business did learn something from the dismantling of Kukje and the slower economic growth of the early 1980s. Investment plans became more focused, and the impulsive leaps into new businesses less frequent. Critics of the chaebol often point out that the government only rarely punishes business. But one does not need to bring down too many big groups for the whole business community to get the message.

Immediately after Kukje's collapse, government officials hinted that other conglomerates might follow. There were rumors that Daewoo, the country's fourth-largest group, was going to be brought down as well. Chun, it was said, was backing those who wanted to winnow out the weak conglomerates. The rumors were so persistent and widespread that Deputy Prime Minister Kim issued a formal statement at the end of February saying that the government did not intend to dismantle any other chaebol. After he left office, however, Kim Mahn Je said that there was truth to the stories that the technocrats had hoped to dismember some of the other groups. The government backed off because of the sluggish economy and the fear that the collapse of another large business group would cost Korea international credibility.[6]

Daewoo was the most obvious candidate for a government-imposed restructuring. The firm was struggling under the burden of heavy interest payments on its Okpo shipyard, which was finished just as the shipbuilding industry entered a long depression. Many people in Seoul believe that Daewoo chairman Kim Woo Choong saved the group only through a brilliant lobbying campaign. The Seoul rumor mill, in one of its more endearing bits of apocrypha, had it that Kim Woo Choong was traveling around the world in February and March 1985 in order to avoid a summons from the Blue House. Stories had Kim traveling from Libya, where Daewoo had large construction contracts, to Latin America on his personal jet, trying to stay one step ahead of Korean Foreign Ministry officials who were instructed to order him to return to Seoul. Kim reportedly remained abroad until his emissaries were able to persuade the president that Daewoo, with a higher international reputation than Kukje, should be allowed to survive, if only for reasons of national pride and Korea's international credit standing.

The dismantling of Kukje showed that the policy pendulum was once again swinging against the chaebol, just as it had in the early days of the Fifth Republic. Yet the government was no more able to control the chaebol in the mid-1980s than it had been at the beginning of the decade. In a series of confused policy announcements, the government managed to anger the large business groups without winning much support from the public.

Kukje's dismemberment was not the first time the government had pulled apart a major corporation. In 1979, after a period of rapid economic growth and growing concern about big business' power in the economy, the issue of the chaebol was sharply pinpointed by the collapse in 1979 of Yulsan, which had been one of the biggest and fastest-growing business groups. Shin Sun Ho had founded Yulsan only in 1975, at the age of thirty-one, with $2,000. Initially he operated out of a hotel room as a sales agent.

By the end of his first year in business Shin had two companies, Yulsan Industrial and Yulsan Aluminum. He set up Yulsan Construction in 1976. Shin expanded his empire by using his influence to take over bankrupt companies or companies on which banks could be persuaded to foreclose. Five companies were set up or acquired in 1977 and another six in 1978. By the end of 1978, Yulsan had fourteen companies in exporting, construction, aluminum, shipping, engineering, electronics, foodstuffs, and construction materials.

Only three years after Yulsan was founded, its gross corporate assets totaled $230 million. Exports, concentrated in basic products such as cement, steel, and plywood, surged from $42 million in 1976 to $165 million in 1977. At the time of its collapse, Yulsan even was planning to move into aluminum refining, prefabricated aluminum buildings, shopping malls, and ready-to-wear clothing. This crazy-quilt approach to business typifies Korean chaebol, which usually will expand into any promising business area where they can secure finance. This is not as irrational as it might seem. Business opportunities in a fast-growing economy like Korea's are usually limited primarily by lack of government permission, money, or managerial capabilities.

The misuse of export promotion loans was one of the major charges against Shin after the collapse of Yulsan. In fact, Yulsan had done nothing worse than other chaebol had in its use of subsidized government export financing to leverage its operations. One of Yulsan's mistakes, however, was that its accountants did not even bother to cover up the misuse of borrowed funds within the group.

For example, Yulsan borrowed 1 billion won from a bank, ostensibly to finance a Yulsan Construction building project. Shin then invested 140 million won of the proceeds to start a shipping company. As soon as registration was complete, the bank lent the new company 140 million won to pay back the loan it had taken out from the construction company. It is estimated that Yulsan used about 10 billion won ($20.66 million at prevailing exchange rates) in export loans in similar pyramid financial deals.

The leverage of the Yulsan group was exceptional, even by Korean standards, with $27 of debt for every $1 of equity. Some of this debt was related to its export activities, which allowed the company to tap concessionary 120-day credits at an annual interest rate that fluctuated between 8 and 9 percent, compared with a free market rate of more than 20 percent. Yulsan's survival depended on continued rapid growth in exports; high growth would ensure its access to the cheap credit that kept its increasingly precarious financial structure from imploding. Exports, however, were no longer expanding rapidly in the late 1970s.

The decisive blow came when the government suddenly banned exports of cement in 1978 to facilitate a crash program of domestic apartment construction, which the president's advisers convinced him was necessary to stave off middle-class discontent with rising real estate prices. This move caught Yulsan by surprise. The company was too far off balance to recover from the ban on overseas shipments of its major export product. Total exports by Yulsan in 1978 amounted to only $150 million, compared with $165 million in 1977 and far short of its export target of nearly $400 million. As a result, its main source of financing, export credits, shriveled. In November 1978, company checks totaling 2.8 billion won bounced at the Bank of Seoul. The bank was, with the assistance of Blue House contacts, persuaded to advance 6 billion won in relief funding.

Yulsan may not have had many exports, but it certainly was not lacking in creativity. By early 1979 Yulsan was exporting ordinary rocks, labeled as commodities and financed by fraudulent letters of credit opened by its overseas branches in order to generate "exports." This would not be the only time a chaebol's far-flung tentacles have helped group companies try to get out of trouble by using fake letters of credit. The problem, of course, was that in the end the goods had to be shipped and in Yulsan's case there was nothing to export. In April 1979, Shin and the president of Bank of Seoul were arrested. The dismembering of Yulsan followed.

The collapse of Yulsan came less from overexpansion than from a deliberate decision by the banks not to provide further credit to overcome the company's liquidity crisis. To bring the banks to this point, it was necessary to convince President Park to dismiss one of his Blue House secretaries; in the ensuing investigation the heads of four of the five commercial banks were forced to resign to take responsibility for lending to a company that broke the rules.

The meteoric rise and fall of Yulsan showed both the open nature of the Korean economy in the 1970s to those who understood the system, and the mercilessness of Korea, Inc. to those who used the system to advance themselves and then stumbled. Yulsan's collapse had parallels with the subsequent dismemberment of Kukje in 1985. Like Kukje, there were rumors that Yulsan had given funds to opposition politicians. Moreover, Yulsan had grown by gaining political influence in the Blue House, bending bank rules, and preying on less well-funded companies.

Apologists for Korea's cozy business-government relationship like to claim that the forced collapse of Yulsan and Kukje proves that the government disciplines nonperformers. But these corporate crashes are the exceptions that prove the rule: The government creates winners in the Korean economy, and those who lose are never punished simply on economic grounds.

Controlling the Chaebol

In an economy as highly leveraged as Korea's, control of the financial system gave the government extraordinary power over the economy. Credit control could be used as a club, as it was when the government cut off Kukje. Or it could be used more benignly, as it was in mid-1985, when the central Bank of Korea stepped in with low-interest loans to rescue the banks from the burden of their nonperforming loans. "If we had not given the special loans to the commercial banks, I think they would have collapsed," a Bank of Korea official said several years later.[7]

The central bank cut its interest rate on these policy loans from 6 percent to 3 percent and funneled 300 billion won in emergency low-interest loans to the banks. It was the first of three special loans to the banks. From 1985 to 1987, these low-interest loans totaled 1.7 trillion won; the actual amounts of policy loans were far higher, because this figure does not include a variety of other special financing funds.

The banks, in turn, used the money to prop up failing companies. The banks had no choice but to channel the money to the companies and hope that the government somehow made up the losses to them at a later date. Ordinary bank shareholders had no idea of the scope of the operation, and would have been powerless to stop it even if they had. The top management of the banks was still appointed by the Ministry of Finance, and bank presidents were personally beholden to the government for their jobs. Many, in fact, were former Ministry of Finance officials.

The rescue operation was conducted in secrecy, although the government let it be known that it was stepping in to save the commercial banks. The economic slowdown may have left the Ministry of Finance and the central bank little choice. But the consequences for South Korea's financial system have been far-reaching. The nonperforming loans, which in mid-1989 still totaled 2.5 trillion won at the five major commercial banks, effectively froze financial reform for several years. (When the Korea Development Bank and other state-owned banks are included, the total may have been as much as twice as high.)[8] Policymakers were afraid to allow competition from foreign banks or other domestic financial institutions until the banks had dug themselves out of the pit of bad debt. That decision, in turn, helped keep interest rates well above world levels and made it more difficult for South Korean manufacturers to compete.

The commercial banks had been nominally privatized in what the Fifth Republic technocrats and bureaucrats speciously claimed was one of the administration's greatest successes in making the economy more market-oriented. But in 1985 the banks were once again used as a government tool to keep the economy from imploding. The dangerous corner of 1985, when it looked as if the economy might come undone, showed how fragile the reforms instituted in the early days of the Fifth Republic were. For all the talk in the early 1980s of encouraging free market forces, the slowdown of 1985 and the fear it sparked in the government reinforced the state's continuing heavy involvement in the economy. This retreat from reform was to occur repeatedly throughout the latter part of the decade, most dramatically with the government's rescue of Daewoo Shipbuilding in 1989.

The government conducted the 1985 rescue operation furtively and stonewalled opposition attempts to unearth details about which companies had received cheap credit. This reflected the elitism of the planners, a thoroughgoing contempt for politicians, and the technocrats' contention that they were scientists in an economic laboratory. The independent *Dong-A Ilbo* newspaper summed up the national mood with an editorial saying, "National consensus should be made with the special loan[s] which will affect greatly the competing interest of the Korean people. That's the most vital step to minimize a possible backlash." It was a prophetic warning. After Chun left office, the technocrats were caught up in the furor over the Fifth Republic. Kim Mahn Je, former Finance Minister and presidential secretary Sakong Il, and others were questioned both by prosecutors and hostile legislators for their role in the collapse of Kukje and the forced restructuring of the shipping and construction industries.[9]

Even at the time, some businessmen and bankers joined opposition politicians and newspapers in criticizing this rescue package. Local newspapers complained that the bailout favored big business, while two banks that had relatively few problem loans, Shinhan Bank and Hanil Bank, argued that the bailout also favored bad bank management. This critique was a prescient one. Because banks knew that the government would rescue them from their bad decisions, and that the easiest policy was simply to follow Finance Ministry orders, the stability of the financial system would continue to rely heavily on the ability of government technocrats and bureaucrats.

The various restructurings presided over by Kim Mahn Je, Sakong Il, and the rest of the team cost the country an enormous amount of money. New bank loans given to acquiring companies totaled 6.8 trillion won, or about $8.5 billion. Interest payments on another 4.2 trillion won of principal were delayed or reduced. Another 986 billion won in bad debt was simply written off. The biggest beneficiaries were those who picked up the pieces of Kukje, but low-interest loans were also used to smooth the reorganization of the shipping and construction industry. Jungwoo Development, known as the "forty-eight-star company" because of all the ex-generals in its ranks and which reportedly had thrived thanks to strong military connections to Chun, was one of the most prominent companies to be brought down. More than 500 billion won of its loans was written off or rolled over to acquiring firms on favorable terms.[10]

Policymakers redoubled their efforts to rein in the chaebol at this time. New credit regulations, announced just before the crash of Kukje, made takeovers of small firms more difficult and restricted growth in unrelated business sectors. At the same time, the government said it would try to control speculative real estate activities by the large groups. These new regulations had no enforcement power, and, as it turned out, the policies were more a sop to public opinion than an effective means of dealing with the very real policy issue of concentrated real estate holdings in densely populated Korea. Introduction of the "real name financial system," which by outlawing the use of aliases in financial transactions would have given some teeth to the stated policies, had been one of Kim Jae Ik's unfinished tasks at the time of his death. But it was not even mentioned in 1985, reflecting how public relations had triumphed over substance.

Business leaders held a meeting with Chun on April 2, 1985, in an attempt to get lower interest rates and defend themselves against the anti-chaebol measures that economic planners were beginning to implement. Present were the heads of all major conglomerates, including Hyundai's Chung Ju Yung, Samsung's Lee Byung Chull, Daewoo's Kim Woo Choong, and Lucky-Goldstar's Koo Cha Kyung. This meeting put the Blue House, the technocrats, and bureaucrats on notice that big business was going to fight aggressively any attempt to impose sweeping restrictions. The relatively modest measures eventually adopted to control the chaebol, many of which were struggling to stay solvent during a period of economic weakness, in part reflected how much business' power had grown since 1980. It took nearly three years of struggle before business was able to get out from under the 1980 forced industrial restructuring, but the effect of the 1985 measures was shrugged off by most companies in a matter of months.

One of the most controversial proposals in 1985 was to allow the Office of Bank Supervision and Examination (OBSE), which polices banks, to set up target net worth ratios and force companies to classify their businesses into mainstream and peripheral operations. The idea was to force companies to concentrate on mainstream activities and, with the help of mandatory credit controls imposed by prime banks, to force companies to shed peripheral businesses by starving them of credit.[11] These ideas were elaborated on throughout the later 1980s and into the early 1990s, with the idea of limiting cross-shareholding, bolstering balance sheets, and encouraging more specialization. They were a dismal failure.

Business leaders attacked the credit control measures as a retreat from the liberalization policies that had been pursued since 1980, and even the normally quiescent Federation of Korean Industries released a position paper opposing the credit squeeze. Hyundai's Chung Ju Yung was the most outspoken executive. "Who can classify the business lines into mainstream or nonmainstream clearly?" he asked. Chung attacked the financial restrictions as unrealistic, commenting that "only one among the Federation's 500 members is in a position to meet the government's net worth guidelines."

Businesses lobbied heavily at all levels of the government and succeeded in blunting the original proposals. The OBSE backed down and waived the requirement that companies sell real estate holdings and other nonmainstream operations to raise funds for new investments in core businesses. Regulators also agreed to allow companies to continue taking up shareholder rights offerings of sister companies, which allowed chaebol to keep equity control of group operations. Most important, bank supervisors made a critical concession by excluding export credits from credit controls, a policy that permitted the massive export boom of 1986–88, when global economic winds blew in Korea's favor.[12]

Kukje's demise, and the debate over the future of the chaebol, took place against a backdrop of economic weakness that left some companies in desperate shape. By mid-1985 it was clear that the threat to the chaebol had passed, if only because of the weakening of the economy. Many areas that had underpinned Korea's economic growth, such as steel, footwear, textiles, and overseas construction, were in trouble. Pusan, Kukje's base and Korea's second-largest city, was hit especially hard. Orders for sneakers, running shoes, and other footwear, whose production employed tens of thousands of people in the city, were slow. Making matters worse, Kukje's footwear subsidiary was for a brief time managed by the company's bankers, who were inexperienced at running a business.

The economic weakness stemmed from a combination of harsh domestic economic management and international factors over which Korea had no control. Internationally, exports suffered because of the dizzying strength of the dollar against the yen and other major currencies. Because the won was loosely pegged to the dollar, this undercut Korea's competitiveness and virtually halted export growth in many areas.

At the same time, monetary growth was at its slowest in many years in 1985 as policymakers concentrated on cutting inflation. The problems in overseas construction and shipping, which had been headaches since the early 1980s, continued to be a drag on the banks and many chaebol. There was hardly a glimmer of good news on the economic front except the success in reducing the inflation rate.

The government's insistence on carrying through its restructuring plans in the midst of this bad economic environment provoked an angry response from the business world, one that lingered through the rest of Chun's term. The private sector was increasingly impatient with the government's tight monetary and fiscal polices and businessmen were going public with their complaints. Hyundai chairman Chung Ju Yung, who as head of the FKI was the country's preeminent business spokesman, repeatedly urged the government to ease up on the economy by lowering interest rates and expanding monetary growth more quickly. Chung urged a cut in interest rates to about 8 percent from more than 13 percent, an unrealistic proposal given the speed at which the economy was growing and its built-in inflationary bias, but typical of what business wanted: lots of cheap credit.

The Biggest Get Bigger

In spite of these economic worries, Korea's love-hate relationship with the chaebol was swinging back against business by the mid-1980s. Most companies had ridden out the austerity measures and the forced restructuring of the early 1980s with surprisingly little damage, and by 1984 the momentum to attack big business was mounting again.

The attacks on big business came from technocrats in the government such as Kim Dae Young, a director general at the Economic Planning Board, and Suh Sang Mok, vice president of the Korea Development Institute, as well as from professors and legislators. They claimed that the big companies had grown fat largely through their government connections, rather than through their entrepreneurial and managerial talents. Critics also complained that there was little professional management and that owners still ran their chaebol like private fiefdoms.[13]

More forceful was the macroeconomic critique that the chaebol relied too heavily on banks for capital and distorted the whole financial system by gobbling up most available loans. Professors and politicians also claimed that the chaebol were too diversified, and, lacking specialization, inefficient. Moreover, critics correctly pointed out that small business could not flourish in an atmosphere in which big business could stifle any promising company. Advocates of limiting the chaebol role also claimed that family control led to inept management.

The government used many sharp sticks to prod business. The Capital Market Promotion Law was used effectively to force firms to sell shares to the public; the Fair Trade Commission policed the relationship between big business and its suppliers in order to give at least minimal protection to smaller vendors; and the growth in bank lending was subject to increasing control.

The chaebol grudgingly sold shares in some of their operations to the public. Hyundai Engineering and Construction had its initial public offering in November 1984. However, according to Kim Mahn Je, the company sold shares to the public only after the government made twenty-seven official requests, and politicians raised a fuss in the National Assembly.[14] In almost no other country in the world is a company prodded to go public in this manner.

Hyundai's Chung Ju Yung offered only 30 percent of Hyundai Engineering's stock to investors. He and other chaebol chairmen had good reason to limit their stock offerings. The stock market was not a vibrant institution, and, even worse, he was forced to issue stock at an arbitrary government-determined price rather than a market valuation. It was little more than good political theater to force the chaebol to sell a few shares, even if most of the buyers were the wealthy speculators who made up the bulk of the players in the tiny local stock market.

There was no talk of a radical corporate restructuring, as there had been in 1980. Instead, sweeping credit controls were seen as the best way to check the chaebol. Gradually an ambitious policy evolved that tried to limit the chaebol, promote small and medium industry, and modernize the banking sector, all at the same time. But, like previous plans, it quickly became little more than a bureaucratic exercise that had no success in changing the top-heavy structure of Korean business.

A muted attack on quasi-taxes signaled a new mood on the part of Korean business during the mid-1980s. The old subservience of business to the whims of government came under challenge. It is hard to date this transition with any precision, but the sources of change are apparent. The economic slowdown; the better quality of new company recruits, who were less likely to tolerate government coercion; and the political, sometimes corrupt, nature of Chun's Blue House all contributed to a more aggressive attitude by business.

The dramatic contraction of the economy in 1980 and the slow growth of the next few years taught companies that they could not simply make their investment decisions on the basis of government projections. After 1981, companies were freer to invest in most industries, although automobiles, textiles, petrochemicals, and some sectors reserved for small and medium industry remained restricted.

But as the chaebol tried to make their own investment decisions for the first time, government policy in the post-Rangoon era began to try to hedge big business in. After appeals by small and medium industry, the Economic Planning Board obstructed several ventures. When Hyundai Heavy Industries decided that the quality of work gloves supplied to its shipyard was too poor, it decided to produce its own. Small manufacturers of work gloves protested, and Hyundai's plan was blocked. Hyundai was forced to take an indirect route and acquire a glove manufacturer surreptitiously. Samsung was similarly stymied by small firms making bottled liquefied petroleum gas (LPG) from getting into that field.

The attempt to encourage small and medium industry was more successful in political than in economic terms. Kim Mahn Je, who was minister of finance from 1983 until 1986, said that Chun "got some mileage" by playing on popular discontent with the chaebol. A bit of political mileage seemed to be about all the government got, although the attempt to nurture smaller companies helped the lucky few firms that benefited from the government's affirmative action program.[15] But it also stimulated the chaebol to sidestep restrictions on their activities by setting up nominally independent companies that they controlled.

There are hundreds of firms related to the chaebol. These companies typically are headed by retired executives or relatives of the controlling family. Nearly all their business is usually done with a particular business group, which often provides technical and sometimes financial assistance and, most important, is a steady customer. These smaller companies are sometimes absorbed into the parent company but, more often, remain legally separate to help the chaebol fulfill the letter of government policy. Banks, for example, are required to make a certain percentage of their loans to smaller companies; this arrangement allows them to give the appearance of complying with the government's directive while still preserving the structure of the chaebol.

For all the pushing and pulling by the technocrats, their restructuring efforts of the early and mid-1980s did not change the big business bias of the economy. By all objective measures, the chaebol maintained their dominance of the Korean economy throughout the 1980s and into the early 1990s, despite the spinning of an increasingly dense web of administrative and legal restrictions designed to hem them in. Big business had been nurtured by government, but it was understood that it would always play a subordinate role. That changed in the 1980s, as businesses became more aggressive and some became too big to fail. Although the technocrats continued to talk about imposing market discipline, they found that there were limits to the punishment they could impose on business. The command planning of the 1970s gave way to negotiated planning, to business-government bargaining, by the late 1980s.

The Debt Dilemma

Along with the chaebol, the most contentious economic issue of the mid-1980s was foreign debt. Politically, foreign borrowing raised questions of Korean independence and sovereignty, which in a visceral way reflected fears that the government was not doing enough to preserve the purity of the race. The debt had resulted from a conscious decision to limit direct foreign investment, so that

South Korean business groups—and, eventually, the whole country—could enjoy the profits of economic success. Economically, the strategy was executed brilliantly. Politically, the policy was problematic because it fed on South Korean fears of dependence on foreign powers.

Dissidents, drawing on Latin American dependency theory, argued that the government's economic polices were making Korea little more than a colony of foreign (especially U.S. and Japanese) capital. They exploited the government's weakness—its close ties to the chaebol—to buttress their theory. "Our first task is to get rid of the military government which is tied up with the vast foreign debt which makes Roh dependent on countries like Japan and the U.S.," said a radical woman unionist in an interview during the summer of 1987. "It's all tied together. The military leads to foreign debt which leads to being subject to foreign countries which leads to dependence."

Radicals spoke of Korea as a nation suffering from "dual dependencies." The chaebol, in this view, were exploited by the foreign multinationals and banks that provided them with capital and technology; small and medium companies were in turn at the mercy of the chaebol, which paid them little and late. Workers, the small fry in this feeding chain of capitalism, were most oppressed. Foreign debt was incurred by export industries, but had to be repaid with the sweat and toil of workers. In the late 1980s, a new element was added—farmers. According to the popular analysis, farmers suffered from import liberalization, which was necessary to appease the United States and thus keep Korea's export pipeline open. Exports, in other words, indirectly destroyed traditional Korean culture. The quixotic solution of stopping exports and developing a nationally based economy appealed on some level even to many Koreans who were not radicals.[16]

There was more here than simply rhetoric. Foreign debt was one of the most critical macroeconomic issues facing Korea in the mid-1980s. Korea's foreign debt had doubled between 1980 and 1984 because of continued spending on troubled heavy industry projects such as the former Hyundai International's Changwon facility and Daewoo's Okpo shipyard. An aggressive nuclear power program, expansion of the Seoul subway and construction of a new subway in Pusan pushed the debt total still higher. The mounting debt prompted criticism both by opposition National Assembly members and dissidents. With $40.1 billion in outstanding debt by mid-1984, Korea was among the largest foreign borrowers in the world, trailing only Argentina, Brazil, and Mexico. As the debt crisis deepened in Latin America and Eastern Europe, Korea also came under the bankers' harsh spotlight.

It was plausible for branch managers in Seoul to argue that Korea was different. The country had never rescheduled its debts, and it had wisely invested most of the money that it borrowed in national development projects that would someday pay a handsome return. But in the head offices of multinational banks, Korea was often seen as just another developing country, one that had an unstable government and faced a strong Communist threat. As one banker put it, "If the

Philippines got into serious difficulties, bankers in the lending centers might conclude that all of Asia was going down and cut short-term loans to Korea."[17]

Because of its heavy reliance since 1979 on short-term debt, Korea was especially vulnerable to such a scenario, one that had in fact affected Brazil when Mexico got into trouble in 1982. The consequences of a disruption in foreign lending could have been a serious problem. Because many banks had reached their exposure limits for Korea, even a short pause in rolling over loans would cause problems in finding new sources of cash.

Although Korea was performing well, it had made a Faustian bargain by hitching its economy to exports. If growth in world trade slowed, Korea's economy would suffer. Korea needed to borrow $6 billion a year, and any hesitation from lenders could trigger default.

The debt also heightened Korea's traditional sense of vulnerability and preyed on its insecurity as a young, weak nation-state. Government officials, business executives, middle-class citizens, workers (radical or not), and farmers would all cite the national debt when the subject of more liberal trade was raised. Koreans consistently said that trade liberalization would have to wait until after the debt was repaid.[18]

The government nurtured the sense of vulnerability, continually reminding South Koreans how weak the country was, and urging them to struggle to meet export targets or national savings goals. While these campaigns achieved their intended purpose, their very success boxed the government into something of a corner as the debt issue took on political significance that authorities were unable to control. Just before he left for Rangoon, Kim Jae Ik said in a private conversation that when the country began running a trade surplus, he would use it to pay down the debt. He made it clear that the reasons were political, not economic.

The dissidents' critique of the debt also reminded Koreans of the fact that their comrades in the North, under the autocratic leadership of Kim Il Sung, had pursued a much more autarkic economic policy. North Korea had borrowed far less money from abroad—although it did default on some $5 billion in foreign debt—and it had not used foreign investment to help it in the process of national reconstruction. On the contrary, the North Korean government's greatest claim to legitimacy was its *juche* policy, which stressed autonomous development of everything from tractors to textiles. Moreover, although South Korean radicals could not say this publicly until 1988, Kim Il Sung had no foreign troops in his country, while South Korea was home to more than 40,000 U.S. troops throughout the 1980s.

Thanks to the rapid increase in exports that began late in 1985, the economy turned so quickly that the debt issue was defused before it became a major political liability. In early 1986, the government predicted that foreign debt would peak at $51.4 billion in 1992, and that the country would become a net creditor only in the year 2000. In fact, Seoul was able to freeze debt in 1986, and it never went above its year-end 1985 level of $46.7 billion. By the end of the 1980s, South Korea looked set to become a net creditor, a decade and an unexpected export boom ahead of schedule.

Notes

1. Author interview, January 1991.
2. Author interview, February 1991.
3. *Far Eastern Economic Review*, August 4, 1988. Also author interviews, Ministry of Finance, July 1988.
4. However, perhaps there were some personal considerations at work, as Yang and Kim reportedly had never gotten along well. Yang, who came from a family of gentleman-farmers, looked down on Kim, who was the son of a bath house owner in Taegu whose considerable ability carried him to the top of Korea's administrative elite.
5. Author interview, January 1992.
6. Author interview, November 1990, for Kim's comments throughout this chapter.
7. Author interview, September 1989. See also *Far Eastern Economic Review*, October 12, 1989.
8. See Lee-Jay Cho and Yoon Hyung Kim (eds.), *Korea's Political Economy: An Institutional Perspective.*
9. The worries about misuse of funds throughout the government apparently were well-founded. One little-noticed revelation of the 1988 National Assembly hearings was the admission by Deputy Prime Minister for Economic Affairs Rha Woong Bae that the Ministry of Defense had diverted 537 billion won to unauthorized purposes in 1984–86. *Korea Times*, October 22, 1988.
10. *Far Eastern Economic Review*, August 4, 1988.
11. All South Korean companies legally must have one main, or prime, bank that is responsible for monitoring the credit channeled to them. The system, which is modeled on a similar arrangement in Japan, is key to the government's control of companies.
12. *Business Korea*, December 1984, March 1985, May 1985, and August 1985.
13. *Business Korea*, December 1984. Also *Far Eastern Economic Review*, December 12, 1985.
14. *Business Korea*, December 1984.
15. Both the Ministry of Finance and the Ministry of Trade and Industry drafted bills—which passed the National Assembly—to promote venture capital firms that were supposed to help fledgling firms. There were no public hearings and, say venture capital executives, no attempt to find out what would be most appropriate for the industry. The bills also conflicted in some aspects. It was yet another example of the attitude of government officials, backed by their academic experts, to presume that they knew what was best for the economy without deigning to consult those whom they condescendingly referred to as "practitioners."
16. Many Koreans also apparently assumed that U.S. banks were subject to Washington's control. Says a former Citibank executive who was based in Seoul for much of the 1980s: "Koreans assume that U.S. banks are run like Korean ones and that we are puppets of the U.S. government . . . and that therefore Korea was controlled left and right by the U.S. It would be unthinkable for the Korean government to leave the banks as alone as the U.S. does." Author interview, April 1994.
17. *Business Korea*, September 1984.
18. This sentiment generally disappeared after the 1988 Olympics, when it became apparent that a favorite Korean phrase—"We are just a poor, developing country"—no longer applied to a nation that had hosted the largest Olympics in history.

17

The Big Boom

In recent years, the world has been dragged into the vortex of economic war reminiscent of the 1930s, which presaged a world war.

—Chun Doo Hwan[1]

Lee Soon Ja, widow of the slain technocrat Kim Jae Ik, was in Washington when she read that South Korea would show its first trade surplus ever in 1986. "I cried," she remembers. "Around 1980, my husband had said that if everything went right, that our trade should be in the black in 1986 or 1987. Everyone thought he was crazy. Even I told him not to say those kinds of things."

At last, the long-awaited "second take-off" had arrived. This boom was the one that the technocrats had promised when they wrung out inflation and forced companies to restructure in the early 1980s. Hyundai cars were whizzing along California freeways, Samsung microwaves were in New York apartments, and Daewoo's Leading Edge computers were in Minneapolis. Korea was flooding the U.S. market with everything from forklifts and aircraft components to televisions and VCRs. Another Japan, it seemed, was rising across the Pacific.

South Korea's economic growth had already been extraordinary. But from 1986 to 1988 it underwent a boom of unprecedented magnitude, with the economy growing more than 12 percent a year for three consecutive years. At the same time, it went through a tumultuous political upheaval, almost a revolution, that brought the country at least the beginnings of a more representative government. Workers, taking advantage of the freer political climate, rose against their bosses and built strong unions, which doubled their wages between 1987 and 1990.

During these years the streets of Seoul became first crowded, then clogged, as South Korean workers were at last able to afford the cars they were making for the rest of the world. Limits on neon signs, long restricted as a waste of energy and an affront to Confucian sensibility, were lifted, and the drab city on the Han River blazed with light. Room salons, the Western-style private drinking rooms so popular among the Korean male elite, became more elaborate, and whiskey prices soared to over $200 a bottle, yet the liquor flowed more freely than ever. The drink of choice was the *poktanju* ("atomic bomb"), a shot glass filled with whiskey floating in a mug of beer, the whole lot downed in one long swallow, a potent brew that was appropriate for the hard-charging Koreans.

Until 1989 Koreans could not travel freely abroad. Passports were distributed only to those who had a good reason for needing them—and tourism did not qualify as a good reason.[2] When restrictions on travel were lifted, Koreans went on shopping and traveling binges from Honolulu to London, earning themselves a reputation for lavish spending and often boorish behavior along the way.

For those who stayed at home, outings became ever more elaborate. Roger Mathus, who was working for Texas Instruments in Seoul, saw the effects of the boom in the Korean countryside. A passionate hiker who used to spend most of his Saturday afternoons and Sundays in the mountains, just as many other Koreans did, Mathus saw what affluence meant to ordinary middle-class Koreans.

> In the early 1980s, people would take a can of fish and cook some soup and drink a bottle of *soju*. Two or three years later they made the soup with pork instead of fish and drank beer. You go a couple of years further and people turned up their noses at pork and had to have [grilled] beef. Instead of *soju*, somebody brought a bottle of scotch. The women, who in the past would never touch anything, started to drink some beer. And instead of going by bus, people would start to take their own cars and rather than basic clothing, people would buy name-brand clothing, boutique-type hiking brands.[3]

The Tiger Roars

At the beginning of 1986, there was little to suggest how dramatically Korea's economy would boom over the next three years. The country had just been through an unsettling year in which the collapse of Kukje, erratic economic policies, and weak export performance had badly shaken business and bureaucratic confidence. But by the end of 1988, Korea had successfully hosted the biggest Olympic Games ever, and the economy was almost half again as large as it had been three years earlier. Among Asia's four tigers, it seemed that South Korea's roar was the loudest in the world economy.

It was during these three years that business people and politicians in Tokyo, Washington, and Brussels began fretting that Korea would become "another Japan," running chronic trade and current account surpluses as a result of policies designed to encourage exports and discourage imports. Trade disputes, especially with the United States and Europe, escalated sharply. Asia, it seemed, had created another economic challenge to the West.

There was good reason for worrying about Korea. Exports doubled between 1985 and 1988, and Korea moved into the ranks of the top twelve trading nations in the world. After running a chronic trade deficit for forty years, Korea quickly began generating large surpluses. These were significant amounts of money—a total of $23 billion between 1986 and 1988. It was an extraordinary turnaround for a country that had never before had a trade surplus, and probably unprecedented in the world if expressed as a percentage of Korea's GNP.

South Korea emerged during this period as the most powerful of the Asian developing economies. Korea had always been lumped together with the other East Asian dynamos, Taiwan, Hong Kong, and Singapore. Yet although the four tigers posted the world's most dynamic growth in the 1980s, they are quite different. With a population almost 50 percent larger than the other three tigers put together, Korea's domestic market alone gave the country a stature none of the others could hope for. Its strength in heavy industries, such as shipbuilding, chemicals, and autos, as well as the scale of its operations in emerging fields such as semiconductors, also helped set Korea apart.

During the second half of the 1980s, Korea solidified its position as the second-largest shipbuilder in the non-Communist world, trailing only Japan, and emerged from technological obscurity to become one of the world's largest suppliers of semiconductor chips. In autos, Korea emerged as the only developing nation capable of designing and producing its own passenger cars for the export market. Posco was the world's third-largest steelmaker—with the world's single biggest facility—and was undergoing an expansion program that would soon make it the second largest. Samsung, Hyundai, and a handful of other companies were expanding petrochemical operations, so that by the early 1990s Korea would claim to have the world's fifth-largest petrochemical capacity—in spite of having not one drop of domestically drilled oil. It was, in other words, during these years that Korea assumed the role of a key new world manufacturing center, a status that none of its other East Asian rivals enjoyed.

Another measure of change was the fear with which the Japanese regarded their neighbor to the west. Executives at Japanese electronics manufacturers openly worried about stepped-up semiconductor production at Samsung. Japanese knitwear makers filed an antidumping suit in Japan charging that Korea was doing to them what Japanese companies had been doing to the West for so many years: selling goods at low prices in order to increase market share. The suit forced the Koreans to negotiate export limits on some apparel products.

The growth in the size of Korean corporations was extraordinary during the 1980s. Hyundai's combined sales grew almost tenfold, from $3.9 billion in 1979 to $32.1 billion in 1989. In 1991 they hit the $50 billion mark. Samsung grew even more quickly, from $3.1 billion to $33.8 billion during the 1980s. Lucky-Goldstar grew a relatively modest sixfold, from $3.9 billion to $22.8 billion. Daewoo grew at about the same pace, from $2.9 billion to $17 billion. Almost all other major groups grew at similar or only slightly lower rates, with most at least quadrupling their sales during the 1980s. By 1989, Korea's four largest business groups had combined sales of $107 billion.[4]

The Three Blessings

How did Korea suddenly accelerate its growth? Good planning was essential for success, but the Korean economy also needed a dose of good luck. And in 1986 it got just that. The year started out on a sour note, as the economy slowly recovered from its worst economic performance since 1981. President Chun was forced to give his annual New Year's address in the heavily guarded Blue House rather than in the National Assembly for fear of protests. The opposition, cheered by its moral victory in the 1985 legislative elections and looking forward to a presidential election in 1987, became increasingly bold in its calls for reform. Chun was now a lame duck president, and his power was waning quickly. The debate on the future of Korea, and of Korea, Inc., was wide open.

While the political front was unsettled, the economic news could not have been better. For late in 1985, the economy of Korea had begun to turn around quite rapidly. The September 1985 Plaza Accord, in which the five major industrial nations agreed to continue driving the dollar lower, marked a critical moment. In 1985 U.S. policymakers, led by Treasury Secretary James Baker, came to believe that the strength of the dollar was aggravating the growing U.S. trade deficit. The dollar had peaked the previous February against most major currencies; the Plaza agreement confirmed a policy switch by the Reagan administration, which had previously viewed the strong dollar as a source of pride.

The weakness of the dollar did not succeed in eliminating the U.S. trade deficit. Instead it did for Korea what advocates like Baker hoped it would do for the United States—it prompted an unprecedented export boom, much of it, ironically, to the United States. Because the won was loosely pegged to the dollar, the devaluation against the Japanese yen and West German mark allowed Korea's new generation of export industries—automobiles, consumer electronics, ships, and steel—to take market share from Japanese and European producers. At the same time, thanks to strong consumer spending in the United States, exports of traditional products, notably textiles and clothes, reached record levels.

The falling dollar was the most important of what the Koreans came to call the three lows, or three blessings. The other two were low dollar interest rates—part of the strategy of driving down the dollar—and low commodity prices, especially on oil. These three blessings did not merely produce a boom of unparalleled magnitude in Korea but also solved two of its chronic economic problems, the current account deficit and foreign debt. Exports produced a surplus, which in turn was used to pay off debt.

The United States traditionally took a little over a third of Korean exports, but by 1986, this proportion had soared to almost 40 percent of a much larger base. In dollar terms, Korean exports to the United States doubled from $10.8 billion in 1985 to $21.4 billion in 1988. Korea was sending an extra $10 billion a year of products ranging from the running shoes and sweaters that its companies had exported for many years to increasingly expensive and sophisticated merchandise like programmable VCRs, personal computers, passenger cars, and microwave ovens. Many of these were products that U.S. manufacturers were having such a difficult time producing profitably. Korea, not surprisingly, became a target of U.S. trade complaints.

As U.S. and European companies were retrenching in much of the consumer electronics market, Koreans were setting up factories in the United States. Both Lucky-Goldstar and Samsung had established factories to make VCRs and microwave ovens in the United States in the early 1980s, primarily as a way of avoiding protectionism. But these ventures also allowed companies to raise money outside Korea without the scrutiny of the Bank of Korea and were another important step in the development of corporate independence. Samsung and Lucky-Goldstar were pioneers in the corporate strategy of escaping government control.[5]

The strength of the boom lay not in government-led efforts but in the new managerial efficiency of Korea's larger companies, sometimes supplemented by partnerships with foreign firms, and stepped-up efforts to market products abroad under their own name or through their own marketing channels. In 1985, Korean companies spent a paltry $4.1 million on advertising in the United States. By 1988, the figure had soared to more than $150 million, reflecting the Koreans' success in marketing and distributing the products it made. Hyundai Motors, which started exports to the United States in 1986, led this upsurge in advertising spending abroad.

These increasingly bold international activities required more senior managers abroad to assess factors as different as marketing opportunities, political risks, and possible trade restrictions. The companies, led by Samsung, also developed political intelligence networks abroad that often surpassed the government's. This was yet another way in which businessmen at large companies were gaining the upper hand in their relationship with the technocrats, since they now had better information and thus no need for government guidance.

The export boom, which was capped by the 1988 Seoul Olympics, erased much of the self-doubt and inferiority that had traditionally clouded the Korean psyche. In little more than a thousand days, Korea underwent a sort of Cinderella transformation, changing from an austere nation, acutely conscious of its backwardness, to a country with a prosperous middle class and a conviction that with hard work anything could be accomplished. That sentiment was summed up in a newspaper headline, "SEOUL OLYMPICS PROVE KOREANS CAN ACCOMPLISH ANYTHING."

This sort of braggadocio quickly caught on among Koreans, especially younger ones. "We Koreans are very flexible," said a general manager at Hyundai Motors. "We learn very quickly. That is where we have an advantage over you in the West and why we have been able to overtake so many countries." Asked if

Korea would overtake even the United States, the executive said, "someday, probably yes." This belief that Asia was destined to inherit the economic mantle as the United States and Europe declined was echoed throughout Korea, especially in business circles.

A crude, arrogant nationalism blossomed in the heady years when Korea grew 12 percent a year. In a typical remark, a senior Finance Ministry official told a visiting investment banker that "there will be no crumbs from the Korean table" for foreign securities firms.

This sort of sentiment was understandable coming from people who had been utterly dependent on foreign capital, but it often degenerated into a crude xenophobic nationalism. It was also, as later events were to show, woefully out of touch with the reality of the Korean economy and its place in the world. But at the time this wishful thinking appeared sound enough.

Export Explosion

A few sets of numbers hint at the magnitude of the change. In this fiercely export-driven economy, exports had nearly doubled in the first half of the decade, growing from $17.5 billion in 1980 to $30.3 billion in 1985. By the standards of most economies, this was a very impressive performance. Yet in the next three years, exports doubled again to $60.7 billion. The increase in exports in 1988 alone ($13.4 billion) was nearly equal to the total exports in 1979, the year Park was assassinated ($14.7 billion).

Incredibly enough, a decade earlier, in 1978, Mexico and Brazil each exported roughly the same amount each year as Korea did. But in the 1980s, Korea outstripped these Latin American rivals. By the late 1980s, in the developing world only Taiwan and Hong Kong had a similar level of exports. By 1987, Korea was a larger exporter than many European countries, including Spain, Ireland, Norway, Finland, Denmark, and Austria, lagging only slightly behind countries like Sweden and Switzerland.

A small company, Trigem, typified the way Korean firms rode the export boom. The company had cobbled together its first primitive computer in 1981 using components bought in the local electronics bazaar. The computer monitor was a standard black-and-white television set, complete with channel selectors. Trigem quickly vaulted out of this primitive stage and, as the won weakened against the yen, Trigem won sizable production orders from the Japanese producer Epson and from Computerland. "We asked Computerland why they chose us," Trigem chairman Lee Yong Teh said. "They said, 'If we ask the Japanese to make a modification [in the computer] it will take one year. If we ask Trigem it will take one week.' "[7]

While many of these products were still made for and marketed by companies like Computerland, Sears, J. C. Penney, and General Electric, increasing numbers of them were marketed by chaebol such as Daewoo, Samsung, or Lucky-

Goldstar. Daewoo, although it has an extensive corporate image advertising campaign, does not sell any consumer products under its own name in the United States. Daewoo did succeed with a computer it sold through Leading Edge Products, a Massachusetts-based firm that was one of the most successful wholesalers of IBM personal computer clones during the mid- and late-1980s. Leading Edge had previously sourced its computers from a Japanese manufacturer, but it abruptly switched to Daewoo Telecom when the yen began to appreciate.

Sales of the Daewoo computer were phenomenally successful. Although shipments began only in 1985, by the middle of 1987 Daewoo was shipping 13,000 units a month. Total exports of its computers were valued at more than $100 million in 1987, more than that of the country's total exports when Park Chung Hee took power in 1961. "The computer was originally accepted in the market because it had a low price tag. Eventually it established an image as a quality product," Daewoo Telecom president Park Sung Kyou said proudly.[8] "This computer made Korea known as a source of more sophisticated products, like computers, in the world market." Daewoo eventually bought Leading Edge outright in 1989.

Korean managers made no claims to be innovative. They were best at exploiting market niches that had been pioneered by someone else and producing goods quickly to meet established specifications. But as Korean manufacturers became more experienced, they began to make the sorts of small design improvements that had earned the Japanese a reputation for quality.

IBM, for example, had always put its on-off switch on the rear panel of the computer, making it cumbersome for users to turn on the machine. Daewoo put the switch in the front, an innovation later adopted by IBM. "We don't have the capability that will make us a leader who comes out with a revolutionary product," said Daewoo's Park. "But we can come up with innovative products."

The large U.S. market, with its relatively simple distribution channels, was much easier to sell to than anywhere else in the world. In other countries it took longer for Korean companies to take advantage of the strengthening yen, but the chaebol did chip away at Japanese market share around the globe. In 1987 the share of Korean exports going to the United States slipped from 40 percent to 38.7 percent as exports to Asia surged.

For Korea, Europe was a more difficult market than either the United States or Asia. While European retail chains gladly bought Korea's less expensive consumer electronics to replace their Japanese lines, European governments took protectionist action much more quickly than the United States had done. At the beginning of 1988 the European Community (EC) suspended the Generalized System of Preference (GSP) benefits, which allowed Korean products preferential import duty rates, in protest against Korea's refusal to provide favorable patent protection for European companies.[9]

Korean companies had already anticipated protectionism in the EC. In 1987, Lucky-Goldstar had broken ground on a microwave oven and VCR factory in

West Germany, hardly a low-cost production site. Usually Lucky-Goldstar, like other Korean companies, preferred to establish a market through exports first. But because of protectionism in the EC, the company made a decision to establish a factory there before the market was developed. "The EC market has been difficult to penetrate," said Kim Song Hwan, director of international finance at the Lucky-Goldstar group. "There is rising sentiment for protectionism. Their administrative restrictions are very efficient at controlling trade. We thought it would be a good idea to make a direct investment early on. We learned a lot from the Japanese experience."[10]

Finance and Freedom

Controlling the chaebol by restricting credit became more difficult for the Korean government. The growing resources that Korean companies commanded as a result of the export boom made them more willing to buck government directives. Moreover, the stock market, which the government promoted as an alternative to heavy dependence on bank borrowing, provided a new source of funds as stock prices surged between 1986 and 1988.

Once seen as little more than a casino, the stock market took on respectability. The number of investors soared from 1.4 million at the end of 1986 to around 4 million in 1989. Middle-aged women carrying bags stuffed with 10,000-won notes and untraceable bearer checks flocked to brokerage offices in the crowded downtown Seoul district of Myongdong, where brokerage houses are concentrated, and in the affluent Kangnam area south of the Han River.[11]

These were heady times for new investors and for the bright young college graduates who flocked to the brokerage business in Seoul, just as they did in New York, London, and Tokyo. The change was more startling in Seoul than it was in the West, for the best and the brightest in Korea had previously gone into the government or academia. Only in the late 1970s did they begin to go into business, but certainly not into the stock market.

A series of government policies adopted after the 1985 slowdown encouraged large firms to raise money in the stock market. Alarmed by the mounting debt-equity ratios of Korean firms, the government adopted policies to force the chaebol to raise more equity and thus make them less vulnerable to swings in the economic cycle. (High debt ratios leave companies vulnerable to economic downturns since fixed interest payments must continue regardless of the health of continuing operations.)

After a period of initial resistance, the new policy was immensely successful. Capital raised on the stock market was negligible in 1985, with the total market capitalization at year-end standing at just under $10 billion. But in 1989 alone, companies raised $20 billion in new capital on the Korea Stock Exchange; the market capitalization soared to more than $130 billion by year-end. That year, more equity was raised on the Korea stock exchange than on the New York Stock Exchange.

This reliance on the stock market for financing was done at the insistence of the Ministry of Finance. But the growing importance of equity finance had an effect the Ministry of Finance had not imagined: As companies became less dependent on banks for financing, they became more independent of the government and far more willing to ignore administrative guidelines.

The process at work was not a simple one. On one side, the government was encouraging reluctant companies to shore up their financial base and compete in a freer market. On the other side, government planners still wanted control over major investment decisions undertaken by large corporations. But the effect was clear enough: The technocrats' policies undercut government control of the chaebol. Although the government publicly proclaimed its support for liberalization, in fact it was extremely uncomfortable at seeing power slip out of its hands.

Any company that announced a new public offering was certain to find it oversubscribed, because Korean authorities tried to ensure that new shares were priced cheaply enough to guarantee profits for initial buyers. (This pricing was another reason companies had been reluctant to go public.) In May 1987, Daewoo Telecommunications, flush with its PC export success, had its initial public stock offering oversubscribed 209 times, the biggest ever in Korea.

Increased corporate resources and the diminished dependence on government-controlled credit emboldened executives. They were more willing to test the government, especially when it came to innovative ways of finding funds. An indication of the new corporate assertiveness came in late 1986 and early 1987 when corporations raised an estimated $150 million through so-called mismatched swap arrangements. The technique, which involved using an artificial rate in the foreign exchange market, allowed foreign banks to sidestep restrictions on foreign capital inflows and lend the money they brought in to Korea to their large corporate customers at rates that were above world levels but below those in Korea.

In the beginning of 1988, Korean companies and aggressive foreign bankers pushed even harder, developing a new technique to skirt the government's tight money policy. In essence, this technique allowed the companies to create money through the use of options on foreign exchange. Because of Korea's high interest rates, both foreign bankers and domestic companies benefited from what was an almost riskless transaction.

After they figured out what was going on, Ministry of Finance and Bank of Korea authorities were angered by this sort of financial gaming; the scheme, after all, swelled the money supply and flouted the government's policy of trying to strictly control monetary growth in order to check inflation. The Bank of Korea belatedly prohibited further transactions and punished the companies by forcing them to buy government bonds at below-market interest rates. There was no legal basis for the central bank's action, and the companies had no right of appeal.

"They stopped the [use of these] techniques," remembers Lee Soon Hak, the Samsung group's chief financial officer. Lee, a graduate of Seoul National

University's elite College of Commerce, was one of the new generation of executives who came into positions of real authority during the 1980s. This generation, especially those who worked at Samsung, was unwilling to passively accept government guidance on financing. "They said we abused the regulations. We did not. We had lawyers check first and then we used the regulations very skillfully. . . . The Korean government was desperate to control the money supply [by prohibiting the option transactions] even though they weren't illegal." This sort of innovative financing, says Lee, "is not to be blamed. It is to be praised."[12]

The governor of the Bank of Korea during most of this period could not have disagreed more. Park Sung Sang coincidentally stepped down as head of the central bank the same month that the disputed options transaction began. He used a telling metaphor when foreigners would suggest that perhaps the Korean financial system needed to be opened up to market forces, and that banks should make credit allocation decisions on their own initiative.

> [Money] is like water in a reservoir. The water should be channeled into the most productive rice paddies. . . . We cannot afford to let this money go into weedy rice paddies or flow into the ground through money games. We have to control very tightly. We need to guide the economy very effectively, with no waste of loanable funds. This is a very scarce resource. We cannot lose the grip.[13]

But the government did lose its grip during the boom years. Liquidity, although eased enough to permit economic growth, did not account for the whole difference. The change came in the form of vast export earnings, which Korea's traditionally cash-starved corporations were accumulating. Probably for the first time ever, Korea's exporters were largely profitable.

Liquidity conditions had eased dramatically in 1985, with M2 monetary growth running at more than twice the level of 1984. With the central Bank of Korea, guided by the Ministry of Finance, pumping more money into the economy, businesses found it easier to borrow. Yet because economic growth in Korea remained so strong, and projected returns on investment were so high, the easier money did not remove corporate complaints.

Quite the opposite happened. As economic growth accelerated, the higher monetary growth was buried under a mountain of cash needs. Businesses needed cash to finance investment in new plants as well as the larger inventories needed for increased production. Worried about inflation, the government shut the door to cheaper foreign borrowing.

The mounting trade surpluses had caught the government off guard. For decades the country's economy, indeed its entire way of thinking, had been predicated on deficits. In hundreds of ways, Koreans were encouraged to preserve foreign exchange in order to make their country strong. They were told to recycle scrap paper and metal, avoid imports, and forego foreign travel in order to save scarce foreign currency for national development. Beginning at the top with

President Park and his old black suits, the cult of austerity dominated the ideology of economic development.

The economic necessity for austerity disappeared with the surplus, yet the technocrats and bureaucrats who were in charge of an increasingly complex economy simply could not keep up with the change. The entire financial structure was based on a scarcity of foreign exchange. But in the late 1980s the problem was suddenly that too much money was coming in, money from overseas Koreans who wanted to invest in stocks, real estate, or the curb market, and from Korean companies bringing more of their foreign earnings back home.

The Ministry of Finance reacted by trying to curtail capital inflows. It was ironic that Korea, a country that had jailed executives in the 1970s for alleged capital flight, now reacted with horror to people who wanted to invest in the country. But this reaction underscored the desire to keep as much government control as possible, for the financial system was one of the last strongholds of government authority.

Unfortunately, a number of short-sighted, politically expedient policies squandered the chance for financial reform in the late 1980s. The government concentrated on repaying—and even prepaying—foreign debt and building up the capital reserves of banks and securities companies. But it did little to change the fundamentally uncompetitive cartel structure of the financial system, which remained dependent on Finance Ministry approval for all but the smallest decisions. The ministry continued, for example, to appoint senior executives of all the major banks, and final decisions were made at the presidential Blue House. Ministry officials also busied themselves with everything from setting insurance rates to pricing new securities issues on both the local and foreign markets.

One ostensible reason for lack of progress was the determination of government planners not to squander the legacy of anti-inflationary growth, which they rightly regarded as one of the major economic achievements of the Fifth Republic. That took a toll on corporations, which were unable to obtain any funds from the banking system. While small groups were particularly vulnerable to liquidity shortages, even large companies were sometimes forced to go to the curb market for working capital. From 1980 to 1988, most companies actually had negative cash flow, which left them no alternative but to borrow or sell assets to raise cash.

This seeming paradox of abundant liquidity, which raised inflationary fears, and some of the highest real interest rates in the world, accompanied by extreme difficulty in securing funds, constituted one of the main points of government-business conflict. It was a growing source of tension as time went on and Korean companies began competing on more equal terms with foreign competitors. As Korea's labor costs rose and its currency appreciated, its competitiveness eroded. But the burden imposed by high financing costs was probably a greater source of lagging international competitiveness than spiraling wage costs.

The Ministry of Finance had repeatedly proclaimed its intention to liberalize the financial system since shortly after Chun had taken power. In reality, liberalization had been sacrificed to the anti-inflation policy and the obsessive desire to keep control of the financial system and the economy. The tight money policy of the early 1980s made liberalization difficult, because the government repeatedly intervened to prop up ailing industries. The reorganization of the shipping and overseas construction industries and the dismantling of Kukje ruled out true financial market liberalization, because if the banks had not been propped up with low-interest loans, they would have collapsed.

Continuing control of the financial sector was a deliberate policy choice in the mid-1980s, driven by the fear that the financial system was so enfeebled by government-ordered policy loans and bad debts that many banks would not survive in a truly competitive market.

Financial authorities in any country rarely give up control voluntarily, correctly arguing that finance is different from other sectors. If banks collapse, the whole economy comes to a halt. But the difficulty of liberalization in Korea was compounded by the arrogance of officials at the Ministry of Finance and the less powerful Bank of Korea.

The harassed bureaucrats still regarded themselves as mandarins and looked down on the "practitioners" who soiled their hands with business. They showed surprisingly little curiosity about how financial markets actually worked, and most were more interested in the power politics of financial control than the policy issues involved in liberalization. The distance between bureaucrats and the world they were charged with regulating became increasingly apparent during the late 1980s.

The Finance Ministry had been moved to an isolated government complex south of Seoul in early 1987, cutting down on opportunities to meet informally with bankers and brokers. As visitors approached the Integrated Government Complex #2 in Kwachon, just over the hills that ring the southern edge of Seoul, they almost could have mistaken it for a California college campus. Broad patches of lawn separated the four six-story office buildings, which nestled on the southern edge of Mt. Kwanak. Tennis courts were off to one side. Only riot police checking visitors' identification hinted that this was a place of power.

Inside, however, was another story. Like other Korean offices, the ministries were cluttered with huge filing cabinets and gray metal desks piled high with papers, and it seemed difficult to believe that this was in some sense the nerve center for the Korean miracle. But this was where plans were drawn up and implemented.

As the economy grew larger, and companies less cooperative, the task of managing Korea, Inc. became more complex. "Until 1985 this was a very simple economy," says banker Alan Plumb. "After 1985 it was like a corner shop turning into a department store."[14] The problem came when the government still insisted on running it like a corner store.

Largely cut off from real information about the markets, Finance Ministry bureaucrats relied instead on academic experts who told them what they wanted to hear, namely that the financial system should be kept as closed as possible for as long as feasible. During the boom years, these experts fretted that hot money would flow in and stoke inflation if the markets were liberalized; as the surplus dwindled, these same experts said that financial liberalization (including the prohibition of aliases) would spur a flood of hot money *out* of the country. What was lacking, above all, was strong political and technocratic leadership to move the reform process ahead. This lost opportunity for reform cost the economy dearly in the years to come.

Government restrictions on bank ownership continued to hamper Korean companies in their ability to secure cheap funds and keep their costs competitive. Financing had not mattered as much when the authorities had generously handed out low-interest policy loans, but as these were trimmed back and wage costs rose, the cost of financing became more critical. The lack of control over banks was a crucial difference between the Korean chaebol and their Japanese counterparts, the *keiretsu* (the successors to the prewar zaibatsu). The keiretsu controlled financial institutions and had access to plentiful low-cost capital, thanks to Japanese policies keeping interest rates on deposits low.

An analysis of three international electronics makers found that Korea's Goldstar used more than 80 percent of its operating income in 1985 to pay interest costs. While its operating profit was 7.8 percent of sales, its pretax profit was only 1.2 percent. The Japanese company Matsushita, by contrast, had a higher operating profit margin (11.1 percent) and actually made money from its financial activities.[15]

The 1986 freeze on most foreign borrowing angered companies because of the disadvantage it put them at in the world market. The prime interest rate in Korea was nominally between 10 and 11.5 percent from 1982 to December 1988. In reality, only a handful of companies could borrow at these rates, since banks customarily tacked on compensating balance requirements and charges that raised effective interest rates to 13–18 percent. At a time when prices were rising less than 5 percent annually, this resulted in some of the highest real interest costs in the world.

As the country's current account switched dramatically from red to black, government economists suddenly had to deal with the problem of a flood of money threatening to wash away their anti-inflation efforts. Their response was a classic one. In the simplest terms, they forced exporters to trade their dollars for won. They then made domestic financial institutions buy low-yielding government securities to soak up the increased supply of domestic currency.

In more technical terms, they tried to sterilize the surplus of dollars (and other foreign currencies) by selling bonds. Financial institutions were coerced, using a variety of measures, to buy the monetary stabilization bonds at below-market interest rates. The result was that domestic interest rates remained high because the surplus was not allowed into the domestic market.[16]

South Korean firms were eager to tap the international financial markets.

With foreign bank borrowing generally out of the question, except for refinanc-
ings and overseas projects, companies looked at other methods. Samsung Electronics issued a $20 million convertible bond in late 1985 in the Euromarket.
This was yet another case where corporations led the government. Although the
Ministry of Finance had drawn up a vague market liberalization plan in the early
1980s, it was only when Samsung finance executives brought a proposal to the
ministry in 1985 that overseas issues started. "We taught them about convertible
bonds," remembers Lee Soon Hak. "We even helped write the regulations."[17]

Over the next four years, the Ministry of Finance allowed only five more
companies to issue convertible bonds. Because of foreign investors' growing
interest in the Korea Stock Exchange, and because of a prohibition on foreign
ownership of Korean equities, the convertible bonds were an extremely attractive
way to raise funds. They generally carried a minimal interest rate (sometimes as
low as 1.75 percent annually) and were convertible into common stock at a
premium of roughly double the underlying stock price. Yet demand for the
convertible bonds still outstripped supply among investors; the issues sold at
huge premiums in the late 1980s. For corporate treasurers used to paying 13–18
percent for bank loans, the overseas issues were virtually cost-free money.

For the Ministry of Finance, obsessed with controlling the money supply and
intent on protecting local securities houses, these financial instruments were
troublesome. The ministry severely restricted the number of companies that
could issue overseas securities, bringing windfall gains to the lucky few firms
that received permission and denying others access to cheap financing. By the
time the ministry reversed its stance in 1990, foreign investors had turned sour
on Korea and some potential issues had to be canceled because of overly aggressive pricing. This was yet another case where overzealous financial regulation
had put Korean corporations at a disadvantage in the world market.

Still, it was great business while it lasted. The late 1980s were heady years in
Korea's stock market, and, just as in other stock markets around the world, greed
was part of the game. Brokers pushed up the underlying prices of shares on the
local market before a convertible bond issue. This meant that the company could
raise money even more cheaply, because the price foreigners paid for the shares
was higher and the firm had to give away a smaller underlying equity share in
the company.

Saehan Media, a manufacturer of videotapes, was the first of a flock of
lesser-known companies to issue convertible bonds. The company was run by
one of Samsung founder Lee Byung Chull's sons, but because it was in a commodity business and its products were virtually indistinguishable from its
competitors', the firm did not seem to have particularly promising prospects. The
only way for a company like Saehan to compete was on price, which meant
profit margins were thin and had little prospect for improvement.

Saehan Media had had a serious fire at one of its factories in early 1988,
about six months before the bond offering—a 25-billion-won fire against which

it had virtually no insurance and which caused it to report a loss for the first half of 1988. Bizarrely, the Ministry of Finance let the company issue its overseas bonds in part because it was due to report a loss for the year. That loss, under the Ministry of Finance's own guidelines, would have made it ineligible to issue convertible bonds the following year. The regulation was supposed to protect investors from flimsy companies. But, in a striking display of form over substance, the ministry simply accelerated the approval process. Local brokers, meanwhile, pushed up the stock price of Saehan Media in the prelude to the issue so that it would be able to raise overseas capital more cheaply, by forming a cartel to buy the stock.

On other deals, local brokers demanded that firms wanting to participate in the lucrative and prestigious underwriting of convertible bonds pay a stiff entry price: They had to buy domestic corporate bonds at a government-mandated issue price, which was far less than the market price. A securities house literally had to buy business, taking a loss on one piece of paper in the hope that it could make a profit on another.

Practices like this can and do occur in the United States and other Western countries, as Michael Milken, Ivan Boesky, and the other insider stock and bond traders of the 1980s proved. But in Korea, like in Japan and Taiwan, these practices are institutionalized to an extent hard to comprehend in the West. The stock exchange is a cozy, clubby world. The number of participants is strictly fixed, because the government regulates the number of securities houses. There were twenty-five Korean securities firms for most of the 1980s, with entry restricted by the government.

Sanctions against insider trading were rare. In the few cases where they were applied—well under a dozen times in the 1980s—the penalty generally consisted of nothing more than repaying the illicit profits. The general mood in the securities industry was so lax that when authorities took the unprecedented step of charging a group of Korea Stock Exchange employees, who were legally not even allowed to buy stocks, with insider trading and manipulation of share prices, their fellow employees backed them up with a sit-down protest.

These sorts of friendly, relationship-oriented transactions, even if they often shaded into illegality, suit government authorities because they facilitate control. The network of relationships, and the deference to government officials, is one way in which control was exercised; but the pattern of consistent abuse of the law, ironically, helped keep everyone in line on the bigger issues, because anyone who challenged the system knew that the penalty was likely to be a tax or securities investigation.

The Ministry of Finance regulated even minor details of corporate life for the securities houses. The number of branches, where they were located, and the commission structure were all subject to ministry approval. If the market began to rise quickly, as it did in 1986, the ministry simply ordered institutions to sell stocks and buy government bonds. When the market fell, the ministry ordered these same institutions to buy stocks. At the end of 1990 and the beginning of 1991, the ministry put together a 6.7-trillion-won government-sponsored support program to prop up stock prices. The Bank of Korea ordered commercial banks to fund much of this artificial buying.[18]

While institutional investors grumbled about ministry restrictions on stock purchases, such as forcing purchases of monetary stabilization bonds to reduce the amount of cash available to buy stocks, they were unwilling to challenge the fundamental structure of control. These men—never women—had gone to the same high schools and universities and were bound by complex webs of loyalty, obligation, and friendship. It was a system, moreover, in which industry still remained in the weaker position. The government appointed the presidents of even "private" banks. Securities companies, banks, and investment trust companies had to go to the ministry for even trivial matters, such as when and where new branches could be opened. While industrial firms went a long way in the 1980s toward breaking away from government control, thanks largely to the pressures of international competition, firms in the country's protected financial industry were still playing by the rules of the old Korea Inc., which required submission to government whims. One of the challenges for the Korean economy in the late 1990s will be to open up its financial sector, just as its manufacturing firms have opened to the world.[19]

Notes

1. Chun Doo Hwan, "President Chun's New Year Policy Statement," January 16, 1986, *Korea Annual*, 1986, p. 374.

2. Government officials, academics attending a conference, businessmen, and students could get passports. Except for older people, tourists could not. Lee Soon Ja's comments are from an October 1991 author interview.

3. Author interview, April 1992.

4. Adapted from *Dong-A Ilbo* survey, published in January 1990. The exchange rates are converted into dollars at current rates, 484 won: $1 in 1979 and 680 won: $1 in 1989. The won amounts are as follows: Hyundai's sales grew from 1.9 trillion won in 1979 to 21.8 trillion in 1989; Samsung, from 1.5 trillion won to 23 trillion; Lucky-Goldstar, from 1.9 trillion to 15.5 trillion won, and Daewoo, from 1.4 trillion won to 12 trillion won.

5. The results of this strategy were dramatically apparent by the end of the decade. For example, the Bank of Korea and the Ministry of Trade and Industry had records of less than $1 million in investments in Mexico in 1990. Yet Samsung alone had invested $12 million in a television assembly plant near the U.S. border and Lucky-Goldstar had a similar facility. Mexican diplomatic sources in Seoul estimated total Korean investment in their country at more than $60 million. Most of these investments were not secret. Samsung boasted about its investment in a corporate newsletter. But it was a dramatic demonstration of how large companies with access to international financial resources were slipping away from traditional government controls.

6. This headline was in the *Korea Times*, September 17, 1989, supplement published on the first anniversary of the opening of the Seoul Olympics.

7. Seoul Foreign Correspondents' Club press luncheon, March 28, 1991.

8. Author interview, June 1987.

9. At the same time, the United States "graduated" Korea from the GSP beneficiary program, on the grounds that the country was developed enough not to need the preferential treatment.

10. Author interview, July 1987.

11. South Korea is a cash society, but one whose largest currency note is worth less than $15. The country has a huge underground economy, estimated at 20–30 percent of the recorded GNP. Many of these middle-aged women, most of whom traditionally invested in real estate, or who put their money into the curb market, were drawn into the stock market on a large scale for the first time during the 1986–88 period.

12. Author interview, January 1991. The reason for this financial gaming was simple: Korea had both a strong and appreciating currency and high real interest rates. Says a former Citibank executive: "Those two things are not supposed to happen [at the same time]. A strong currency should have low interest rates. A strong currency with high interest rates is inevitably going to lead to capital inflows. I brought in money and invested in MSBs [Monetary Stabilization Bonds] at 18% and took it out at a better exchange rate. That is what caused the imbalance and that is what caused these crazy controls [and the different schemes to get around the controls]. These schemes were just disguised dollar loans." Author interview, April 1994.

13. Author interview, November 1987.

14. Author interview, January 1990.

15. Prudential-Bache Securities; 1987 corporate report on Goldstar.

16. The reasons for Korea's high interest rates are complex and hotly debated. Arguably, the surplus of savings over investment should have forced rates down in the late 1980s. It seems that the extreme segmentation of the credit market—especially in the form of preferential lending for special interests—effectively crowded out other borrowers and raised the cost of money. The high demand for funds, especially in the real estate market (where many of the transactions are not reported), also kept rates high.

17. Author interview, January 1990.

18. This broke down into a 2.7-trillion-won program announced on December 12, 1989, which was funded by the commercial banks and funneled through the country's three investment trust companies, and a 4-trillion-won stock market stabilization fund that was more broadly funded by a variety of financial and nonfinancial institutions.

19. It would be a mistake to note only the many shortcomings of the Ministry of Finance's capital market policies, for the development of a real stock market during the 1980s had great significance for corporate Korea. Says a former Citibank executive: "The Korean chaebol in the early-to-mid 1980s were dangerously overleveraged. They couldn't absorb any bad shocks. . . . If it hadn't been for the stock market, you could have had much more bad news. Daewoo would have been a dead duck. Daewoo Securities became the gold mine for the group. The development of a capital market was one of the notable achievements of the 1980s. The other was the phenomenal expansion of the savings rate, which carried them into the surplus." Author interview, April 1994.

18

Shifting into Overdrive

> We wanted to run the company our way, but GM wanted to run the company their way. That was the point of disagreement. We are very happy to go with Mitsubishi because we can run the company our way. They don't touch on management. This way we can do better business than arguing with the partner all the time.
>
> —Hyundai Motor president Chung Se Yung[1]

When Hyundai's Chon Sung Won was just another hungry young executive in the early 1970s, he bounced around the world looking for buyers. With just one suitcase and—perhaps even more unusual for a Korean executive—only one aide, Chon spent much of 1974 and 1975 trying to find export markets for Hyundai's new Pony model. Chon traveled to more than thirty countries, sometimes sleeping in airport terminals as he waited for connecting flights, other times hanging around embassies for visas because South Korea, something of a pariah state, had no diplomatic relations with many third world countries. This was the Hyundai can-do spirit at work, pitting sheer persistence against a lack of experience. "We didn't have any basic knowledge on exports," remembers Chon. "We just thought that someday we should export. That was the natural thinking in South Korea at that time."

By the early 1990s, Chon was sitting in a spacious office in the Hyundai building in downtown Seoul, overlooking a fourteenth-century palace and the fabled Secret Garden that for centuries was reserved for royalty. The unscuffed soles of Chon's shiny brown shoes looked as if they have hardly set foot on a piece of pavement.

For Chon by then headed one of Korea's best-known companies, the only automobile company outside Japan, Europe, and the United States that had be-

254 • TROUBLED TIGER

come a player in the world auto markets. Like other Korean success stories, Hyundai Motor made it into the big leagues with a combination of grit, guts, and good luck.[2]

In the 1960s, the government wanted an auto business, for the same tangled reasons of national pride and imagined economic advantages that it wanted a steel mill and a petrochemical complex. Like their counterparts in many developing nations, Park Chung Hee and the founders of Korea, Inc. thought that any self-respecting country should make its own cars. Although Korea alone has succeeded in this ambition, it is easy to forget how close its auto industry came to being stillborn, a victim of the mismanagement, inconsistent government policy, corruption, and lack of technology, capital, and managerial know-how that plague too many Korean companies.

After the liberation in 1945, many Koreans already had a fair amount of technical knowledge, reflecting the fact that, after Japan, Korea had been the most industrialized nation in Asia in the 1930s. Toyota, Nissan, and Isuzu were among the Japanese companies producing auto parts such as piston rings, springs, bodies, and bearings in Korea during the Japanese colonial period. These Japanese enterprises spawned a host of smaller companies. One of those who ran an independent operation was a young man named Chung Ju Yung, who had just turned twenty-four when he bought the "Ado Service" auto repair shop in the Sodaemun district of Seoul in 1940. The shop had twenty workers when Chung took over; it employed seventy by the time the Japanese nationalized it in 1943.[3]

Korea started making its own vehicles in the mid-1950s out of U.S. military discards. Cast-off U.S. military jeeps served as the chassis while the bodies were made from flattened steel drums that the U.S. military had thrown out. The Cheval (sometimes known as Sibal) Auto Company's nine-seat taxis, usually crammed with passengers, were a common sight in the Seoul of the 1950s. Cheval's founder, Choi Mu Song, received some help from the government, but his attempts to strike a technology transfer agreement with a foreign partner were frustrated by frequent ministerial changes at the Ministry of Commerce and Industry. Choi's situation went from difficult to impossible after Park Chung Hee seized power. A threat to levy punitive back taxes forced Choi to turn over his company to what became the Shinjin Motor Company.[4]

The government took a keen interest in building up the auto industry. During the first five-year plan, imports of finished autos were prohibited—a prohibition that was to last until 1987. Tariffs on imported auto parts and components, however, were eliminated, as they were on many other favored industries, in order to encourage local assembly operations.

Tellingly, the auto industry was caught up in factional struggles among Korea's new military rulers. KCIA founder Kim Jong Pil's faction first seized control of the newly formed Saenara ("New Nation") auto company as a way of generating funds for the Democratic Republican Party. Founded in 1962, Saenara had a technical cooperation agreement with Nissan, whose automobile kits were assembled in Korea and sold domestically. However, Saenara also managed to smuggle in 1,642 fully assembled Datsuns and sell them for twice their landed price. The smuggling operation required a good deal of official connivance and resulted in a windfall for Saenara.

The government shut down Saenara in 1963, as a result of a foreign exchange crisis and unhappiness within the ruling elite over Kim's maneuvering. In 1965, after the restoration of diplomatic ties with Japan, the newly formed Shinjin Automobile Manufacturing Company took over Saenara's facilities. Shinjin was a joint venture between the Korea Spicer Group and Toyota. Daewoo would later take over the operation, which would become an unhappy alliance between Daewoo and General Motors known as Saehan ("New Korea") and later as Daewoo Motor.[5] From the start, the auto industry was both a symbol of national pride and a victim of factional infighting among groups trying to control a business through which large amounts of cash flowed.

When Chung Ju Yung was building the new Seoul-Pusan highway in the mid-1960s, Park Chung Hee supposedly asked him, "Do you know anything about cars?" When Chung said that he had run an auto repair shop in Seoul during and after World War II, Park encouraged him to start producing passenger cars. "You're building the road. Now we need cars," the president is said to have told Chung. In the final days of 1967, Hyundai Motor officially opened its doors. In 1969 production began when Hyundai started assembling knocked-down kits of Ford's Cortina model. At that time Kia, which later emerged as the number two auto company, was making nothing more ambitious than bicycles.

In the late 1960s, Ulsan was simply a mid-sized city on the eastern coast, a jumble of low mortar and cement buildings, with open sewers and little running water or electricity. It took a leap of faith to build a motor industry in a city that had virtually no roads. "I visited the Ulsan plant three days after I joined the company in November 1969," remembers Kim Nwae Myong, who later became the managing director of export marketing. "We used to say that the road from downtown Ulsan to the plant was the worst road in the nation." After a bone-rattling ride on a pitted, unpaved track, visitors to the plant saw nothing but a primitive assembly operation next to the port.

But Hyundai had big ideas. Although it had the joint venture with Ford, the company was determined to build a Korean car. Chon Sung Won remembers the thinking that lay behind the risky decision to create an independent, export-oriented auto industry. "The government tried to develop an auto industry. [Government and business thought] it should not be just an assembly operation, [but that] we should have our own car. It was a fundamental government policy." Hyundai management, says Chon, quickly figured out that simply running an assembly operation would neither be profitable nor do much to develop the country's industrial structure.[6]

Hyundai thought that the domestic market was too small to support the development of a home-grown model. Unlike automakers in large countries such as Japan,

Korea's manufacturers did not have the luxury of first developing models for the domestic market and then developing overseas sales. "No one thought we could make our own industry because the market was so small and the industrial level was so low," says Chon. At the time, Hyundai's production was less than 5,000 cars a year, all for the domestic market. "That's one day's production now," chuckles Chon.

Hyundai engaged in classic bargaining with the government when it was building its plant. "We wanted to be able to build 50,000 cars a year," remembers Chon Sung Won. To do that, Hyundai had to come up with sales figures to justify what at the time seemed like enormous capacity. The company made optimistic five- and ten-year demand projections and presented them to skeptical government officials. "I picked the figures out of a hat," Chon conceded in a 1991 interview. Whether he was brilliant or simply lucky, the numbers were astoundingly accurate. "At that time no one believed us. All the people said Hyundai was crazy." Characteristically, however, Park Chung Hee was willing to believe Hyundai, and he allowed the company to gamble on developing a new model.

With the help of technical assistance from Japan's Mitsubishi, along with British and Italian design and production experts, Hyundai in fact did build its own auto in the early 1970s, using a simple four-cylinder engine. Few outsiders took Korea's quixotic dreams of becoming an industrial producer seriously. A BBC documentary of former British Leyland executive George Turnbull, who along with a team of British engineers helped design and build the Hyundai factory, found it rather amusing that these earnest Asians actually believed they could build a car that would compete in the world market.

The company proudly trumpeted this first Korean-designed car with advertisements showing its Pony model poised grandly with Notre Dame cathedral in the background. Although production started only in December 1975, this was the car that the globe-trotting Chon Sung Won had been trying to sell in the early 1970s.

The effort cost Hyundai a tremendous amount of managerial attention and money at a time when both were in short supply in Korea. "Between 1972 and 1978 Hyundai Motor was essentially a bankrupt company supported by other Hyundai companies," remembers another senior Hyundai executive.[7] The Shinjin venture dominated the auto market, with a market share as high as 80 percent in the early 1970s.

The audacity of Hyundai's auto gamble is even more striking given what else the company was doing. The 1970s was a decade when Hyundai was building its huge shipyard just up the road from the auto plant on the outskirts of Ulsan and its construction unit was racking up $6 billion in Middle East construction contracts.[8]

More difficulties came with Chun's 1980 takeover and the attempt to rationalize excess capacity in the auto and other businesses. Chun ordered Hyundai to give up its heavy industrial facility (Hyundai International) at Changwon and merge with the Daewoo–General Motors venture. Although Hyundai fought off the order to merge with GM, it was a close scrape as the Korean company sparred with General Motors over the Detroit automakers' demand for a 50 percent share in the venture as well as overall management control. Given GM's strategy of trying to build a world car, which involved centralizing design and production decisions in Detroit, such an alliance would have been fatal to the Korean motor industry's dreams of independence. After six months, the negotiations ended when the Blue House agreed to let the two companies remain separate.[9]

A senior Hyundai executive said that the management effort required to deal with the "nonsense" put forward by the "military guys" who were trying to streamline the auto industry cost the company several years' delay in beginning exports to North America.[10] But the company kept what mattered most—its independence.

Even in the tough environment of the early 1980s, as the technocrats squeezed credit and tried to prune many of the huge heavy industrial enterprises started in the 1970s, Hyundai kept pouring more money into expanding its capacity. "We were losing money continuously for three years," remembers Chon Sung Won. "But at that time we invested a lot of money in Excel, including a new factory with 300,000 units of [annual] capacity."

Tough antipollution regulations made it imperative for Hyundai to find help if it was to break into the U.S. and Canadian markets. The decision to look for a full-fledged foreign partner was a big step for Hyundai, which alone of the major chaebol had virtually no foreign joint ventures.[11] Talks with Mitsubishi began in 1979, but they did not really get going until Mitsubishi chairman Kubo Tomio visited Korea in August 1980. Kubo insisted on visiting Puyo, the capital of the ancient Paekche kingdom, and made what was for a Japanese the extraordinary statement that as a native of the southwestern Japanese island of Kyushu (closest to Korea) he had to be part Korean. The following January, after a second meeting between Kubo and Chung Ju Yung, Mitsubishi agreed to give Hyundai the emission control technology it needed, as well as other important technical assistance, in exchange for allowing the Japanese auto company to buy an initial stake of 10 percent in Hyundai Motor, which was later increased to almost 15 percent.

In 1984 Hyundai started sales in Canada, which it intended as a sort of dry run for the U.S. market. In any event, its Pony model did not meet U.S. safety and emission standards and the launch of the Mitsubishi-based Excel was still several years off. The company figured on selling 5,000 cars the first year in Canada. Thanks to the car's low price, Hyundai sold over 25,000, making the Pony Canada's fifth most popular import vehicle behind three Japanese makes and a Volkswagen model. In 1985 almost 80,000 of the low-priced, fuel-efficient Ponys were sold, catapulting it to first place among imports.

Hyundai executives predicted sales of 100,000 cars in 1986. But the tide turned against the South Korean automaker. Ponys started literally falling apart, as hubcaps rattled off and cassette decks gobbled up tapes. The new Stellar, based on the Pony, was so underpowered that a critic complained of having to turn off the air conditioner to merge onto the highway. Deliveries of the Excel model were delayed as dealers tried to sell off the 30,000 Ponys still in stock.

Moreover, Canadian officials began talking about removing a tariff exemption for Korean cars, which effectively gave the Koreans around a 10 percent price advantage against their Japanese competitors, and saved Hyundai some $200 million (Canadian) in duties.[12] While sales north of the border were falling, however, Hyundai readied its jump into the huge and demanding U.S. market.

The launch of Hyundai's Excel model in the United States could not have been better timed. Initial shipments began in 1986, just a few months after the Plaza accord, which had accelerated the slide of the dollar. The yen shot up, and the Korean won followed the dollar down. The rise in the price of Japanese cars, which reflected the Japanese strategy of selling more expensive cars because of quotas in the U.S. market, gave Hyundai Motor a generous price umbrella. While the Korean press had been pessimistic about Hyundai's chances in the U.S. market, the company easily exceeded its initial export targets.

Hyundai Motor set a record for first-year auto exports to the United States, shipping 168,882 units of its Excel model in 1986, giving it a stunning 7.1 percent share of the subcompact market. "In our first year, we managed to achieve sales which took Honda and Toyota individually seven years to reach," bragged Hyundai managing director Lee Bang Joo. The following year—when it was hampered by strikes and parts shortages—Hyundai nonetheless sold over a quarter of a million Excels in the United States. Korea's success as an auto exporter landed it in the ranks of a select group of nations.[13]

Sales for the auto company soared from $1.5 billion in 1984 to $5.8 billion in 1989. This catapulted Hyundai Motor to the lead position in the Hyundai group. Combined group sales were $23 billion in 1988 (and about $50 billion in 1991), making Hyundai one of the largest corporations in the world. Its other operations included the world's largest shipyard and substantial electronics and engineering operations. By the end of 1989, Hyundai Motor alone had 37,000 employees, most of them production workers at Ulsan.

Hyundai Motor, Hyundai Heavy Industries, Hyundai Mipo dockyard, and eleven other Hyundai companies quickly transformed Ulsan from a mid-sized fishing port into one of the incubators of Korean industrialization. By 1989, the city had a population of 600,000; of these, 80,000 worked for Hyundai, mostly at the shipyard and the auto plant.[14] By the beginning of 1992, Hyundai counted 170,000 employees around the world.

By the 1980s, Ulsan had been turned into the sort of industrial cauldron rarely seen now in industrialized countries. At night eerie flames flickered from smokestacks, and during the day a pallid haze clung to the three- and four-story buildings through the sprawling city. The area was so polluted that by the late 1980s Hyundai executives began to refuse transfers to the area, preferring instead to commute from Seoul, where they kept their families so that their children could attend better schools. Ulsan became one of the tribal homelands of South Korea, a witness to the gulf that separated workers from Seoul's white-collar elite of managers and intellectuals.

Pollution was even worse at the Onsan chemical complex, which formed the southern boundary of Ulsan, than in the city. The government moved nearly 10,000 families to new homes in the late 1980s as a result of chemical contamination. These people, most of whom had been farmers, were assured by authorities that the new chemical plants being built next to their houses would be completely safe. But as fruit withered on trees and rice shriveled in paddies, even the Chun government had to concede that the living conditions next to the chemical complex were intolerable.

Until the late 1980s, however, these sorts of problems were largely overlooked in the rush to development. The success of Hyundai's car sales was a milestone for Korean exporters because of the control that the company exercised over the sales and marketing of its cars. One of the great weaknesses of Korea's export-oriented companies was—and remains—their reliance on foreign buyers who then controlled the sales and marketing of the products. Hyundai, however, established its own network of dealers. Each dealer had to build an exclusive showroom for Hyundai cars, a strategy that Hyundai management and independent analysts thought was key to the company's success.

It took considerable financial resources to establish this brand-name presence in the U.S. market, resources that had simply not been available even a few years earlier. Hyundai and its dealers spent $55 million on advertising its cars in 1986. Total U.S. advertising for the other three major chaebol was under $5 million, less than one-tenth of what Hyundai's auto campaign cost. The spending on marketing kept climbing. In 1987, Hyundai's ad campaign for its cars cost almost $100 million and in 1988 more than $135 million. Expensive though this campaign was, it succeeded in carving out a respectable niche in the U.S. auto market for Hyundai. Its share of the subcompact market rose from 7.1 percent in 1986, the year exports to the United States began, to 11.2 percent in 1987.

By contrast, Daewoo Motor, the 50–50 joint venture between the Daewoo group and General Motors, showed the dangers of relying on a foreign partner for sales and marketing abroad. Daewoo's LeMans model, which was based on the West German Opel Kadett, was sold in the United States exclusively through GM's Pontiac dealers. The modestly priced LeMans was used as a way of enticing buyers into the showroom, where dealers then tried to sell customers more expensive, more profitable models—which were not made by Daewoo. By the end of 1989, Daewoo had all but pulled out of the U.S. market.

The Daewoo–General Motors alliance had been in trouble even before Daewoo took over Shinjin Automobile Manufacturing Company. Shinjin had been owned by the same group that controlled Korea Heavy Machinery Manufacturing, which Kim Woo Choong had resurrected. Although Shinjin dominated the domestic market in the 1970s, it was slow to respond to change. The company's flagship model during the decade was a gas-guzzling model introduced shortly before the first oil shock, which lost market share to Hyundai's fuel-efficient Pony.

In the 1980s, Daewoo executives complained bitterly that General Motors had prevented them from taking the necessary steps to turn the operation around. Finally, in the late 1980s Daewoo set up a new motor operation without General Motors (and with technical help from the Japanese automaker Suzuki) as a result of disagreements over future strategy.

Why did Hyundai succeed where its competitors in other countries had failed? Part of the reason was as simple as being ready with the right product at the right time. The U.S.-Japanese auto agreement, under which the Japanese "voluntarily" restrained their exports, presented a clear opportunity for the Koreans to sell cars in the U.S. market. The export quotas gave the Japanese an incentive to sell increasingly more stylish and expensive cars, which provided larger profits. This opened up new opportunities for economy cars in the U.S. market. "We were sucked into a vacuum," says Chon Sung Won. "We were lucky. We had every reason to succeed."

But timing alone was not enough, for at the same time that Hyundai was succeeding, two of its competitors were faltering. The Yugoslavian-made Yugo flopped on the U.S. market, while the Malaysian Proton had such severe problems that the government had to ask Japanese partner Mitsubishi to take over the management. Assembling and marketing an auto for the international market is no simple task, as these two failures showed. Hyundai, for example has more than 400 parts makers supplying it with the 20,000 components that are assembled into a single car.

Hyundai tried to produce as many parts domestically as possible, cutting its reliance on Japanese suppliers. As part of its export push, Hyundai invested $300 million in an automatic transmission plant, which saved it more than 100,000 yen (about $700) in import costs on every car when it was completed in late 1987. In 1991 it started producing its own engines, and in the early 1990s it began a joint development project with Mitsubishi, on remarkably equal terms, to develop a new model. Hyundai's policy of developing its own manufacturing capabilities shows that in spite of worries about continuing overdependence on Japanese technology, Korean companies can win a fair degree of autonomy.[15]

Hyundai executives, reflecting the Korean notion that hard work alone can accomplish almost anything, say that a fierce determination to succeed, coupled with a vigorous long-term investment program, underpinned the company's success. Hyundai's Lee Bang Joo noted, in a typical Korean remark, that "the key [to our success] is an unshakeable commitment." They proudly point to the decision to go ahead with construction of the Excel plant at a time when, as another manager put it, "every day we worried about bankruptcy."[16] It is this relentless push for expansion, for top-line growth at almost any cost, that was (and in most cases still is) the defining characteristic of South Korean industry, for what Hyundai was doing in passenger cars, other Korean companies were doing in consumer electronics, textiles, footwear, ships, and other mass-produced goods.

South Korea's tremendous economic success had been accomplished under the pressure of overwhelming state control for the quarter-century after Park Chung Hee seized power in 1961. But prosperity generated pressure for change. South Koreans were tired of being treated like infants or criminals by an illegitimate military government. In June 1987, as the economic juggernaut rolled on, the middle class took its protests to the streets and almost brought the government down.

Notes

1. *Asian Wall Street Journal,* April 23, 1982.

2. Brian R. Gold, "The Entry of Hyundai Motor into North America," p. 28, says that Hyundai produced 54 percent of all the autos produced by the industry between 1962 and 1986, 1,432,046 out of a total 2,614,219.

3. Ibid., pp. 18, 29–30, citing Kim Chuk Kyo and Lee Chul Hee, "The Growth of the Automobile Industry," in Park Chong Kee (ed.), *Macroeconomic and Industrial Development in Korea* (KDI, 1980), pp. 279–80. The Chung Ju Yung information (Gold, p. 19) comes from a *Hankuk Kyongje Shinmun* article on February 16, 1986 (interview with Chung Ju Yung).

4. Thanks to Chi Jung Nam for the information on Sibal, which he tells on the authority of Choi's nephew, Park Jae Wan. Additional information on the early days is found in Gold, "The Entry of Hyundai Motor into North America."

5. In 1972, Toyota pulled out of South Korea, because of the Japanese company's desire to do business in China, and was replaced by General Motors. China enforced an economic boycott against South Korea after Zhou Enlai issued the Four Principles designed to punish South Vietnam and its allies. At that time the Toyota-Shinjin venture accounted for 80 percent of domestic sales (Gold, "The Entry of Hyundai Motor into North America," p. 23); a fuller account of this is found in Chang Dal-joong, *Economic Control and Political Authoritarianism,* pp. 180–83. Hyundai, at least, came to see Toyota's pullout as ultimately a good thing, because it left the field open for a hungry domestic competitor (Gold, p. 24, citing a Hyundai corporate history). General Motors and Daewoo eventually had a bitter divorce, which was completed in 1992. See Chapter 8 for an account of how General Motors acquired Daewoo as a partner.

6. Author interview, November 1991. Unless noted, this is the source for all of Chon's quotations.

7. Author interview, March 1991.

8. The $6 billion figure is from Carter J. Eckert et al., *Korea Old and New,* p. 399.

9. Because of Hyundai's ties with Ford, enforcing the Blue House's edict would have meant a merger between a GM venture and a Ford venture.

10. Lee Sang Il, general manager of Hyundai Motor's North American operations, quoted in Gold, "The Entry of Hyundai Motor into North America," p. 33.

11. The exception that proved the rule was the Hyundai Mipo dockyard, in which Kawasaki Heavy Industries had a mere 5 percent stake, of no importance as far as management control was concerned. Hyundai Motor's tie-up with Ford was more a sourcing arrangement than a full-fledged partnership; Ford owned none of Hyundai's equity. Gold, "The Entry of Hyundai Motor into North America," pp. 34–5, on Mitsubishi. Gold also notes that in the late 1970s Hyundai had talked with both Renault and Volkswagen about some sort of alliance, but no deal was struck.

12. Gold. *The Entry of Hyundai Motor into North America*, pp. 44–45. The threat prompted Hyundai to build an assembly facility in Bromont, Quebec, that chronically lost money and was shut down indefinitely for "re-tooling in 1993. The company eventually took a write-down of 280 billion won in 1996 to cover the costs associated with this ill-thought-out venture.

13. It also produced an Excel model that was sold under Mitsubishi's name; including these sales, Hyundai sold 330,000 units in the United States in 1988, the peak year during the 1980s.

14. Author interviews with Hyundai Corporate Culture Department general manager Park Il Kwon, April 1990 and January 1992 (for number of employees at the beginning of 1992).

15. The relationship with Mitsubishi came at a heavy cost. In 1988, for example, about $20 million of the $25 million in royalty payments that Hyundai made were to Mitsubishi. Hyundai Motor Company prospectus, February 7, 1990, p. 32.

16. Author interview, January 1989.

19

Surrender

> If I have any personal desire, it is to be recognized by my fellow countrymen as the former president and as the one who firmly planted a democratic system in Korean soil for the first time and is recorded as such in history.
>
> —Chun Doo Hwan[1]

It was an acrid taste, the stinging taste of discontent, that Korea's elite got as they left a party at the Hilton Hotel to celebrate former general Roh Tae Woo's selection as the ruling party's presidential candidate on the muggy summer evening of June 10, 1987. Tear gas fired to quell demonstrators a few hundred yards down the hill from the hotel filled the air, leaving politicians and businessmen sneezing, wheezing, and teary-eyed as they dashed for the air-conditioned comfort of their chauffeur-driven Hyundai Grandeurs and Daewoo Princes.

The forces for change had been building up for years, but it was on this day, with Roh's formal nomination as the Democratic Justice Party's presidential candidate, that the battle began in earnest over the "peaceful transfer of power" that Chun had promised since 1980.

The nominating convention itself was a carefully crafted affair held on the southern edge of Seoul, in a gymnasium built for the upcoming 1988 Olympics. The president was delayed, so the band struck up a seemingly apt tune: "My Way." Helium balloons were released on cue, confetti was scattered, and a band played as the two former generals clasped their hands and held them aloft. Designed to look as if it were a spontaneous outburst celebrating democracy, in reality the convention was as predictable as a Swiss watch.

Because of a skewed voting system, which virtually guaranteed the election of the ruling party candidate, this was more of a coronation than a simple nomination. Some countries declined to send their ambassadors to what was seen as a transfer of royal power rather than the kick-off to a democratic election. However, U.S. Ambassador James Lilley's presence was carefully noted by both the government and the opposition.

But by the time the guests left the Hilton Hotel—a showplace owned by the Daewoo group—it became clear that, even with tens of thousands of riot police on the streets, Chun was going to have a hard time getting his way. Opposition to Chun, which had been pushed underground for the first half of the 1980s, had been building more openly since the 1985 legislative elections. In 1987 it would come to a head, stoked by the torture death of a student in January, Chun's backtracking on political liberalization in April, and, the night before the nomination, the wounding of Lee Han Yol, a Yonsei University student demonstrator. Lee was hit in the head at point-blank range by a rifle-launched tear gas grenade and lay in a coma. He would die before the month was out. But it would be a long month for both police and protesters: A staggering total of 351,000 tear gas canisters and grenades were fired in June alone.[2]

The Salaryman's Revolution

The tear gas that drifted up to the Hilton from Namdaemun (South Gate) was only one sign of the protests that had erupted throughout downtown after police had blocked a noontime rally at the Anglican Church to protest Roh's nomination. Several days earlier, hundreds of riot police, clad in their trademark bulky green uniforms and dark helmets, began sealing off the narrow streets leading to the church, which is just off City Hall plaza in the center of the city, in order to prevent demonstrators from assembling. On the day of the demonstration even office workers in adjacent buildings were prohibited from going to work. At noon, there was a weird calm in the church courtyard, as about two dozen clergy and lay supporters who had secreted themselves in the compound held a brief, mute walk around the cathedral. They were the silent center of the storm.

Out on the main streets of Seoul, on the other side of the police lines, something extraordinary was happening. Traffic was halted on the main boulevard running by National Treasure No. 1, the historic South Gate, as demonstrators clashed with police. Throughout the central business district, from the chic Myongdong shopping area to the gritty streets around the Seoul railroad station, groups of demonstrators would gather, chant antigovernment slogans, and then scatter under the inevitable barrages of tear gas. They would then regroup, and the cycle would begin again. To beat the chronic tear gas, people took to walking the streets with plastic food wrap over their eyes and surgical masks over their mouths, both sealed around the edges with toothpaste, which for some reason cut the sting of the tear gas.

These demonstrations, small and peaceful though they were, represented an unprecedented challenge to Chun. Although numerous demonstrations had taken place during the seven years he had been in power, they had usually been confined to university campuses. For the June 10 demonstrations, though, radical students had slipped out of campus areas singly or in small groups and met at prearranged points in downtown Seoul. The students' successful shift in tactics, which took the demonstrations out of the isolated campuses and into the heart of the capital, proved decisive in rallying public support.

For nearly three weeks this pattern of demonstrations continued. Small groups of chanting demonstrators would taunt policemen with protest slogans. The gathering would be broken up by fleet-footed "grabbers" (combat policemen trained in taekwondo and clad in civilian clothes, running shoes, and helmets) and clumsy squads of riot policemen, only to re-form almost immediately at a nearby location. It was extraordinary that the protesters could keep up the momentum day after day. But what worried the government most was that these hit-and-run demonstrations were not made up only of students and dissidents.

For the streets of Seoul were increasingly filled with white-shirted salarymen from downtown office buildings who would pour out of their offices at lunchtime to watch the action, and occasionally join in. Middle-aged women berated the young riot policemen for their indiscriminate use of tear gas. Store owners in the crowded Namdaemun market hid students from the police who were pursuing them. In the past, the middle class had not usually put itself on the front lines during demonstrations, but in June 1987 it left no doubt where its sympathies lay.

A classic example of the middle class' passive-aggressive part in the protests occurred on the evening of June 19 between the Chosun Hotel and the broad ten-lane Namdaemun Boulevard in the center of the city. (At the time, a massive sit-down protest by thousands of people shut down the boulevard itself.) Demonstrators, mostly students but with some office workers and older citizens mixed in, chanted slogans at a group of about a dozen riot police they confronted. This was center stage. But only a few feet away, ringing this drama, several hundred office workers and bystanders, mostly in their thirties and forties, watched closely. A low roar was heard from the onlookers, but few moved their lips. Everyone and no one was criticizing this government, these police, the whole unfair political system. It was like a Greek chorus roaring its disapprobation of an unjust ruler.

The riot police, who were vastly outnumbered by the crowd, would periodically wheel around and confront a group of people behind them, or off to the side. A hush would fall over the bystanders when they were confronted directly by the police, but then the rest of the crowd, now safely out of the policemen's gaze, would take up the roar of disapproval, and the riot police would wheel again. Periodically the riot police, who were young, frightened military conscripts, would panic and fire tear gas, scattering the crowd. Then the demonstrators would gather again and the cycle of taunts and the roar of anger and the volleys of tear gas would begin anew.

The police had every reason to be afraid. In several cases, but most dramatically at a major intersection in front of the Shinsegae department store, protesters simply surrounded and overwhelmed the riot police, stripping them of their shields, tear gas rifles, clubs, helmets, and masks, leaving them half-clothed and exposed to taunting protesters.

No one, it seemed, supported Chun. A group of workers from the government-owned Korea Exchange Bank formed an organization called the Democratic Workers of Korea Exchange Bank, to raise money for the demonstrators. "We fully support the patriotic students' and civilians' struggle against the government," they said in a statement. "We are now discussing the best way for workers to join the protests. In our minds our aspiration for democracy is growing and growing. We have gathered a sum of money, though tiny, to support the movement for democracy and the brave fighting against the government."[3]

Moreover, anyone associated with the administration was tainted. A boycott developed against Korea Explosives, allegedly responsible for making the tear gas. Sports fans boycotted a baseball team whose corporate owner allegedly had a connection with Lee Soon Ja and thus had won a lucrative contract selling instant noodles to the riot police.

This direct challenge to the state could not go on in a country that valued order and authority. The Chinese idea that rulers have the "mandate of heaven," which gives them the legitimacy to rule, was well accepted in Korea. Chun had clearly lost heaven's blessing, and therefore the right to rule.

Torture, Suicide, and a "Grave Decision"

By 1987, Chun's claims to leadership, always fragile, had eroded altogether. His purification and anticorruption campaign years earlier had led to the Madame Chang curb market scandal and the shakedown of business to fund the Ilhae Institute. His wife's relatives had systematically enriched themselves; his brothers were, in a cruder form, looting state organizations and extorting money from private businessmen.

Ironically, Chun's authority was also undermined by his promise to step down after a single term in office and Korea's successful bid for the Olympics, Chun's other claim to legitimacy. As early as 1985, after the government party's poor performance in legislative elections, the president began to be regarded as something of a lame duck, and jockeying for the post-Chun era began in earnest. When the protests gathered force in 1987, the impending Olympics made a harsh crackdown politically impossible.

Nineteen eighty-seven had started badly for the South Korean government. A student at the elite Seoul National University who had been taken in by security agents was killed during interrogation. Police maintained that the death was accidental. But a copy of the government's secret autopsy report was leaked to the *Dong-A Ilbo* newspaper. The autopsy showed that twenty-one-year-old Park

Chong Chol had been tortured to death, his windpipe smashed on the edge of a bathtub in a secret interrogation room.

Brutal interrogations were common in Korea, and dissidents had long tried to rally public support against torture. In a well-publicized 1986 case, labor activist Kwon In Suk sued a policeman she said had sexually abused her while she was being questioned for labor union activities.

Kwon was a union organizer, a Seoul National University student who had lied about her educational background, pretending not to have gone to university so that she could be hired as a blue-collar worker. It is a crime in Korea to understate one's educational background. This law reflected one of the government's biggest fears, that well-educated radicals would infiltrate the country's workplaces and spur the workers to rise. As a result, security agents compiled blacklists, which they regularly distributed to employers in an effort to prevent activists from getting employment.

"I needed to hide my university background in order to get a job," Kwon said. Although her case attracted a good deal of attention, her torturer initially escaped punishment while Kwon was stigmatized as a radical and jailed for more than a year on charges of fabricating an official document.[4]

Park Chong Chol's case was too brutal to ignore. He was dead at the hands of the government. A linguistics student at Seoul National University, Park was at the top of the nation's intensely competitive educational hierarchy. He was the son of a man who ran a water pumping station in Pusan. The family lived in a simple apartment above the pump house, but he had taken advantage of the upward mobility that Korea's educational system allows.

When government agents killed Park Chong Chol, they did more than murder a student activist. They struck at the hopes and dreams of parents around the country whose greatest wish was that their sons might go to Seoul National University. That the government had killed one of the best and the brightest of the young generation only thickened the patina of revulsion and mistrust covering the Fifth Republic.

An unrelated event several months later underscored the popular perception that Chun had lost even the few shreds of legitimacy that still clung to him. In April a prominent businessman jumped to his death from his tenth-floor office suite in central Seoul. The suicide of Park Ken Suk, chairman of the troubled Pan Ocean shipping company and brother of Koreagate figure Tongsun Park, coincided with an investigation into tax evasion and currency smuggling charges against the company.

A week after Park's suicide, the Office of National Tax Administration revealed that Park and Pan Ocean president Hahn Sang Yon had smuggled $16.4 million out of the country since 1979. The two senior executives had feuded and were informing on each other to tax authorities at the time of Park's death. Han was subsequently convicted on capital flight and tax evasion charges.

The Pan Ocean affair was another affront to the traditional mores of Confucian Korea. Stashing money overseas, cheating the taxman, and living lavishly were, of course, nothing new, but people began to mutter that corruption was spiraling out of control as the country became richer. The torture death of Park, Chun's continuing hard-line posture, and the Pan Ocean scandal signaled to many that the Fifth Republic was rotten within and without.

By the spring of 1987, there was a widespread sense that something was very wrong. The country's economy was booming, and people were getting ready for the 1988 Olympic Games. But politics remained stuck in the dark ages. Chun stunned the nation with an April 13 telecast in which he said he was suspending talks on constitutional revisions. That ended hope for a direct presidential election, and paved the way for Chun's hand-picked successor to follow him in office. Chang Se Dong, who had been head of the National Security Planning Agency (the NSPA, the successor to the KCIA) since February 1985, had reportedly urged Chun to take this tough line, arguing that the government could easily ride out the predictable protests that would follow this self-styled "grave decision."

At the end of May 1987, the struggle for power came to a head. Chang Se Dong, who had been considered a rival to Roh for the presidential nomination, was forced out of office in a wide-ranging cabinet reshuffle just two weeks before the ruling Democratic Justice Party was set to hold its nominating convention.

The stock market fell sharply when news of the cabinet reshuffle was announced. There were fears that the shake-up reflected divisions in the military and that Chang was leading a coup against Chun. One of the wilder rumors—and it is impossible to give it more credibility than that—had Chang Se Dong initially refusing to leave his NSPA office and firing several bullets into the ceiling to prove his point.

The Korea Stock Exchange composite index fell 3.2 percent, one of its sharpest drops ever, on rumors of the power struggle. Only when the state-run television showed President Chun hosting foreign diplomats at a cocktail party that evening did rumors of a coup dissipate. Although the military had been weakened as Korea became richer and more diverse, the May 26 incident showed that both foreigners and Koreans still worried almost obsessively about the military and hard-liners in the intelligence agencies. Moreover, with memories still fresh of how Park Chung Hee had left office on a hospital litter, even the wildest rumors could not be discounted altogether.

If the political situation seemed to be deteriorating, or, conversely, if more liberal forces seemed to be getting the upper hand within the ruling party, Koreans would whisper speculation of an impending coup. The stock market was especially sensitive to rumors of right-wing or military maneuvering, and would periodically plummet on reports of military rumbling. For while Koreans dreamed of political change, they were afraid of what opposition leader Kim Dae Jung referred to as "the military veto group."[5] Given the military's power grabs in 1961 and again in 1979–80, these fears were not unfounded. South Korea had not had a single example of a lasting peaceful transfer of power.

In 1987, though, officers were far from a united group. Many believed that their time in politics had passed. Any military intervention also would have to weigh the questionable loyalty of the troops. In 1979 and 1980 there was never any question but that conscript soldiers would follow orders. In 1987, especially by mid-June, it was unclear whether either the combat police or rank-and-file soldiers could be relied on. They were conscripts, and they were better educated than their predecessors had been in 1980. By 1987, they were more likely to be from the city than the country; many empathized with the protesters and, indeed, had themselves been protesters before induction into the military.[6] Ironically, the very economic success that the government had worked so hard for eroded government political control. By 1988, the national economy was more than twice as large as it had been when Chun took power. People were better educated, and young people had grown up thinking that their country deserved a more modern political system to go along with its astounding record of economic growth. A pompous ex-general was not most Koreans' idea of a suitable leader for their increasingly prosperous and self-confident nation.

The Generals Surrender

Even more suddenly than it began, the wave of demonstrations ended when Roh, the ruling party presidential candidate, shocked the nation with a dramatic Monday morning announcement that essentially bowed to all the protesters' demands. Major points of Roh's June 29, 1987 declaration included a direct presidential election, the release of political prisoners, and the lifting of political bans on opposition leader Kim Dae Jung and other prominent politicians.

After falling sharply on rumors of a coup at the end of May, the stock market had nervously jumped up and down during much of June in response to the political situation. But on June 29, it posted its biggest rise ever, gaining 16.68 points. Of the 399 companies listed on the exchange, 378 posted gains, with 286 up their maximum for the day.[7]

"I've never seen it like this," a young Korean stock analyst who supported Kim Dae Jung said. "It's great news. Real democracy is coming. Koreans have been disappointed over and over again by the government. Now Koreans believe that they are the citizens and the government is listening to the people. If the ruling party announced nothing today, then the next opposition rally would have been bigger because the movement was snowballing."

The country was euphoric. "Today is democracy day in Korea," said the president of one of the country's securities companies, as he lifted his tumbler of scotch in a posh room salon in Seoul's wealthy Kangnam district. These extremely expensive watering holes are a modern elaboration of the *kisaeng* (Korea's version of the *geisha*), a place where executives unwind with copious quantities of scotch in the company of attractive young women. While the *kisaeng* houses are in traditional buildings and often serve exquisite Korean cuisine, the room salons usually are done up in a more modern fashion, with oversized chandeliers and low leather-and-chrome couches. Women feed the men snacks of nuts, dried squid or fruit and a madame periodically comes in to make sure that everyone is happy—or at least that the men are. These are very much places for the rich, with the minimum bill about $100 per person and a more typical tab running several hundred dollars a head. The depth of the antipathy toward Chun even among the elite was nowhere more apparent than in the booming business Kangnam's watering holes did on the night of June 29.

Chun ratified Roh's democratization announcement on July 1. But as if to reinforce the message about how much Koreans wanted democratic change, hundreds of thousands of people poured into the streets of Seoul on July 9 for the funeral of Lee Han Yol, the student who was fatally injured when he was struck by a tear gas shell a month earlier. After several weeks in a coma, Lee had died on June 28, on the eve of Roh's dramatic announcement.

Joining the student mourners for Lee were thousands of middle-aged and elderly women, most of whom were mothers and grandmothers of students. The cortege route through downtown Seoul was lined with a cross-section of Seoul residents. Shop and office workers peeked out of doorways, leaned out of windows, and crowded onto rooftops to watch the procession of several hundred thousand people, which swelled to include elderly men and women in traditional white *hanbok*, in the largest demonstration in the country's history. Protesters took over City Hall plaza in the heart of downtown and tore down the Korean flag that flew over the municipal building. If Chun and his advisers still had any doubt about the costs of a crackdown, or the depth of support for democratic change, this peaceful demonstration dispelled them.

Chun managed to stay on at the Blue House until his term finished on February 25, 1988. But he was spent as a political force after Roh's June 29 democratization announcement, which marked a watershed in modern Korean political history. While the country still had a long way to go to fulfill Roh's promises, his speech signaled that hard-line forces could no longer block change. What Roh's speech did not do, however, was lay out any clear road map for reform. Nowhere was this more apparent than in the booming Korean economy, which had relied on top-down direction for nearly three decades of rapid growth. Following Roh's promise of democracy came a kinder face of authoritarianism. But first would come a challenge from the workers who were the muscle of the Korean economy.

Notes

1. Chun Doo Hwan, "President Chun's New Year Policy Statement," January 12, 1987, in *Korea Annual*, 1987, p. 365.

2. *Physicians for Human Rights Record*, Issue 1 (Fall 1987), p. 1, quoted in William Shaw (ed.), *Human Rights in Korea*, p. 208.

3. Author notes, June 1987.

4. Kwon's quotation is from a 1990 press briefing at the Seoul Foreign Correspondents' Club. Although she was only successful in winning damages after the democratic reforms of 1987, the simple fact that she received support from some lawyers and that her case was covered in the controlled Korean press, even in a muted fashion, marked an important change. She used the 30 million won she received in damages to start a labor counseling center.

5. It is possible that the military would have vetoed Kim Dae Jung's election, had he won. A senior military official told the local press during the 1987 presidential campaign that "something bad might happen" to Kim if he were elected. Moreover, a Western intelligence source told the author (in 1991 interviews) that credible reports had been received in 1987 that if Kim won the popular vote, a coup would be mounted to prevent him from taking office.

6. Indeed, after 1987 conscripts grew increasingly bold about speaking out against the often violent conditions in the military. See *Far Eastern Economic Review*, February 6, 1992.

7. This section is based on author interviews and notes, June 1987.

20

Workers

From a broad perspective, labor unrest is an indication that the economy is advancing. Because of economic advancement, human resources are growing scarce. To employ workers under such circumstances, you have to pay better wages, don't you? In a sense, this is the price of economic development.

—Roh Tae Woo[1]

Chung Ju Yung and other businessmen had always been able to count on taking care of labor activists with a telephone call to intelligence agencies. An uppity worker would be hauled off for questioning or thrown out of her rented room. If things got really tough, riot police would stand guard while pro-management employees assaulted workers; if need be, the police would lend a helping hand. But in the summer of 1987, Korea started playing by a new set of rules.

So it was on a sweltering day at the end of July that the septuagenarian Chung found himself held hostage by workers at his Hyundai shipyard. Confident of his ability to resolve anything with his personal touch, Chung went down to the company town—his company town—of Ulsan in response to workers' demands that they negotiate directly with the founder and honorary chairman of the group. But angry workers refused to let Chung leave until he had agreed to their demands for an independent union. It was a shaken and embittered man who left the shipyard by helicopter late that day, vowing never again to negotiate with men whom he considered dangerous radicals. A stunned nation saw pictures of one of the country's most powerful men at the mercy of his workers with the once-almighty security forces unable to act.

Hyundai Pays the Price of Democracy

Workers let the country know just what they thought democracy meant when they took advantage of the more liberal political climate to press their demands in wildcat strikes at thousands of factories and work sites across the country in the wake of Roh's June 29 liberalization announcement. But it was at Hyundai that the struggle to define what democracy meant for the economy was played out most dramatically.

On July 7, little more than a week after Roh Tae Woo's announcement promising political reforms, workers at the Hyundai Mipo dockyard tried to form an independent trade union, the first at any of Hyundai's manufacturing companies. However, as a group of workers was on its way to the Ulsan District Labor Office to register the new union with the authorities, thugs snatched the union documents.

Harassing workers was a typical tactic for dealing with budding union activism. For much of the 1980s, similar ploys commonly had been used to prevent unionization. Those employees who made a good faith effort to comply with cumbersome government registration and approval requirements had documents stolen, or found that a group of pro-management workers had suddenly registered a "union" a few hours earlier. Police officials either were of no help or actively supported management in blatantly illegal antiunion activities.[2]

But in the wake of Roh's democratization pledges the structure of Korean labor and management was turned upside down. On July 15, government pressure on Hyundai forced the company to return the documents to the workers. Local labor officials, in contrast to the past practice of delaying or denying approval, quickly registered the new union. This was an extraordinary event and a reflection of the fact that some authorities were taking calls for reform seriously.

Chung's attempts at negotiation did not solve the fundamental problem of whether or not workers would be able to choose their own union representatives. So workers again took to the streets. In a dramatic showdown on August 18, thousands of workers at Hyundai Heavy Industries commandeered forklifts, bulldozers, and heavy trucks from the company's massive shipyard. Many wore heavy protective clothing, including welding shields, giving the group the appearance of a medieval army.

They marched out of the shipyard and toward the center of Ulsan, a little more than ten miles away. Thousands of riot police took up positions on the road at the top of a pass that lay between the shipyard and the town. The two sides prepared for what looked likely to be a bloody conflict. On one side were thousands of military conscripts clad in Darth Vader helmets and shields, their shins swathed in greaves. They were armed with clubs and backed by tear gas. Against students in Seoul this usually was protection enough, but it promised to be insufficient if the tough, militant Hyundai workers attacked.

At the last minute, just as the workers began their assault, the government forces withdrew from the pass. To avert the danger of violent street confrontations, riot police allowed some 30,000 workers to take over the municipal stadium. That evening, with worker militance still stoked by singing and chanting, the personal intervention of the deputy minister of labor resolved a situation that some Koreans feared could provoke military intervention. Han Jin Hee cajoled his way into the stadium with the help of the Ulsan mayor and police chief to announce that the government would see that Hyundai cede to workers' demands for independent unions at eight of the group companies.

The government insistence that Hyundai recognize independent unions was a stinging rebuff to a group that had prided itself on operating virtually without limits under Park Chung Hee, and it was done without talking to Hyundai management. Although Hyundai's power had been trimmed under Chun's tenure, the group had survived the 1980 restructuring of the chaebol nearly intact, and, along with Samsung, was solidly entrenched as one of the two most powerful groups in Korea. The government's decision to side with the workers was particularly unnerving for the chaebol, given Chung Ju Yung's humiliation at the hands of radical workers who had held him hostage only a few weeks earlier.

Chung still tried to avoid recognizing the independent unions. Even after Han Jin Hee announced government support for the workers, Hyundai demurred, with a company spokesman insisting that the agreement was only between the government and the workers and that Hyundai had not accepted the principle of union recognition. Even Chung could not indefinitely resist the combined pressure from workers and government, however, and over the next few years the company grudgingly tolerated the emergence of independent unions. Along the way, there were kidnappings staged by company executives, beatings by company-hired thugs, and at least one death.

The government's decision to weigh in on the side of workers was only one of several demonstrations to the country's business executives that the country was entering a new era. On August 18, the same day the Ulsan crisis was temporarily resolved, Chun Doo Hwan issued an unprecedented statement signalling support for union activity. "The current labor unrest can be attributed to the growing desire of laborers for fair distribution of wealth and more autonomy," Chun said. "This must be accommodated as a necessary pain to be experienced in the course of industrialization."

Part of the turnaround was due to the upcoming election. The ruling party went to extraordinary lengths during the second half of 1987 to make sure that Roh won the election. Workers made up a huge block of voters who could easily turn away from the ruling party. The only way to stave off a mass labor vote for the opposition was with a progressive labor policy.

After the election, surprisingly, the government kept this more neutral stance toward labor until the spring of 1989. This was mostly an attempt to buy peace at a time of weakness for the ruling party, but part of it was antipathy toward the chaebol executives. Many government officials had little patience for Hyundai's Chung Ju Yung, who epitomized a primitive form of industrial management. The moderate stance toward labor also reflected the reality that the country's first popularly elected government in nearly three decades could not simply flout the will of the people.

The state's intervention in the Hyundai strike was not only powerful evidence that authorities were tilting away from a knee-jerk pro-management stance for the first time in the forty-year history of the Republic of Korea, but also a reminder that the rule of law still counted for little. There was no legal process to take away the right of representation from the old union, no vote by workers to choose a new union, but simply a government decision to sue for peace. The unionists who had registered the first union in July, at the Hyundai Mipo Dock-yard, were tossed out in August as insufficiently radical. Government intervention in all areas of the economy could have its advantages, but it had the distinct disadvantage of being whimsical and erratic.

The government-imposed settlement did not succeed in imposing order. A few weeks later, after a predawn raid on September 2, in which 103 Hyundai Heavy Industries workers were arrested as part of a nationwide crackdown, Hyundai unionists rampaged through the Ulsan town hall, inflicting serious damage. The cycle of militant action and government counter-action at Hyundai continued for more than five years. In 1989 only an amphibious assault on the Hyundai shipyard by 10,000 government troops ended a 109-day sit-down strike that had shut down the facility. A similar raid took place in 1990 after a shorter strike and, in 1992, only the threat of police storming the plant dislodged Hyundai Motor strikers.

Hyundai had long been notorious for its antiunion attitude, but it was largely a difference of degree that separated it from other Korean companies. Its founder, Chung Ju Yung, is among the most autocratic of South Korea's business leaders and a man who treated his production and construction workers as if they were military conscripts. Chung's temper is legendary. A former Hyundai executive recalls him hurling ashtrays at senior executives in rage. Several of the U.S.-trained Ph.D.s who were lured back to Korea to work for Hyundai Electronics were slapped in the face by "the old man," as he is known to top managers.

"He poured his physical energy into working harder," remembers a man who for a time headed one of the biggest Hyundai units. "He could kick a general manager in the shins and then go out drinking with him and be his buddy. It was a combination of money, personal threats, and personal attention" that Chun used to motivate his managers.

This hierarchical, militarized corporate culture extended all the way through the business group, and it came as little surprise that Hyundai bred some of the country's most militant unionists. The pictures of uniformed Korean workers lined up in military formation that symbolized Korea's industrial might were, if not Posco employees, usually Hyundai shipyard or construction workers. A bitter strike by Hyundai construction workers in Saudi Arabia in the mid-1970s, in which two managers were killed and $48 million in heavy equipment was destroyed, testifies to the resistance that Hyundai's treatment of its workers could incite.

Labor Lashes Out

Athough Hyundai's troubles in 1987 were among the most serious and protracted in the country, they were by no means unique. Almost as soon as the protests by students and dissidents stopped at the end of June, the government faced an explosion of wildcat strikes. More than 3,000 strikes erupted across the country during the summer and autumn of 1987, more than in the previous ten years combined. All the strikes were technically illegal under South Korea's restrictive labor laws.

Labor scholar Mario Bognanno estimates that 32 percent of all manufacturing firms with 300 or more employees were struck in 1987 and that 1.225 million workers were involved in strikes between June and October 1987. Perhaps most tellingly, two-thirds of the country's large factories (those with more than 1,000 employees) were hit by strikes. Having promised democracy, the government now had to deliver it, not just to relatively well-off city dwellers but to those who had been disenfranchised.[3]

The primal passions unleashed in the wake of Roh's democratization announcement were as puzzling to most outsiders as they were frightening to middle-class Koreans who watched the demonstrations on television from the safety of their comfortable apartments in Seoul. The old rules had crumbled. Workers would administer a rough justice to their masters, just as peasants had in the uprisings that had swept through rural Korea in the late nineteenth century.

Since 1945, the country's labor situation had swung between enforced passivity and euphoric outbursts of strikes and general political action. Every period of political opening had seen an upsurge of labor activity. U.S. occupation forces faced a strong union movement in 1945, which was crushed in 1946–47 after a general strike. Labor had been active after the April 1960 uprising that had forced Syngman Rhee from office. In 1979, disagreement about how to handle demonstrations in Pusan and Masan had indirectly led to Park's death, and the outburst of labor activity that occurred during the spring of 1980 was one of the justifications Chun used to impose martial law.

Harsh government policies meant that labor's voice was muted during most of Chun's Fifth Republic. In 1980, labor organizers were prime targets of the government's "purification" campaign. The union movement was gutted that year, with almost 200 union officials purged and more than a dozen sent to the military's brutal re-education camps.

Throughout the Fifth Republic, unions were neutered through government laws and policies that ensured that the movement would remain fragmented and ineffective. Every company, or workplace, had to have a separate union. That meant, for example, that workers at Hyundai's automobile factory could not forge any links with either auto workers at Daewoo or workers in other Hyundai subsidiaries. Even assistance from the Federation of Korean Trade Unions (FKTU), the government-sanctioned umbrella group for the union movement, was severely limited. Until December 1986, the FKTU was prohibited from providing any help, even negotiating expertise, in a wage dispute, under a bizarre ban on so-called third-party involvement in labor conflicts.

National union officials were under the close watch of the Ministry of Labor; individual companies controlled their local union leaders. Unionists were often bought off by employers, who paid their salaries, gave them an office, a car, a driver, and other benefits.[4] The government could unilaterally, and subjectively, dissolve a union and force out its officers.

The Ministry of Labor determined annual wage increases through semi-official wage guidelines, and it acted as the final arbiter of disputes. Thus the backlash in 1987 should have come as little surprise. "Our government is the nation's 'pattern setter' " for labor relations, one "highly placed source" told Mario Bognanno. "But it is also the greatest violator of our labor laws. An illogical industrial relations system is the result."

Administrative guidelines gave the Ministry of Labor the right to review all documents, even internal union material, and the right to disband unions that were considered too militant. "There were daily, routine, administrative orders, guidelines, and collaboration" between national union officials and the ministry, said an official who worked for the FKTU during the first half of the 1980s. In addition, the union movement came under the close scrutiny of National Security Planning Agency agents stationed in the FKTU headquarters to monitor the federation and, in at least one case, order the dismissal of several of the more outspoken staff members. Those who regularly visited the FKTU offices in Seoul also included officials from the Defense Security Command (the presidential security arm that Chun had once headed), the Labor Ministry, and the Seoul Metropolitan Police. The government helped favored candidates running for union office and impeded others.

The few instances of union activity to occur during Chun's reign rattled the government and were dealt with harshly. Organizers at Daewoo Motors's Pupyong plant were fired and jailed after leading a wildcat strike in 1985. Three years earlier, Control Data had closed its disk drive subsidiary in part because of government pressure on the U.S. company not to give in to workers' demands. Workers at smaller companies who tried to exercise their rights within—or, often, outside—the country's repressive labor law usually found themselves up against the intelligence service and sometimes riot police. A blacklist made it difficult for activists to obtain employment.

The complicity of employee representatives was sometimes comic. The government said that large companies had to establish labor-management committees, which were supposed to allow the two sides to work out differences in an amicable fashion. These committees were legally required to meet four times a year. In one case documented by a labor relations attorney, the group met only once a year. But it brought three changes of clothes, took four photographs of members in the different outfits, and used the pictures as proof that they were meeting quarterly. It was a quintessential demonstration of the Korean capacity for form over substance.

A Model Worker

What did this system mean for ordinary workers? It meant that in spite of paltry wages they had no recourse if their employer did not pay them on time, or did not pay them overtime, or forced them to work inhumanely long shifts, sometimes twenty-four hours straight.

The story of Chung Dong Keun epitomized the hardships workers faced during the Fifth Republic. Chung, who in 1987 was a slightly built man in his early thirties, had always considered himself a model worker. "I reported to work thirty minutes early, without pay, to clean around my work site," he remembered later. "I did not support workers' grievances. I opposed the strikes some workers wanted." Chung said that his job at a small electronics assembly factory in Seoul was the best work he had ever found. Hired in early 1984, Chung started near the top of the pay scale. But he still only made about $2,000 a year, typically working seventy-eight-hour weeks.

Trouble started when the company fell behind on its wage payments. "On Christmas Eve, 1984, we stayed late, because the company promised they would pay us our October wages [which were two months overdue]. At midnight, a foreman told us we would not be paid that night. Along with some of the other older workers, I cried all night in our dormitory, in despair at life and the company."

Several days later, the company made a partial payment of the back wages. "The president of the company said we should continue to believe in him and the company. He repeated what he had said many other times—that his dream is that when he made money he would build a school to educate our children. I was still filled with anger and rage. I stood up and said what we needed and wanted was not a school to teach our children. What we wanted was our back wages." The company president was a man who enjoyed some political influence, serving as a local official for the ruling Democratic Justice Party.

After Chung's outburst, he was called into the manager's office and warned that if he was going to continue being a troublemaker it would be best if he left the factory. Instead, Chung and a group of three workers formed a study group to find out what their legal rights were. Eventually the group grew to twenty people, about 10 percent of the employees.

"By February [1985], the wages for November, December, and January had not been paid. The Lunar New Year was coming up. Most of us had no money to visit our parents. We had no choice but to strike." Management, police, and officials from the Labor Ministry tried to evict the workers from the factory, where they held a sit-in. After a five-day strike, the company agreed to pay back wages and give the workers three days off for the Lunar New Year holiday. The situation deteriorated after the strike. Management tried to break up the union by intimidating employees, especially young women workers. By May, the wages for February, March, and April had not been paid, and the workers staged another strike, a fifteen-day sit-in protest in front of the factory.

"We had reached this point only after we had tried everything. We had gone to the newspaper, the police, the Ministry of Labor, and the company management. We had gone to anyone who would listen to our plight. Only after our strike could we get our back pay." The workers also succeeded in reducing the work week from 78 to 66 hours and the company recognized the union. However, later in the year, the wages stopped again, and in December, once more, the workers went on strike. Chung was arrested that month during a sit-in outside a government office in Seoul. When he was released from prison four-and-a-half months later, the company had gone out of business.[5] This, for many workers, was the reality of the Korean miracle.

Birth of the Working Class

By 1987, there were many more workers than there had been when Chun took power. Korea had about 3 million manufacturing workers for most of the early 1980s. By 1987, it had 4.4 million. More than a million new manufacturing workers were added during the three boom years of 1986 to 1988 alone.

The national economy was two-thirds again as large in 1986 as it had been in 1980. By 1988, it was more than twice the size it had been when Chun took power.[6] There were more permanent employees, more middle-class salarymen, and fewer farmers.[7] There were now world-scale factories and industrial sites, like Hyundai Motor, which in 1988 employed more than 30,000 people, and the nearby Hyundai Heavy Industries which employed 20,000 more. Workplaces such as these were the cauldrons in which a radical labor movement was forged. Yet in spite of the growth of the work force, membership in the government-sanctioned FKTU plummeted from 1.1 million in 1980 to three-quarters of a million in 1985, because of organized labor's enforced impotence during the Chun years.[8]

These millions of new workers, mostly young, many part of the great wave of migrants leaving their family farms to be part of the first generation of wage laborers, were a critical part of the militant labor movement that exploded in the summer of 1987. The younger workers came of age during a time when political dissent was still sharply restricted, knowing nothing of the privations of the Korean War or its aftermath and increasingly cynical about political restrictions. They were the muscle of a powerful economic machine, thanks to their high level of education, and the long hours and relatively low wages that they had little choice but to accept. They also had imbibed a bitter sense of entitlement to the riches they saw being created around them.

During the 1988 National Assembly hearings into the misdeeds of the Fifth Republic, the head of Poongsan Metal, a company that made coin blanks and bullets, conceded that he had donated 3.45 billion won ($4.3 million) to the Ilhae Foundation and other government-controlled organizations in five years. But the company had wanted to pay the family of a worker who was killed at one of its plants only 30 million won ($37,500) rather than the 90 million won the family wanted. From 1976 to 1988, sixty Poongsan employees had been killed while working for the company, reflecting a breathtaking disregard for basic safety conditions.

In criticizing the company head, opposition lawmaker Noh Moo Hyun said, "I'm telling this not to you alone but all [the] other wicked businessmen in this country who are willing to donate billions to the dictator while haggling over the compensation for the death of a worker who died while earning money for you."

The stunting of the labor movement allowed no room for the development of trained unionists. Those who came to the fore were radicals who had thrived on the underground existence they had been forced to lead during the Chun years. The greatest failure of Chun's labor policies—and perhaps his entire economic policy—was the inability to build a moderate union leadership. The security-minded people around Chun were mainly responsible for these short-sighted labor policies, but the technocrats are also to blame for not having given enough attention to labor policy.

When the political environment changed, the past policies of repression meant that there were almost no legitimate union leaders at either the local or national levels. Because of deliberate fragmentation of unions, with weak national unions and the prohibition of outside assistance, there could be no control from the center. As a result, after 1987 the unionists who had been active during the earlier Chun years were almost uniformly tarred as collaborators with an "evil" government. There was a fierce scramble for power among new union leaders, with the structure of the new situation favoring the most radical voices. There was no sense of limits, no sense of political or economic trade-offs, only a tremendous feeling of entitlement, a belief that workers had been exploited for decades and that now was their chance to even the score.

After Roh Tae Woo's June 29, 1987 democratization speech, workers began talking more openly about class-based political action. Kim In Chol, a union activist in the port city of Inchon, spoke for many in the radical labor movement when he said that the primary task was to develop class consciousness among workers.

"The Korean economy is subjugated to world forces and strengthening of internal monopolies. The Korean economy is very dependent on importing foreign capital and this trend has been worsening," Kim told a group of visitors only a few days after Roh's dramatic statement. "The characteristic aspect of the Korean economy is its dual structure. There is the agricultural sector and the industrial urban sector. There are conglomerates, and there are medium and small businesses. Korean workers are engaged in a double oppression. Because of subcontracting, the burden of paying workers falls on small and medium-sized companies."

This sort of jargon had a visceral appeal to workers emerging from the harsh years of Chun's rule. When the time for change came, it was no surprise that moderates were swept away. Unfortunately, this turmoil and lack of established leadership had an extremely corrosive effect on the union movement. Unionists would periodically purge their leaders, even those who had been elected as radicals, out of suspicion that they had sold out to the management. This cycle of purges was especially serious at large heavy industrial firms such as Daewoo Shipbuilding and Hyundai Heavy Industries.

The labor activity that surfaced so dramatically in the summer of 1987 was one of the biggest challenges that Korean economic planners and corporate executives had to deal with in the latter part of the 1980s. Although the impact of labor strikes peaked in 1989, it is still uncertain what form the country's labor-management relations will take.

The antibusiness, antiwealth ethos of the labor movement also reflected an idealized sense of being Korean, a belief that because Koreans are ethnically homogeneous, there should be rough equality among them. "The unique thing about our labor problem is that we are only one race," says Ssangyong chairman Kim Suk Won. "Labor unions asked, 'Why should you order us around?' " The reality is that the country is factionalized, fractious, and riven by class and regional divisions. But this national myth of equality and homogeneity still fuels workers' anger.

What Is Democracy?

"Democracy Day" came and went in Korea. But after the whiskey glasses were emptied and the revelers staggered out of the room salons, Koreans woke up to the sober reality that democracy was hard work. For decades "democracy" had been little more than a mantra to chant, a rallying call to mobilize antigovernment forces. Very little in the authoritarian, hierarchical structure of Korean life has prepared people for the clumsy power-sharing, the sloppy give-and-take, and the compromises that are at the heart of representative government.

Koreans have been accustomed to framing issues in terms of absolute good or evil rather than as a series of imperfect choices. They have deified the idea of a wise, just patriarch who made decisions selflessly, for the good of the nation. They are uncomfortable with the idea of interest groups shamelessly fighting to advance their own agenda.

Roh's bombshell announcement sparked a furious debate about democracy and what it meant for Korean workers, businessmen, and officials, and for the top-down system of economic control that the technocrats guided and the bureaucrats implemented. But if the government did not continue to act as the economic traffic cop, as it had done for almost three decades, who would?

The old economic structure of Korea had sometimes been arbitrary, even in its treatment of the elite of officials and executives, and it had often been brutal for workers, but authoritarianism at least was moderately efficient. Now the claims of equity vied with those of efficiency in a babble of competing interests.

Through the quarter-century of Korea's relentless march to industrialization, labor had been sacrificed on the altar of growth. The management-labor councils and other institutional devices designed to give labor some measure of protection against employers were usually a sham, a legalistic fig leaf designed to cover up the terrible human costs that Korea's workers were paying for their country's economic success. When the political environment eased in 1987, workers were quick to seize the chance to lash out, just as they had been in 1980. So, too, were ordinary citizens quick to pounce when they had their chance to go after Chun and his family. But first came elections.

As the labor movement began to subside temporarily in the autumn of 1987, thanks to relatively quick wage increases, the presidential campaign began in earnest. Huge crowds greeted Kim Dae Jung as he made his first public appearances in many provincial areas since the 1971 election campaign. Just as they had in 1971 and 1980, Kim Dae Jung and Kim Young Sam dueled for the allegiance of opposition-minded voters. They tantalized their supporters with hints of a compromise in which one would step down in order to unite the antigovernment forces, but in the end the lust for power seduced both of them. The two Kims split the vote with a third Kim, former Park Chung Hee loyalist Kim Jong Pil, allowing Roh Tae Woo to win the election, although he received less than 37 percent of the vote.

All the candidates made similar promises about democratizing society and the economy and ushering in a new era of freedom and prosperity. All wooed voters with gifts, ranging from traditional Korean meals to cookware sets and quilts and mattresses. On the stock exchange, share prices for paper and beer stocks soared. Beer consumption was up because of the pre-election wining and dining. Paper makers worked to the hilt to supply stock for leaflets and handbills. Campaign spending laws were openly flouted, and the government itself later admitted that it had illegally donated close to $100,000 in cash to Roh's campaign. This was little more than spare change in an election that was estimated to have cost the four candidates a total of around $1 billion.[9]

Each of the major candidates staged massive rallies, with some one million people each. These were not spontaneous events, especially in the case of the ruling party candidate. Government and chaebol employees were given the day off and pressured to attend Roh's rally in Seoul to swell the crowd size. Other people were paid a small fee by ruling party organizers to come to the rallies.

This vote offered a choice between change and continuity. Most Koreans apparently wanted change, but thanks to the division of the opposition, Roh Tae Woo won the election. The dramatic gamble of his June 29 reform package had paid off. Rather than coming into office as the illegitimate hand-picked successor of a dictator, Roh assumed the presidency as a legitimately elected candidate.[10]

Euphoria and fear were mixed as Roh Tae Woo took office on February 25, 1988. There was still some fear that the military might step in and abort the move toward political liberalization. The stock market, ever sensitive to any threat of right-wing interference, fell sharply on the day Roh was inaugurated. Part of the reason was whispers of a possible military coup, but many market analysts also believed that Chun's wife was taking the last opportunity to sell off shares in the market using secret channels to which she would no longer have access.

Everyone expected that there would be a reckoning after Roh took power and that people who were injured during the Chun years would try to take revenge. But the speed and intensity of this backlash nonetheless stunned Koreans. Within days of Chun's retirement, his younger brother, Chun Kyung Hwan, came under fire on corruption charges.

"Baby Chun," as the local press called him, had grossly abused his power as head of Saemaul. Under Chun Kyung Hwan's stewardship, which lasted from 1980 until 1987, Saemaul came to symbolize almost everything that was wrong with the Fifth Republic. An organization that, whatever its faults, had been a pillar of Korea's nation-building program was diverted from its original purpose. Money was wasted, or siphoned off for the younger Chun's personal use. Although the opposition had attacked Saemaul during the Fifth Republic, prosecutors and government auditors had done nothing.

In mid-March 1988, only weeks after Chun left the Blue House, the younger Chun slipped out of the country to Japan as local prosecutors launched an intensive investigation into the Saemaul movement. His aides tepidly said that he had traveled abroad to study sales and marketing.[11] Following a public outcry, he returned to face questioning by prosecutors.

Notes

1. Press conference with the Blue House press corps, April 21, 1988.
2. Under South Korean labor law, forming a union required the signatures of thirty workers (or 20 percent of the work force, whichever was less) and permission of the local authorities. No voting was necessary, and the new union could exclude anyone it wished. Workers could, and often did, find themselves in a situation where they could neither form a union nor join an existing one. Samsung was particularly adept at setting up these paper unions. Workers would go to register a union and find that a small cadre of pro-management workers had registered just before them. With only one union allowed per work site, workers were prohibited from forming a union by this sort of company trickery.

See Asia Watch, *Human Rights in Korea*, pp. 203–7 and 207–71, for case studies of typical harassment of union activists.

A good summary discussion of South Korean labor history and labor law in the pre-1987 period is James M. West, "South Korea's Entry into the International Labor Organization: Perspectives on Corporatist Labor Law During a Late Industrial Revolution." More general, and tendentious, treatments are George Ogle, *Liberty to the Captives: The Struggle Against Oppression in South Korea*, and *South Korea: Dissent Within the Economic Miracle*.

The most extended treatment of labor during the Park years is by Choi Jang Jip in his *Labor and the Authoritarian State: Labor Unions in South Korean Manufacturing Industries, 1961–80*.

This chapter also draws heavily on Mario F. Bognanno, *Korea's Industrial Relations at the Turning Point*.

For a discussion of labor relations practices at multinational firms in Korea, see Ronald A. Rodgers, "Industrial Relations Policies and Practices in the Republic of Korea in a Time of Rapid Change: The Influence of American-Invested and Japanese-Invested Transnational Corporations," and Ronald A. Rodgers [note: his name is misspelled as Rogers in the article], "An Exclusionary Labor Regime Under Pressure: The Changes in Labor Relations in the Republic of Korea Since mid-1987," *Pacific Basin Law Journal*, Spring 1990, vol. 8, no. 1, pp. 91–163. This article provides the most complete English-language treatment of labor in the late 1980s in Korea.

3. Manufacturing and transportation accounted for 90 percent of strikes, but less than 20 percent of establishments. Bognanno, in *Korea's Industrial Relations at the Turning Point*, estimates that 32 percent of all manufacturing firms with 300 or more employees were struck in 1987 and that 1.225 million workers were involved in the June–October 1987 period (pp. 41–43, using survey data from Ministry of Labor).

The Federation of Korean Trade Unions picked up more than half a million members from the end of 1986 to mid-1988: Membership rose from 938,921 to 1,525,088; the number of locals increased from 2,263 to 5,062 (ibid., p. 63).

The government determined annual wage increases through semi-official wage guidelines and it acted as the final arbiter of disputes (ibid., p. 17; p. 30 on wage guidelines).

4. Ibid., pp. 28–29.

5. This information came from a July 1987 author interview. For an extended analysis of labor standards and legal practices, see Ronald A. Rodgers, "An Exclusionary Labor Regime Under Pressure: The Changes in Labor Relations in the Republic of Korea Since mid-1987."

6. In constant prices GNP grew from 52.3 trillion won in 1980 to 78.1 trillion in 1986 and 111.6 trillion in 1988. Data from Economic Planning Board, *Major Statistics of the Korean Economy*, 1989.

7. While the member of production line workers increased 65 percent between 1980 and 1988, the number of professional, technical, administrative, and managerial workers, the heart of the middle-class salarymen, rose 82 percent, and clerical workers 56 percent. Farmers declined 29 percent in number.

8. Chun and his technocrats at least reaped some economic benefits from these antilabor policies, as productivity growth outstripped wage increases.

In 1980–81 productivity grew 36 percent more quickly than wages, while in 1982–86 productivity growth was 16 percent higher. Coupled with currency devaluations from 1980 to 1985, the competitiveness of the export sector was greatly enhanced. Overall, productivity grew twice as quickly as did wages from 1980 to 1986.

9. Prime Minister Kang Young Hoon admitted that the government illegally donated 55.2 billion won to Roh's campaign (*Korea Herald*, July 4, 1990). The $1 billion figure

is, of course, an imprecise one, but it represents the lower end of consensus estimates privately made by knowledgeable Korean and non-Korean sources for the author. The ruling party alone was generally believed to have spent some 400 billion won.

10. Most Koreans, at any rate, saw him as legitimate. Hard-core dissidents, and some opposition figures, believed that pervasive vote-rigging and a pattern of dirty tricks invalidated the election results. Although there certainly were irregularities, most Koreans appeared willing to accept the results of the election. Kim Dae Jung and Kim Young Sam called for street protests, but their calls were largely ignored, in large part because of public disgust with their failure to unite.

11. In August 1986, around the time of a brutal nightclub murder in which one of his associates was involved, Chun had left the country allegedly to pursue his studies at Harvard. Although he was accepted by the university, Selig S. Harrison found that Chun seems never to have formally attended classes, but instead spent much of his time playing tennis with his bodyguard. *Washington Post*, January 25, 1987.

21

Purges and Medals

> My dear people, I am truly sorry.
>
> —Chun Doo Hwan[1]

An unruly crowd of several hundred spectators crowded around Chun Kyung Hwan when he arrived at the prosecutor's office next to Toksu Palace in downtown Seoul on the morning of March 29, 1988, barely a month after his brother had stepped down as president. As guards escorted him through the crowd, a man shouted "you bastard," and slapped the forty-six-year-old Chun in the face, later saying that he had hit Chun because "he did not show any sign of contrition or remorse." Others shouted "kill him" at the man they called "Baby Chun." After forty hours of interrogation, Chun was jailed early on the morning of March 31. On April 16 prosecutors formally indicted the younger Chun on eight counts of corruption, charging that he had embezzled 7.4 billion won.

The younger Chun's ability to divert money seemed to be limited only by his imagination. Prosecutors listed 128 different instances of corruption. He stole 500 million won from funds donated to boost the morale of Saemaul leaders and smaller amounts from the Leaders' Promotion Foundation and the Saemaul training center. Chun took a straight bribe of 200 million won from a construction company executive in return for awarding his firm a contract. "Baby Chun" also broke foreign exchange regulations with his purchase of a house in the United States.

Money was diverted from a Saemaul newspaper; there were illegal transactions involving a used ship and improper sales of land. Chun apparently had considered investing in a gold mine in Australia and another gold venture in Brazil. Moreover, prosecutors said Chun helped his associates improperly get bank loans.

Chun Kyung Hwan became a lightning rod for the anger that people felt toward the Fifth Republic. At his trial, Chun was escorted into court in the traditional white jacket and white pants worn by criminal suspects, with his hands ceremoniously tied in front of him with a thick piece of rope. Spectators at the trial hissed and hit him. "Chun [Kyung Hwan] abused something sacred to us," said a senior Foreign Ministry official. Even the unrepentant former president felt obliged to offer his apology, unconvincing though it was. "I failed to control my brother," said Chun Doo Hwan. "It is because of my lack of virtue." The ex-president had cut short a trip to the United States as indignation over his brother mounted, returning to Korea to announce his resignation from the Council of Elder Statesmen and the ruling Democratic Justice Party on April 13.

In September, Chun Kyung Hwan was sentenced to seven years in jail, fined 3.2 billion won, and ordered to forfeit 989 million won worth of property. Although Chun was released after less than three years in prison, it was an ironic coda to an administration that had once punished an official for accepting a 5,000 won gift.[2]

It was not just Chun Kyung Hwan, or a few relatives of the former president and his wife, who were involved in scandals and corruption. What became apparent after Chun left office was the depth of corruption and the degree to which it had been quietly tolerated, even expected. The pervasive corruption is another of the ugly legacies bequeathed by the Fifth Republic. Corruption had long been part of the Korean system, but Chun did the country a tremendous disservice by allowing his relatives to prosper. For all his faults, Park had never allowed his family to profit personally from his position. Unfortunately, the Chun and Lee families set an example of egregiously corrupt behavior that still undermines the Korean social contract.[3]

As Chun's younger brother was being questioned by prosecutors, another alleged victim of the Fifth Republic stepped forward. Yang Chung Mo, former chairman of the Kukje group, filed for the return of his businesses, claiming that the takeovers were illegitimate because he was forced to hand over stocks in the firms under pressure from the government.[4] While Kukje's collapse had prompted whispers that Chun was taking political revenge, Yang's lawsuit was the first time that these charges had been aired publicly. Yang painted a vivid picture of coercive fund-raising by the president's younger brother and a petty, vindictive Blue House. These charges against the government by a businessman were unprecedented. In part, Yang's boldness reflected the disrepute into which Chun's Fifth Republic had fallen. But they also signaled something more fundamental, a new assertiveness on the part of business that reflected broader political changes.

In April 1988, for the first time in the forty-year history of the country, the ruling party failed to win a majority in elections for the legislative National Assembly, garnering only 125 of the 299 seats at stake. With 71 seats, Kim Dae Jung's Party for Peace and Democracy emerged as the largest of the three opposition parties. Along with two other opposition parties, one led by opposition parties. Along with two other opposition parties, one led by opposition warhorse Kim Young Sam and the other by former Park Chung Hee stalwart Kim Jong Pil, the opposition controlled enough of the legislature to pass laws, although not enough to override a presidential veto. This would force the government to compromise as never before.

Through the summer of 1988, Korea wrestled with the problems of democracy. A new breeze of openness and accountability blew through stuffy government offices. In one of the most notable examples, the Ministry of Finance released details of the 1985 corporate bail-out of the construction and shipping industries. At the same time, Seoul prepared to host a giant coming-out party, an Olympiad that would signal Korea's emergence as a major economic force in the world and celebrate its new democracy.

Son Ki Jong ran into the graceful Chamshil Olympic stadium early on the afternoon of September 17, 1988. As viewers around the world watched, the aging runner did a very un-Korean jig, sprinting a few steps with the Olympic torch before handing it off to Lim Choon Ae, the woman runner whose notorious beating at the hands of her coach a year earlier had prompted a national uproar. Half a century before, Son had won the marathon at the 1936 Olympics in Berlin, where Korea's colonial status forced him to run as a member of the Japanese team. The independent *Dong-A Ilbo* newspaper deleted the Japanese Rising Sun emblem on his shirt when it ran a photo of the victorious Son. For this act of defiance the newspaper was shut down and two of its senior journalists jailed. Now, half a century and a civil war later, South Korea was at the center of the world's stage, the host of what was at the time the biggest Olympiad in history. Commandos parachuted from the sky, landing to form multicolored Olympic rings, and hundreds of taekwondo experts lined up in formation smashed boards in unison on the field of the main stadium—both appropriate reminders of the warlike economic machine that the country had put together.

On October 8, 1979, less than three weeks before Park Chung Hee was assassinated, Seoul Mayor Chung Sang Chon told a stunned press conference that the city would bid for the 1988 Olympics.[5] Like so many of the grandiose schemes during Park's tenure, this idea seemed preposterous; it was resisted by many officials throughout the government, especially at the Economic Planning Board. After Chun took power, he considered dropping the bid, but decided that it would be taken as a sign of weakness if South Korea did not to go ahead with it. Chun was not a man who under any circumstances wanted to look weak.

At the International Olympic Committee meeting in Baden-Baden, West Germany, in September 1981, there was not much competition for the dubious honor of hosting the 1988 Olympiad. Montreal had lost about $1 billion on the 1976 games, and the 1980 Moscow games had been marred by the U.S. boycott. In fact, there had not been a placid Olympiad since Tokyo had hosted the 1964 Games: Mexico City's 1968 Games, symbolized by the clenched fists of black U.S. medalists, opened shortly after more than one hundred student demonstrators at the University of Mexico had been killed; the 1972 Munich Games witnessed the murder of eleven Israeli athletes; Africans boycotted the Montreal Games in protest against the New Zealand rugby team's tour of South Africa; and the 1980 boycott of Moscow by the West was to be followed by the 1984 snub of Los Angeles by the Eastern Bloc.

In any event, at Baden-Baden only Seoul and Nagoya, Japan, vied for the right to host the 1988 Olympiad. Nagoya made a number of mistakes. Its lobbyists were extremely arrogant, spending more time disparaging the South Korean bid than promoting their own. The Japanese were so cocky that when it came time for the final voting, they already had their victory banquet arranged.

The Koreans pulled out all the stops to win over delegates. They played for sympathy from developing nations, reminding delegates that Japan had already hosted an Olympics and that it was time for an up-and-coming state like Korea to have a chance. The Koreans were supremely organized. They brought five former Miss Koreas and ten of the most beautiful Korean Air hostesses to Baden-Baden. Hyundai's Chung Ju Yung rented three huge houses, "almost like chateaux or castles," remembers Shin Yong Suk, a member of the Korean delegation.

"Chung Ju Yung spent several million dollars, but he never wanted to profit from the Olympics. He just did it out of patriotism . . . Chung mobilized resources," says Shin. "He did it the same way he won construction contracts in the Middle East. [He would ask delegates,] 'Do you want an airplane ticket, a woman, money?' "[6]

Korea could also boast that its preparations were already 60 percent complete, thanks to an ambitious infrastructure development program, which included plans for a riverside sports complex. Nagoya's facilities existed only on blueprints. However, when the results of the vote were announced on September 30, 1981, the outcome stunned even the Koreans: They won by a 52–27 margin. The Olympics gave Koreans a tangible goal to work toward, for the Games would coincide with Chun's promise to step down at the end of his term.

Although some dissidents derided the Olympics as, in the words of one, an attempt by the United States to solidify the position of South Korea as its "forward base in Northeast Asia," the domestic and international effect was overwhelmingly positive. The Korea Development Institute joined most Koreans when it boasted that the Seoul Games were "the most successful Olympics ever."[7]

The Games ultimately trapped the government. They made it virtually impossible for Chun to crack down on protesters during the hot summer and autumn of 1987, for the eyes of the world were on Seoul. Two soccer matches in Seoul were interrupted by tear gas during June 1987, a number of athletes were expressing misgivings about going to Seoul, and there was talk from Los Angeles that the city would be ready to host the Games again, if Seoul could not. It is a virtual certainty that Chun would have imposed some form of limited martial law had it not been for the impact such a draconian step would have had on the Olympics.

In a country where targets and goals are the typical way of motivating people, the Olympics had a tremendous catalytic effect. A total of 2.4 trillion won was spent directly and indirectly on the Olympics.[8] The government cleaned up the Han River, which runs through the capital, and built extensive parks along its banks. Expressways and subway lines were constructed, as were graceful sports stadiums and athletic facilities. Korean engineers wrote software to time the events, and Korean contractors built housing for the Olympic athletes and officials.

When the Olympic Games opened in Seoul on September 17, they were the largest in history. Athletes from 161 nations participated, including many from countries that had long been staunch enemies of Korea, such as the Soviet Union and China. The South Koreans, tasting forbidden fruit, were enraptured with the Chinese and the Soviet teams. Ironically, the opening ceremonies came almost five years to the day after the Soviet flag had been burned by a group of employees from the Korea Explosives group and hundreds of thousands of passionate protesters had screamed slogans against the Soviet Union for its downing of KAL flight 007. Somehow, though, most Koreans found it easy to ignore Stalin's backing for Kim Il Sung, easy to forget about the Chinese People's Liberation Army "volunteers" who streamed over the border and drove the UN forces south. But Americans found it rather unsettling to see U.S. athletes jeered and the Soviet team cheered during an Olympic basketball match.

The Games gave Korea an opportunity to develop better relations with Eastern Europe, the U.S.S.R., China, and other socialist countries. Although there had been some doubt as to whether the Communist bloc would even come to Seoul, a diplomatic offensive gave the Roh Tae Woo government a stunning coup with the announcement in early September that Hungary would establish formal diplomatic relations with South Korea. In what had been one of the world's most virulently anti-Communist countries, this exuberant embrace of Communist bloc athletes was surreal. Even the normally staid Korea Development Institute researchers were carried away by euphoria, proclaiming that the Korean-Soviet contacts were worth an "extra-venue gold medal."[9]

During 1989 and 1990, South Korea established relations with almost every other Communist country. The U.S.S.R., Poland, Yugoslavia, Czechoslovakia, Romania, and Bulgaria recognized the Republic of Korea. These diplomatic ties, of course, reflected domestic changes in these countries as much as the Roh Tae Woo administration's diplomatic skills, but they were nonetheless a powerful boost for South Korea's self-esteem and provided new economic opportunities.[10]

By the end of 1990, China was the only major country not to have diplomatic relations with South Korea. But trade offices were exchanged in early 1991 in the first quasi-official contacts. Sporadic charter flights between South Korea and China began in late 1990, as did regular passenger ferry service. Ethnic Koreans living in northeastern China became a familiar site in Seoul, selling traditional Chinese medicines in front of the Toksu Palace or in subway stations. Relations between the two countries were formally established in August 1992.

As always in Korea, there was a slightly sour edge even in the midst of success. With more than 150,000 visitors in town for the Games, this was the biggest invasion of foreigners since Korea had been prised open by colonial powers more than a century earlier. Given its level of economic development, Korea was undoubtedly the most parochial country in the world. Only one out of every four South Koreans had ever been in an airplane, and far fewer had traveled outside their Indiana-sized country. Although during the Olympics taxi drivers assiduously practiced their English and ordinary citizens refrained from the pushing and spitting that usually characterize street life in Seoul, many ordinary Koreans found foreign ways a bit baffling. There were complaints, for example, that athletes dressed too scantily.

However, it was a quintessentially Korean event, a sit-down strike, that galvanized this antiforeign sentiment. South Korean boxer Byun Jung Il was angry when a New Zealand referee penalized him for head-butting during a match with Bulgarian Alexander Hristov. When Hristov was declared the victor, chairs and bottles were tossed into the ring. Referee Keith Walker was attacked by a crowd of South Korean officials, including a security guard who was supposed to protect him. The Korean team manager urged the largely Korean crowd to join in the attack on the referee.

Walker managed to escape, but Byun staged a sixty-seven-minute sit-in to protest his loss. This was only the second such incident in Olympic history: the first occurred at the 1964 Tokyo Olympics when another South Korean boxer protested a decision. "This is the most disgraceful incident I have ever seen in boxing," fumed Anwar Chowdhury, president of the International Amateur Boxing Association.

The incident did not end when Byun left the ring. NBC had televised the event, triggering a storm of complaints about the United States trying to make Korea look bad. Somehow, many Koreans forgot that Byun's protest had prompted the coverage.[11] "Why did you have to show it so many times," a Korean asked a visiting journalist. "That's the way journalism works, it reacts to the story," he answered. "But you are not in your home now, you are in ours," said the Korean. "We call it good journalism. They call it ridicule," wrote *Washington Post* reporter Tony Kornheiser, summing up the divide between Korean and American perceptions of the incident.[12]

South Korean Olympic head Park Seh Jik and ruling party secretary general Park Jun Byung—both extremely powerful and prominent members of the ruling elite—complained about the incident and helped stoke domestic criticism of the United States in general and American media in particular.

A few days later, a group of U.S. swimming medalists were jailed because a couple of them, as a prank, stole an inexpensive statue from a bar at the Hyatt Hotel in the Itaewon district. Although the hotel wanted to drop charges, this harsh treatment, South Korean prosecutors said, was retaliation for NBC's televised coverage of the boxing incident.

Feelings ran so high that both Roh Tae Woo and Prime Minister Lee Hyun Jae soon urged Koreans to cool their tempers and not let the incident exacerbate tensions with the United States. "Even if the reports of NBC included something that hurt our self-esteem, we should put up with it, since most of the network's reports were affirmative," said Roh.[13]

The Olympics, coming as they did in the midst of an unprecedented export boom, signaled Korea's coming of age. But mood swings between euphoria and sullenness quickly made it clear that the country was going through the awkward growing pains of adolescence. Nowhere was this clearer than in relations with the United States.

Booing the U.S. basketball team while rooting for the Soviet team typified South Korea's cocky attitude. The incident highlighted the widespread belief that Korea had succeeded in its struggle to be a developed nation and was now ready to break free of the United States.

Not surprisingly, this sort of adolescent thumbing of the nose did not sit well with most Americans. "This is the thanks we get for saving them from communism, protecting them from Russian-supported North Korea for 40 years," complained a visiting U.S. official. "It's going to be a long time before Americans are ready to forgive this slap in the face." U.S. Ambassador James Lilley was only slightly more temperate in his remarks: "I don't think Korea's ever going to be the same again," he said. "I see a more assertive, nationalistic Korea emerging from [the Olympics]. I don't think things can ever return to the status quo between us now."[14]

The spasm of anti-Americanism aside, the psychic importance of the Olympics can hardly be overstated. When Seoul was chosen in 1981 it was a controversial choice, and there were doubts that the country could pull off the feat. The success of the Games, held during stunningly beautiful autumn weather, merged in Korean minds with a freer political climate, double-digit economic growth, and the opening of relationships with Communist countries.

The Olympics came to symbolize a high-water mark in South Korea's history. It was one of the few times that Korea, a little country usually shoved into the shadows, took center stage. The Korea Development Institute study, for example, painstakingly detailed the exchanges that occurred around the Olympics, noting for example that Soviet President Mikhail Gorbachev's Krasnoyarsk speech, in which he said, "There is a possibility that economic exchanges with [South] Korea could be established," occurred the day before the Olympics opened. Tellingly, the Korea Development Institute study also—erroneously—claimed that the capital and foreign exchange markets were liberalized on the occasion of the Olympics, "qualifying [Korea] for advanced country status."[15]

At the end of November, toward the close of a long and bitter year, Chun Doo Hwan's fall from dictator to disgrace became complete. In September, he stayed away from the opening ceremony of the Seoul Olympic Games—a day that he had hoped would symbolize one of his great achievements—for fear that he would be booed by the crowd.

Koreans, however proud they were of hosting the Olympics, treated the Games mostly as a spectacle for foreigners. Busloads of Koreans had to be brought in to fill the stadiums for many events, because the Olympiad was a sideshow to the main spectacle, a diversion from the reckoning that was being forced on Chun and his hated Fifth Republic.

A truce between the warring political camps was called in Seoul during the Olympics, just as it had been in ancient Greece. But in the weeks before and after the Games, witnesses paraded before the National Assembly to denounce Chun and his men for their bloody seizure of power. Legislators and witnesses screamed and cried and pounded tables as they described the infamous Kwangju massacre, in which some 200 people had died as Chun tightened his grip on power; the purges of politicians, journalists, and government officials that followed; the brutal "re-education" camps where men crawled over broken glass or were trussed and dragged along the ground by army jeeps; and the crude corruption and extortion of money from the country's businessmen during Chun's administration.

The country had never seen anything like this drama, and far more people watched this show than the carefully choreographed Olympics. In almost every building lobby in Seoul, passers-by and office workers crowded the television set that broadcast the spectacle. In bars and restaurants, in buses and taxis, televisions and radios were tuned into the hearings. Sometimes the testimony went past midnight, and the whole country stayed up late watching the passion play of this man who had overreached himself, who had risen so high and fallen so far. It was hard to remember that the economy had doubled in size during his eight years in power.

At last, on November 23, 1988, seven weeks after the Olympic flame had been extinguished in Seoul, with both his brothers under arrest and no end to investigations into his family in sight, an exhausted and bitter Chun Doo Hwan went before a nationwide television audience. Wearing a dark suit, sober tie, and white shirt, he stood in his living room and looked straight into the camera.

He apologized for his relatives' misdeeds, for the deaths of scores of people in the re-education camps set up after he seized power, for the purges he engineered, and for the brutality inflicted by government troops during the Kwangju uprising. Chun said he was "pained and ashamed about my past. . . . I am branded as a power-abusing president. . . . So now I have nothing more to hide and no further excuses to make." Chun then walked out of his house and down a twisting stone staircase. An aide opened the right rear door of a black Hyundai Grandeur, and the ex-president mustered as much dignity as he could to ease himself in to the seat of Korea's most luxurious car. His wife, many of whose relatives were in jail on corruption charges, followed him down the stairs and into the automobile. A gaggle of photographers snapped shots of her weeping in the back seat as the car drove off.

The couple was driven to a remote Buddhist monastery in the mountains, where they spent two spartan years in internal exile, shunned by the people of a nation they had so recently ruled. Chun underwent a 100-day Buddhist purification ritual, and pictures of him and his wife harvesting potatoes were circulated to show the depth of their repentance. Back in Seoul, a tidal wave of anger crashed down on almost everyone associated with Chun's Fifth Republic. The president's two brothers and many of his former associates were jailed while quicker-witted aides and former ministers fled to comfortable exile in Washington or California. Chun himself was largely wiped out of history, as the government rewrote school textbooks in a campaign to wipe away what were called the "evil legacies" of his administration.

From the new president to the humblest farmer, Koreans proudly proclaimed that the purge that accompanied Chun's humiliating fall from grace would usher in a new age of democracy and an end to the arbitrary exercise of power. In its simplest outline, Chun's bloodless fall and the proclamation of a gentler Korea was a simple triumph of good over evil, with a democratic opposition joined by many millions of ordinary Koreans forcing an authoritarian military leader to crumble. Koreans often like to think of it as their version of "People Power," the popular uprising that swept the Marcoses out of power in the Philippines. Others, like Chun's successor Roh Tae Woo, have simply preferred to call it a "miracle," a political fairy tale that somehow naturally grew out of the country's economic success, and leave it at that.[16] But the story was not that simple.

Notes

1. From his apology on November 23, 1988. *Asian Wall Street Journal*, November 24, 1988.

2. The prison sentence was cut by more than half, thanks to a February 1991 presidential decree.

3. Corruption involving the Blue House was so common that people who claimed to have influence with the president commanded a large fee, whether or not they actually had influence.

In one of the more pathetic newspaper pictures from this period, Chun Sun Hwan, the president's cousin, was photographed as he sat glumly in the back of a car after being arrested in November 1988 on charges of receiving 10 million won in bribes to get permission to build a golf course. He was to have received 1.5 billion won if the construction permit were actually issued. The case came to light only because the disgruntled businessman who bribed Chun filed a suit against him after Chun could not deliver on his promise but refused to return the money. During the Fifth Republic, Blue House permission was needed to build a golf course, and developers were a major source of political funding. Golf courses were invariably lucrative investments because memberships were sold for tens—or hundreds—of thousands of dollars in a country in which the elite were infatuated with golf.

Chun's older brother, Chun Ki Hwan, was also arrested on corruption charges. Both the former president's brothers served time in prison, while Lee Soon Ja's relatives escaped unscathed. Many Koreans believed, however, that the Lee family had been much more systematic in its corrupt activities. Chun's brothers were generally held to be inept, petty crooks by comparison.

4. *Korea Herald, Korea Times*, and other local newspapers, April 3, 1988. Yang's charges are detailed in the discussion of Ilhae in Chapter 15.

5. Park did this at the urging of his close associate, "Pistol" Park Jong Kyu, who fittingly enough headed the hosting of the 42nd World Shooting Championships, which were held in South Korea in 1978. Park Chung Hee hosted a banquet for about a dozen International Olympic Committee delegates who came to Seoul for the shooting championships; in their thank-you letter they suggested that Seoul consider bidding for the Olympics. The idea was embraced by Park Jong Kyu and Park Chung Hee. After Park Chung Hee's assassination, Park Jong Kyu convinced a skeptical Chun Doo Hwan to press ahead with the Olympic bid by first winning over Roh Tae Woo.

6. Author interview, December 1990.

7. Jong Gie Kim et al., *The Impact of the Seoul Olympic Games on National Development*, p. 2.

8. Ibid., p. 39.

9. Ibid., p. 11.

10. It was perhaps typical of the South Koreans' self-absorption that Roh and many other senior Korean officials claimed that South Korea's democratic reforms of 1987–88 had provided the East Europeans with a model for their popular uprisings.

11. The state-owned Korean Broadcasting Service, by contrast, pulled back and showed the sit-in only with a long, wide camera shot.

12. *International Herald Tribune*, October 12, 1988. Almost anyone in Seoul could report similar experiences, from being accosted by upper-middle-class women in hotel coffee shops to hearing taxi drivers complain about the incident more than a year later.

13. *Asian Wall Street Journal*, October 1, 1988. Kim et al., *The Impact of the Seoul Olympic Games on National Development*, cites the "biased" reporting of NBC; mentions "the American government's support and protection of a dictatorship" and trade disputes as catalysts for anti-American feelings that surfaced during the Olympics (pp. 22–23). The work also says that feelings toward the United States were the only ones that suffered during the Olympics (pp. 24–25); on p. 92 the report again blames anti-Americanism on NBC.

14. *Asian Wall Street Journal*, October 3, 1988.

15. Kim et al., *The Impact of the Seoul Olympic Games on National Development*, pp. 11, 67, 94.

16. Ironically, South Korea ended the 1980s just as it began, with Chun Doo Hwan on center stage. On December 31, 1989, a brisk, winter Sunday, Chun left his hideaway at a Buddhist temple in the mountains for his first trip to Seoul since he had been hounded into internal exile more than a year earlier. He was driven to the huge domed National Assembly building on Yoido in hopes that his appearance would banish the legacy of the Fifth Republic that still haunted the new administration.

Chun testified to a crowd of assemblymen and a nationwide television audience that he had done nothing wrong during the Kwangju uprising, that he had taken no money improperly from corporations during his time in office, and that while errors were made during his administration, he had little to apologize for. After a year of meditating in the monastery on his wrongdoings, Chun told the nation that he had committed no errors of substance.

The former president read his statement in a monotone, its answers designed to do no more than fulfill the letter of the agreement with the National Assembly that Roh had struck without him. Angered by Chun's lack of contrition, one opposition legislator hurled a name plaque at him, while another threw an ashtray. Several rushed to the podium, one yelling that he was a murderer, another that he was a liar. Once again, Chun was driven away, forced to read the end of his statement to the press outside the assembly chambers in the hours just before midnight on New Year's Eve.

Then Chun was driven back to the monastery in the mountains. A few days later, after the opposition legislators were criticized for demeaning the former president, the fury subsided and the potency of Chun as an issue dissipated. A few weeks into the 1990s it seemed almost as if Chun had never existed. A broad ruling-party coalition, including much of the opposition, was formed, and Koreans seemed anxious to forget their past differences. The new Democratic Liberal Party (DLP) included Roh, Kim Young Sam, and Kim Jong Pil. Modeled on Japan's ruling Liberal Democratic Party, which writes its name with identical Chinese characters, the DLP still must show that it can encompass a wide variety of factions within one party.

22

Coping with Success

Seoul Olympics proves Koreans can do anything.
—*Korea Times*[1]

Dan Gunter hadn't planned his trip to Seoul. Gunter, an agricultural scientist and the executive director of Florida's citrus department, had hopped a plane for the long trip to Korea only after reports of carcinogenic Florida grapefruits had threatened one of the state's newest and fastest-growing export markets. Gunter was a scientist, not a slick public relations man, and he was totally unprepared for what the Korean press hit him with.

At issue was a claim that American grapefruit growers had used alar—a growth hormone for apples—on fruit shipped to Korea. The Korean market had just been opened to grapefruit imports, and sales had boomed until the alar reports hit the papers. The tempest began after a local consumer protection group, whose major goal was to protect domestic farmers, misinterpreted a test result. For more than a week the government refused to clarify the situation or to temper the hysteria in the press. Sales stopped almost overnight, and grapefruits rotted in crates.

The questions—speeches, really—that Korean journalists hurled at Gunter during an early morning press conference made it seem as if America itself was on trial. The Koreans refused to accept Gunter's contention that alar was not used, if only because it was ineffective on citrus, and the press conference turned into a quintessential display of the conspiratorial, xenophobic side of the Korean character. One journalist wanted to know if alar was put only on export fruit, as opposed to grapefruit consumed in the United States, or if it was possibly added during shipping; another said that even if it were true that the grapefruit contained no alar, other nasty chemicals almost certainly were used, perhaps arsenic or lead. The unstated theme of many questions was that Korean consumers were being singled out by American farmers and food companies who were trying to poison them in order to increase profits.[2]

Tellingly, the local press accounts did not mention that Korean farmers used more than 3,000 metric tons a year of alar on the apples and pears that make up a traditional Korean dessert plate.

Korea had enjoyed its Olympics, which gave it the chance to strut its stuff on the world stage. But for all its claims of being a "developed nation," a phrase that Koreans took very seriously, battles over everything from grapefruit to automobiles showed that Koreans did not think that opening their market to imports was part of the bargain.

Koreans believed that they deserved to have the same chances to take advantage of the world trading system that Japan did, a sort of affirmative action program for a developing nation. The idea that autoworkers in Detroit or farmers in Florida might not see it that way was alien to most Koreans.

In 1988, South Korea had the fourth-largest and fastest-growing trade surplus with the United States, trailing only Japan, Taiwan, and West Germany. Yet the prevailing Korean view was, and to a large degree still is, that no restrictions should be placed on Korean exports, but that the rest of the world should understand Korea's "special situation" and not press to open markets. Korea always wanted more time, special deals, and favored treatment from the United States.

As the U.S. trade deficit swelled, Washington focused more attention on the countries like Korea that were following the Japanese model of neomercantilist trade policies. The United States had long been Korea's largest market; Korea started running a trade surplus with the United States as early as 1982, four years before its trade as a whole shifted to surplus. Korea, which had only a fraction of the financial resources of Japan and Taiwan and depended on U.S. military support, was in a relatively weak position to resist trade pressure.

"There is a sense in the administration, which I believe Congress shares, that we should not make the same mistakes with Korea that we did with Japan," said Deputy U.S. Trade Representative Lynn Williams. "Korea has political problems, but so do all countries, including the United States. Korea and other countries will have to stand up and face trade issues, not hide behind 'the relationship.' "[3] Trade negotiators felt pressure from both an increasingly impatient Congress and American producers, who with increasing frequency filed suits under Section 301 of the 1988 U.S. Trade Act, which allowed stiff retaliation against unfair trade actions. To Koreans, all this maneuvering was just another form of gunboat diplomacy.

The United States and Korea: From Guns to Butter

Although as early as the Kennedy administration concerns had been raised about Korean textiles, it was not until the mid-1980s that the United States really focused attention on allegedly unfair trade practices by Koreans. Koreans responded with outrage. After an antidumping suit in the United States against Korean photo albums crippled exports to the United States, sidewalk vendors in Seoul advertised the photo albums with handwritten signs asking buyers to support Korean album makers in their struggle for economic justice. These sentiments about debt and trade, along with unhappiness over the U.S. support of Chun Doo Hwan, fused into Korea's first public displays of anti-Americanism.

In 1985 came two incidents that would have been unimaginable in the past. In the eastern port city of Kangnung, a U.S. diplomat was hit on the back of the head by a beer bottle in a crowd and knocked unconscious; police could find no witnesses. In Inchon, just west of Seoul, an American was beaten up as he stepped off a train. In 1979–80, demonstrators had protested for civil liberties and human rights; but by 1985 the focus of their protests turned to the Chun government and its U.S. backers. Although protesters were few in number, the antiforeign sentiments they tapped were widespread.

For many years South Korea had been almost eerily pro-American. The opposition was criticized not because it was anti-American, but because its language of human rights made it seem too pro-American, with the Park administration sometimes accusing dissidents of "toadyism." This was, as many U.S. observers noted, unlike just about any other developing country.

The trade talks united Koreans in their unhappiness with U.S. policies and left a residue of bad feelings on both the American and Korean sides of the negotiating table. The deterioration in U.S.–South Korean relations was puzzling to many Americans because it occurred in a country that U.S. policymakers considered one of their major foreign policy successes of the postwar years.

On the other side, the average Korean simply could not understand why a big, rich nation like the United States, a country that had sacrificed more than 54,000 American lives in the Korean War and subsequently poured billions of dollars in aid into their country, should care about petty items like meat, wine, and cigarettes—beef, butts, and booze, cynics scoffed. For Koreans, ever conscious of hierarchy, the United States was their big brother who would always be there to lend a helping hand. "They thought that the special relationship we had would overcome all," says a U.S. diplomat who served in Seoul during the late 1980s. "They thought the rules didn't apply to them."[4]

The United States was unhappy with the cocksure attitude of the Koreans and their often adolescent assertions of national pride. Even after contracts and trade agreements were signed, foreign firms found themselves hampered by obscure regulations seemingly designed to frustrate imports. "In Korea a signed agreement is simply the beginning of negotiations," diplomats and foreign businessmen warned newcomers.

This shift from security to economics—from guns to butter—prompted aggressive action by the United States on a variety of issues, ranging from agriculture to intellectual property rights, on cases including everything from the Batman logo to semiconductor designs.

Cigarette imports remained a notably bitter issue even after the two countries signed an agreement in 1987. U.S. trade negotiators said that the issue was simply one of free trade and equal access to markets, but Korean critics pointed out the hypocrisy of the U.S. government's discouraging smoking at home while promoting it abroad. "This is Korea's version of the Opium War," fumed a senior official of the National Young Men's Christian Association Federation who was active in a boycott campaign against foreign cigarettes. Korean women dressed in traditional white linen clothing passed out leaflets protesting the cigarette sales on busy streets in downtown Seoul. Smokers were told not to smoke foreign brands, because "the smell of foreign tobacco is the smell of the destruction of our farmers," in the words of the YMCA anti-import campaign.[5]

The campaign had broad public support. Tobacco marketers found that most foreign cigarettes were sold at vending machines, because buyers did not like to buy them from a Korean clerk. One of the biggest cigarette companies in the world, British-American Tobacco, did not even put its name on individual cigarettes in Korea in order to allow smokers to puff in anonymity. Smokers of foreign cigarettes hid the packs in an inside jacket pocket, slipping the unmarked cigarettes out one by one.

There were, not surprisingly, coercive aspects to the campaign as well. Retailers who sold foreign cigarettes were harassed, advertisements for foreign cigarettes were destroyed, and vending machines vandalized. A promotional event at the Haeundae beach resort near Pusan was disrupted by a gang of toughs. It was an assault organized by the state-owned tobacco monopoly's in-house union. Local governments also urged citizens to smoke Korean cigarettes, because a substantial part of local revenues given out by the central government was based on consumption of Korean cigarettes.

Both sides were hypocritical. Korea exports significant quantities of raw tobacco to the United States. Moreover, South Koreans are already extremely heavy smokers. Three out of every four men smoke. Yet the Finance Ministry, which depends on cigarette taxes for revenue, has resisted attempts to require stronger antismoking warnings.

More broadly, agricultural imports became an extremely knotty issue in trade negotiations during this period. Public protests against beef imports slowed down government attempts to reopen the market after it was illegally closed in 1985. Ironically, beef farmers had suffered because of a disastrous import campaign led by none other than the president's younger brother, Chun Kyung Hwan, during the early 1980s. In yet another of his corrupt schemes as head of Saemaul, Chun had encouraged large imports of live cattle (more than 24,000 head in total) to build up domestic herds. The increase in supply, one of the fastest build-ups of livestock herds anywhere in the world, pushed domestic beef prices into a free-fall when the animals were slaughtered for market. Farmers were forced to sell their cattle for less than they had originally paid. Many of them lost a substantial part of their life savings; they took to the streets in 1985 in what was at the time one of the largest antigovernment demonstrations during the Fifth Republic. Beef imports were quickly banned.

The broad public support for continued import bans underscores the way in which Korea, like Japan, is a country organized to benefit producers, not consumers. Even consumer groups support import restrictions, although it means they pay significantly higher prices for their food. Although rice is the staple of the Korean diet, with per capita rice consumption of 121 kilograms a year, Korean consumers pay five times the U.S. price for rice. Nonetheless, support is nearly unanimous for a continued ban on imports as a way of supporting farmers and ensuring security of food supplies.[6] Only when Japan agreed in 1993 to import rice as part of the Uruguay Round of GATT did Korea grudgingly follow suit. Characteristically, the agriculture minister resigned to take responsibility.

Democracy took its toll on market-opening measures. Most working-level bureaucrats had always opposed import liberalization. Now they were joined by politicians, who wanted to protect domestic interest groups, and farmers, who knew they could not compete in many traditional products. Consumers, too, supported restrictions on imports. "We are Koreans," said the director of the Citizens Alliance for Consumer Protection in Korea, explaining the organization's unwillingness to back rice imports even if it would benefit consumers.

Roots of Anti-Americanism

Americans were proud of saying that Korea would not have survived without their help. David Cole, an economist who worked in Korea in the 1960s, said that from the Korean War until the mid-1960s, "large amounts of U.S. assistance, $2.6 billion, made the difference between growth and no growth, and probably between survival or collapse of South Korea as an independent country." At the time, there was virtually no anti-Americanism. "This is the one country I have been in, and I have been in a great many developing countries, where I never experienced the kind of 'Americans go home' expressions that are common elsewhere—for that matter not even among dissident elements in the country," Cole told a U.S. congressional hearing in 1978. "The Korean concern was that Americans should not go home prematurely."[7]

Chun's seizure of power after Park Chung Hee's assassination forever undermined this pro-American sentiment. To support their arrest of martial law commander Chung Seung Hwa on December 12, 1979, Chun and Roh Tae Woo ordered troops off front-line positions on the DMZ and into Seoul. Those troops, along with most of the South Korean army, were under the operational control of a U.S. general, under a complicated arrangement intended to make sure that the forces were most efficiently integrated. That did not mean that the United States always had effective control over the troops.

The U.S. commander, John Wickham, was livid at Chun's action. "He was not happy with anything that happened" on December 12, said a confidant of the general. "He viewed Chun Doo Hwan as a murderer. He was [also] unhappy with the abrogation of the chain of command."

Wickham shunned Chun for two months. Finally, after rumors began to circulate of a potentially disastrous countercoup by older officers, Wickham agreed to speak with Chun on February 14, 1980, in a meeting that illustrated the limits of U.S. power. When Chun arrived at Wickham's headquarters at the Yongsan military base, the Korean officers treated the young Korean general with the protocol normally reserved for the president. Even though Chun was only a two-star general, the Korean four-star general at the Combined Forces Command went down to meet his car, a highly significant gesture in a country as obsessed with protocol as Korea. Wickham, by contrast, declined even to stand up to meet Chun when he came into the room.

The U.S. general had carefully rearranged his office in preparation for Chun's visit. He had taken his Bible from the credenza behind his desk and placed it on the otherwise empty coffee table that the two generals and their two interpreters sat around. This was designed to show Chun Wickham's belief in a higher power, although its impact was almost certainly lost on the South Korean general. Wickham was dressed for the occasion in his fatigues, not a Class A dress uniform. He meant business.

"He sat back in his big chair with his boots on the table right in Chun's face," remembers a source familiar with the meeting. This was a crude, calculated insult in a country where it is considered extremely bad form to display the soles of one's feet. "Chun told Wickham that he was not taking power. He lied through his teeth. What do you do when a man in power lies? There is no way to contradict him."[8]

One way to counter these sorts of power grabs is through publicity. But the United States remained silent through the spring of 1980, as it was to do for seven more years. When the bloodshed came at Kwangju, the United States was restrained in its comments. South Korean papers were intimidated into not running U.S. expressions of concern during the incident, giving many Koreans the clear impression that the United States had acquiesced in the violence. The United States also declined requests by dissidents for help in mediation, a step that might have reduced casualties.

In fact, the South Korean paratroopers who conducted the initial assaults were from a special warfare unit that was not under U.S. operational control. The troops who went in to clean up did so under a procedure which gave the United States no authority to stop them. But none of this was made public until William Gleysteen, who was ambassador to Korea in 1980, belatedly gave his account in 1987.[9]

Throughout his term Chun somehow bullied the United States, especially Ambassador Richard "Dixie" Walker, with the threat that revealing the U.S.

version of what happened when Chun took power would threaten the special relationship that the two countries enjoyed. It certainly would have undermined Chun's relations with Washington, but it would have gone a long way to cure the festering wound caused by the bloody events of 1979–80. Instead, Walker only managed to inflame anti-Americanism further by being quoted as saying that the dissidents were "spoiled brats."[10]

The United States had long put more emphasis on security issues than on democracy in Korea. Under the U.S. military government, which ruled the country from 1945 until 1948, democracy took a back seat to the problem of establishing political control in a country that was coping with extreme poverty and spiraling toward civil war. Economist Paul Kuznets, speaking of this period, noted that "it was not an issue of supporting or promoting democracy. It was an issue of keeping people alive. It was as simple as that."

Later, U.S. concerns over democracy were downplayed because of the threat from the North. For example, U.S. diplomats in Seoul had tried to block Park Chung Hee's 1961 coup, but abandoned their effort largely because they were afraid the North would try to take advantage of any weakness in the South. Paul Cleveland, a former political counselor at the U.S. embassy in Seoul, summed up U.S. policy by saying that "we have disassociated human rights and security assistance on the grounds that security assistance is an overriding need and that we should not make that connection [between military help and democracy]. I know that there are some who hold a different view, but that, I think, has essentially been our Government's position."[11] Official U.S. gratitude for South Korea's help in Vietnam, where it sent troops, also helped soften pressure for political reforms throughout the 1960s and 1970s.

By the 1980s much had changed. The unwillingness or inability of the United States to stop Chun from taking power had disillusioned a younger generation of Koreans. Fused with trade pressure from Washington, the image of the United States changed from big brother to big bully. Americans rightly felt that they deserved better for saving South Korea from absorption by the Communist North. But any country that was the younger sibling in the sort of big brother–little brother relationship that the United States and Korea had would have been unhappy.

This anti-Americanism was also stoked by the presence of a U.S. military base, about the size of New York's Central Park, in the heart of downtown Seoul. Just as Americans would not welcome a Japanese takeover of Central Park, Koreans' resentment of this base was understandable. Indeed, no other country in the world has a foreign military base in its capital. The United States has pledged in principle to move out by 1996, but the large tract of foreign-occupied land in the midst of one of the world's most densely populated cities constantly reminds Koreans that Korea is not completely their own country. Even though most South Koreans would be unhappy if U.S. troops simply packed up and went home, there is nonetheless a powerful undercurrent of resentment at their presence.

The United States, and especially the U.S. military, had an impact in Korea that would have surprised and astonished most Americans. Until 1994, the U.S. military television channel was broadcast on the sweetest spot of the broadcast band—channel 2—beaming everything from *Wheel of Fortune* to *Nightline* into South Korean homes and restaurants. Products as diverse as Johnny Walker whiskey and Spam acquired cachet, thanks to the thriving—and quietly tolerated—black market.

The U.S. military disclaimed involvement in South Korean politics, but Koreans noticed that their presidents for thirty years came from retired generals who had worked in one way or another with the Americans. It was, after all, the U.S. military that had helped build the South Korean military into such an effective fighting force. The United States wanted to take the credit, but not the responsibility, for South Korea's military.

Richard Stilwell, former commander-in-chief of the U.S. forces in Korea, boasted that the United States "had an extraordinarily large hand" in shaping the Korean armed forces. "Over the years we have totally controlled the pace of modernization of those forces, at least up until 1975, for the very simple reason that we were providing the financial resources for those forces.... Our role historically since the end of World War II—first, to establish a constabulary; then, a fledgling military establishment—has been a greater role of participation, I might say a greater responsibility, than with respect to any other free world armed forces."[12] Yet for all its influence, the United States had proved unable to keep the military out of politics.

The U.S. military also had a tremendous impact on the South Korean economy and political structure. The Korea Military Academy's four-year course was modeled on the U.S. Military Academy at West Point; the academy's nickname was East Point. Although Chun Doo Hwan and Roh Tae Woo are its best-known graduates, the diffusion of military techniques has spread throughout Korean society. Joel Bernstein, who worked with the U.S. AID effort, noted that the briefings he received at Korean companies all followed the same pattern.

> I would be sat down in a chair, and tea was served, and they would begin a briefing with a flip chart and graphs around the wall, and the briefing was straight out of U.S. military briefing manuals. "Here is our problem and our goals, and here are the resources we are deploying to achieve the goals." Sometimes the data on the charts at that time wasn't very good, because they didn't have very good data, but that isn't important. The point is that there had been inculcated throughout Korea a sort of problem-solving approach, which is not in its traditional culture. It is not the normal way people approach a problem in traditional cultures. And the military obviously had a great deal to do with that. In addition, you found many officers leaving the Korean military going into management of private companies, in large numbers, so a lot of

management skills that were learned in the military were then transferred to the civilian economy.[13]

U.S. military power often shaded into contempt for the natives. Don Lee, a Korean-American whose father worked for the foreign service, remembers watching a team of Blue Angels, the daredevil Navy pilots, performing their tricks over the Yongsan base in central Seoul.

> The Phantom F–4s flew acrobatic stunts over a field and then, for the finale, buzzed the Han River—dry at the time, and a stone's throw from the base— and dropped napalm onto the sandbars, terrific billows of flames rising into the air. At the time, I loved it. I was a kid like any other. But later, as an adult, I thought about this militaristic demonstration—dropping bombs during peace-time into the river of a foreign capital, in the middle of the city, for a show. Could anything have been more arrogant? It characterized how Americans treated Koreans in general. They paid no respect to local customs, cut ahead of lines, demanded special service at shops, routinely belittled their servants. Ugly Americanism in all its glory. And there was an epithet for Korean women who were the girlfriends or wives of enlisted men: "moose."[14]

For Americans who expect some gratitude for their role in allowing South Korea to survive as a nation, it is instructive to remember how the Koreans treated China's decisive role in repelling Japanese invaders at the end of the sixteenth century. Steven Linton, a U.S. scholar who was raised by missionary parents in Korea, notes that at first the Chinese role was openly acknowledged, but as time went on it was minimized. Today, few Koreans know about the critical Chinese help. "When the Chinese military are mentioned at all, accounts of their arrogance, cowardice and duplicity make up most of the coverage while victory is attributed to Admiral Yi Sun Sin and his famous turtle boats."[15]

Japan and Korea: Unhappy Neighbors

When Japanese Prime Minister Miyazawa Kiichi visited Seoul at the beginning of 1992, he was met by crowds of wailing elderly women, demanding compensation for having been forced into service as prostitutes—sex slaves, really—during World War II. The Japanese government had long denied that the tens of thousands of "comfort girls" had anything to do with the Japanese government. The forced prostitution rings, according to the official Japanese position, were strictly a private affair arranged by entrepreneurs. But a few days before Miyazawa's visit, documents emerged showing that the Japanese government was officially involved in enlisting elementary school girls—as young as twelve years old—into the comfort corps. This revelation, which was accompanied by the sort of studied and grudging apology that characterizes Japanese-Korean relations, inflamed public opinion and undercut Miyazawa's visit.

Japan and South Korea have a uniquely troubled and ambiguous relationship, one in which Korea is very much the weaker partner. Forty years of Japanese occupation left a bloody and brutal legacy, but this period also witnessed the beginning of Korean industrialization. By the late 1930s, Korea was the most industrialized country in Asia after Japan, with massive chemical works, a developed machinery industry, and substantial textile enterprises. Korea's abundance of hydropower and mineral resources of rare earths even made it home to Japan's embryonic nuclear program shortly before the end of the war.

Diplomatic relations between the two countries were cut at the end of World War II, although Japanese industry benefited greatly from procurement orders for the Korean War. Park Chung Hee's decision to re-establish relations with Japan, strongly urged by the United States, nearly brought down his government in 1964. The cabinet resigned, and martial law was declared. In 1965, when the normalization bill was hurriedly pushed through the legislature, opposition members were physically barred from the National Assembly. When students hit the streets in protest, the government took the unusual step of sending troops onto the campuses of two universities to shut the schools down.[16]

In spite of this antagonism, Japan had an extraordinary impact on the development of the Korean economy. Steelmaker Posco was built with Japanese help and funded with the reparations agreed to at the time of the 1965 normalization agreement. The Japanese decision to establish a potential competitor was all the more surprising, given the massive overcapacity and price-cutting that the Japanese steel industry was suffering from during the late 1960s. Japanese firms invested in South Korea's Masan Free Export Zone, located just across the narrow Tsushima Strait, which Park Chung Hee set up to earn foreign exchange for Korea by offering Japanese companies a docile, cheap, and hard-working labor force.

Japan also helped establish South Korea's heavy industries. From 1969 through 1975, as the big push into heavy and chemical industries began, Japanese companies invested a total of $110 million in petrochemical projects alone. The auto industry, which benefited enormously from Japanese investment and technology transfers, would not have existed without Japanese help. Mitsubishi's stake in Hyundai Motors, and its decision to provide it with critical emission control technology in the early 1980s, was a milestone in the development of Korea's automobile industry. Mazda and Itochu (formerly known as C. Itoh) own a combined stake of 10 percent in Kia Motors, the country's second-largest automaker, and Mazda has provided Kia with key design and manufacturing assistance.

Japanese firms also helped launch South Korea's consumer electronics industry in the early 1970s. Tie-ups between both Goldstar and Samsung and Japanese producers were particularly prominent. In the late 1980s, the integration took a new twist with an agreement between Goldstar Electron and Hitachi. The Japanese firm supplied the production know-how, helping Goldstar set up its fabrication facility, naturally enough using almost exclusively Japanese equipment. Goldstar had a guaranteed market for many of its DRAM semiconductors, and Hitachi had a reliable source of lagging-generation chips, freeing up capital resources for the next generation of chips.

This is not an altogether happy partnership. The Koreans complain that the Japanese are reluctant to transfer technology and that they keep their markets closed. "There are many invisible barriers to trade," complains Samsung executive vice president Lee Kil Hyun. His complaint is a familiar one: Japanese distribution channels, Lee says, are "as complex as a man's body." Ssangyong chairman Kim Suk Won sees "unseen Japanese efforts" that bar entry to South Korean goods. These are friends of Japan, not Japan-bashers, talking. Lee worked in Tokyo for more than a decade, and Kim, who for a time headed a Korean-Japanese business association, attended high school in Japan.

The Japanese, for their part, have a mouthful of complaints about the Koreans. They complain that Korean firms are rigid and formal, even by Japanese standards, and that there is not enough of the sort of teamwork that makes Japan successful. The Koreans also look to government to solve too many of their problems, the Japanese complain. "Politics and economics are combined too closely," says an executive with a large Japanese trading company. South Korea, he adds, "has been against communism, but in practice it has been [a] . . . centrally planned economy. It's very strange. People need to stand on their own and take more self-responsibility."[17]

As recently as 1991, South Korea and Japan were each other's largest Asian trading partners. But Japan was running a large and growing trade surplus with South Korea. In 1991, Korea's deficit was a record $8 billion. The deficit persists in spite of South Korea's blanket bans on several hundred Japanese goods, ranging from passenger cars to washing machines. Although the restrictions are blatantly illegal under international trade rules, the Japanese know that to challenge them would cause more political trouble than it is worth. They also know that this sort of policy is, after all, based on the Japanese model.

If they could work together more, the Koreans and the Japanese would make a powerful combination. The two countries control about two-thirds of the world shipbuilding market, and as shipbuilding prices hit rock bottom in the late 1980s they cooperated in a loose cartel to push up prices, with shipbuilders exchanging detailed information on bids that were being prepared for international customers. But they have a long way to go. Anti-Japanese feeling is strong in Korea, and the Japanese unwillingness to come to grips with its past simply fuels suspicion.

The Japanese penchant for making insensitive statements is by no means limited to salvos lobbed at America. A Japanese scholar, writing in 1990, sought to minimize Japan's bloody occupation of Korea by noting that "it is by no means rare to witness ethnic genocide by colonizers such as the massacre of Tasmanians by the British in Australia and racial extinction of many tribes at the hands of Spanish settlers in Latin America." In another instance, author and television commentator Takemura Kenichi told an international conference in 1990 that "an all-out invasion of Japan by Korea is inevitable if Korea is reunified." His solution: Japan should help North Korea so as to prevent reunification.[18]

Austerity

By Korean standards 1989 counted as a recession, a throbbing post-Olympic hangover, with growth slowing to 6.7 percent. After three years of 12 percent growth it was inevitable, even salutary, that the economy would cool off. Wages in dollar terms had nearly doubled since 1987, thanks to a strong labor movement and currency appreciation. Property and stock prices were shooting up, and Korea looked as if its bubble might burst. Yet Koreans had come to think that double-digit economic growth—or something close to it—every year was normal. Even many of the country's Ph.D.s, who certainly should have known better, termed it a recession or stagflation. Koreans burrowed deeper into their antiforeign shell as the economy slowed, and Roh Tae Woo himself called the situation one of "total crisis." This near-panic prompted a sweeping and ill-thought-out cabinet reshuffle in March 1990.

The new ministers promised to get the economy back in the fast lane again by jump-starting the export machine and forcing consumers to cut down on spending. This cabinet was made up primarily of holdovers from the Park Chung Hee days, men who were used to a relatively small, primitive economy in which an authoritarian government could easily control all the key players. They made some basic macroeconomic mistakes by overstimulating the economy, but their biggest international failure was a politically inspired campaign to restrict consumer imports at the same time that they wanted to boost exports.

The new ministers worried that the country was importing too much. They tried to enforce a campaign of austerity—backed up with administrative guidance and punitive tax investigations—that they figured would cut imports without attracting too much attention from trading partners. Minister of Trade and Industry Park Pil Soo was outspoken in his determination to limit ostentatious displays of wealth. "We have lived in a poor situation for many years. Some made money, mostly by speculation, [and now] they want to have a very expensive bed and to drink champagne," he said. Park complained that a store displayed a bottle of cognac on sale for 1.35 million won. "This I don't like. And there are more than 100 different [kinds of] wines imported, even though many Koreans are not wine drinkers. Is it acceptable? No. . . . The haves should . . . [learn] the spirit of austerity. . . . They spend just too much."[19]

The opaque ties that hold Korea, Inc. together were visible once again, as importers simply stopped bringing in many foreign goods. Ford was one of those hit hardest. The U.S. automaker had introduced its Mercury Sable autos to the Korean market in December 1989. Imports of foreign cars were legalized only in mid-1987, but stiff duties and taxes had kept the flow of foreign autos to a trickle. The Sable was the first import that was cheaper than a comparable Korean car, Hyundai's high-end Grandeur model, and it quickly became the best-selling auto import. The numbers were tiny, only a few hundred cars a month, but the imports still alarmed government officials and domestic automakers.

The government quietly told Kia, which had been importing the cars, to trim its sales effort. In April 1990, sales started to slow; by June they were running less than a third of their levels early in the year. Kia, a South Korean automaker that is 10 percent owned by Ford and made the Ford Festiva for export to the United States, had invested several million dollars in a service network and advertising campaign, but its executives simply agreed to go along with the dictate from the government.

An official at the Ministry of Trade and Industry admitted that the government had asked Kia to cut its sales of the cars. "We tell the companies that they have to understand the sensitivities of the people and for the good of the country restrain their sales of luxury goods," he told a reporter. The MTI official was one of the few who was clumsy enough to admit what the government was doing.[20] An official at the presidential Blue House said privately that while the government did not explicitly tell officials to discriminate against imports, the Blue House would not object if the policy were interpreted that way. In a country as politically attuned as Korea, explicit orders do not need to be given for people to start toeing the policy line.

Just in case consumers did not get the message, anonymous tax agency officials said that buyers of imported autos risked tax audits, a strong threat in a country where tax audits are typically punitive and the use of the tax agency as a political tool is taken for granted. These threats appeared in most major newspapers within the space of a few days. They were apparently based on leaks from tax officials to the small group of journalists who cover the tax office. No tax officials would ever confirm these statements to foreign diplomats or journalists, and government officials brushed aside the reports as "misunderstandings" by irresponsible local reporters. But no denials were ever issued and, most important, Koreans believed the threats and took them seriously. Sales of the Hyundai Grandeur climbed as those of the Sable sank.[21]

The Sable case was not an isolated example. Tax agents ordered the proprietor of a Gucci boutique in the wealthy Apkujong neighborhood to remove many goods from public display after she was quoted in a *Washington Post* article on South Korea's consumer boom. The store eventually closed, in part because of continuing harassment from government officials.

By 1990, Korea was one of the world's twelve largest trading nations. Along with its East Asian neighbors, it had benefited tremendously from the freer trade. But, like Japan, Korea often seemed to think that free trade was a one-way street.

For all that South Korea has opened up to foreign products and foreign ideas, despite hosting the Olympics and establishing ties with its former Communist enemies, Korea remains deeply suspicious of the rest of the world. This was perhaps nowhere more evident than in the country's response to the Uruguay Round of GATT trade negotiations, which were intended to liberalize world trade. The proposed trade opening meant some adjustments for South Korea, but overall the country is one of the greatest beneficiaries of free trade.

Many Koreans did not see it that way. Opposition to the Uruguay Round was stirred up by government officials and local journalists in the early 1990s. The press told Koreans that their country was a "defendant" in the trade talks, which Koreans were led to believe would lead to the domination of their economy by foreign interests. Koreans luridly discussed the possibility that the Uruguay Round of trade liberalization would mean that, along with a flood of foreign dentists, undertakers, and doctors inundating South Korea, prestigious universities like Harvard would set up Seoul campuses to skim the best students away from Seoul National University and destroy Korea's national identity.

Nothing better demonstrated this blind, unthinking xenophobia than the sporadic harassment of Uruguayan diplomats and protests at the country's embassy. Although Uruguay had been only the host country for the beginning of the trade talks, Koreans figured that the country was somehow to blame. Korean manufacturers' reliance on an open trading system was hardly discussed in this hysterical campaign. Trade became, "a hate-the-foreigner issue," in the words of a U.S. trade negotiator. "The press was rotten, inaccurate and misleading."[22] Politicians were little better.

Korea, Inc. Under Attack

The proto-revolutionary rumblings of labor, the grumbling of a discontented business community, the tattoo of corruption charges and the impossibility of a military clampdown put Roh Tae Woo's young Sixth Republic in a difficult situation. Technocrats displayed a palpable sense of doubt about how to confront the new Korea. This striking loss of self-confidence among the technocracy was unwittingly underscored in a 1989 study by the Korea Development Institute, the government think tank that had provided much of the intellectual underpinning for the policies of the 1970s and most of the 1980s.

Describing Korea's situation during the Fifth Republic, the study said there was "a legitimacy crisis, a consolidation crisis, a distortion crisis and a development crisis." That is quite a mouthful from the people whose policies were so closely identified with the government.

> The distortion crisis was based on the mistakes of the eighties stemming from the growth of the sixties and seventies. The government's development strategy created structural imbalances among industries, classes and regions. The distortion was deeply rooted in the *chaebol* (large corporations) economy, neglect of the masses [sic], and high dependence on foreign countries.[23]

This sort of thinking among the policy elite testified to the loss of direction among policymakers.

The economic experts who had guided the economy were too cowed by the prevailing anti-Chun mood to defend their accomplishments, their legacy of low inflation and sustained growth. They were powerless to stop policies designed to buy off voters with pork-barrel spending projects and subsidies.

The most notorious case in which sensible economics ran up against special interests was in Korea's rice paddies. Korea's policy of encouraging rice production by subsidizing farmers had made a good deal of sense during the 1970s, when, despite importing large quantities of grains, Korea was still forced to limit rice consumption to five days a week. (This policy ended only in 1976.) But as rice surpluses mounted during the 1980s, it was folly to keep raising rice support prices, particularly because consumer prices were lower than what farmers received. Every year the government paid more for rice, selling what it could to consumers at a loss. Meanwhile, rice consumption was dropping as the Korean diet became more varied.

In 1987, technocrats wanted to raise rice prices 6 or 7 percent. But farmers, flushed with enthusiasm for sharing the spoils of democracy, demanded a figure well into the double digits. Finally, a compromise was reached, wherein rice prices rose the same amount as civil service salaries, 14 percent. The one had nothing to do with the other, but it was typical of the sloppy policy-making that came to characterize the late 1980s and early 1990s. On top of this generous price rise, at a time when inflation was only 3 percent, the government bailed out farmers with an expensive and indiscriminate loan package, at a cost of $6 billion over ten years.[24]

Korea's situation was similar to that of Japan. Rice farmers have a special place in both countries, thanks to family and emotional attachments to the land. Both countries worry that they could go hungry in the event of a war or a cut-off in international supplies if they are not self-sufficient. Japan is an island and, for all practical purposes, so, is South Korea. In both countries, the government was unable to provide the political leadership needed to restructure the agricultural sector. Off-farm income as a percentage of farmers' total earnings in Korea lagged far behind that of Japan and Taiwan. Welfare handouts replaced the sort of practical economic policies that had enabled Korea to prosper. This loss of leadership hurt the country, coming as it did when economic restructuring was needed.

In an attempt to win support for their continuing reform of the economy, technocrats convinced Roh to form a Presidential Commission on Economic Restructuring. The aim of the group was to debate, for the first time publicly, the future of the Korean economy and to adopt long-term economic policies. On paper it worked well enough, and the commission promised a solid diet of liberalization, internationalization, and economic reform. The reality was that on virtually every front, Roh's politically weak government backtracked on its promises of reform or failed to carry through promised initiatives.

Roh, for example, had pledged a sweeping privatization program as part of his effort to free the economy from the heavy control that had characterized it for nearly thirty years. This, like many of his other efforts, was a triumph of form over substance. If measured by the yardstick of increasing competitiveness by forcing more accountability, it was a failure. Minority stakes were sold in the state-owned steelmaker, Posco, and in the electricity monopoly, Kepco, but nothing changed in the operations of these companies. Posco was already run efficiently, even though it was hemmed in by price controls, but Kepco was not.[25]

Financial reform was another failure. Sakong Il, who remained finance minister until December 1988, managed to win presidential approval for a banking and securities reform package on the day before he was relieved of his job in a cabinet reshuffle. The cornerstone of the banking reforms was a plan to decontrol interest rates, beginning with loans. Although this was done on paper, in fact the Ministry of Finance enforced a cartel freezing rates slightly above where they had been. They remained at that level for more than three years, even as officials proclaimed in speeches at international conferences that interest rate reform was evidence of their liberalization of the financial sector.

Progress on liberalization took another step backward on June 29, 1990, the third anniversary of Roh's democratization announcement, when the Finance Ministry ordered short-term finance companies to cut their interest rates. These institutions, which were far more market-oriented than banks, were doing too good a job at competing, and they were taking business away from the big, slow-footed banks. Because authorities at the Finance Ministry did not believe in competition, they effectively tried to shut down the short-term finance companies. In 1991 these firms were encouraged to become either banks or securities companies.

The result of such inconsistent policies pleased no one. "Economic discipline has deteriorated significantly under the present regime," complained Suh Sang Mok. Suh was the vice president of the Korea Development Institute for much of the 1980s, before joining the legislative National Assembly in 1988 as a member of the ruling party. "Look at the policy loans. In the 1970s, it was the heavy and chemical industries. Now we have new ones, to give money to agriculture, small and medium industries and housing. In the last few years agriculture and housing have increased significantly. If you squeeze credit, what is going to suffer? Manufacturing. It is the sector we do not want to suffer. So there is a dilemma."[26]

Roh Tae Woo tried to put some of the muscle back into the Korean system when he engineered a stunning merger of two opposition political parties with his ruling Democratic Justice Party at the beginning of 1990. Long-time opposition warrior Kim Young Sam and his party joined Roh, as did Kim Jong Pil, Park Chung Hee's long-time ally and a key player in the 1961 coup. This was Korea's attempt to establish a Japanese-style political coalition of the sort which existed until 1993, where a strong ruling party could rule indefinitely while taking only minimal account of opposition demands.

It did not work out quite as Roh had hoped, yet despite the tumult of labor unrest and political uncertainty, the economy kept humming along. The dip to 6.7 percent growth in 1989 was less surprising than the rebound to 9 percent growth in 1990, followed by 8.4 percent growth in 1991. For an economy the size of Korea's, at a time when many of its other Asian competitors were recording growth rates of half that level, strong growth at a time of rapid political change seemingly proved the long-term viability of the Korean system. Underpinning this strength was a handful of Korean companies, buoyed by a tremendous pool of hard-working employees and heavy capital spending, which surged to positions of world leadership.

Notes

1. September 17, 1989, Olympics Anniversary Supplement.
2. The controversy arose after the Citizens' Alliance for the Protection of Consumers in Korea sent some grapefruit to be tested by the state-run Agricultural Chemical Research Unit. The state-run testing agency said that it could detect traces of alar at concentrations of 0.5 parts per million and above; the finding came back negative but was marked on the test sheet as "less than 0.5 parts per million." This was interpreted incorrectly by the consumer group as a positive finding.
3. *Electronics Korea*, December 1989.
4. Author interview, April 1990.
5. *Far Eastern Economic Review*, March 29, 1990, and April 19, 1990.
6. In mid-1991 the price for high-grade japonica was 1,560 won per kilo. Equivalent rice sold for $5 for a 25-pound bag at the U.S. commissary in Seoul. Korean farmers received $1,850 a ton for rice compared with $300–325 in world markets. Unpublished data prepared by the U.S. Department of Agriculture, Seoul.
7. U.S. Congress, House, *Hearings before the Subcommittee on International Organization of the Committee on International Relations*, 95th Congress, 2nd session, Part 6, Hearings July 19 and August 2, 1978, pp. 43, 47.
8. The description of this meeting is based on an account to the author by a source with intimate knowledge of the encounter.
9. Later, in 1989, the United States prepared a fuller account in response to a request from the National Assembly.
10. Walker later insisted that he had been misquoted.
11. U.S. Congress, House, *Hearings before the Subcommittee on International Organization of the Committee on International Relations*, Kuznets is quoted on p. 101; Cleveland on p. 103. Both testified on August 2.
12. Ibid., p. 26.
13. Ibid., p. 54.
14. Don Lee, *Village Voice*, February 19, 1991, pp. 42–43.
15. Stephen Linton, *Coverage of the United States in Korean Textbooks (An Analysis of Educational Policy, Tone and Content)*, p. 48.
16. See David C. Cole and Princeton N. Lyman, *Korean Development, The Interplay of Politics and Economics*, especially Chapters 3 and 5 for a detailed discussion of the normalization treaty and its domestic consequences.
17. Author interview, October 1990.
18. Nigel Holloway, ed., *Japan in Asia*, pp. 24–25.
19. Author interview, April 1990.

20. *Wall Street Journal,* June 12, 1990.

21. See American Chamber of Commerce, *Doorknock 1991,* for more details. This account, however, is based primarily on author interviews.

22. Author interview, February 1990.

23. Jong Gie Kim et al., *The Impact of the Seoul Olympic Games on National Development,* pp. 70–71.

24. The figure comes from Koo Bohn Young, a secretary for economic affairs to Roh Tae Woo in a commentary published in the *International Herald Tribune,* January 18, 1990.

25. Underscoring the close state-business ties, Park Tae Joon, who had headed Posco since its founding, became the chairman of the new Democratic Liberal Party when it was formed at the beginning of 1990.

26. Author interview, March 1991.

23

Joining the Big Leagues

I do not think that the businessmen who were accused of illicit wealth accumulation are criminals.... I propose that the accused businessmen be given an opportunity to build factories and donate their share to the state. It will not be too late for the state to evaluate them and decide the criminal sanction later when they complete the construction.

—Lee Byung Chull to Park Chung Hee[1]

After a young researcher named Lee Young Woo joined Samsung in 1968, one of his first projects was working on vacuum tubes for radios, about as close as South Korea's primitive electronics industry got to the cutting edge of technology. By 1988, however, Samsung had not only become one of the world's largest electronics companies but it was the largest non-Japanese firm in the bruising global battle to sell semiconductor memory chips. In a generation, South Korea had vaulted from a lagging, primitive economy to one with pockets of world-class technology and production methods. Nowhere was this more apparent than at Samsung's Kiheung plant, about an hour south of Seoul.

A visitor to the Samsung plant must navigate the rough, narrow streets in the village of Kiheung. Traffic is often clotted, as farmers driving cultivators vie for space with trucks carrying multimillion-dollar shipments of semiconductors. Cows, which still form a substantial portion of the assets of many villagers, graze next to modest farmhouses.

Twenty years after he joined Samsung, Lee Young Woo proudly showed visitors a mock-up of the company's impressive semiconductor production facility—including a planned expansion that would double production capacity by

1991 at the cost of many hundreds of millions of dollars. At a time when most U.S. manufacturers had ceded the mass-market DRAM semiconductor business to the Japanese, Samsung was charging ahead, confident that it could give Japanese companies like NEC, Hitachi, and Fujitsu a run for their money.

The next few years proved that Samsung's confidence was well-placed. In 1991 a team led by Lee, who was in charge of semiconductor research at the company, finished in a dead heat with Japan's Toshiba in the race to design the world's first 64-megabit DRAM semiconductor. By 1993, only a decade after Samsung began selling semiconductors in earnest, it was the world's biggest DRAM manufacturer.

South Koreans had proved that they could produce steel, ships, and cars of world-class quality at competitive prices. But the emergence of Samsung and, to a lesser extent, other Korean electronics producers near the front of the pack in high-technology fields signals a new level of sophistication in the Korean economy and among Korean corporations.

Although it specializes in high-volume production of memory chips, in total semiconductor sales Samsung is among the world's top six producers. Its other competitors are all Japanese: Toshiba, NEC, Hitachi, Fujitsu, and Mitsubishi. Like its Japanese competitors, Samsung is a one-stop electronics shop, making everything from consumer gadgets like so-called fuzzy logic washing machines and vacuum cleaners, which use rudimentary artificial intelligence software, to microwave ovens, televisions, telecommunications switching systems, and computers. Samsung Electronics is the centerpiece of the Samsung group, which vies with Hyundai for the right to call itself South Korea's largest chaebol, a group with combined annual sales of $87 billion, whose interests span from a securities house and the country's most prestigious golf club to petrochemicals and construction operations.

From Rice Mill to Semiconductor Plant

Lee Byung Chull was born on the fertile Naktong River delta, in the southeastern corner of Korea, in 1910, the year that Japan formally annexed his country. Lee's father was a wealthy landowner in a village that counted about 300 households, and the younger Lee received a classical Chinese education until he was ten years old. Lee Byung Chull wanted to get a modern education, and his parents allowed him to go to a primary school in Seoul. He spent much of the 1920s in Japanese-occupied Seoul before moving to Tokyo, where he attended the elite Waseda University. He dropped out, apparently because of poor health, and returned to Korea. He seems to have been somewhat aimless for the first few years after his return, spending his time, according to a biographer, "wandering around Seoul doing nothing in particular."[2]

Backed by money that he inherited from his parents, Lee started a rice mill in Masan, near his home village, in 1936. It was an uncharacteristically hasty decision, and Lee later said that he was not sure why he chose that business. Two years later he moved to Taegu and founded Samsung. The name literally means "Three Stars." Fittingly, Samsung was to be crushed three times and, like a phoenix, rise from the ashes three times.

Lee's highly leveraged trucking and real estate business went bankrupt when loans were squeezed after the Japanese invasion of Manchuria. But by the time of the liberation in 1945 Lee's businesses were thriving again. Besides trucking and real estate, his company was involved in domestic trading (including the shipment of goods such as fish and dried apples to Manchuria), milling rice, brewing, and noodle-making. He was one of Kyongbuk Province's largest tax-payers by the time of the liberation.

After the departure of the Japanese, Lee thought that setting up some sort of international trading business would be profitable, so he moved to Seoul and set up the Samsung Moolsan ("Trading") Company in November 1948.. He is also reputed to have been one of those who benefited from the disorderly sale of Japanese assets after 1945. Lee's bet on trade was a good one. By the time the Korean War erupted in June 1950, his company was among the ten largest trading companies in the country.

The trading company was destroyed by the invasion of Seoul, and North Korean occupation forces in Seoul put Lee on their wanted list. He went into hiding and slipped down to Pusan, the only city still controlled by allied forces, where he re-established the trading firm in January 1951. The reborn Samsung concentrated on imports and grew seventeenfold during its first year, thanks to windfall profits from the war. Those profits prompted Lee to think about manufacturing; in 1953 he set up the Cheil (First) Sugar Company in Pusan. The company was South Korea's only sugar refiner and enjoyed large profits. Money from the sugar company was reinvested in the Cheil Wool Textile Company, founded in 1954.

Like Cheil Sugar, the textile company benefited from Korea's import-substi-tution policies of the 1950s, which nurtured domestic producers by limiting imports. The textile company quickly became the core of the group and contin-ued to enjoy that status until the late 1970s. Koreans grumbled that Samsung prospered thanks to the "three whites"—sugar and flour, cement and fertilizer, and cotton yarn—and accused Lee of being a profiteer. By the end of the 1950s, Lee owned about half the shares in South Korea's recently privatized commer-cial banks, including 85 percent of what became Hanil Bank, almost 50 percent of Chohung Bank, and 30 percent of the Commercial Bank of Korea. He also controlled a significant part of the insurance market thanks to his acquisition of Ankuk Fire and Marine Insurance and Dongbang Life Insurance.[3] While the rough-hewn Chung Ju Yung built up Hyundai as an industrial company, by contrast Lee's Samsung looked more like the property-and-trading combines common among the overseas Chinese of Southeast Asia.

Lee Byung Chull later said that the biggest shock of his life came when he picked up a newspaper in Japan in May 1961 to find that Park Chung Hee had seized power. As the richest man in Korea, Lee was a prime target for the anticorruption campaign staged by the new government. Later, the government officially calculated Lee's wealth at 800 million won, or nearly one-fifth of the national total of allegedly illicit wealth. He was also accused of donating 64 million won in political funds and evading 451 million won in taxes during the 1950s.

Claiming poor health, Lee initially begged off when he was asked to return to Korea. Finally, after nearly a month had passed, he flew back to Seoul. He was met at the airport by martial law command representatives and taken to meet Park, interrogated, and then jailed. But the wily Lee, who already had survived the Japanese occupation, U.S. military government, a North Korean invasion, and the corrupt administration of Syngman Rhee, was able to strike a deal with Park. The deal between the young general and the country's most successful businessman laid the foundation for modern Korea.

Lee Byung Chull promised that he would win the cooperation of the business community in Park's economic development plans. As part of the deal, Lee "voluntarily" offered to donate most of his wealth to the country; accepted the expropriation of his bank shares by the government; and became the first head of the Federation of Korean Industries, the main business group. He also reputedly suggested the idea for an industrial estate, such as the one that was later built at Ulsan.

Lee helped arrange a $40 million loan to finance the world's largest fertilizer plant in the mid-1960s. However, the Korea (Hankuk) Fertilizer Company, which was financed by Mitsui and twenty other investors, nearly caused his downfall. In September 1966, a major scandal erupted when a rival politician claimed that one of Lee Byung Chull's sons, Lee Chang Hi (later head of the huge videotape maker Saehan Media), had diverted some of the imported raw materials for the fertilizer company to the black market. Imported fixtures intended for employee dormitories at the plant were also found on sale in Korean stores. Lee Chang Hi was forced to sever his ties with the group as the result of this incident. Park Chung Hee ordered an investigation, and Lee offered to "donate" 51 percent of the shares in the company to the government in penance. Samsung's name was blackened in the public's mind for some years after this incident. Perhaps as a result, Lee never developed the rapport with Park Chung Hee that Hyundai's Chung Ju Yung enjoyed. Kim Seok Ki, who is both a chaebol scholar and a relative of the Lee family, claims that Samsung's political connections were seriously damaged by the incident and that it was excluded from large investment opportunities until the early 1970s.[4]

Samsung's more cautious attitude may also have hurt Lee's relations with the gung-ho Park Chung Hee. Although by Western standards Lee and Samsung were freewheeling gamblers, they represented the epitome of conservatism compared to Hyundai. While Hyundai was setting up its auto plant in Ulsan and plunging ahead with international construction contracts in Thailand and Vietnam, Samsung was quietly minding its traditional businesses. Aside from the botched fertilizer effort and a paper company acquired in 1965, Samsung set up no manufacturing businesses from 1952 until the late 1960s, when Samsung Electronics was founded.

During the 1960s Lee continued building domestically oriented businesses with quick payback periods or low fixed assets, such as a department store (Shinsegae, now one of the country's largest) and a real estate development company. He also set out to cultivate influence by setting up the *Joongang Ilbo* (one of the nation's leading newspapers); the Tongyang Broadcasting Company (seized by Chun Doo Hwan in 1980 with only nominal compensation); and the Samsung Cultural Foundation. The group also acquired Sungkyunkwan University.

Samsung's financial base had been weakened by the Korea Fertilizer scandal, and Samsung moved very cautiously in capital-intensive industries. Lee Byung Chull wrote in his memoirs that he wanted "to avoid trial and error" in fields where mistakes are expensive.[5] Samsung took part in the build-up of the HCI program, but on a much smaller scale than Hyundai or Lucky-Goldstar. A joint venture with Amoco and Mitsui, Samsung Petrochemicals, makes purified terephthalic acid (PTA), a key material used in making polyester fiber. This fit in nicely with Samsung's position as the dominant textile manufacturer in Korea, a country whose textile industry was particularly strong in synthetic fiber production. (It was only in late 1988, a year after Lee Byung Chull's death, that Samsung plunged into petrochemicals. The $2 billion investment in a naphtha cracker and associated petrochemical refining facilities cost the company dearly when it came on stream in the early 1990s and exacerbated a regional glut of petrochemicals.)

Samsung acquired a shipbuilding unit in 1977 at the government's request. Although Samsung's is the third-largest shipyard in the country, it is far smaller than Daewoo's or Hyundai's yards. Samsung kept the scale small and thus limited its exposure to the world shipbuilding cycle. At the end of the 1980s, construction, chemicals, and heavy industry made up less than one-fifth of the company's sales.

Given Lee Byung Chull's fluent Japanese and his education at Waseda, it is not suprising that Japanese partners have provided key help for Samsung. Besides the ventures already mentioned, Toray helped Samsung start a synthetic textiles operation in 1973; a group of Japanese investors led by the trading firm Nissho Iwai provided 19 percent of the investment for the prestigious Shilla Hotel in Seoul, with the balance held by Samsung; Toyo Engineering helped set up Korea Engineering in 1978 for industrial plant exports; and Hattori Seiko is a partner in Samsung Watch. Samsung's VCRs are produced under license from Japan's Victor, which for a time prohibited exports by Samsung, and facsimile machines are made under a license from Toshiba. Japanese companies are both suppliers and competitors. Other early joint venture partners included Sanyo and Nippon Electric (later called NEC).

Unlike Daewoo or Lucky-Goldstar, which have failed to grab leadership positions in most technology areas, Samsung is at the top of the global pack in the semiconductor memory area.

Birth of the Electronics Age

At the end of the 1960s, Lee Byung Chull picked electronics, not heavy industry, as the manufacturing area where Samsung could make its mark. Lee was apparently impressed by Goldstar, a spinoff from the chemical manufacturer Lucky, which had started making radios in the late 1950s and enjoyed success in the local market. In 1970 the first black-and-white televisions slid off the assembly line at Samsung's Suwon plant. Refrigerators and washing machines followed. But it was not until 1977 that the company even started making anything as basic as color televisions. In 1979 Samsung had started producing VCRs, making Korea only the fourth country in the world to produce what was to become a hit product in the 1980s.

In 1980 it started making what was to become another success, microwave ovens. The microwave oven production was typical of the way that Samsung went after a product. One visitor to the Suwon facility in 1977 described it as looking like "a dilapidated high school science classroom."[6] Although South Korea was still more than three years away from color television broadcasting, Samsung engineers were starting to produce a color television. Tearing apart television sets manufactured in the United States, Europe, and Japan, Samsung's researchers were reverse engineering—copying—the innards so that they could produce as many of the sophisticated components as possible in Korea. This ambitious localization program saved precious foreign exchange and helped develop more advanced R & D and production techniques.

Samsung was also starting to design its own microwave oven with a research team that was given a small corner of the primitive lab—about fifteen square feet of working space. The research team was headed by a scientist who had failed at his last assignment, producing an electric skillet. After a year of working ten or twelve or more hours a day, six or seven days a week, Chu Yun Soo turned on his prototype microwave oven. The plastic cavity melted. After more eighty-hour weeks, he tried again. This time a shaft melted. At a time when the Japanese and Americans were selling more than 4 million microwave ovens a year, Samsung could not even produce a working prototype.

Samsung managed to make its first working prototype for a microwave oven in June 1978. The first export order came from Panama, for 240 ovens. It was not until 1980 that Samsung managed to win its first U.S. order, from J.C. Penney, for several thousand ovens. The production team virtually lived at the factory, with senior managers sleeping on cots. The line ran during the day, producing fewer than ten units a day at first, while the fine-tuning was done at night. In 1980 the company made just over 1,000 microwaves. In 1981 production leaped to more than 100,000 units. It doubled in 1982, but Samsung was still dissatisfied with a world market share of less than 4 percent.

Back in the United States, General Electric was alarmed by its slipping share of the microwave market. Japanese manufacturers, who had built up their production capacity ahead of GE, were taking General Electric's market share on its home turf. GE started looking around for a lower-cost source. In 1983, it cost GE $218 to make a microwave oven, but Samsung could do it for $155. As expected for a low-wage competitor, part of that difference was labor, which cost GE $8 and Samsung only 63 cents. But most of the difference came in overhead costs, which were $30 versus 73 cents, and in management costs, which ran at $10 per oven for GE and two cents for Samsung, wrote consultants Ira Magaziner and Mark Patinkin. From GE's perspective, "what the companies got for their money was the most disturbing figure of all. GE got four units per person per day. Samsung got nine."[7]

"Traditionally, low-wage countries have been content to let their factories lag a decade behind countries like the United States," wrote Magaziner and Patinkin. "They make bicycles in the age of the automobile, black-and-white televisions in the age of color. Samsung was one of the first Third World companies to take a new approach, to compete directly in modern products."[8]

The Samsung Men

Toward the end of his life, Lee Byung Chull used to winter in Japan. He was attracted not only by the mild weather, which allowed him to golf all year, but a culture he felt comfortable with. Lee prided himself on being a cultured man, typified by his success in building up the country's finest private art collection. Whereas Hyundai's Chung Ju Yung used to engage in traditional *ssirum* wrestling with new recruits, Lee Byung Chull had a more refined idea of the Samsung man. Until the early 1980s, Lee used to participate in final interviews with every new white-collar hire.

As the company grew and Lee aged, he decided to institutionalize the Samsung spirit through a training center set in the same complex as his art museum and his tomb. Here all new male recruits undergo an intensive training period.

Most major Korean companies—and even many smaller ones—put their employees through initiation rituals, but Samsung's is particularly intense. Employees start the day at ten minutes before six by singing the national anthem and then going for a quick jog around the grounds. Discipline, cleanliness, and an attention to detail are underscored by a twelve-point checklist in the dormitory rooms, where the men sleep three or four to a room. Courses include conflict resolution, role-playing, leadership and management classes, and computer and quality-control training. Employees who are going overseas attend intensive twelve-week training programs that include everything from business and politics to office and table manners.

Samsung is the most disciplined of the Korean groups. As early as the 1950s, Lee Byung Chull set up a powerful secretariat reporting directly to him. This secretariat, which now has 125 senior executives who are rotated for two- or three-year stints, gives Samsung a degree of control and centralization that no other major chaebol enjoys. Although Korean chaebol chairmen exercise tremendous control at all companies, no other group has the sort of professional staff to coordinate strategy.

After Lee Byung Chull's death in November 1987, the Samsung style proved itself as third son Lee Kun Hee took over with a minimum of disruption. The younger Lee wields a strong hand in promotions, and there is grumbling that he favors the "Samsung military" (those whose entire working life has been at Samsung). But he has left the business of running the company largely to the extremely competent corps of professional managers his father recruited. These include not only graduates of the best universities in the country but politically well-connected men. During the administration of Roh Tae Woo, the senior ranks of Samsung included former Prime Minister Shin Hyon Hwak and former Deputy Prime Minister Kim Mahn Je.

No other company is challenging Japan head-on the way Samsung is. Koreans like to say the Japanese are lazy, and Samsung is one company that hopes to take advantage of any weakness shown by the Japanese. Lee Kun Hee told an interviewer that "the day when South Korea can surpass Japan is when that country becomes afflicted with social malaise—when it loses its spirit and social values."[9]

Samsung is the only one of the major chaebol in South Korea that is free of independent unions. It pays above-average wages and provides some of the best working conditions and employee benefits in the country. It also will use virtually any means to stop the formation of independent unions.

Wee Choi Hak, a worker at the Samsung Heavy Industry shipyard in Okpo, found that out the hard way. Wee claims that he was kidnapped by company officials when he and a group of workers tried to organize a union. The group that hustled him into a Hyundai Pony sedan in June 1988, he says, included a director of the company and two officials in the personnel department. These sorts of cases are not atypical in Korea, and Wee was eventually released. (He claims he was held for ten days.)

In a lengthy interview, Wee said he simply wanted society "to treat laborers as human beings, as people with the same worth as people with capital, to give us the same social position as well as economic benefits." To Lee Kun Hee, Samsung's chairman, who had said that Samsung's workers do not need a union, Wee said that he "would just like to remind him that the entity which decides whether or not a union is needed is not the chairman but the workers. I want him to wake up from this illusion he has that he knows what is best."

In June 1988, Samsung shipyard workers who wanted to unionize were at first prevented from leaving Koje Island, where the shipyard was located. Finally, after driving all night to Seoul, they arrived at the Labor Ministry in Kwachon, on the southern edge of the city. Strangely, someone had just registered a union. But no meetings were ever held and no elections were allowed. Because South Korea allows only one union per workplace—and it can be as exclusionary as it likes—the workers were frozen out. This ended, for all practical purposes, the most serious unionizing attempt Samsung faced during the tumultuous late 1980s.[10]

Challenging Japan

By 1992, not only was Samsung the world's largest DRAM producer, but it had staked out substantial positions in key electronics products. It was the world's largest computer monitor maker, the second-largest VCR maker, the third-largest microwave oven producer, and the sixth-largest producer of color television sets. Its factories ringed the globe, from Indonesia to Mexico to Portugal. Its huge production facilities were backed up with an impressive commitment to spending on new factories as well as research and development. From $400 million in 1986, capital spending at Samsung Electronics grew in succeeding years, to about $1 billion annually during the late 1980s and early 1990s—as much as $1.3 billion some years—on new plant and equipment.

Most of that money went to its semiconductor business. Semiconductor capital spending accelerated as the company solidified its position as the world's largest DRAM producer, with two-thirds of 1992's $1 billion in capital spending going to semiconductors.[11]

Samsung's spending has paid some impressive dividends. Samsung Electronics' sales totalled $15.8 billion in 1996 and it ranked as the world's seventh largest semiconductor producer. Thanks to strong chip sales, Samsung Electronics' *profits* alone totalled more than $3 billion in 1995, though the collapse in chip prices sliced earnings 93 percent to 164 billion won in 1996. By 1996, Samsung was the largest maker of DRAMs (with 17 percent of the world's market), microwave ovens (18.8 percent market share), computer monitors (12.2 percent market share), and Static-RAM computer chips (15 percent market share). It also had a significant presence in faxes, color televisions, VCRs and camcorders.[12]

Samsung Electronics is the group's core company, and the group has a strong focus on technology-oriented businesses. But it is placing some big bets on new businesses in the future, bets that seem out of character with Lee Byung Chull's conservative approach. Although it had no aerospace experience, Samsung became the prime contractor for Korea's ambitious program to build F–16 fighter planes for its air force. This decision was made by President Chun himself in 1986, as a result of a strenuous lobbying effort led by Lee Byung Chull. Samsung Aerospace, which is primarily a consumer camera maker, will spearhead the government's effort to jump-start the country's fledgling aerospace business.

The $2 billion Samsung invested in a petrochemical refining complex in the late 1980s and early 1990s seems to have been driven by rivalry with the Hyundai group, which was building the same type of plant literally next door to Hyundai's facility in Sosan. "It was a macho thing," conceded a senior Samsung executive. "The business had been very profitable, but regulated. When it was deregulated, everyone wanted to jump in. Once you announce a project you can't just back down, so we had to go ahead."[13]

Samsung is, by Korean standards, a well-run company, and it is among the more profit-minded of the chaebol. But even Samsung cannot shake the impulse to boost sales at almost any cost. Samsung launched what looked like an attempt to make a hostile takeover of Kia, one of South Korea's three passenger car manufacturers, in late 1993 and it has repeatedly expressed an interest in manufacturing automobiles. Given the ruthless nature of competition in both electronics and automobiles, it seems preposterous to think that Samsung could succeed in both.[14]

Too Much of a Good Thing

Bigger might have been better when Korean companies were struggling to get a toehold in world markets. But as the Korean economy becomes more internationalized, and more open to foreign competitors, Samsung and the other chaebol will have to focus their efforts on what they do best. Without a protected local market, being big will no longer be enough. "Even in the Olympics there aren't gold medalists who can win in both swimming and basketball," said Ahn Hyo Young, the late head of McDonald's in Korea.[15]

For it is not only Samsung that is expanding as if sheer size alone will guarantee success. Hyundai, Kia and Daewoo had production of 3.3 million cars in 1996, a figure that they expect to double by the year 2000. Samsung's expansion will come on top of that. Total domestic capaicty in 1997 was 4.2 million autos while demand was less than half, 1.7 million units.

Hyundai's Chung Ju Yung has traveled to the former Soviet Union almost a dozen times since 1989 in search of natural resource ventures that his group can tap. In the early 1990s, Chung said he was prepared to invest $3 billion in what was then the U.S.S.R. to develop massive timber, oil, coal, and natural gas projects. "Korea is short of natural resources and the U.S.S.R. will contribute to stabilizing this situation," said Chung. "Korea is viewed by the Soviet Union as an economic collaborator."

Even many Koreans worry that Chung is wildly optimistic about doing business in the former U.S.S.R., but Chung says the skeptics should consider the record of success that South Korean companies like his have had in the past. "About fifteen or twenty years ago when we had an opportunity to get into the Middle East, we had no capital, no technology, and no experience. People in advanced countries expected the South Korean efforts would be a failure. We surprised them."[16]

A smaller group, Kumho, which does not even rank among the top dozen chaebol, plans to spend $7 billion nurturing its fledgling airline subsidiary during the 1990s, mostly on a fleet of four dozen new Boeing jets. The company, which started with two taxicabs in 1946 and is best known for its bus company, received a license to start an airline only in 1988. Since then, its Asiana subsidiary has

embarked on an expansion program that is almost unprecedented in world avia-
tion history. At the same time, it is pouring hundreds of millions of dollars into
expanding its chemical operations, and it has branched out into building golf
courses and hotels.

Hyundai, Samsung, and even Kumho can afford to be so aggressive in part
because of the unwritten assumption that the largest chaebol have simply become
too big to fail. For all the talk of competition and free market forces, there is a
government guarantee on the biggest companies. Kukje showed the difficulties of
breaking up the biggest business groups. But it was in 1988, when Daewoo teetered
on the financial precipice, that this policy of protecting the biggest companies was
confirmed.

Daewoo Shipbuilding's billion-dollar-plus debt load threatened to push the whole
group into bankruptcy after a decade of weak orders and continuing mismanagement. Daewoo, however, had taken over the Okpo shipyard in 1978 on President
Park Chung Hee's orders, and Daewoo chairman Kim Woo Choong contended that
the government had an obligation to help his company. Workers, who knew precisely how Korea, Inc. functioned, pressed for wage increases of between 25 and 55
percent a year during the late 1980s, even as the firm stood on the edge of insol-
vency. They knew, as one of them said, that "if Daewoo goes bankrupt someone else
will take over the company" and that their jobs would be secure. Eventually, the
government did rescue Daewoo, with a package that wrote off some debt and
extended repayment terms on the remainder.[17]

Daewoo remains among the most aggressive Korean *chaebol*, leading many
observers to believe founder Kim Woo Choong is trying to ensure that, whatever
difficulties the company encounters, it will always remain too big for the government to allow it to fail. Although it debt is three times its equity, and its $391 million
in profits in 1996 were little more than one-half of one percent of the groups' $68
billion in combined sales, Daewoo's relentless expansion continues. Kim Woo
Choong expects to invest $15 billion overseas by 2005, up from $2.8 billion at the
end of 1996. In early 1997, Daewoo opened a $1.1 billion, 320,000-annual capacity
auto factory in Kunsan, South Korea. Though the Korean auto industry is staggering
under excess capacity, Daewoo Motors plans to keep piling on the investments,
boosting worldwide production to 2.5 million units by the turn of the century from
its mid-1997 level of 1.7 million, in a bid to become one of the worlds' ten largest
auto makers.[18]

Hyundai and Samsung, too, know that if their massive bets in petrochemicals or semiconductors go badly wrong the government will help
salvage their groups, for Korea remains less a market economy than a
negotiated one. When the technocrats and the colonels tried to restructure
the business groups in 1980, there was a chance that some of the biggest
groups might not survive in any recognizable form. But businesses, or at
least the biggest businesses, now are sitting at the bargaining table as near-
equals with the country's economic mandarins.

This close relationship with the government engenders resentment, even hostility, from many Koreans. Indeed, one of the most striking facets of Korea is the antipathy toward the chaebol, despite their central role in Korean economic development, on the part of both government officials and the general public. The following editorial, which lashed out against one of many practices by which the chaebol used their connections with banks to fund real estate purchases, is typical of public sentiment:

> The immodest and irregular mode of operation of these large-scale enterprises in collaboration with major banks is a reproach to the integrity of our business community. . . . Rather than trying to strengthen the structure of their capital, they have been bent on drawing more money from banks to multiply their commercial lines for shady profit. . . . Equity and justice in the economy are vociferously called for these days. Our financiers and industrialists must regain a sense of morality to work toward these ends.[19]

This problem will take at least another generation to solve, for the chaebol are likely to be resented as long as they are identified with the families that founded them. Hyundai's "Chung Ju Yung is a king" to his staff and "his words are law," complained a Blue House official during the Roh years; Chung's sons are watched carefully as they rise to the top of the group. Staff at the Lucky-Goldstar group spend much of their time assessing the "royals," as they call the Koos and Huhs whose families founded the group and whose relatives are scattered throughout the group. Until the late 1980s these young princes had a dedicated personnel department watching over their advancement within the group.

The increasing importance of chaebol families sours egalitarian-minded Koreans and keeps these multibillion-dollar organizations very personal affairs. Intermarriages between chaebol and political families became common during the 1980s, capped by Roh Tae Woo's daughter's marriage into the family that owns Sunkyong. The conglomerate used its political protection, or the general appearance of that protection, to extend the sweep of its business. Most controversially, Sunkyong won a coveted license for a cellular telephone network in late 1992; in the ensuing outcry, then-candidate Kim Young Sam forced the cancellation of the contract.

Daewoo's chairman Kim Woo Choong speaks for the misunderstood Korean businessman.

> Traditionally in Korea, businessmen have not been respected; rather, they have been people to look down on or to keep your distance from. There may be a lot of reasons for this, and perhaps the greatest is the deeply-rooted Confucian tradition of social rank: the scholar, the farmer, the artisan and the merchant, in that order, with the merchant at the bottom of the ladder. Another reason can also be found in more recent trends where, for some businessmen, the end— the accumulation of wealth—justifies the means.[20]

The antipathy that Koreans feel toward businessmen is far more complicated than Kim admits. It is rooted in a primitive notion of equality, a sense that Koreans suffered together and in turn should share equally in the fruits of prosperity. This instinctive egalitarianism can be seen in the bitter opposition of workers to companies, even foreign ones, which introduce merit-based pay scales, and demands that all pay rises be based on seniority. But the unhappiness with business also stems from the fact that most leading businessmen were political entrepreneurs, dependent on their political skills as much as their business acumen. True or not, many Koreans believe that Kim Woo Choong would not have attained such prominence had his murdered father not been Park Chung Hee's teacher. It is this alliance between business and government that is at once the Korean economy's greatest strength and its most pronounced flaw.

Notes

1. Kim Seok Ki, "Business Concentration and Government Policy: A Study of the Phenomenon of Business Groups in Korea, 1945–1985," p. 106. This is from an interview with Lee Byung Chull, where Lee describes his meetings with Park immediately after he returned to Korea after Park's 1961 coup.

2. Leroy P. Jones and Sakong Il, *Government, Business and Entrepreneurship in Economic Development: The Korean Case*, p. 352. This section is based on Jones and Sakong, pp. 349–54; *Far Eastern Economic Review*, June 4, 1982; and Samsung Company and Samsung Electronics prospectuses published in 1991 and 1992.

3. Kim Seok Ki, "Business Concentration and Government Policy," esp. pp. 73–85 for the development of Samsung in the post–Korean War period.

4. Ibid., pp. 111–12; this has Lee Byung Chull's account of the incident, in which he claims that the material was smuggled with the consent of Park Chung Hee and the knowledge that it would be a source of political funding. The problem, Lee says, came when a powerful politician was unhappy with the division of the spoils.

5. Quoted in Jones and Sakong, *Government, Business and Entrepreneurship in Economic Development*, p. 349.

6. Ira Magaziner and Mark Patinkin, "Fast Heat: How Korea Won the Microwave War," *Harvard Business Review*, (January–February 1989), pp. 83–84.

7. Ibid., p. 89.

8. Ibid., p. 84.

9. *Far Eastern Economic Review*, June 4, 1982.

10. Author interview, February 1989. See also *Far Eastern Economic Review*, June 1, 1989.

11. Impressive as Samsung's resources are, they are overshadowed by its biggest international competitors. IBM, for example, spent more than $16 billion in capital investment from 1989 through 1991, including more than $5 billion in 1991 alone. IBM's research and development spending ($6.6 billion in 1991) was twice the total South Korean spending on R & D. But Samsung's scale is impressive when compared with that of any of its rivals from the developing world.

12. Company data; market share figures are from Samsung Group, February 14, 1997, press release.

13. Author interview, February 1992.

14. Samsung denied that it was trying to mount a hostile takeover, although after a public outcry it did promise to sell the 10 percent stake it had amassed in Kia. It subse-

quently struck a technical tie-up with Nissan and says it will start selling passenger cars in 1998, more than a decade after the government turned down its original request to start making cars with Chrysler.

15. Author interview, December 1988.

16. Author interview, September 1990. *Far Eastern Economic Review*, September 20, 1990. Hyundai's activities in Russia were scaled back following the collapse of the Soviet Union.

17. The quotation about bankruptcy comes from a February 1989 author interview with a labor activist at Daewoo Shipbuilding and Heavy Machinery.

In the end, the shipyard bailout paid handsome dividends, as Daewoo benefited from the appreciation of the Japanese yen—which made its Japanese rivals less competitive—and increased demand in the global shipbuilding industry. In 1992, Daewoo Shipbuilding and Heavy Machinery reported a net profit of 211 billion won, which accounted for virtually all of the group's total income of 232 billion won. In 1988 and 1989 the shipbuilding unit lost 263 billion. Daewoo Corporation prospectus, dated October 1993, p. 48.

Daewoo was rescued from bankruptcy, thanks to government intervention. It was a messy solution, one in which politicians were involved. However, the openness of the process, notwithstanding the accusations of backroom deals, gave the outcome a measure of legitimacy and ensured that the Daewoo rescue did not become a political issue after Roh Tae Woo left office. That very openness, however, also politicized the process, with legislators drawn into policy-making. The affair was messier than it would have been in the old authoritarian days of Korea, Inc. but nonetheless healthier in terms of the legitimacy of government and business.

For the background on Daewoo Shipbuilding's problems see *Asian Wall Street Journal*, November 9, 1988. Kim Woo Choong claimed in that article, as he had on other occasions, that at the time Daewoo took over the shipyard the Korea Development Bank had promised to inject 400 billion won in equity into the shipyard but put in only 200 billion. As a result, he said, the capital base was permanently crippled. True or not, most analysts say that until the brush with bankruptcy, the shipyard was also poorly managed. The emphasis was on sales rather than profits. See also *Far Eastern Economic Review*, November 10, 1988; December 8, 1988; and February 23, 1989.

18. *Far Eastern Economic Review*, May 1, 1997.

19. *Korea Herald*, September 22, 1989.

20. Kim Woo Choong, *Every Street Is Paved with Gold*, p. 35.

24

The End of the Beginning

Politicians are the culprits and businessmen are accomplices.

—Chung Ju Yung[1]

One man was a disgraced corporate chieftain, the other a senior North Korean on the run. Although both captured the attention of a fascinated South Korean public in early 1997, at first glance they could hardly have seemed more different. Yet the very different sagas of Chung Tae Soo, the founder of the Hanbo group, and North Korean defector Hwang Chang Yop were two strands of the Korean thread. The corrupt corporate head and the fugitive ideologue between them epitomize Korea's two great challenges: building a transparent, competitive, modern economy and overcoming the painful division of the country.

The spectacular collapse of the Hanbo group in January 1997, which easily won the dubious distinction of being Korea's largest financial scandal ever, served as a measuring stick to show how far short of the mark President and former opposition leader Kim Young Sam's reforms had fallen. The Hanbo debacle exposed the mountain of bad loans at Korea's banks and raised again the question of how professional and competitive Korea's giant chaebol really are. Short-term foreign debt soared, and analysts began talking about a Mexican-style collapse. Rating agencies slashed credit ratings for Korean banks, forcing them to pay more for borrowing on international markets. Another big group, specialty steel–maker Sammi, quickly followed Hanbo into bankruptcy. The giant beer-and-*soju* maker Jinro was saved from what would have been the third collapse among the thirty largest chaebol only by a government-orchestrated rescue. In an unprecedented move for a large Korean company, Ssangyong Motor said it would look for a foreign partner to take 49 percent of the company after racking

329

up losses of 228 billion won in 1996; the Ssangyong group staggered under debts that were *eighty-six times* its equity. Other large groups, including auto giant Kia, tottered on the edge of bankruptcy and began the unusual step—for Korea—of selling assets in a struggle to stay afloat. Despite brave talk about moving to a more market-oriented economy, the government stepped in and encouraged banks and other financial institutions to keep pumping funds into large troubled groups.

For corporate Korea, it was the worst crisis since the early 1980s. The roots of the problem lie in the chaebol's growth-at-any-cost strategy. High debt and slim profit margins—usually well under one percent of sales—mean that the chaebol are vulnerable to anything that crimps their cash flow. Falling semiconductor prices and the weakness of the Japanese yen, which introduced intense pricing pressure, did just that. So did excess capacity in two other big export items, steel and petrochemicals. The downturn was unprecedented, for by the mid-1990s, Korea was too big to overcome the problem simply by cutting expenses and increasing exports. And because Korea had become a high-cost economy, productivity and efficiency mattered as never before.

The revelations about Hanbo's Chung, who had been a major ruling party fundraiser during the administration of Roh Tae Woo and remained on good terms with political heavyweights, showed the fundamental corruption that runs through Korea's system. Credible reports claim that Hanbo donated more than $60 million to Kim Young Sam's 1992 presidential campaign. The ironically named Hanbo, or "Korean treasure," had piled up nearly $6 billion in debt by the time it went bust, thanks to corrupt and incompetent bankers and high-level political backing. Its borrowing binge came although the company had virtually no shareholder's equity and it was headed by a man who had already been imprisoned twice on corruption charges relating to his activities on behalf of former president Roh Tae Woo. Whether or not senior officials or Kim's relatives are legally culpable, there's no doubt that their friendship helped Chung secure continued funding for Hanbo. Hanbo's bankruptcy points up a banking system that continues to rely on political connections more than hard-headed credit analysis. The Hanbo affair also forced into the open the prominent role that Kim's second son, Kim Hyun Chul, played in Korea's moneyed politics and led to widespread calls for the resignation of the president himself.

Even as the Hanbo scandal dominated newspaper coverage, a drama that could have even more far-reaching consequences for South Korea was playing out in Beijing. Hwang Chang Yop, the architect of North Korea's *juche* policy and a long-time associate of Kim Il Sung, fled to the South Korean embassy in a successful bid for political asylum. Hwang was for many years among the two dozen most powerful people in the country. It was as if Thomas Paine had fled to London during America's Revolutionary War. His defection, by far the most significant in the history of divided Korea, hinted at deep problems in the North's leadership.

North Korea's days have been numbered since the collapse of the Soviet bloc and, with it, access to bartered raw materials. But since the death of the charismatic Kim Il Sung in July 1994, the economy has deteriorated more sharply. North Korea is tottering. The only question now is whether it will go with a bang or a whimper—and when that will happen. The consequences for Northeast Asia are immense. A North Korean collapse could unleash a wave of millions of refugees. An attack on South Korea, though unlikely, would result in enormous casualties. Even the most benign outcome, a North Korea that embraces economic growth and opens to foreign investment, will pose immense challenges for its neighbor in the South. For it is South Korea that will be called upon to provide much of the cost of rebuilding the North Korean economy, which could run on the order of $1 trillion. This isn't just a question of money: South Korea's continuing internal divisions will be put to new tests as the country grapples with rapprochement with its impoverished, estranged fellow Koreans to the North.

Much has changed in the decade since hundreds of thousands of South Koreans, including Kim Young Sam, took to the streets in June 1987 and forced the government to hold open presidential elections. Korea's press is freer, labor has been unshackled, and local elections have given voters their first taste of grassroots politics. The change is most evident on a personal level. Passports were not generally available until 1989; now hundreds of thousands of Koreans travel abroad every year, with many of them heading to China, a country that was vilified a decade ago for its communism but is now embraced both as a potential market and as a cultural soulmate. A decade ago it was illegal to import wine; now Seoul's trendy cafés are filled with wine drinkers. Then, few Koreans could afford cars. The sporty little Kias driven by young women were such a startling change from the traditional boxy, black, chauffeur-driven car owned by an executive's company that they prompted much comment on the "my car" phenomenon. Now the highways are clogged on weekends with families out for a drive in their Hyundais, Daewoos, and Kias.

But much has not changed. Indeed, Korea clings to its authoritarian past in so many respects that it raises the question of whether or not the country of 45 million people is really on the road to democracy. Democracy is not simply the showy institutions of a political system where elected office is fiercely contested but genuine debate and dialogue are stifled. It is the ability to thrash out issues in public, to have decisions made in a transparent fashion, and to have coercion and corruption kept to a minimum. It is the ability to accept defeat in elections, and the grace to go into opposition. It is an understanding that power is not an all-or-nothing equation, but something that is shared and consensual. It is the self-discipline by those in power not to use their position to hound their opponents.

By these standards, Korea still has a long way to go. Railroading critically important national security and labor legislation through a secret pre-dawn National Assembly session, where the opposition was not present, is not democratic. But that is what happened on the morning of December 26, 1996, in a move that set off the most extensive round of protests since Kim Young Sam took office. Using the prosecutors and tax inspectors as political tools to punish enemies is not democratic. But the Kim Young Sam administration repeatedly has done just that.

More broadly, South Korea's continuing use of authoritarian power politics calls into question the popular notion in the West that economic development necessarily leads to Western-style political freedom and democracy. Power continues to flow down, from a presidential palace that allows little scrutiny of its activities and from a bureaucracy that believes its role is to command everyone from businessmen to farmers to students. Korea remains a divided country, not just between North and South, but between labor and business, between people of different regions, and between government and the people. Economically, the tasks are less grand, but nonetheless compelling. The pace of economic liberalization is picking up, thanks to promises Korea made in order to gain entry to the Organization for Economic Cooperation and Development (OECD) in late 1996. But it has far to go. Its troubled banks, burdened by bad loans, must be cleaned up while its chaebol must become more competitive. This is Korea's legacy, its unfinished business.

Kim Young Sam: Failed Reformer

When Kim Young Sam took office in February 1993, the first Korean president in more than thirty years without a military background, no one could doubt that he had pulled off a stunning coup in winning the presidency. Derided as an intellectual lightweight by many of Seoul's elite and reviled as a turncoat by his former colleagues in the opposition, cynics expected little in the way of substantial change from dissident-turned-ruling party leader Kim Young Sam. After all, most of the old guard of the Chun Doo Hwan and Roh Tae Woo years had, in the end, rallied around Kim, following the merger of his opposition party with the ruling party at the beginning of 1990. It seemed far more likely that they would co-opt him than that he would make any bold moves.

How wrong that skepticism initially seemed. Almost as soon as Kim took office, he required senior officials to disclose their assets. The disclosures incited a public outcry when it became apparent how much wealth had been amassed by politicians and bureaucrats and allowed Kim to engineer a broad purge of the tainted old guard. More than 3,000 officials stepped down or were forced out of their jobs, including three ministers, five vice-ministers, and the mayor of Seoul.

The most spectacular domestic political event of the Kim administration has been the convictions of former presidents Chun Doo Hwan and Roh Tae Woo on various charges ranging from corruption (together they accumulated more than $1 billion in ill-gotten assets) to sedition in connection with the December 1979 coup and the May 1980 Kwangju massacre. Chun originally received a death sentence, commuted to life imprisonment, while Roh's sentence was seventeen years in prison. Nearly three dozen other business, political, and military figures were also convicted in the highly charged 1996 trial. Among them were Daewoo founder Kim Woo Choong and the heads of the Dong Ah and Jinro business groups.

The casualties of Kim's campaign included Park Tae Joon, head of Posco Steel, erstwhile rival to Kim for president and controller of the fat ruling party campaign purse. After he had fled to Japan to avoid standing trial, Park suffered the ignominy of seeing his house in Seoul seized to pay fines for tax evasion.[2] Former finance minister Rhee Yong Man also moved to Japan to escape prosecution on corruption charges stemming from his conduct while in office. Other casualties included another former political rival, Roh's nephew and former prosecutor Park Chul On, who was convicted on charges stemming from his ties to gangsters.

The list of those purged went on. Former defense minister Lee Jong Koo was fined 180 million won and sentenced to three years in jail for corruption in military procurement. Roh's national security adviser fled to the United States to avoid questioning on similar grounds. The chief prosecutor and the chief justice of the Supreme Court were forced to step down. It was the most sweeping purge since Chun had taken power.

Koreans and outsiders alike applauded the changes. "The transition from hard-as-nails authoritarianism is just stunning," said Chalmers Johnson, a longtime East Asia watcher and the author of the seminal work *MITI and the Japanese Miracle.* "Korea is without doubt the most democratic country in Asia right now."[3]

In early August, less than six months after he took office, Kim Young Sam appeared on nationwide television to announce his boldest economic step: an emergency decree outlawing the use of aliases in financial transactions. For more than a decade, economic reformers had proposed just such a change. Time and again, influential interests in the ruling party had blocked the idea. That Kim Young Sam dared make such a move showed, according to his boosters, that he was truly intent on laying the groundwork for a new Korea. Certainly, investors took him seriously. The benchmark Korea composite stock price index fell 4.5 percent, its largest one-day drop in history, after the announcement.

It is tempting to applaud this reckoning, for it seemingly showed that no one was above the law. But did it really? It was so heavily tainted with partisan politics that Kim's crusade in many ways resembled nothing more than another Korean vendetta designed to place his cronies in power by using corruption charges to sweep out those of the old crowd who had fallen out of favor. Indeed, as the Kim administration went on, it looked more and more like those of his disgraced predecessors. Even the much-vaunted introduction of the real-name financial system remained open to abuse because of the continuing use of borrowed names, and its extension to real-estate transactions in 1994 was considerably less dramatic and less effective.

Even in the early days of the Kim Young Sam administration, at the height of the anticorruption crusade, bribery remained rife. The prosecutors, whose zeal in ferreting out corruption was lauded by the media, were themselves on the take. "The prosecutors have interesting ways of taking bribes," a lawyer working in Seoul said a year after Kim took office. "You play cards with them, except you're supposed to lose. Or you go to a restaurant where they say they already have run up a tab of two or three million won and you buy them a meal and clear the tab. They give a kickback to the restaurant owner, because the outstanding bill is usually false, you get a tax deduction for the business expense, and they keep the cash."

Sadly, as Kim's administration draws to a close, it is becoming clear just how far short of the mark he has fallen in wiping out corruption. Hanbo is only the most notorious case. In October 1996, Defense Minister Lee Yang Ho was fired from his job on corruption charges involving senior Daewoo executives. Lee was sentenced to four years in prison. In November the wife of a former health and welfare minister was arrested on charges that she accepted 160 million won in bribes from an optometrists' association, which was lobbying for a law that would give its members a monopoly on selling eyeglass frames. Senior officials at the Fair Trade Commission and the Securities Supervisory Board also were sacked for corruption.

The Kim administration's politically motivated trials show that Kim has yet to demonstrate a healthy respect for his opponents. He may have felt that he had little choice with Park Tae Joon and Park Chul On, both men with powerful political bases who could have come back to wound him. Yet the prolonged persecution of Chung Ju Yung and the Hyundai group smacked of an atavistic impulse for revenge.

The Securities Supervisory Board, a nominally independent body whose members know how to read political winds, refused to allow three Hyundai subsidiaries to go ahead with planned public stock offerings despite repeated requests during 1992 and 1993. The ostensible reason, reflecting the continuing micro-management of the financial sector, was that the stock market was too weak to absorb all the new shares. Giving the lie to the official explanation, the Korean Composite Index market nearly doubled between August 1992 and the end of 1993. Indeed, in November 1993, just a few days after Hyundai's latest request to list shares had been rejected, the Finance Ministry ordered financial institutions to sell their shares to slow down the market's rapid rise. The treatment of Hyundai was yet another reminder that Korea remains a country ruled by men, not laws.

The administration's impotence on the economic front adds to the sense that Kim Young Sam will be remembered as a disappointing transitional figure. Although he spent many years in opposition, Kim is very much a creature of the Korean system and lacks the intellectual firepower or political courage to make fundamental changes in the cumbersome, corrupt, and inefficient chaebol-dominated economy.

Korea has gone onto the wrong track. What worked when it was playing catch-up no longer makes sense. The unwillingness to embrace more drastic reforms will cost the country, which for nearly four decades has contentedly followed a modified version of the Japanese model. Japan's difficulties should have been a warning to policymakers and managers in Seoul, but Korea seems determined to repeat the mistakes of sticking with a statist, top–down economic model long after it has outlived its usefulness. The obsession with capital-intensive manufacturing of semiconductors, steel, and petrochemicals, for example, reflects an inability to move toward a higher value-added, more innovative economy. Korea will continue to grow, but it is choosing to be a low-margin economy characterized by lumbering, heavily indebted giants. Even when the economy booms, Korea suffers: Although exports soared in 1994–95, the trade deficit actually widened because of Korea's dependence on imported capital goods and components.

Korea's primitive finance system, long a way of channeling funds into favored industries, now is retarding growth. The country's banks, still under the government's thumb despite more than a decade of brave talk about reform, are staggering under the impact of bad loans that are estimated to total an extraordinary 12–25 percent of total assets.[4] Despite more than a decade of talking about financial reform, and even some meaningful change, the system remains woefully inadequate. South Korea is facing a make-or-break period in the financial sector, as it once again studies financial reform. If reforms are carried through, "Korea would probably emerge ... as the strongest, most dynamic economy in Asia," say analysts at Hong Kong's Political & Economic Risk Consultancy. Unfortunately, warns the group, "this is not a prospect people who have been working closely with Korea for years think is the most likely."[5] Korea's political and bureaucratic elite is simply unwilling to give up the power that comes with control. And, at heart, the people who run Korea simply don't trust free markets, especially financial ones.

Like Chun and Roh before him, Kim embraced a series of policy measures ostensibly designed to trim the chaebol. Even more threatening, from the point of view of the chaebol heads, he attacked the traditional way of doing business by putting chaebol executives on trial for corruption. Although prosecutors won a number of convictions, almost all the sentences were suspended. Whatever the embarrassment for Daewoo head Kim Woo Choong and others who were convicted, in a broader sense these trials proved to be much ado about very little: The chaebol continue to dominate the South Korean economy and the fundamental pattern of corruption remains deeply ingrained. With more than a decade of government policy having failed to check the chaebol, it is time to try something new. The most obvious choice would be to invite in foreign competition. But that prospect apparently strikes Koreans as even more unpalatable than continued chaebol dominance of an economy with deep structural problems.

A characteristic example of how Korea's bureaucracy frustrates what would be considered normal economic activity in most countries came when authorities detained a shipment of $250,000 worth of Snickers and Skittles candy bars at the port of Pusan in 1992. The imported candy lacked a quarantine certificate testifying that the sweets adhered to new "internal guidelines," although these products had been imported for several years with no problems. The guidelines were never made public.

The official who held up the shipment "said that if he informed us of the regulations, we would have evaded them," said Donald Gregg, who was U.S. ambassador to Korea at the time. Although the candy eventually was imported, the regulations remain secret. "You can never be too careful," says the official, who was promoted to director of the Health Ministry's international cooperation division following the incident.

Kim Young Sam was supposed to do away with this sort of behavior. Yet in June 1993, just four months after Kim took office, prosecutors arrested seven executives from Amway and Sunrider International. Sunrider's top executive in Korea was jailed for operating a multilevel, or pyramid, sales network, which special prosecutor Kwak Young Chul said could lead to "serious social disorder." Kwak complained that Sunrider and Amway, each of which operates in a similar fashion without legal problems throughout the world, were taking advantage of Korea's family networks and eroding the country's work ethic. The real problem seems to have been that the two foreign companies were encouraging consumption and shaking up traditional retailing methods.

Another example of how the Kim Young Sam administration relied on traditional forms of control: The president of any Korean company applying for special loans designed to help small businesses had to say what kind of car he drove "so the banks can assess whether he is managing his business prudently and not living beyond his means," said an administration official. "Our goal is a free market economy . . . but our first priority is to clean up the country. . . . In a country like Korea, you have to distinguish between the good people and the bad people."[6] Heavy pressure from U.S. trade representatives led to a 1995 agreement to open up the auto market to more foreign competition, but after the current account deficit widened in 1996 the atavistic reaction to clamp down on foreign imports reappeared. Police stepped up their ticketing of drivers of foreign cars on spurious charges and authorities resorted to the timeworn tactic of using anonymous leaks to the press to threaten retaliation against foreign car owners.

Senior officials claim to know that the quasi-military pattern of development, which was so effective in a compact, relatively homogeneous country playing catch-up, is not going to work as the economy becomes more complex and its companies are competing on something more than cheap labor. Kim Young Sam grandly proclaimed that he wanted to preside over a "five-year plan for the new economy," that, in his words, would make Korea "the best place in the world to do business." Key to the reforms were promises to deregulate, internationalize, and liberalize the Korean economy by cutting away at restrictions on everything from land ownership by foreigners to construction of factories. Although government officials mouth the slogans of change, in their hearts many of them still believe that the state knows best. As a government publication says: "In order for this deregulation policy to be successful, the behavior of officials should change toward one that is meant to help business, not hinder it."[7]

Despite the talk of globalization and liberalization, old habits die hard. In 1997 Korea stepped up the campaign to discourage consumer goods imports because of alarm over the record $23.7 billion current account deficit in 1996. Shipments of Guinness beer were held up at the docks. Authorities designed more cumbersome labeling regulations for clothes and food along with the old standby—the threat of tax investigations—to deter spending on imports and expensive foreign travel, despite the fact that so-called luxury imports—which include golf clubs, automobiles, and home appliances—totaled only about $2 billion, or 8.8 percent of imports.[8] That these sorts of juvenile tactics occur in one of the world's largest economies reflects opaque regulations and a xenophobic mentality among large sections of both the government and the country as a whole.

These parochial, mercantilist attitudes ensure that foreign involvement in the economy remains minimal. Inward investment as a percentage of the economy, to take one measure, was only half the level of that of the United States in 1993.[9] This unwillingness to create the conditions for a more open economy reflects a sense among many Koreans that economics—and trade—is a zero-sum game and that more competitive practices or technology brought by foreigners will do nothing but drain the country of its wealth and take profits that should be Korea's to enjoy. Although Korean officials periodically court foreign investors, the underlying hostility to foreign involvement in the economy remains strong. A policy of encouraging foreign involvement (not just investment) in the economy would not be a matter of simply changing a few regulations but of reorienting overall economic policy from the highest levels down to the lowest ranks of the bureaucracy. The stiff resistance to even modest reforms of the financial system, especially by the Finance Ministry, is a continuing reminder of how difficult this task would be even for the most determined administration.

Ironically, Korea's problems may force it to act more boldly. Even more than most people, Koreans are best at acting when they face a crisis. The tottering of the giant chaebol, the gaping current-account deficit, the parlous condition of the banks, and the evident exhaustion of a state-led system of growth may force a more radical restructuring. The last major crisis Korea endured was nearly two decades ago, in the tumultuous months following the assassination of Park Chung Hee as the economy sagged under the weight of spending on the heavy-industry program and the second oil price hike. That was also the last period of serious economic reform.

Hard though it will be to enact sweeping economic change, it will be more difficult still to sink deep-rooted changes in Korea's harsh political climate. The manner in which the labor law was rammed through the legislature reflects a belief that power matters far more than process, a distrust of the cut-and-thrust of democracy as the country struggles to reach a national consensus. It is understandable why the administration wanted an overhaul of the labor laws. The country has had ten years of annual wage hikes averaging 15 percent, well above increases in productivity. As Korea prices itself out of markets, the country's giant business groups want the freedom to lay off workers and to use employees more efficiently. Fair enough. Workers—and the OECD—in return wanted to do away with the monopoly on worker representation that a government-sanctioned trade union enjoyed and fewer restrictions on organizing. Indeed, that is what the OECD thought Korea had agreed to when it agreed to admit Seoul in late 1996. But the new labor law railroaded through in December 1996 delayed an easing of restrictions on organizing until 2000, hardly the sign of a good faith effort by the government. When Kim Young Sam's team could not reach a consensus, it resorted to the legislative equivalent of force. The opposition thought that it had no choice but to take to the streets. So much for a new spirit of democracy.

The Challenge of Change

The devastation of war and the desperate attempt to escape from poverty were powerful goads to growth. The threat of chaos, even though it was often exploited by linking it to "Confucian" ideals of harmony, was credible only because of the historical agonies that still burn in the memory of any Korean born before 1950. Yet this top–down, militarized development model does not fit South Korea's high-valued-added, high-technology ambitions for the 1990s and beyond.

South Korea is no longer a cheap-labor country run by an authoritarian president whose primary goal is playing economic catch-up. Its years of massive export expansion are finished, a victim of rising wage costs and increased protectionism. The heroic days of building huge shipyards and steelmills are past, and the era of naked authoritarianism is over. Yet it was, of course, under just such a forced-march campaign to build up heavy industry that Korea turned in such stunning growth. The task of the late 1990s and beyond will be to come to grips with these changes. So far, the result has been uninspiring.

The past thirty years have been good to South Korea, whose businessmen eagerly seized the opportunities presented by increases in world trade volume. But the 1990s are a decade in which overcapacity is rampant (especially in the mass-market products in which Korea has traditionally excelled), technological change is accelerating, and competing multinational firms have radically reshaped themselves to become more competitive. Contrast the upheaval at General Electric and IBM with the stasis in the ranks of the Korean chaebol and it is clear why the chaebol are falling further behind. While American firms have flattened management levels and pushed responsibilities and decision-making down their lean white-collar ranks, Korea's chaebol salarymen remain, like their Japanese counterparts, overstaffed and underemployed.

The focus merely on top-line growth, with little regard for profits, is a strategy that is not working in the low-inflation, low-growth environment of the 1990s. Those of South Korea's chaebol that do not radically reorient themselves are courting trouble. Even if the government guarantee against bankruptcy continues, and there is no certainty of this, the lumbering chaebols risk irrelevance in an increasingly competitive world economy. There may be a future in providing mediocre goods at mediocre prices, but it is not the one that Koreans say they want.

Although its chaebol have staked out leading positions in some key sectors, these are primarily mass-market commodity products where the Koreans have little pricing power. Their corporate structure, despite some attempts at managerial reforms in recent years, does not have the nimbleness of either its U.S. or its Taiwanese competitors. Worse, Korea finds itself in this developmental cul-de-sac at a time when it has nothing like the capital or technology base of its Japanese neighbor. Its companies are smaller and more vulnerable than their Japanese competitors; the country as a whole is still a net debtor and, unlike Japan or even Taiwan, it has not run up large trade and current account surpluses. Japan and Taiwan have some of the world's largest foreign reserves. South Korea's reserves barely meet international minimum comfort levels. For all its success, Korea's economy remains very fragile.

The signs are clear that Korea is facing an economic reckoning. Its glory days are past. The question is whether it settles down to a steady jog, with the economy growing on the order of 5–6 percent annually for another decade or more, or it essentially stalls out, as the Japanese economy has done. The first alternative would ensure it a growth rate that would be double the expected OECD average but is almost certain to mean a painful restructuring of the economy. To anyone familiar with the extraordinary energy of the Koreans, it is the most likely alternative, but a wholesale reorientation of the economy to focus more on productivity and profitability is not likely to happen until Korea gets closer to the brink of a major financial crisis than it is to date.

Economic growth in 1992 and 1993 was the lowest in more than a decade, with annual growth rates of 5.0 and 5.8 percent, respectively. Part of this was a healthy cyclical slowdown after the rapid growth years of the late 1980s, but it reflected broader changes as well. Korea is having trouble clawing its way into the ranks of more developed nations with sophisticated products, yet it is no longer a cheap manufacturing site. It already has large shares of world markets in its main products, so simply revving up production to grab more market share is not an option. Growth picked up quite strongly in 1994 and 1995, reflecting strong semiconductor demand and, above all, the strength of the Japanese yen, which allowed Korean companies more pricing freedom on the many products in which they compete directly—such as ships, steel, semiconductors, petrochemicals, and automobiles. But it was a false boom.

As the yen weakened against the dollar, going from a high of 80 yen to the dollar after its April 1995 peak to 115 yen to the dollar by mid-1997, Korean exporters were hammered. Indeed, the dismal economic performance in 1996 laid bare the structural problems that plague the economy. Earnings at listed affiliates of the thirty largest chaebol dropped a staggering 90 percent. Plunging prices for DRAM semiconductors trashed earnings at Samsung, Hyundai, and the LG group (the erstwhile Lucky-Goldstar). In 1995 semiconductors accounted for nearly one-fifth of Korea's entire exports. Almost all of the Samsung group's earnings had come from DRAM chips, and senior management had counted on chip profits to fund its ambitious plans to start making automobiles. One senior official said privately in mid-1995 that the company was willing to lose $1 billion annually for ten years in automobiles—and that it would be financed by earnings from semiconductors. Samsung soldiered on with its embryonic auto venture, which it says will begin shipping cars in 1998, despite seeing profits at flagship Samsung Electronics fall more than 90 percent in 1996.

The yen appreciation laid bare Korea's chronic structural problems—its obsession with top-line growth, its inability to make the transition to more niche-oriented products, its overreliance on debt, much of it extended on the basis of connections rather than credit analysis—in early 1997. Despite their problems, steel, semiconductors, and other capital-intensive industries are Korea's best hope for continued growth because its labor-intensive producers already have been pummeled by lower-cost manufacturers in China, Vietnam, and Indonesia. Pusan's shoe industry, once the world's largest thanks to huge orders from companies like Nike and Reebok, largely closed up shop in the early 1990s. The Kukje shoemaking factory in Pusan, which at its height in the mid-1980s employed 20,000 people and was the largest in the world, went bankrupt in 1993. The site was turned into an apartment building, a fitting symbol for the new Korea.[10]

The failure of Korea's producers of higher-value-added goods to hold on to the gains they made during the 1980s calls into question just how sustainable Korea's growth remains. All the major business groups built large personal computer factories, but none could sustain international success. Instead, their competitors in Taiwan came to dominate personal computer production by the early 1990s, and the Koreans effectively dropped out of the international market. Korean-manufactured personal computers' share of the U.S. market dropped from 11.8 percent in 1990 to 6.8 percent in 1992. Taiwanese computer makers had quicker design and production times and could sell their wares for less: A typical Korean notebook computer cost 28 percent more than a comparable Taiwan-made model. Samsung's expensive and ineffectual purchase of AST, a former high-flier that fell on hard times in the mid-1990s, pointed up the difficulty that Korean companies have in adapting to the fast-moving pace of the personal computer marketplace. For all their resources, the chaebol, much like their Japanese counterparts, are unable to react to changing market conditions swiftly and decisively.

In consumer electronics, the picture has been every bit as dismal. Although Korea is the world's largest producer of home appliances after Japan, Korean companies have been unable to break out of a crude me-too pattern of imitation that faltered as labor costs rose. Wages in the sector jumped 143 percent from 1985 to 1990, while they increased only 18 percent in Japan during the same period. Not surprisingly, market shares dropped. The Korean share of the U.S. color television market fell from 6.8 percent in 1990 to 4.5 percent in 1992.

In only one important product area, DRAM semiconductors, is Korea likely to seize the lead from the Japanese. Korea's global market share for these key semiconductors increased from 14 percent in 1990 to 24.3 percent in 1992. By 1996, the Koreans had about one-third of the world market. Samsung Electronics led the global DRAM market with a 17 percent market share and the $21 billion company was ranked by U.S. market researcher Dataquest as the world's seventh-largest semiconductor producer. Not coincidentally, DRAMs are a product where the design rules are extremely clear and little market agility is required. The business plays to Korea's strengths, requiring as it does large, continuing capital investments and a willingness to cut prices to win market share.[11]

Set against this pessimistic reading are the obvious signs that South Korea's chaebol are maturing through their increasingly large international investments. Hyundai Electronics broke ground in March 1997 on the first phase of a planned $3.9 billion semiconductor plant in Scotland, Europe's largest single inward investment. That followed by just a few months LG Semicon's groundbreaking ceremony at a similar-sized plant in Wales. "Make no mistake, these guys mean business," says Dataquest semiconductor analyst Richard Gordon. "To vendors heavily reliant on DRAM, 1996 was a disaster, yet both Hyundai and LG Semicon have pressed ahead with major DRAM investment plans without hesitation." Hyundai and Samsung are each building major chip plants in the United States. Daewoo beat out its estranged partner General Motors to take over a Polish auto plant. The Koreans inside of a decade have become major foreign investors, and this will impose discipline of a sort that they did not face at home.

South Koreans are extremely ambivalent about the role of the chaebol. They rightly fear the economic concentration that comes with ceding control of the economy to a few score business groups, but they are not certain how to restructure the chaebol without damaging the underlying economy. If Korean policymakers are serious about solving the problem of the chaebol's dominance in the economy, they should liberalize the market, particularly to foreign competitors. More foreign competitors—and easier access to capital for both foreign and domestic firms—would force the chaebol to concentrate on what they do best. But there is no sense of urgency to reform. When the economy turns down, Koreans are more eager than ever that the chaebol prosper.

There are signs that some of the chaebol are starting to take these competitive imperatives more seriously. But even Samsung, without doubt one of the most professionally managed groups in the country, has been seduced by the Korean penchant for bigness, as witnessed by its multibillion-dollar investment in a money-losing petrochemical complex and its announced intention to start making passenger cars.

Sadly, South Korea's leaders have not been able to build a culture of trust, a sense of shared purpose. Park Chung Hee and Chun Doo Hwan tried to impose it from above, but it didn't stick. Unlike the Japanese, among whom the sense of the common good is much more deeply ingrained, Koreans too often have a greediness, a sense of atomistic individualism that makes common cause only with others with whom one has an existing connection, such as the family, schoolmates, or coworkers. The consequences of this are seen in the singular tendency of Koreans literally to bump into strangers on the street. Tragically, it was evident in the spirit of the contractors who built the Sampoong Department store in the upscale Kangnam district of Seoul, which collapsed in June 1995 killing more than 650 people. Shoddy construction and corruption caused the disaster. It was not an isolated incident: Less than a year earlier the rush-hour collapse of a bridge in Seoul killed thirty-four people in an accident with similar roots. These are not unique disasters but the manifestation of symptomatic problems.

Korean Reunification: Dream or Nightmare?

To end with the beginning: the division of Korea and its eventual reunification. North Korea provided the rationale for South Korea's militarized, forced-march development, the enemy without which South Korea as we know it would not have developed. South Korea produced one of the world's most impressive rates of economic growth because Park Chung Hee and his coterie of businessmen, bureaucrats, and generals were goaded by North Korea. North Korea provided the deadly threat needed to justify the forced-march growth program and repressive political policies. Park and, later, Chun wanted to be strong enough to defend against the North, and they sought economic prosperity as a way of proving the legitimacy of their often harsh rule. Indeed, it was the fear that they might have to go it alone that prompted Park and his men into the fateful embrace of heavy industries in the early 1970s, a step that continues to color Korea today.

Ironically, now that the North is tottering, South Korea has no clear policy. Its leadership is torn between an atavistic wish to see the North prostrate and the fear the Pyongyang regime's collapse will mean a huge bill for reunification, much of it footed by South Korea. The South passionately fears yet desires the North's collapse. This schizophrenic policy is making it even more difficult to think clearly about Pyongyang in its dying days.

Certainly, it is time for the South to think more coherently about what will be done as the North disintegrates. Paramount leader Kim Il Sung's sudden death in July 1994, one of the most significant events in the half-century following the division of the Korean peninsula, removed the buttress of revolutionary leadership and legitimacy underpinning the government's survival despite deepening economic trouble. Since then, the economic situation has continued to deteriorate while second-generation leader Kim Jong Il has yet to demonstrate that he wields the shrewdness and authority to guide the country through its worst crisis since the Korean War.

Events in the first few months of 1997 point to a North Korean government in a state of unprecedented turmoil. The defection to South Korea in January of Hwang Chang Yop, one of the twenty-five most senior officials in the North Korean leadership, marked an extraordinary turn of events. Hwang's defection, which took place at South Korea's embassy to China in Beijing, preceded a series of tremors in the secretive North. Defense Minister Choe Hwang died, and Prime Minister Kang Song San was replaced. A younger generation is stepping to the fore, but it shows no signs of being more outward-looking. Despite talk of economic opening and attempts to develop a special economic zone in the remote northeastern part of the country, it is clear that the North's leadership refuses to make the hard choice between economic opening and continuing isolation. That's no surprise: Either choice could mean the death of the regime.

It might be tempting to dismiss the internecine power struggles, were it not for a worsening economic situation that led the North to make a series of unprecedented moves in efforts to obtain food. The North's economy has contracted by about one-third since 1990. Its erstwhile socialist allies have embraced the market and have stopped barter trade. Although China continues to provide substantial food aid to North Korea, Russia no longer provides oil on a barter basis. North Korea's heavy industrial base has all but closed up shop because of the chronic energy shortage.

Food shortages have led to widespread hunger. State-run media have trumpeted the virtues of foraging for edible bark and roots among an increasingly hungry population. Two years of disastrous grain harvests in 1995 and 1996, totaling only about 3.5 million metric tons each year, provided only about half what the nation needs. Rations in Pyongyang, whose residents are the nation's best-fed, declined from 700 grams a day in autumn 1995 to 500 grams a day in February 1996. The situation is far grimmer in North Korea's depleted countryside. A survey by the United Nation's World Food Program in July 1996 found that in rural areas the daily food ration for adults was only 190 grams of grain a day. That's less than the international minimum for human survival, which is 300 grams, providing about 1,000 calories. Worse, only employed adults received this ration. Schoolchildren received a reduced ration and the unemployed, such as the elderly, received no ration.[12]

Reports suggest that the situation has deteriorated since then. "I was stunned by what I saw ... and by how much worse conditions have gotten since I was there last August," U.S. Congressman Tony Hall, a Democrat from Ohio, said after a four-day trip to the North in April 1997. Said Hall, "Evidence of slow starvation on a massive scale was plain." Hall witnessed families eating grass, bark, and weeds and children whose growth was stunted by hunger and disease. In what was certainly not a coincidence, the same day that Hall met the press in Tokyo after his trip, North Korea said for the first time that some children had died of malnutrition and that about 15 percent of all children were suffering from malnutrition-related problems. The previous day, word leaked out that U.S. grain giant Cargill had reached agreement to send about 20,000 tons of grain to North Korea in exchange for 4,000 tons of zinc in the first direct shipment of U.S. grain to North Korea since the Korean War.

Although there is little doubt that the North faces unprecedented trouble, North Koreans are tough, and the implosion of the economy has as yet prompted no documented political rumblings from below. The graphic evidence provided of the North's problems is a stunning turnaround for a country that has long trumpeted its achievements. But it does not represent a decision to open to the outside world. Instead, it is a last-ditch attempt to preserve the power of the country's totalitarian rulers. North Korea may continue to stagger from one shipment of food relief to the next for some years to come. Pyongyang's residents are the elite of a country that is ruled by a communist-Confucian doctrine that is uniquely well-suited to maintaining power. They have much to lose from an upheaval. The country's peasants are weak and isolated, like grains of rice scattered across the hillsides. In their hunger and misery they are more likely to flee northward across the border to China, as they have been doing in increasing numbers, than to foment an uprising in the capital.

So it is hard to imagine the spark that would ignite a popular uprising. Already, the Pyongyang regime has weathered its troubles with far more resilience than almost anyone predicted. Before Kim Il Sung died, it was popular to say, as one senior U.S. official put it, that Kim Jong Il would last "somewhere between two months and two years." It is possible that the North can continue to limp along for some years to come, relying on handouts of rice and oil from the international community. The resilience of the country, given its ruthless security forces and its internally compelling ideology, should not be dismissed lightly. The ability of Iraq and Cuba to weather international isolation and continuing economic difficulties illustrates how long even weak countries can last. But it will not survive in its present form indefinitely. Despite all the headaches that North Korea causes, neither the United States, Japan, China, nor Russia seem interested in pushing for change. China is happy with a friendly state on its border that provides a buffer against the U.S. troops in South Korea, and it worries that North Korea's collapse could unleash a flood of refugees streaming into its ethnic Korean enclaves. Japan, too, worries that North Korean refugees would pose a big threat to it, with officials warning about a flotilla of boat people and perhaps even pro-communist sympathizers washing ashore.

Yet with the North looking wobbly, the South is increasingly jittery. South Korea has gone from a euphoric anticipation of union in the wake of Germany's reunification to a sober and often sour assessment of how much unification will cost and the disruption that it will mean for the South. Although the most likely assumption is that North Korea will either collapse or undergo a major upheaval in the near future, planners do not seem ready to think about the big decisions necessary in the event of rapid change.

It probably matters less than most people think whether the North goes with a bang or a whimper, lashes out in a desperate death rattle, opens up to investment and assistance from abroad, or simply collapses as a result of worsening food shortages and internal power struggles. What counts in terms of a reconciled Korea's future prosperity is how South Korea, the United States, and South Korea's neighbors—China, Japan and Russia—deal with the aftermath. There's no question that the Korean peninsula could become one of the globe's hottest trouble spots, if things go badly. Handled properly, though, unification or confederation may prove far less painful than most people imagine.

The pessimists' case is simple and superficially compelling. The two Koreas are much farther apart than the two Germanys were, in everything from per-capita income to simple human contact. There is in Korea no Berlin, a city where both sides could have some contact. North Korea has remained far more hermetically sealed than Germany—and for far longer. The Berlin Wall stood for only twenty-eight years, while the Korean peninsula already has been divided nearly twice that long. There have been only a few family reunions, and travel remains virtually impossible. In thinking, in food, even in everyday speech, the North and South are far apart.

The two sides are locked in an embrace of mutual hostility that provides both their governments with a good measure of legitimacy. The North has never renounced armed force against the South, and its bombastic propaganda regularly invokes the possibility of conflict. The most notable of the North's recent verbal bombshells came in March 1994, when a North Korean negotiator walked away from talks aimed at defusing the North's nuclear program with the threat that "if a war breaks out, Seoul will be turned into a sea of fire." In March 1997 the Committee for the Peaceful Reunification of the Fatherland lashed out at a report in a South Korean newspaper that Kim Il Sung had died of a heart attack after a furious row with Kim Jong Il, as "a declaration of war."

This is not just hollow rhetoric or a holdover from the bombing of the Korean Air Line jet in 1987 or the 1984 Rangoon bombing, which killed seventeen South Korean officials. In September 1996 a North Korean commando submarine ran aground near Kangnung, on South Korea's northeastern coast. Eleven crew members were murdered, apparently by the ship's commandos. Thirteen North Koreans were killed by South Korean troops, one was captured alive and one escaped. Fourteen South Koreans, mostly soldiers, were killed either by the infiltrators or accidentally by South Korean forces. In February 1997, shortly after Hwang Chang Yop took refuge in South Korea's Beijing embassy, two assassins believed to be North Korean hitmen gunned down a prominent defector in the southern outskirts of Seoul.

In turn, South Korea's structure of power, with its insistence on obedience and deference to those in a position of authority, is heightened by continuing tensions with North Korea. The two countries are still technically at war, although active hostilities ceased in 1953. Although South Korea has plainly won the contest, the security establishment in the South routinely cracks down on anyone who tries to overstep the current government line. Prosecutors asked for a lengthy jail sentence for a novelist who went to the North in 1996 (as they have for other visitors to the North), they have accused labor protesters of being influenced by the North, and they have threatened to arrest anyone who accesses Pyongyang's Web page on the Internet. This use of the supposed North Korean threat at a time when, in broad political terms, the North is more an irritant than a threat is a transparent way of trying to keep political control.

If Germany has had such a hard time with unification, and Korea is so much more divided, it is easy to see why conventional wisdom has it that a national trauma is in the making. But if the two Koreas can squarely face the greater distance between them—and that is the crucial if—there's a lot that can go very well. First, they must forget about quick integration. They should think instead of working toward a "one country, two systems" arrangement. That is likely to require some quick action, probably in the midst of a splintering by North Korea. It presupposes some sort of reform-oriented administration in the North—possibly under the tutelage of the South. As soon as any crisis develops, officials throughout Northeast Asia, working with Washington, will have to prevent a refugee exodus from starting. That will require both the stick of continuing immigration controls and the carrot of quick economic development, one that quickly raises living standards.

For some time to come, the border would not be open, and travel between North and South would remain restricted. North Korea would be set up as one special economic zone offering generous tax and other incentives to investors. Investments, both from multinationals and the chaebol, would jump-start the economy. Japanese money would be pivotal. The North's industrial and infrastructure base would be completely rebuilt, as if it were after a war. Which, in a sense, it would be. The South would channel some of its prodigious defense spending to help develop the North, much of which could go toward employing the hundreds of thousands of demobilized North Korean soldiers on infrastructure projects.

Given the shortage of disciplined, skilled, low-cost workers in Asia, an economically open northern Korea would almost certainly draw substantial sums of capital. The chaebol, which are investing heavily abroad, would channel more investments to the North in everything from sweaters to sneakers to stereos. Consumer goods companies like Coca-Cola and Nestlé, which already have been sniffing for opportunities, would help build up a light manufacturing base. Multilateral lending agencies, such as the World Bank and the Asian Development Bank, would chip in along with private sector infrastructure funds to build modern roads, ports, apartment buildings, and railway lines. North Korea has only about one-sixtieth the population of China, for which it is taken for granted that reform and economic development will continue apace. North Korea's average educational level is higher; it has none of the ethnic or religious divisions that could fracture China; and its government exercises far more effective control. By comparison with most of the world, economic reform and development in northern Korea could be relatively easy. South Korea will almost certainly avoid Germany's three major mistakes: immediate currency unification, an immediate opening of the border, and a promise to raise East German living standards to the level of the West's within a short period of time. Lower social spending in South Korea also means that Korea's government will have fewer calls for heavy welfare spending than Germany faced.

Economic development does not even depend on a change in government. Unlikely though that now seems, it could happen with a more open North Korean leadership—in other words, a North Korean Park Chung Hee—that won the trust of Seoul and Washington. Given the resistance to change by North Korea's leadership, the very clear sense that economic reformers are only marginal players in the North, and the bitter distrust between the two Koreas, it is unlikely that this rosy scenario will play itself out under Kim Jong Il's leadership. Still, the continued quiet progress of a 1994 deal under which North Korea halted its purported nuclear weapons program in exchange for international assistance is a ray of hope. The Korea Energy Development Organization, a multilateral body with a U.S. head, broke ground on a $5 billion nuclear power complex in August 1997, financed mostly with South Korean and Japanese money. South Korea is supplying most of the project's engineers and technicians, and the endeavor has opened direct telephone and postal links between the two Koreas for the first time since 1950.

Whether they come with a bang or a whimper, radical changes are on the way in North Korea. Responding to them will require leadership and clarity of a sort seldom seen in Seoul. Among other issues, Korea will have to sort out how those in the North are dealt with. Should they be tried as criminals? Given amnesty in exchange for telling the truth? From Eastern Europe to Latin America to South Africa, there are numerous precedents for what Korea is likely to endure. Different as all these cases are, they all suggest that reconciliation and integration will be painful and drawn out.

Washington, too, will play a key role. The North craves legitimacy from Washington and shows signs of wanting to counterbalance China's weight in the region. Washington can play a role brokering peace between the two Koreas, although this will inevitably lead to friction with Seoul, which will resent not taking the lead in relations with Pyongyang. Washington also will have to assure

China that, even in the event of a reunified Korea, it does not intend to use the peninsula to threaten China. That will probably require, at a minimum, no deployment of U.S. troops in what is now North Korea. A peaceful transition is not likely. But it is not impossible.

Much of this work is about the problems that Korea faces. It is designed to explode whatever remains of the myth that consensus and harmony underlay the success of this often-troubled East Asian tiger. But give Korea its due. Per-capita income in 1996 was about $11,500, putting the country squarely in the ranks of the well-off. If there is any doubt that the country has done extraordinarily well, think back to 1961, the year Park Chung Hee seized power, when Koreans were poorer than Indians. In 1996, the economy's gross national product topped $500 billion, the eleventh-largest in the world and not far behind China, a country that has twenty-five times its population.

The years following Park's assassination have been tumultuous and volatile. Hopes of democracy after Park's death were dashed by a 1980 military coup that stunted political development for most of the decade. Yet Chun's militarized administration left office eight years later in the first lasting peaceful transfer of power in modern Korean history; whereas the early 1980s saw purges of journalists and unionists, less than a decade later Korea had the freest press and most militant labor movement in its history. During this time, South Korea continued its record of astonishing economic growth and emerged from the pack of developing nations to become an OECD member and one of the fastest-growing of the middling rich countries.

For all their weaknesses, the country's chaebol are global giants on a scale unmatched by their peers in any other country that has developed in the past half-century. Most of the population has gone from grinding poverty to middle-class affluence. And the Koreans are driven to perform. Their feisty, contentious character combined with an unusual ability to work within a structured, hierarchical system makes it likely that the country will continue to show a growth rate that is above the OECD average, even if it is substantially below the growth of the past thirty-five years. The feeling of insecurity that Koreans in the North and South share, of being sandwiched between China and Japan, acts as a sharp spur. No matter how well they do, Koreans will always feel uneasy. Using economic growth and measures of prosperity as a yardstick, whether it is average height or the "piano supply ratio," remains a favorite Korean pastime. Although the post–Korean War generation is far more cynical about the top–down appeals to work hard and consume less, there is no sign that South Koreans' obsession with growth or willingness to work extraordinarily hard is fundamentally slackening. The savings rate remains high, which will help provide funding for the country's capital-hungry businesses.

Koreans have shown time and again their ability to overcome adversity. More than most people, they excel when faced with a serious challenge. As one of the world's oldest nations, Korea has survived in the face of continuing threats. At the time of its colonization by the Japanese in 1910 it had survived as an independent nation virtually without interruption for over twelve hundred years. Yet its sense of identity is based on the notion that it is a tiny country under siege. Reunification of the two Koreas, and the rebuilding and reconciliation that must accompany it, could develop a more positive sense of the country and banish many of the divisions that now run through South Korea. That is an optimistic assessment, but not an altogether improbable one.

The task of economic and political reconstruction is more subtle than Koreans, with their focus on size and power, grasp. Korea must accept the challenge of change so that it does not fall victim to the weight of the past and become increasingly irrelevant in the world's fast-growing region. Korea has had one of the fastest economic starts in history. But the race for development is a marathon, not a sprint, and Korea will have to adjust its stride now that it has drawn nearer to the leaders of the pack.

Notes

1. Korea Newspaper Editors' Association; cited in the *Korea Herald,* April 18, 1992.
2. What goes around often comes around in Korea. As Kim Young Sam's fortunes plummeted in early 1997, Park Tae Joon restarted his political career with the announcement that he would run for a National Assembly seat.
3. *Business Week,* April 26, 1993.
4. Thomas F. Cargill, "Implications for Korea of Japan's Financial Problems," in *Korea's Economy 1997* (Washington, D.C.: Korea Economic Institute of America, 1997), p. 33.
5. Political & Economic Risk Consultancy, Hong Kong, December 11, 1996.
6. These examples come from Steve Glain, "Korea's Elite Bureaucrats May Be Stifling Economy." *Asian Wall Street Journal,* August 11, 1993.
7. Ministry of Trade, Industry, and Energy, *Korea's "New Economy": Internationalization & Deregulation* (Seoul: Ministry of Trade, Industry, and Energy, 1993).
8. *Asian Wall Street Journal,* "As Growth Slows, Korea Scapegoats Foreign Firms," March 10, 1997; and *Financial Times,* "Guinness Import Bar Puts Seoul Revelles in a Paddy," and " 'Unpatriotic' Buyers Lie Low," March 10, 1997.
9. Young Sae Lee, "The Globalization of Korea: Prospects, Problems and Policy," in *Korea's Economy 1997* (Washington, D.C.: Korea Economic Institute of America, 1997), p. 37.
10. Daewoo's huge textile mill in Pusan, also once the world's largest, cut employment from 5,650 in 1988 to 3,900 in late 1993. By late 1993 the company sourced 45 percent of its production outside Korea, largely from Bangladesh, Burma, and Sudan. And the proportion is expected to keep rising.
11. Samsung Electronics data are from a February 1997 company release. The earlier data are reported in "Korea Falls Behind in World Economic Pace: KDB Report," *Korea Economic Weekly,* December 13, 1993. The source is a Korea Development Bank study entitled "Korea's Industries."
12. This data are drawn from C. Kenneth Quinones, "Food and Political Stability in North Korea," in *Korea's Economy 1997* (Washington, D.C.: Korea Economic Institute of America, 1997).

Bibliography

American Chamber of Commerce. "Doorknock 1991." Seoul: unpublished photocopy, 1991.

Amsden, Alice H. *Asia's Next Giant*. New York and Oxford: Oxford University Press, 1989.

———. "A Specter is Haunting South Korea—The Specter of Anglo-Saxonization." Lee-Jay Cho and Kim Yoon Hyung, eds., *Korea's Political Economy: Past, Present, and Future*.

Amnesty International. *South Korea: Violations of Human Rights*. London: Amnesty International Publications, 1986.

Asia Society. *Korea Briefing: Toward Reunification*. Armonk, NY: M.E. Sharpe, 1997.

Asia Watch. *Human Rights in Korea*. New York and Washington: Asia Watch Committee, 1986.

———. *A Stern, Steady Crackdown*. New York and Washington: Asia Watch Committee, 1987.

Asian Coalition for Housing Rights. *Battle for Housing Rights in Korea*. Bangkok: author, 1989.

Balassa, Bela, and Williamson, John. *Adjusting to Success: Balance of Payments Policy in the East Asian NICs*. Washington, DC: Institute for International Economics, 1987.

Ban Sung-hwan, Moon Pal-yong, and Perkins, Dwight H. *Rural Development*. Cambridge: Harvard University Press, 1980.

Bank of Korea. *Monthly Statistical Bulletin*. Seoul: author, various years.

———. *Economic Statistics Yearbook*. Seoul: author, various years.

Bank of Korea Research Department, Division 2. *Comparison of the Economic Power of Korea With Japan in the Years in Which the Olympic Games Were Held*. Seoul: author (photocopy), 1988.

Bello, Walden, and Rosenfeld, Stephanie. *Dragons in Distress: Asia's Miracle Economies in Crisis*. San Francisco: Institute for Food and Development Policy, 1990.

Boettcher, Robert, with Freedman, Gordon L. *Gifts of Deceit*. New York: Holt, Rinehart and Winston, 1980.

Bognanno, Mario F. *Korea's Industrial Relations at the Turning Point*. Seoul: Korea Development Institute, Working Paper No. 8816, 1988.

Bunge, Frederica M. *South Korea, A Country Study*. Washington, DC: U.S. Government Printing Office, 1982.

Chang Dal-joong. *Economic Control and Political Authoritarianism*. Seoul: Sogang University Press, 1985.

Cheon Kum Sung. *Chun Doo Hwan, Man of Destiny*. Translated by W. Y. Joh. Los Angeles: North American Press, 1982.

Cho, Lee-Jay, and Kim, Yoon Hyung (eds.). *Economic Development in the Republic of Korea*. Honolulu: East-West Center, 1991.

———. *Korea's Political Economy: An Institutional Perspective*. Boulder, CO: Westview Press, 1994.

Choi Jang Jip. *Labor and the Authoritarian State: Labor Unions in South Korean Manufacturing Industries, 1961–80*. Seoul: Korea University Press, 1989.

Christian Institute for the Study of Justice and Development. *Lost Victory*. Seoul: Minjungsa/Christian Institute for the Study of Justice and Development, 1988.

Clark, Donald (ed.) *The Kwangju Uprising*. Boulder, CO., and London: Westview Press, 1988.

Cole, David C., and Lyman, Princeton N. *Korean Development, The Interplay of Politics and Economics*. Cambridge: Harvard University Press, 1971.

Cole, David C., and Park Yung-chul. *Financial Development in Korea 1945–1978*. Cambridge: Harvard University Press, 1983.

Cotton, James, and Neary, Ian (eds.). *The Korean War in History*. Atlantic Highlands, NJ: Humanities Press International, 1989.

Cumings, Bruce. *Korea's Place in the Sun* . New York, NY: W.W. Norton, 1997.

Daewoo Corporation. Preliminary Offering Circular. October 1993. Barclays de Zoete Wedd Limited; Ssangyong Securities Europe Limited; Daewoo Securities (Europe) Limited.

Deyo, Frederic C. (ed.). *The Political Economy of the New Asian Industrialism*. Ithaca, N.Y. and London: Cornell University Press, 1987.

Eckert, Carter. *Offspring of Empire: The Koch'ang Kims and the Colonial Origins of Korean Capitalism, 1876–1945*. Seattle and London: University of Washington Press, 1991.

Eckert, Carter J., et al. *Korea Old and New: A History*. Seoul: Ilchokak Publishers for the Korea Institute, Harvard University, 1990.

Economic Planning Board (Republic of Korea). *Major Statistics of the Korean Economy*. Seoul: author, various years.

———. *The Economy in 1972*. Seoul: author, 1973.

Gold, Brian R. "The Entry of Hyundai Motor into North America," Master's thesis, Harvard University, 1989.

Grajdanzev, Andrew J. *Modern Korea*. New York: John Day, 1944.

Halliday, Jon, and Cumings, Bruce. *Korea: the Unknown War*. New York: Pantheon, 1988.

Hart-Landsberg, Martin. *The Rush to Development: Economic Change and Political Struggle in South Korea*. New York: Monthly Review Press, 1993.

Hatada, Takashi. *A History of Korea*. Translated and edited by Warren W. Smith Jr., and Benjamin H. Hazard. Santa Barbara, CA: American Bibliograpical Center, Clio Press, 1969.

Henderson, Gregory. *Korea, The Politics of the Vortex*. Cambridge: Harvard University Press, 1968.

Henthorn, William E. *A History of Korea*. New York: Free Press, 1971.

Hicks, George. *The Comfort Women*. Singapore: Heinemann Asia, 1995.

Hinton, Harold C. *Korea Under New Leadership*. New York: Praeger, 1983.

Hofheinz, Roy, and Calder, Kent E. *The Eastasia Edge*. New York: Basic Books, 1982.

Holloway, Nigel, ed. *Japan in Asia*. Hong Kong: Review Publishing, 1991.

Hoston, Germaine A. *Marxism and the Crisis of Development in Prewar Japan*. Princeton: Princeton University Press, 1987.

Hughes, Helen (ed.). *Achieving Industrialization in East Asia*. Cambridge: Cambridge University Press, 1988.

Jacobs, Norman. *The Korean Road to Modernization and Development*. Urbana and Chicago: University of Illinois Press, 1985.

Janelli, Roger L., with Dawnhee Yim. *Making Capitalism: The Social and Cultural Construction of a South Korean Conglomerate*. Stanford: Stanford University Press, 1993.

Johnson, Chalmers. *MITI and the Japanese Miracle*. Stanford: Stanford University Press, 1982.

Jones, Leroy P. *Public Enterprise and Economic Development: The Korean Case*. Seoul: Korea Development Institute, 1975.

Jones, Leroy P., and Sakong Il. *Government, Business and Entrepreneurship in Economic Development: The Korean Case*. Cambridge: Harvard University Press, 1980.

Kearney, Robert P. *The Warrior Worker*. New York: Henry Holt, 1991.

Keon, Michael. *Korean Phoenix*. Englewood Cliffs, NJ: Prentice-Hall International, 1977.

Kim Bun-woong and Rho Wha-joon. *Korean Public Bureaucracy*. Seoul: Kyobo Publishing, 1982.

Kim, Bun Woong, Bell, David S., Jr., and Lee Chong Bum. *Administrative Dynamics and Development: The Korean Experience*. Seoul: Kyobo Publishing, 1985.

Kim Byong-kuk. *Kim Woo-choong: Schumpeterian Entrepreneur*. Seoul: Bobmun, 1988.

Kim Chong Shin. *Seven Years With Korea's Park Chung-hee*. Seoul: Hollym, 1967.

Kim Dae Jung. *Mass Participatory Economy*. Lanham, MD: Center for International Affairs, Harvard University, and University Press of America, 1985.

Kim Dong-ki and Kim Linsu. *Management Behind Industrialization: Readings in Korean Business*. Seoul: Korea University Press, 1989.

Kim, Ji-hong. *Korean Industrial Policies for Declining Industries*. Seoul: Korea Development Institute, 1989.

Kim, Jong Gie, et al. *Impact of the Seoul Olympic Games on National Development*. Seoul: Korea Development Institute, n.d. [1989].

Kim Joon-suk. *The State, Public Policy and NIC Development*. Seoul: Dae Young Moonwhasa, 1988.

Kim, Joungwon Alexander. *Divided Korea: The Politics of Development, 1945–1972*. Cambridge: East Asian Research Center, Harvard University, 1976.

Kim Kihwan. "Kim Jae-Ik: His Life and Contributions." Unpublished manuscript, 1987.

———. *The Korean Economy: Past Performance, Current Reforms, and Future Prospects*. Seoul: Korea Development Institute, 1985.

Kim, Kwang-suk, and Park Joon-kyung (eds.). *Sources of Economic Growth in Korea: 1963–1982*. Seoul: Korea Development Institute, 1985.

Kim, Kyong-dong (ed.). *Dependency Issues in Korean Development*. Seoul: Seoul National University Press, 1987.

Kim, Seok Ki. "Business Concentration and Government Policy: A Study of the Phenomenon of Business Groups in Korea, 1945–1985." Ph.D. dissertation, Harvard University, 1987.

Kim Suk Jo and Baker, Edward J. "The Politics of Transition: Korea After Park." Unpublished manuscript, East Asian Legal Studies, Harvard Law School, 1980.

Kim Woo Choong. *Every Street Is Paved with Gold*. Singapore and Kuala Lumpur: Times Books International, 1992.

———. Speech delivered at Small Business Conference, Seoul, September 17, 1990.

Kirk, Donald. *Korean Dynasty*. Armonk, NY: M.E. Sharpe, 1994.

Korea Annual. Seoul: Yonhap News Agency, various years.

Korea Development Institute. *Industrial Policies of Korea and the Republic of China.* Seoul: Korea Development Institute, 1989.

Korean Labor Data. Seoul: photocopy manuscript from church sources of documents relating to the labor movement, 1987.

Korean Overseas Information Service. *The Fifth Republic of Korea and President Chun Doo Hwan as Seen from the Press.* Seoul: author, 1983.

———. *A Handbook of Korea.* 6th ed. Seoul: Seoul International Publishing House, 1987.

Krause, Lawrence B., and Kim Kihwan (eds.). *Liberalization in the Process of Economic Development.* Berkeley: University of California Press, 1991.

Lee Chong-Sik and Langford, Mike. *Korea: Land of the Morning Calm.* New York: Universe Books, 1988.

Lee, Ki Baik. *A New History of Korea.* Translated by Edward W. Wagner with Edward J. Shultz. Cambridge and London: Harvard University Press for the Harvard-Yenching Institute, 1984.

Lee, Kyu-uck (ed.). *Industrial Development Policies and Issues.* Seoul: Korea Development Institute, 1986.

Linton, Stephen. *Coverage of the United States in Korean Textbooks (An Analysis of Educational Policy, Tone and Content).* Seoul: Photocopy manuscript prepared for the U.S. Information Agency, October 1988.

Luedde-Neurath, Richard. *Import Controls and Export-Oriented Development: A Reexamination of the South Korean Case: 1962–1982.* Boulder, CO: Westview Press, 1986.

Macdonald, Donald Stone. *The Koreans.* Boulder, CO, and London: Westview Press, 1988.

Magaziner, Ira, and Patinkin, Mark. "Fast Heat: How Korea Won the Microwave War." *Harvard Business Review* (January–February 1989), pp. 83–84.

Mason, Edward S., et al. *The Economic and Social Modernization of the Republic of Korea.* Cambridge: Harvard University Press, 1980.

McCormack, Gavin, and Selden, Mark (eds.). *Korea, North and South.* New York: Monthly Review Press, 1978.

Ogle, George E. *Liberty to the Captives: The Struggle Against Oppression in South Korea.* Atlanta: John Knox Press, 1977.

———. *South Korea: Dissent Within the Economic Miracle.* London: Zed Books, 1990.

Paik Sun Yup. *From Pusan to Panmunjom.* Washington, DC: Brassey's (U.S. Inc.) A division of Maxwell Macmillan 1992. [The Original is "Kun Gwa Na" (Army and I). Seoul: Daehan Textbook, 1989.]

Palais, James B. *Politics and Policy in Traditional Korea.* Cambridge: Harvard University Press, 1975.

Park, Chung Hee. *The Country, the Revolution and I.* Seoul: Hollym, 1970.

———. *Korea Reborn: A Model for Development.* Englewood Cliffs, NJ: Prentice-Hall, 1979.

———. *Our Nation's Path.* Seoul: Dong-A Publishing, 1962.

———. *To Build a Nation.* Washington, DC: Acropolis Books, 1971.

Park Tae Joon. The "Separated" Familes & Other Essays. Seoul: Su Jung Dang Printing, 1988.

Porter, Michael E. *The Competitive Advantage of Nations.* New York: Free Press, 1990.

Presidential Commission on Economic Restructuring. *Realigning Korea's National Priorities for Economic Advance.* Seoul: author, 1988.

Pye, Lucian W. *Asian Power and Politics.* Cambridge and London: Belknap Press of Harvard University Press, 1985.

Rhee, Yung W., et al. *Korea's Competitive Edge.* Baltimore and London: Johns Hopkins University Press, 1984.

Rodgers, Ronald A. "Industrial Relations Policies and Practices in the Republic of Korea in a Time of Rapid Change: The Influence of American-Invested and Japanese-Invested Transnational Corporations." Ph.D. dissertation, University of Wisconsin, 1993.

———. "An Exclusionary Labor Regime Under Pressure: The Changes in Labor Relations in the Republic of Korea since mid–1987." *Pacific Basin Law Journal*, Spring 1990, vol. 8, no. 1, pp. 91–163.

Sakong, Il. *Korea in the World Economy*. Washington, DC: Institute for International Economics, 1993.

———. (ed.). *Macroeconomic Policy and Industrial Development Issues. Essays on Korea's Fifth Five-Year Plan Vol. I*, Seoul: Korea Development Institute, 1987.

Samsung Electronics Co. Ltd. November 1993 prospectus; Merrill Lynch & Co., global coordinator.

Satterwhite, David. "The Politics of Economic Development: Coup, State and the Republic of Korea's First Five-Year Plan (1962–66)." Ph.D. dissertation, University of Washington, 1993.

Shaw, William (ed.) *Human Rights in Korea*. Cambridge: Harvard Council on East Asian Studies with Harvard University Press, 1991.

Song, Byung-nak. *The Rise of the Korean Economy*. Hong Kong: Oxford University Press, 1990.

Steers, Richard M., Shin, Yoo Keun, and Ungson, Gerardo R. *The Chaebol: Korea's New Industrial Might*. New York: Harper & Row (Ballinger Division), 1989.

Taylor, Lance. *Varieties of Stabilization Experience*. Oxford: Clarendon Press, 1988.

U.S. Congress, House. *Hearing Before the Subcommittee on International Organizations of the Committee on International Relations*. 95th Cong., 1st and 2nd sess.

U.S. State Department. *Foreign Relations of the United States*. Washington, DC: Government Printing Office, 1948.

Wade, Robert. *Governing the Market: Economic Theory and the Role of Government in East Asian Industrialization*. Princeton: Princeton University Press, 1990.

West, James M. "South Korea's Entry into the International Labor Organization: Perspectives on Corporatist Labor Law During a Late Industrial Revolution." *Stanford Journal of International Law* 23, no. 2 (1987).

Whang, In-Joung. *Role of Policy Research Institutes in National Econmic Management: The Korean Case*. Seoul: Korea Development Institute (unpublished photocopy), 1988.

Woo, Jung-en. *Race to the Swift*. New York: Columbia University Press, 1991.

World Bank. *Korea: Managing the Industrial Transition*. 2 vols. Washington, DC: author, 1987.

———. *World Development Report 1989*. New York: Oxford University Press, 1989.

———. East Asia & Pacific Region Country Briefing Note (Korea). Washington, DC: 1993.

———. *East Asia and the Pacific Regional Development Review: Sustaining Rapid Development*. Washington, DC: author, 1993.

———. *The East Asian Miracle: Economic Growth and Public Policy*. New York: Oxford University Press, 1993.

Yoo, Jung-ho. *The Government in Korean Economic Growth*. Seoul: Korea Development Institute, Working Paper No. 8904, 1989.

———. *The Industrial Policy of the 1970s and the Evolution of the Manufacturing Sector in Korea*. Seoul: Korea Development Institute, Working Paper No. 9017, 1990.

Index

Economy *(continued)*
government rescue of, 329, 330
Japanese model and, 335
Kim's reform of, 333, 334–35, 336–37
Marxist ideology and, 52–53
real estate prices and, 132–33, 137*n.9*
standard of living, 331
U.S. Federal reserve cautions and,
171–72
wages and, 129, 136*n.4*
see also Chun Doo Hwan, economy
under: before Rangoon; Chun Doo
Hwan, economy under: after
Rangoon; Economy; Kim Young
Sam; Park Chung Hee, economic
growth under; Park Chung Hee,
economic slowdown under; Roh
Tae Woo, economy under
Education, 11, 49
see also Seoul National University;
Student movement
Eisenhower administration, 8, 125–26*n.2*
Electricity production, 43, 95, 185, 186,
187–88, 192*nn.27,33*
Electronics industry
Heavy and Chemical Industries (HCI)
program and, 105
Korean companies in U.S. of, 240
semiconductors and, 238, 315–16,
323–24, 341
see also Samsung Electronics
EPB. *See* Economic Planning Board (EPB)
Export Credit Guarantee Department
(ECGD), 191*n.24*
Export Day, 56, 103
Exports
1979 decrease in, 133
1986–88 increase in, 229, 234, 236–43,
245, 251*n.4*, 252*n.9*
1994–95 increase in, 335
1996 decrease in, 340
currency value and, 174–75, 177
economic growth tied to, 6, 54–61,
65*n.30*, 112*n.19*, 206, 233, 339–40
of people, 57
to U.S., 242
U.S.-Korea trade deficit and, 237,
239–40, 298
see also specific company; Trade

F

Family Code, 166, 170*n.7*
Federation of Korean Industries (FKI), 201
1985 credit control measures and, 229
Chung Ju Yung and, 214
formation of, 40
Lee Byung Chull and, 318
Park Chung Hee's corruption and, 93
Federation of Korean Trade Unions
(FKTU), 277, 284*n.3*
Fifth Republic. *See* Chun Doo Hwan
Finance
1983 new commercial banks and,
207–208
1985 credit control measures and,
226–30, 235*nn.9,11*
1985–1988 reduction of, 239–40, 251*n.5*
Bank of Korea and, 4, 38, 40
convertible bonds and, 249–50
foreign deficit and, 171–72
foreign investment and,
the curb market and, 102–104
government control of, 245–46, 337
hesitancy of investors and, 171–72,
182
in Korean Stock Exchange, 249
size of, 182, 191*n.11*, 232–35
Madame Chang affair and, 194–200,
202*nn.5,8,9*
mis-matched swap arrangements and,
244–45, 252*n.12*
Park Chung Hee control of, 61–62,
66*n.39*
real-name system, 333
security house regulation and, 250–51
through stock market, 243–45, 252*n.12*
U.S. aid and
Kennedy administration and, 39, 44*n.7*,
65*n.35*
Nixon administration, 88
Park Chung Hee economic policy and,
41, 45, 51, 77
Five Mores campaign, 8
Five year plan
first, 49–52, 53, 58, 67, 69–70, 178
second, 52, 58–59, 60, 70, 74
third, 52, 74–75
fourth, 110, 179

Mark Clifford covered South Korea as a correspondent for *Far Eastern Economic Review* from 1987 to 1992, where he was also a frequent contributor to BBC World Service. He is a past president of the Seoul Foreign Correspondents' Club, which taught him more about Korean labor relations than he ever wanted to know. A graduate of the University of California at Berkeley and a former business editor at the *Far Eastern Economic Review*, he is currently based in Hong Kong as Asia Correspondent for *Business Week*.